Stock market anomalies

Stock market anomalies

Edited by
ELROY DIMSON
London Business School

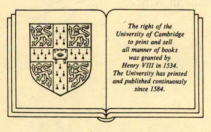

The right of the
University of Cambridge
to print and sell
all manner of books
was granted by
Henry VIII in 1534.
The University has printed
and published continuously
since 1584.

CAMBRIDGE UNIVERSITY PRESS

Cambridge
New York   New Rochelle   Melbourne   Sydney

Published by the Press Syndicate of the University of Cambridge
The Pitt Building, Trumpington Street, Cambridge CB2 1RP
32 East 57th Street, New York, NY 10022, USA
10 Stamford Road, Oakleigh, Melbourne 3166, Australia

First published 1988
Reprinted 1988

Printed in Great Britain by the University Press, Cambridge

British Library cataloguing in publication data

Stock market anomalies.
1. Stock exchange. 2. Stocks – Prices
I. Dimson, Elroy
332.63'22   HG4551

Library of Congress cataloguing in publication data

Stock market anomalies.
Includes index.
1. Stock-exchange. 2. Capital market.
I. Dimson, Elroy, 1947–   .
HG4551.S82 1988   332.63'2   87-6622

ISBN 0 521 34104 3

To Daniel

The contributors to this collection have donated their royalties to
Sport Aid for the relief of famine in Africa.

CE

Contents

Contributors

Robert Ariel is Assistant Professor of Finance at Baruch College of the City University of New York. After receiving his BA in chemistry from Dartmouth College and MA in physics and philosophy from Oxford University, he pursued graduate work in the philosophy of science at the University of Minnesota before earning his PhD in Finance from the MIT Sloan School of Management. His research interests include stock pricing anomalies and the impact of institutional structures on security pricing.

Ray Ball is Professor of Finance at the Graduate School of Management at the University of Rochester. He was formerly Foundation Professor of Management in the Australian Graduate School of Management. Ray Ball co-edits the *Journal of Accounting and Economics*. He was the founding editor of the *Australian Journal of Management* and is a member of the editorial board of the *Journal of Accounting Research*, the *Journal of Banking and Finance* and the *Journal of Business Finance and Accounting*. His principal teaching, research and consulting interests are in accounting, the securities industries, corporate finance and the behaviour and role of markets in general.

Giovanni Barone-Adesi is Associate Professor of Finance at the University of Alberta. His research and teaching interests include equilibrium models of capital markets, option pricing and applications of the theory of option pricing to corporate finance.

Stan Beckers is Senior Vice-President of BARRA International London, specializing in the applications of risk management and control for major institutional investors, market makers and traders. He has published widely in academic and professional journals on portfolio risk measurement and option pricing. Dr Beckers also holds an appointment as a visiting lecturer at the City University Business School, London.

Willem Max van den Bergh is Assistant Professor of Finance at the School of Economics of the Erasmus University, Rotterdam, The Netherlands. His research on foreign exchange risk and hedging strategies has been published in several professional journals. His current interests are in the area of capital structure and the use of artificial intelligence in corporate financial policy.

John Bowers is Senior Lecturer in Finance at the Australian Graduate School of Management, and Associate Director of the AGSM's Centre for Research in Finance. His research interests include the product market determinants of financial parameters and the effect of taxes on financial decisions. During 1986, John was a visiting faculty member at the London Business School.

Nai-fu Chen is Associate Professor of Finance at the Graduate School of Business, University of Chicago. He is currently an Associate Editor of the *Journal of Financial and Quantitative Analysis*. His research has centred on asset pricing models and the relation between the macroeconomy and the stock market.

Leda Condoyanni is a doctoral student in the Department of Accounting and Finance at the University of Lancaster, England. Her research centres upon the identification of anomalies in the Greek equity market.

George Constantinides, Professor of Finance at the University of Chicago, wrote his contribution while he was Marvin Bower Fellow at Harvard University. He is an Associate Editor of *Journal of Finance*, *Journal of Financial and Quantitative Analysis* and *Journal of Financial Research*; and he is a board member of the American Finance Association. His current research interests are in asset pricing theory; information in corporate finance; corporate and personal taxation; and options, convertibles and other contingent claims.

Thomas Copeland is Associate Professor of Finance at the Graduate School of Management, University of California at Los Angeles. He is co-author, with J. Fred Weston, of *Financial Theory and Corporate Policy* and of *Managerial Finance*. Dr Copeland's academic publications include articles on stock splits, receivables policy, leasing, a theory of the bid–ask spread and pension fund management. His current research focuses on portfolio performance measurement and experimental economics. He is active in executive education and has twice been designated the best teacher in the UCLA MBA program.

Albert Corhay is a doctoral student at the School of Business Administration, University of Liège, Belgium, where he was formerly a research assistant in Finance and Accounting. His doctoral research, dealing with stock market anomalies, is financed by the College Interuniversitaire d'Etudes Doctorales dans les Sciences du Management (CIM), Brussels, Belgium. His research interests are in the areas of portfolio management and capital markets.

Elroy Dimson is Senior Lecturer in Finance and Prudential Research Fellow in Investment at the London Business School, where he is Director of the MBA Programme. He has taught at the universities of California (Berkeley), Chicago and Hawaii. He is a Visiting Professor in Finance at the European Institute for Advanced Studies in Management, Brussels, and is on the editorial board of the *Journal of Finance*, *Midland Corporate Finance Journal* and the London Business School's *Risk Measurement Service*. Dr Dimson's research interests include empirical research on active and passive portfolio investment strategies and case studies on corporate financial management.

Dan Givoly is Senior Lecturer in Accounting at Tel Aviv University. He has taught at Columbia University and Carnegie Mellon University. Dr Givoly has published in leading academic journals and his current research focuses on the effect of financial information on market expectations and security prices.

Lawrence Harris is Assistant Professor of Finance and Business Economics in the School of Business Administration at the University of Southern California. Dr Harris' academic research centres on price–volume relations in financial markets, the measurement of effective bid–ask spreads from common stock transaction data, and on other uses of transaction data in financial research.

Gabriel Hawawini is Professor of Finance at the European Institute of Business Administration (INSEAD) in Fontainebleau, France, where he directs several senior executive development programmes. He is a Vice-President of the French Finance Association and the editor of *Finance*, the Association's journal. He has taught at New York University, the City University (also New York), Columbia University, the Swedish School of Economics and the University of Geneva. His research and published work have centred on the efficiency of financial markets, security pricing, financial innovation and economic decision making under uncertainty.

Donald Keim is Assistant Professor of Finance at the Wharton School of the University of Pennsylvania. His research deals with the relation between stock returns and predetermined variables such as size of the firm and dividend yield, calendar-related patterns in security returns, tests of asset pricing models and the pricing of low-grade bonds.

Josef Lakonishok is Professor of Finance at the University of Illinois at Urbana-Champaign, and was formerly on the Faculty of Management, Tel Aviv University. He wrote his contribution while visiting the Graduate School of Management, Cornell University. He has published extensively in leading professional journals. His recent research concerns motives for stock trading, seasonalities in the stock market and financial analysts' forecasts of earnings.

Maurice Levi is Bank of Montreal Professor of International Finance at the University of British Columbia. He is an Associate Editor of the *Journal of International Money and Finance* and the author of a number of books including *Economics Deciphered* (Basic Books, 1981) and *International Finance* (McGraw-Hill, 1983). Dr Levi's research interests include econometrics, monetary theory, financial institutions and international finance. He is particularly interested in the role that man-made institutional factors such as taxes, laws, payments, practices, regulations, and so on, play in the financial marketplace.

Mario Levis is Lecturer in Financial Management at the School of Management, University of Bath. His research interests are in the field of capital market investments and corporate finance.

Paul Marsh is Professor of Management and Finance at the London Business School, where he is Faculty Dean. He is a Governor of the School, and is Joint Editor of the LBS' *Risk Measurement Service*. His research interests include strategic investment decisions, investment in smaller companies, the analysis of unit trusts and other managed portfolios, and the evaluation of analysts' brokers' and share tipsters' forecasts. He is a consultant to a number of leading companies, public bodies and financial institutions.

David Mayers is Professor of Finance at the Graduate School of Management, University of California at Los Angeles. He is an Associate Editor of the *Journal of Financial Economics*. His research interests have included asset pricing, portfolio performance measurement and various topics on insurance markets.

Pierre Michel is Professor of Finance and Accounting at the School of Business Administration, University of Liège (Belgium). He has taught at the Free University of Brussels. Dr Michel serves on the editorial board of the French Finance Association's *Finance* Review. He is a past Secretary General of the European Accounting Association. His books and articles are in the areas of financial analysis and planning, the efficiency of capital markets and the econometric estimation of financial models. His current research focuses on stock market anomalies.

John O'Hanlon is Lecturer in Accounting and Finance at the University of Lancaster, England. Prior to becoming an academic, he worked for firms of professional accountants in both London and Mexico City. His research interests are in the area of international finance and currently centre on stock market anomalies in European and Far Eastern equity markets. He is an examiner for the Society of Investment Analysts in the UK.

Anthony Saunders is Associate Professor of Finance at the Graduate Business School, New York University. He is also Research Adviser to the Federal Reserve Bank of Philadelphia and has acted as a consultant to the IMF, World Bank and the Office of the Comptroller of the Currency. His major field of research interest is in the area of financial institutions. He is currently editor of the Salomon Brothers Center *Monograph Series in Economics and Finance*.

Richard Stapleton is a Fellow of Churchill College, Cambridge and a visiting professor at Manchester Business School and at the European Institute for Advanced Studies in Management. He is a co-editor of the *Journal of Banking and Finance* and a past president of the European Finance Association. His current research interests are in the dynamics of security prices, the valuation of option and various aspects of corporate finance. His research has been published widely in the leading finance journals.

Seha Tinic is J. Ludwig Mosle Centennial Memorial Professor of Finance at the Graduate School of Business Administration, University of Texas at Austin, and previously served on the Faculties at the University of Alberta, University of British Columbia and Dartmouth College. He is a past president of the Western Finance Association and a former member of the Policy Advisory Board of the *Journal of Financial and Quantitative Analysis*. He has co-authored two books, *The Economics of the Stock Market* and *Investing in Securities: An Efficient Markets Approach*, and published more than a score of articles in leading finance and economics journals. His recent research deals with valuation models, investment banking and new securities issues.

Thomas Urich received his PhD from New York University Graduate School of Business Administration, and is currently an Associate Professor of Finance at Baruch College, City University of New York. His major area of research has been financial marketing and investment, where he has published numerous articles in professional journals.

Theo Vermaelen is Associate Professor of Finance at the Department of Applied Economics, Catholic University of Leuven and Research Fellow at the European Institute. He has taught at the University of Chicago and the University of British Columbia. His research has concerned such topics as taxes and finance, new issues, stock repurchases, empirical tests of signalling hypotheses, portfolio performance evaluation and the market for corporate control.

Charles Ward is Professor and Head of the Department of Accountancy and Business Law at the University of Stirling. He was previously employed in the University of Lancaster and the City of London Poly-technic. Research interests include property investment and financial markets. He is co-author (with Professor K. V. Peasnell of the University of Lancaster) of *British Financial Institutions and Markets*.

Roberto Wessels is Associate Professor of Finance at the School of Economics of the Erasmus University, Rotterdam, The Netherlands and adjunct Professor of Finance of the Graduate School of Management of the University of Rochester. He has also several times been Visiting Professor of Finance at the Graduate School of Management of the University of California, Los Angeles. His research interests are in the fields of corporate financial policy and the efficiency of financial markets.

Roel Wijmenga is Assistant Professor of Finance at the School of Economics of the Erasmus University, Rotterdam, The Netherlands. He has a degree in Operations Research and is currently working on a study of the efficiency of the Dutch Stock Exchange.

Foreword

RICHARD STAPLETON

This volume contains the proceedings of a symposium organized by Dr Elroy Dimson at the European Institute for Advanced Studies in Management. Dr Dimson, with the help of a generous travel budget from the Institute, put together a program of outstanding quality which is fully reflected in this volume. The contribution of the conference was to bring together a great proportion of outstanding researchers in a well-defined and important field.

In recent years, tests of the various asset-pricing models have uncovered a variety of anomalies or regularities in the data. It has long been an established fact that small companies have higher average stock returns than large companies. This is referred to as the 'small firm effect'. Further investigation has revealed that much of this excess performance can be attributed to the initial trading days of January. This fact has naturally become known as the 'turn-of-the-year effect'. The availability of masses of data in computer readable form has led to more and more investigation of seasonalities such as these. Thus, we have the 'weekend effect' and even studies of 'time-of-day effects'.

To what extent are these regularities explainable by theory? Do they persist through time and across countries? What are the implications for empirical researchers? The purpose of the EIASM symposium was to review the evidence on stock returns and to attempt to find an answer to these questions. Although some of the questions were not resolved, I think all those who took part left with a greater understanding of the issues involved and with an appreciation of the international empirical evidence.

The conference was organized by Elroy Dimson. He invited the speakers, put together the program and has now edited this volume. I think he has done a great job and produced a volume of proceedings which genuinely adds to the literature in the field. On behalf of Elroy, and all the participants, could I thank the EIASM for their support of the conference. The surroundings and organization at Brussels are perfect for running this kind of event. I hope, and am assured, that this conference will be but the first in a series of such events.

I
STOCK MARKET ANOMALIES:
AN OVERVIEW

1   Introduction

JOHN BOWERS and ELROY DIMSON

1 The asset pricing paradigm

The subject of a competitive equilibrium rate of return on assets has been extensively studied by financial economists. The dominant paradigm is that due to Sharpe (1964) and Lintner (1965) and extended by Merton (1973), commonly known as the capital asset pricing model, or CAPM. The simple version of this asset pricing model, in a world without taxes, is formalized as:

$$E(r_s) = r_f + \beta[E(r_m) - r_f] \tag{1}$$

where:

r_s is the yield on a risky asset (such as shares)
r_f is the yield on a riskless asset (such as government bonds)
r_m is the yield to the average risky asset (or market index)
E is the expectations operator, and
β is the relative risk measure (beta) for the risky asset, defined as

$$\beta = \mathrm{Cov}(r_s, r_m) / \mathrm{Var}(r_m) \tag{2}$$

In the Sharpe–Lintner single-period version of the CAPM, equation (1) holds iteratively over discrete time periods whose definition is left to the empirical researcher. In the Merton version of the CAPM, equation (1) holds in continuous time and the rates of return are defined instantaneously.

The theoretical elegance of the CAPM led to its early acceptance despite the fact that initial tests of derived propositions were not unambiguous in their results. With hindsight it is clear that the likelihood of a Type I error being made in these tests was high, due to the hypotheses contained in equation (1) being accepted against very weak alternatives. For example, the coefficient on beta in cross-sectional explanations of mean *ex-post* returns was of only marginal significance in the early studies of Black *et al.* (1972) and Fama and MacBeth (1973).

One pervasive problem was, and still remains, that conventional tests of the CAPM are in fact joint tests of equation (1) and of the proposition that security markets are informationally efficient. This latter proposition has come to be known as the efficient market hypothesis, or EMH. The concept owes much of its articulation to Fama (1970), who also provides a review of the evidence to that point in time. The joint nature of testing the CAPM and the EMH arises because the use of *ex-post* asset returns in testing a model of equilibrium in the capital markets implies of necessity that these observed returns do in fact represent a series of information equilibria; and conversely any attempt to test the informational efficiency of the market process will require a benchmark, which is provided by the equilibrium model of returns.

Among other things, the EMH requires that capital market returns should be characterized by a lack of any *ex-post* regularities. The existence of a market regularity, such as a seasonal in returns, would imply informational inefficiency since a market participant could use the regularity to devise a trading strategy that would yield above-normal returns. The only observed regularities that are compatible with the paradigm are those clearly caused by institutional constraints (such as transactions costs) or other known market imperfections (such as taxes). For quite a long time – approximately the fifteen years to 1980 – such a lack of empirical regularities was widely believed by financial economists to be true. However in recent years this position has changed.

2 Empirical regularities

The first empirical regularities to be noted for modern capital markets appeared in the work of Officer (1975) on seasonals for the Australian share market, and that of Rozeff and Kinney (1976) in the case of the US market. Then Basu (1977) detailed in the academic literature a price/earnings anomaly that had long been popularized by practitioners. A series of unexplained results in a variety of event studies led Ball (1978) to speculate that researchers might be facing a set of anomalies with respect to the current paradigms of the finance discipline. An early indication of a small firm regularity was reported by Marsh (1979) for the case of the London share market.

Then, during the early 1980s, finance researchers began to report an increasing (and increasingly bewildering) array of anomalies with respect to the joint hypotheses of the CAPM and the EMH. French (1980) reported anomalous behaviour of share market returns around periods of non-trading at weekends, and then Banz (1981) documented an anomaly in the performance of equity returns when classified by firm size. Reinganum (1981) presented evidence on an anomaly based on earnings yields. Subsequent years have seen an explosion of both theoretical and empirical interest in such anomalous behaviour. Empirical confirmation and extension of the anomalies has now taken place for many of the world's capital markets.

These anomalies take the form of observed capital market regularities that are not explained by theory or institutional practice. Some of these empirical regularities are not truly new, in that they have existed as market folklore (sometimes even weakly documented) for many years. However it is only in the last five years that financial economists have sought to examine rigorously the earlier folklore and search actively for new anomalies.

By the end of the first half of this decade, sufficient evidence on capital market regularities had been accumulated that it became clear that an international symposium could be of great value in bringing together many of the researchers interested in this topic. Such a symposium was organized under the auspices of the European Institute for Advanced Studies in Management, and held in Brussels during December 1985. The present book is a direct result of the research papers presented at this symposium. It also includes several chapters contributed by scholars who were unable to come to Brussels.

Participants in the symposium came from twelve different countries. Some crossed the seas from as far afield as Australia, the United States (including California, the mid-West and the East), Canada and Israel. Others represented most of the countries in the EEC, as well as some other European countries.

The organization of the meeting was novel. In each session, two or three related papers were presented and discussed. This task was undertaken by a single speaker, who was not the author of the research. This speaker's task was to summarize the contributions of the session papers, as well as to present any critical analysis. The authors responded, and the discussion was then widened to include other participants. This format facilitated informed debate, and also resulted in the present volume containing a number of survey chapters in addition to a selection of the original contributions.

3 Introduction to the collection

The chapters which comprise this collection have been divided into four categories, forming parts I, II, III and IV of the volume. Part I contains, as well as the present introduction, a survey chapter which synthesizes much of the evidence and theory regarding anomalous behaviour in the world's capital markets. Parts II and III contain chapters which document particular observed empirical regularities. The distinction between

parts II and III is that the former contains evidence on regularities which
might be supposed to be due to imperfections in the trading process itself
(day-of-the-week and half-of-the-month effects), whereas the latter
contains evidence on regularities which are of more general economic
concern (the small firm effect, the turn-of-the-year effect, and others).
The collection concludes with part IV, which is reserved for a new class of
research which is beginning the task of determining the impact of known
regularities on empirical research methods used in finance.

Part I: overview

The remainder of part I consists of chapter 2 by Don Keim which
provides a synthesis of the evidence concerning, and explanations for,
the anomalous behaviour of capital markets which has been identified to
the present time. The author is particularly well qualified to write this
survey chapter, since he was an early (and prolific) contributor to the
debate. He begins his survey with a discussion of the theoretical
development and testing of the CAPM, before proceeding to discuss in
turn the anomalies associated with the firm size effect, the price to
earnings ratio effect and what has become known as the Value Line
enigma. The interrelation of these effects, which is crucial to a proper
understanding of the extent of the anomalies, is then treated in some
detail. Keim goes on to discuss unexplained seasonalities in returns,
including the turn-of-the-year, the day-of-the-week and the half-of-
the-month regularities. He concludes by outlining some of the potential
explanations which have been advanced, and identifies the studies which
test these explanations.

Part II: seasonalities in daily returns

Chapter 3 in part II is by Maurice Levi and contains a survey of the
day-of-the-week effects observed in share price returns. The author
points out that the nature of this regularity depends very much on the
country and the time period studied, and questions whether the observed
patterns are in fact inconsistent with economic behaviour on the part of
market participants. In this connection he stresses the importance of
distinguishing Type I and Type II errors in testing the hypotheses
contained in the asset pricing models of finance theory. He also notes the
importance of understanding the institutional setting within which seasonalities are observed. As part of this survey, the author provides critical
assessment of the remaining chapters in part II.

Leda Condoyanni, John O'Hanlon and Charles Ward, in chapter 4
containing evidence on the international extent of day-of-the-week

effects, show that a version of this anomaly is the worldwide norm, rather than being US specific. They note that the pattern of the day-of-the-week effect appears to be strongly related to different time zones, thus raising the possibility that the different countries are all manifestations of the same underlying cause. In particular, they analyze the hypothesis that the rest of the world's behaviour is due to lagged correlation with the US markets. As an aside to their investigation, the authors report that they do not find any international evidence of a turn-of-the-year effect.

Anthony Saunders and Thomas Urich have provided chapter 5 which examines regularities in the cash market, rather than the equity markets, of the US. They point out that the Federal Funds market plays a pivotal role in the US financial system, and hence any institutional peculiarities are likely to show up as regularities in interest rates and/or volume of transactions. They are in fact able to make a case for regularities on Wednesdays and on Fridays based on institutional practice.

Chapter 6, by Ray Ball and John Bowers, tests for daily seasonals in both equity and fixed interest returns in the Australian markets. These authors note that the existence of seasonals is not of itself surprising if there are supply or demand parameters which are subject to seasonal variation, and hypothesize a weekend effect due to a non-constant marginal efficiency of capital over days of the week. Such an effect (albeit lagged to Tuesday) is found in the equity return data, but is not confirmed by the interest rate data. Ball and Bowers also point to the fact that there is a seasonal in the variance of equity returns, as well as in the mean return, with weekend equity market variance being low compared to the rest of the week.

Chapter 7 in part II is that by Lawrence Harris, which adds to the list of anomalous behaviour of US equity markets by reporting an intra-day seasonal for returns of stocks traded on the NYSE. Harris reports that differences among weekday returns appear to be contained entirely in the first 45 minutes of trading on each day, and that there is an anomalous tendency for the last trade of the day to result in a price rise. The author also notes cross-sectional differences in intra-Monday returns.

Part II concludes with the report by Robert Ariel (chapter 8) on evidence of an intra-month seasonal in stock returns in the US. This seasonal does not appear to be driven only by the January effect (which is known to be concentrated in the early part of that month), and does not appear to be a dividend effect. The author notes that while there is an intra-month difference in mean returns, there is no evidence of intra-month differences in variance of return. He speculates on this anomaly being due to the institutional practices of US pension funds leading to a price pressure effect.

Part III: the small firm, turn-of-the-year and other anomalies

Part III also begins with a survey chapter, this time by George Constantinides (chapter 9), who surveys the chapters in this part (as well as the extant literature) which relate to the turn-of-the-year seasonal. He discusses tests of the tax-loss selling hypothesis, pointing out that an observed effect on trading volume does not automatically result in an effect on stock returns. International comparisons are a clever way to test the tax-loss selling hypothesis, and this leads to a survey of the chapters containing international evidence. The author then turns to an alternative explanation for the turn-of-the-year effect, namely that the expected risk premium is itself subject to seasonal fluctuation. He surveys a number of works which have made contributions along these lines, but points out that such work, although very promising, is only just beginning.

The next two chapters in part III are also concerned with returns seasonality. Seha Tinic and Giovanni Barone-Adesi (chapter 10) present evidence of a significant January seasonal in the Canadian equity markets. Interestingly, the existence of this seasonal does not appear to be affected by the introduction of a capital gains tax in Canada during the time period studied. Using a Fama and MacBeth type of two stage test, the authors report that the CAPM is not supported by the data in the Canadian case, and that there is only weak support for the tax-loss selling hypothesis.

Using a rather different methodology, in chapter 11 Willem Max van den Bergh, Roberto Wessels and Roel Wijmenga find that the tax-loss selling hypothesis is not supported by data from the Amsterdam stock market. Their technique is to regress prior holding period returns against the January effect in an attempt to find a distribution of holding periods which is consistent with tax-loss selling. No such distribution is discovered, and the authors consequently reject the tax-loss hypothesis.

Chapter 12 in part III is by Mario Levis, who is concerned with the relation between size related anomalies and trading activity by institutional investors. Using data for the UK market, the author first confirms a size effect for this market. He then uses Box–Jenkins techniques to relate institutional trading volume variables to returns data. The results do not support the hypothesis that there is a returns impact of trading activity, but rather suggest that institutional trading appears to follow market returns (especially those for large firms). In chapter 13, Theo Vermaelen provides a useful discussion and critical analysis of Levis' contribution.

An example of changing risk premiums is provided by Nai-fu Chen (chapter 14), both in the context of the firm size effect and the January seasonal. Chen first reports the use of a multi-factor model in which firm size is itself used as an instrumental variable in the estimation process. Size is used here as an instrument for an unknown risk factor, within the structure of an arbitrage pricing theory (APT) model, on the presumption that changing aggregate risk for the economy will have a differential effect on small as opposed to large firms. The empirical result of this technique is that the size effect is captured by the resulting multi-factor pricing equation. The author also discusses whether the size effect can be captured by a single-factor model in which size is used as an instrumental variable in beta estimation. The author then turns to the turn-of-the-year effect, again with emphasis in the discussion on research which has interpreted this effect as one of seasonals in risk premiums.

In the final chapter of this part, Albert Corhay, Gabriel Hawawini and Pierre Michel (chapter 15) present some evidence on risk premium-seasonality in the UK. These authors also use the Fama and MacBeth methodology. Their results are that the relationship between mean return and beta is positive only in April and negative only in May, which suggests a tax year-end effect for the UK. However if risk is measured by total rather than just systematic risk, there is a general positive relationship with mean returns. The authors also report a size effect for their UK data set. After controlling for size, the premium for systematic risk becomes positive for April but negative for the months of May and June.

Part IV: the impact on empirical research methods

The final part of this collection also begins with a survey chapter, this time by Josef Lakonishok (chapter 16), who analyzes the other four chapters in part IV. The author points out that the existence of a size effect does not mean that we should always make an adjustment for size when performing empirical research in finance. The decision to make a size adjustment should depend on whether size was a decision variable for the economic actors whose performance is being evaluated. Further, it is not clear that small companies will outperform large companies in the future.

Elroy Dimson and Paul Marsh, in chapter 17 studying the effect of published stock market tips in the UK, demonstrate that CAPM and market model adjustments can give misleading measures of longer-term post-event performance. In their study they found that whether or not these tips achieved superior performance depended on the index (value or equal weighted) which was used as the control benchmark. They show that such size-related distortions can be avoided by a size control portfolio technique. After controlling for size, it turns out that there is no economic value to the published tips.

In a similar vein, Stan Beckers (chapter 18) argues in favour of adjustment for the full range of factors which are empirically related to *ex-post* returns. Chapter 18 illustrates this technique in the context of a case study, again of stock market tips in the UK. Beckers demonstrates how performance attribution using a multi-factor model allows the disaggregation of total returns in terms of the actual decision variables. He makes the point that if fund managers are required to manage an unbalanced portfolio, then their performance should be evaluated against an appropriate benchmark. Again, it turns out that with these adjustments the published recommendations are of little economic value.

A more general treatment of multi-factor portfolio performance methodologies, including comparison with single-factor techniques, is provided in chapter 19 by Nai-Fu Chen, Thomas Copeland and David Mayers. Using the Value Line database, the authors report that using five factors rather than one hardly changes the estimate of cumulative abnormal returns, and does not markedly improve the standard errors. However, when portfolios were based on firm size, the pattern of abnormal returns for the single factor model exhibited negative serial correlation, whereas the multi-factor residuals did not. Further, the multi-factor approach does improve the mean square error, hence leading to better predictive power when assessed by this parameter. The predictive power of the multi-factor methodology is superior for well-diversified portfolios.

The final chapter in this volume is that by Dan Givoly and Josef Lakonishok (chapter 20), who study the US stock market response to earnings signals. The authors find that market reaction to unexpected earnings becomes weaker as a measure of earnings uncertainty rises. The uncertainty measures used in the studies are derived from forecasts of financial analysts. Particularly for unfavourable earnings, the evidence supports the notion that earnings uncertainty will mollify stock price response to earnings signals. This result has implications for past earnings announcement studies.

4 Directions for the future

It is clear from this introduction that the chapters in this volume are representative of a growing body of evidence on stock market regularities. These phenomena appear amongst a variety of securities, in different markets around the world, and in many of the time periods which have been studied.

In his contribution, Maurice Levi warns us to beware of reading too much into the recent evidence of stock market regularities. Some of these regularities are artefacts caused by institutional factors such as ex-dividend, tax and liquidity effects. Other regularities, however, may have been discovered by empirical researchers who, recently, have sometimes been a little too keen in sifting through large databases until eventually they find another 'anomaly'.

In thinking about the disconcerting evidence on stock market anomalies, it may therefore be appropriate to limit our comments to the best substantiated regularity. The small firm effect has been in evidence in many of the world's security markets, and over long time periods. In published studies of the American, British, Australian, Canadian, Japanese, Dutch and Finnish equity markets, the average returns on smaller firms' stocks are higher than any known pricing model predicts (see Banz (1981) for the USA; Dimson and Marsh (1987) for the UK; Brown *et al*. (1983) for Australia; Berges *et al*. (1982) for Canada; Kato and Schalheim (1985) for Japan; Van den Bergh and Wessels (1983) for Holland; and Wahlroos and Berglund (1983) for Finland). In North America, though not necessarily elsewhere, a very large part of this high return occurs in January, at the turn of the calendar (and fiscal) year (see Keim, 1983).

Institutional factors, such as transaction costs and differential tax rates, cannot provide straightforward explanations for the anomalous behaviour of small company stocks. In considering directions for future research, it is therefore likely that we have reached the stage of diminishing marginal returns from documenting the magnitude of known empirical regularities. The existing (and growing) evidence on these regularities should stimulate further developments, both empirical and theoretical.

5 Theoretical models[1]

In terms of theory, we would ideally wish to construct a model, consistent with rational behaviour on the part of all actors, which can explain observed market behaviour. In such a model, managers for whom it is rational to act in the interest of shareholders decide on an optimal size for the firm. Investors purchase the shares, and for rational reasons price them so that returns are high. In such a model, the size of the firm will be an endogenous decision variable driven by some exogenous factors (technology, information, etc). The same exogenous factors will also result in higher returns.

There are a number of difficulties in constructing such a model. First, we do not know what determines the scope of operations within a company. In other words, we do not have a *theory of the size of the firm*. Second, we do not know why people trade securities; and in particular, how to explain the volume of trading, its seasonality and the linkage (if any) with returns. While we often assume tax-induced transactions, and also liquidity- and information-motivated trading, theories here are incomplete.

Previous research on firm size has been the province of a branch of economics often overlooked by the finance profession. In two important articles on the size distribution of firms, Herbert Simon, in collaboration with Bonini (Simon and Bonini, 1958) and Ijiri (Ijiri and Simon, 1964) discussed the stochastic process governing firm growth. Their work led to further confirmation of Gibrat's law, the assertion that the percentage rate of firm growth is independent of its size (as measured by sales, employment or assets). On a related topic, Henry Manne (1965) observed that the distribution of firm sizes is a solution to the problem of how to allocate productive factors over managers of different ability so as to maximize output. Acquisitions, share repurchases, mergers and spinoffs can therefore be viewed as mechanisms by which talented managers vary firm size as they seek to acquire productive factors. Robert Lucas (1978) constructed a model which formalized these ideas. In Lucas' model, the size distribution of firms is a competitive equilibrium solution to the extremum problem of producing at the minimum resource cost.

A useful model of firm size might therefore be devised with size as the decision variable. The latter would be a device to achieve some goal such as maximization of market value, maintenance of owners' control, etc. This decision about size would simultaneously determine the feasibility of, say, various methods of takeover; and as in Milt Harris' and Art Raviv's (1985) paper, these takeover methods would imply excess returns. Other mechanisms which are related to abnormal returns may, of course, be postulated.

While models may be developed to explain the relationship between firm size and returns, they are unlikely to predict a January seasonal. For the latter, we will have to look for factors which are related to the turn of the year. The interplay between tax-loss selling and informational asymmetries may provide a possible explanation. One recent paper that tries to exploit this idea is by Joseph Williams (1986).

6 Empirical implications

A quite different direction for future work lies in extending the boundaries of empirical research. There is clearly a role for continued documentation of the small firm and related regularities in various markets around the world. But the recent availability of different national databases presents other, hitherto unexploited, opportunities, especially for international comparisons.

The world's security markets operate within different institutional settings, they transact shares in companies exposed to differing tax systems, and the extent of information production and dissemination varies across economies. Even the definition of what constitutes a 'small' company varies so much that a stock which is too small to gain a listing on, say, the NYSE is larger in value than a 'big' firm on many European stock exchanges. International comparisons make it possible to test whether variables that are alleged to be important in, say, the US are also important elsewhere. Such tests are particularly useful, since explanations for stock market regularities, which are supported by empirical evidence in only one country, are likely to be incorrect!

Stock market anomalies provide a challenge to both the theorist and the empiricist. But the challenge to the empirical researcher lies not only in the realm of identifying anomalies and testing possible explanations for them. There is also a serious question mark posed about the integrity of much of the methodology of financial research.

In particular, existing methods used for specifying the 'normal' return on a security are flawed. In the presence of a size-based (or any other type of) regularity, the capital asset pricing model breaks down. Without an accepted model for expected returns, much of the empirical literature on performance measurement and on market efficiency is suspect. Some of the research reviewed by Josef Lakonishok (chapter 16) moves towards developing improved empirical techniques in the light of the small firm and related effects. But we have only just begun the process of determining the impact of stock market anomalies on the finance research paradigm. There is much still to be done.

7 Acknowledgments

This book would not have been possible without the encouragement and help of many people. Colleagues at the European Institute for Advanced Studies in Management were instrumental in sponsoring the original symposium, and we are especially grateful to Gerry Dirickx–Van Dyck, in Brussels, for her help. Thanks are also due to all those who participated at the symposium, and to others who have subsequently contributed to this volume. It was because of the high quality of their work that the current volume came into being.

At the London Business School, Anitra Hume-Wright shared responsibility for organizing the initial conference, and laboured enthusiastically on preparing the manuscript. Helpful suggestions were received from George Constantinides, Don Keim, Josef Lakonishok, Maurice Levi, Paul Marsh, Art Raviv, Cecilia Reyes and Dick Stapleton, while Francis Brooke of Cambridge University Press provided much-appreciated advice. Other suggestions were received from Jono, Susie, Benjy and Daniel Dimson. The Editor, however, remains responsible for any errors or omissions which remain.

Notes

1 This section incorporates some ideas put forward at the EIASM symposium by various colleagues, especially Art Raviv.

References

Ball, R. (1978) 'Anomalies in Relationships Between Securities Yields and Yield-Surrogates', *Journal of Financial Economics*, June–September, 103–26.

Banz, R. (1981) 'The Relationship Between Returns and Market Value of Common Stocks', *Journal of Financial Economics*, 9, 3–18.

Basu, S. (1977) 'Investment Performance of Common Stocks in Relation to their Price-Earnings Ratios: A Test of the Efficient Markets Hypothesis', *Journal of Finance*, June, 663–82.

Berges, A., McConnell, J. and Schlarbaum, G. (1984) 'The Turn-of-the-Year in Canada', *Journal of Finance*, March, 185–92.

Black, F., Jensen, M.C. and Scholes, M. (1972) 'The Capital Asset Pricing Model: Some Empirical Tests'. In M.C. Jensen (ed.) *Studies in the Theory of Capital Markets*, Praeger.

Brown, P., Keim, D., Kleidon, A. and Marsh, T. (1983) 'New Evidence on the Nature of Size-Related Anomalies in Stock Prices', *Journal of Financial Economics*, June, 105–27.

Dimson, E. and Marsh, P. (1987) *The Hoare Govett Smaller Companies Index for the UK*, London: Hoare Govett Limited.

Fama, E. (1970) 'Efficient Capital Markets: A Review of Theory and Empirical Work', *Journal of Finance*, May, 383–417.

Fama, E. and MacBeth, J. (1973) 'Risk, Return and Equilibrium: Empirical Tests', *Journal of Political Economy*, May/June, 607–36.

French, K. (1980) 'Stock Returns and the Weekend Effect', *Journal of Financial Economics*, March, 55–69.

Harris, M. and Raviv, A. (1985) 'Corporate Control Contests and Capital Structure', Working Paper, J.L. Kellogg Graduate School of Management, Northwestern University, August.

Ijiri, Y. and Simon, H. (1964) 'Business Firm Growth and Size', *The American Economic Review*, March, 77–89.

Kato, K. and Schalheim, J. (1985) 'Seasonal and Size Anomalies in the Japanese Stock Market', *Journal of Financial and Quantitative Analysis*, February, 243–60.

Keim, D. (1983) 'Size Related Anomalies and Stock Return Seasonality: Further Empirical Evidence', *Journal of Financial Economics*, March, 13–32.

Lintner, J. (1965) 'The Valuation of Risk Assets and the Selection of Risky Investments in Stock Portfolios and Capital Budgets', *Review of Economics and Statistics*, February, 13–37.

Lucas, R. (1978) 'On the Size Distribution of Business Firms', *Bell Journal of Economics*, Autumn, 508–23.

Manne, H. (1965) 'Mergers and the Market for Corporate Control', *Journal of Political Economy*, April, 110–20.

Marsh, P.R. (1979) 'Equity Rights Issues and the Efficiency of the U.K. Stock Market', *Journal of Finance*, September, 839–62.

Merton, R.C. (1973) 'An Intertemporal Capital Asset Pricing Model', *Econometrica*, September, 867–87.

Officer, R. (1975) 'Seasonality in the Australian Capital Market: Market Efficiency and Empirical Issues', *Journal of Financial Economics*, March, 29–52.

Reinganum, M. (1981) 'Misspecification of Capital Asset Pricing: Empirical Anomalies Based on Earnings Yields and Market Values', *Journal of Financial Economics*, March, 19–46.

Rozeff, M.S. and Kinney, W.R. Jnr (1976) 'Capital Market Seasonality: The Case of Stock Returns', *Journal of Financial Economics*, 379–402.

Sharpe, W.F. (1964) 'Capital Asset Prices: a Theory of Market Equilibrium Under Conditions of Risk', *Journal of Finance*, September, 425–42.

Simon, H. and Bonini, C. (1958) 'The Size Distribution of Business Firms', *The American Economic Review*, September, 607–17.

Van den Bergh, W. and Wessels, R. E. (1985) 'Stock Market Seasonalities and Taxes: An Examination of the Tax-Loss Selling Hypothesis', *Journal of Business Finance and Accounting*, 12, 515–30.

Wahlroos, B. and Berglund, R. (1983) 'The January Effect on a Small Stock Market: Lumpy Information and Tax-loss selling', Working Paper, Northwestern University.

Williams, J. (1986) 'Financial Anomalies under Rational Expectations: A Theory of the January and Small-Firm Effects', Working Paper, New York University GSB, July.

2 Stock market regularities: a synthesis of the evidence and explanations

*DONALD B. KEIM**

1 Introduction

The capital asset pricing model (CAPM) has occupied a central position in financial economics over the twenty years since its origins in the papers by Sharpe (1964), Lintner (1965) and Treynor. Given certain simplifying assumptions,[1] the CAPM states that the expected rate of return on any asset is related to the riskless rate and the expected market return as follows:

$$E(R_i) = R_Z + [E(R_M) - R_Z]\beta_i \tag{1}$$

where:

> $E(R_i)$ is the expected rate of return on asset i;
> R_Z is the rate of return on the riskless asset in the Sharpe–Lintner–Treynor model and is the rate of return of an asset with zero correlation with the market in Black's (1972) extension;
> $E(R_M)$ is the expected rate of return on the market portfolio of all marketable assets; and
> β_i (beta) is the asset's sensitivity to market movements.

If the model is correct and security markets are efficient (Fama, 1970), security returns will *on average* conform to the above relation. Persistent departures, however, represent violations of the joint hypothesis that both the CAPM and efficient market hypothesis are correct.[2]

The strict set of assumptions underlying the CAPM has prompted numerous criticisms. Although any model proposes a simplified view of the world, that is not sufficient basis for its rejection; the rejection or acceptance of the theory should rest on the scientific evidence. Sophisticated tests of the propositions of the CAPM were made possible by the creation of a computerized data base of stock prices and distributions at the University of Chicago in the 1960s. Numerous studies were conducted in the early 1970s, the most prominent being those conducted by

Black *et al.* (1972), Blume and Friend (1973) and Fama and MacBeth (1973). The results of these studies were generally interpreted as supportive of the CAPM, although the coefficient on beta – representing an estimate of the market risk premium – was only marginally important in explaining cross-sectional differences in average security returns.

Although the early tests lend some credence to the CAPM in its basic form, Roll (1977) raises some legitimate questions regarding the validity of these tests. Very briefly, Roll argues that tests performed with any market portfolio other than the true market portfolio are not tests of the CAPM and that tests of the CAPM can be extremely sensitive to the choice of market proxy. He also points out that the need to specify an alternative model to the CAPM in some of the early tests – e.g. the Fama and MacBeth test of whether residual variance or beta squared are relevant for explaining returns – can lead to faulty inference. That is, the CAPM may be false, but if residual variance or beta squared do not explain the violation, the test will not reject the CAPM. In response to Roll's first point, Stambaugh (1982) constructs broader market indices that include, for example, bonds and real estate, and finds that such tests do not seem to be very sensitive to the choice of market proxy. The second point has been addressed in the work of Gibbons (1982), Stambaugh (1982) and others, which introduced the use of multivariate tests that do not require the specification of an alternative asset pricing model when testing the CAPM. These multivariate tests have not, however, yielded conclusive results regarding the validity of the CAPM.

Since the CAPM is not unambiguously supported by the tests, researchers have formulated alternative models. Many have developed equilibrium models by relaxing some of the CAPM assumptions. For example, Mayers (1972) allows for non-marketable assets such as human capital and Brennan (1970) and Litzenberger and Ramaswamy (1979) relax the no-tax assumption. Others have examined more *ad hoc* alternatives to the CAPM in the spirit of Fama and MacBeth. For example, Banz (1981) examines the importance of market value of common equity and Basu (1977) examines the importance of P/E ratios in explaining beta-risk-adjusted returns.

The remainder of this chapter discusses such alternatives to the CAPM. The next section addresses models that relax the no-tax assumption of the CAPM. Section 3 contains a discussion of the empirical evidence relating to the ability of market value of equity, E/P ratios and other *ad hoc* variables to explain violations of the CAPM. This evidence is followed by a rather lengthy section on potential explanations that addresses, among other issues, the exaggerated occurrence of these effects in January. Section 5 discusses other persistent patterns in security returns; the chapter ends with some concluding remarks.

2 After-tax asset pricing models

A well-known extension of the CAPM explicitly recognizes the complexity of the tax laws in many countries. For example, higher marginal tax rates of dividend income versus capital gains should make taxable investors prefer a dollar of pre-tax capital gain to a dollar of dividends. Under such conditions as exist in the US, Brennan (1970) and Litzenberger and Ramaswamy (1979) extend the CAPM to include an extra factor, dividend yield. The hypothesis is that, holding risk constant, the higher is a stock's dividend yield, the higher is the required before-tax return to compensate taxable investors for the higher tax liability.

There are, of course, counter-arguments. Miller and Scholes (1978) argue that the tax code has provisions that permit investors to transform dividend income into capital gains. If the marginal investors are using these or other effective shelters, then the before-tax rate on dividend-paying stocks may be no different from stocks that do not pay dividends even though the tax law appears to penalize dividends. Nevertheless, the tax differential has prompted some tax-exempt institutions to 'tilt' their portfolios toward higher yielding securities with the hope of capturing the benefits of the supposedly higher before-tax returns without bearing the costs of the higher implied taxes.

The effectiveness of such a strategy, of course, hinges on whether these after-tax models are supported by the evidence. The general form of the after-tax CAPM is

$$E(R_i) = a_0 + a_1 \beta_i + a_2 d_i \tag{2}$$

where d_i is the dividend yield for security i and a_2 is an implicit tax coefficient that is independent of the level of the dividend yield. The question is whether a_2 is reliably positive and consistent with realistic tax rates.

Empirical testing of the hypothesis that $a_2 = 0$ presents the researcher with a number of difficult problems. For example, since asset pricing models are cast in terms of expectations, the researcher needs to arrive at a suitable *ex-ante* dividend yield measure. Further, he must ask whether the tax effects that motivate the model occur at a single point in time (i.e. the ex date) or whether they are spread over a longer period. Finally, most researchers, based on the models of Brennan and of Litzenberger and Ramaswamy (1979), have assumed a linear relation between dividend yields and returns, even though the relation might be more complicated.

Table 1 *Summary of implied tax rates from studies of the relation between dividend yields and stock returns*

Author(s) and date of study	Test period and return interval	Implied tax rate (%) (*t*-statistic)
Black and Scholes (1974)	1936–66, monthly	22 (0.9)
Blume (1980)	1936–76, quarterly	52 (2.1)
Gordon and Bradford (1980)	1926–78, monthly	18 (8.5)
Litzenberger and Ramaswamy (1979)	1936–77, monthly	24 (8.6)
Litzenberger and Ramaswamy (1982)	1940–80, monthly	14–23 (4.4–8.8)
Miller and Scholes (1982)	1940–78, monthly	4 (1.1)
Morgan (1982)	1936–77, monthly	21 (11.0)
Rosenberg and Marathe (1979)	1931–66, monthly	40 (1.9)
Stone and Barter (1979)	1947–70, monthly	56 (2.0)

Studies have employed a variety of definitions of dividend yield and methodologies in addressing these issues. In the interest of brevity, we forego discussion of the methodological subtleties and simply summarize the major results. Table 1, adopted from Litzenberger and Ramaswamy (1982) and updated, reports estimates of the dividend yield coefficient a_2. In each instance the estimate of a_2 is positive indicating that, holding beta risk constant, the higher is the dividend yield the higher is the before-tax rate of return for common stocks. Although not all of the coefficients are significantly different from zero (e.g. Black and Scholes, 1974; Miller and Scholes, 1982) and not all authors attribute the positive coefficients to taxes (e.g. Blume, 1980; Gordon and Bradford, 1980), the evidence in many of the studies appears to be consistent with the after-tax models.

The story may not be as simple, though, as the models of Brennan (1970) and Litzenberger and Ramaswamy (1979) suggest. Blume (1980) and Litzenberger and Ramaswamy (1980) find that the yield–return relation is not linear for some definitions of dividend yield. They find that the average return for non-dividend paying firms is higher than for many dividend paying firms. Further, Keim (1985, 1986a) finds that this non-linear relation is primarily due to the exaggerated occurrence of the effect in January. Keim (1985) uses a definition of dividend yield similar to Blume and estimates dividend yield coefficients separately in January

Table 2 *Mean daily returns (standard errors) and estimated betas for ten size portfolios of NYSE and AMEX firms, 1964–1978**

Portfolio	Mean daily mean (%)	Average median market value ($ million)	OLS beta	Dimson beta
Smallest	0.142 (0.015)	4.7	0.75	1.69
2	0.092 (0.015)	11.1	0.87	1.64
3	0.079 (0.014)	19.8	0.90	1.55
4	0.064 (0.140)	31.5	0.96	1.50
5	0.058 (0.014)	48.3	0.98	1.46
6	0.053 (0.013)	75.4	0.97	1.39
7	0.046 (0.013)	120.4	0.95	1.31
8	0.042 (0.013)	213.4	0.97	1.24
9	0.035 (0.012)	436.3	0.95	1.13
Largest	0.024 (0.012)	1086.0	0.98	0.97

*Table adapted from Reinganum (1982).

and non-January months. The estimated coefficients are positive and significant in January *and* non-January months, but the January coefficient of 1.15 $[t(a_2^{JAN}=0)=5.6]$ is significantly larger $[t(a_2^{JAN}-\alpha_2^{F-D})=4.6]$ than the non-January coefficient of 0.18 $[t(a_2^{F-D}=0)=3.3]$. Such a finding is not entirely consistent with the simple tax-related models and is suggestive of the possible manifestation of other anomalous effects that exhibit January seasonals, such as the size effect.

3 Other observed asset pricing regularities

The size effect

Considerable interest has been generated in the financial and academic communities by the finding of a significant relation between common stock returns and the market value of common equity, commonly referred to as the size effect. Other things equal, the smaller is firm size the larger is the stock's expected return. Banz (1981) was the first to document this phenomenon. For the period from 1931 to 1975, Banz estimated a model of the form

$$E(R_i) = a_0 + a_1 \beta_i + a_2 S_i \tag{3}$$

where S_i is a measure of the relative market capitalization ('size') for firm i. He found that the statistical association between returns and size is negative and of approximately the same magnitude as that between returns and beta, documented in, for example, Fama and MacBeth (1973).

Reinganum (1981, 1982), using daily data over the period from 1963 to 1977, found that portfolios of small firms had substantially higher returns, on average, than large firms. Table 2, adopted from Reinganum (1982), reports average returns and other characteristics for portfolios comprising the ten deciles of size for NYSE and AMEX firms. The difference in returns between the smallest and largest firms is about 30 percent annually. In response to Roll's (1981) conjecture that this size effect may be a statistical artifact of improperly measured risk due to the infrequent trading of small firms, Reinganum (1982) estimates betas according to methods designed to account for these problems (see Scholes and Williams, 1977; Dimson, 1979). He finds that the magnitude of the size effect is not very sensitive to the use of these estimates. (The Dimson estimator is reported in table 2). Blume and Stambaugh (1983) demonstrate, however, that the portfolio strategy implicit in Reinganum's paper (requiring daily rebalancing of the portfolio to equal weights) produces upward-biased estimates of small-firm portfolio returns due to a 'bid-ask bias' that is inversely related to size. Blume and Stambaugh show that the size-related premium is halved in portfolio strategies that avoid this bias.

Two reservations are usually expressed regarding implementation of these findings – the market for the smallest capitalization firms is rather illiquid and the firms in this market do not meet minimum capitalization requirements for many institutional investors. The average market values reported in table 2 demonstrate that such potential constraints may not be binding. The table shows that the effect is approximately linear in the decile of size, meaning that portfolios of securities with successively smaller firm values yield successively larger risk-adjusted returns. The evidence suggests a wide array of possible portfolios with higher average returns (in some cases, substantially higher returns) than a portfolio of large firms such as the S&P 500 – a typically-used performance benchmark in the investment industry.[3] In other words, the abnormal return opportunities presented by smaller firm stocks are not confined to the very smallest and least liquid stocks on the NYSE and AMEX.

Table 3 *The firm size effect: international evidence**

Australia (1958–81)[a]		Canada (1951–80)[b]			Japan (1966–83)[c]		United Kingdom (1956–80)[d]		
Size portfolio	Return % (std error)	Size portfolio	Return % (std error) 1951–72	1973–80	Size portfolio	Return % (std error)	Size portfolio	Return % 1956–65	1966–80
Smallest	6.75 (0.64)	Smallest	2.02 (0.27)	1.67 (0.58)	Smallest	2.03 (0.35)	Smallest	1.27	1.00
2	2.23 (0.39)	2	1.48 (0.22)	1.66 (0.56)	2	1.50 (0.32)	2	1.18	0.89
3	1.74 (0.31)	3	1.14 (0.22)	1.41 (0.59)	3	1.38 (0.29)	Largest	0.98	0.84
4	1.32 (0.27)	4	0.99 (0.23)	1.39 (0.56)	4	1.17 (0.27)			
5	1.48 (0.24)	Largest	0.90 (0.23)	1.23 (0.58)	Largest	1.14 (0.27)			
6	1.27 (0.24)								
7	1.15 (0.24)								
8	1.22 (0.24)								
9	1.18 (0.25)								
Largest	1.02 (0.29)								

Note: *Monthly returns are reported for each country.
Sources:
[a]Brown et al. (1983b).
[b]Berges et al. (1984).
[c]Nakamura and Terada (1984).
[d]Reinganum and Shapiro (1983)

Table 4 *Temporal behavior of the size effect*

Average differences (*t*-statistics) in daily returns (percent) between portfolios constructed from firms in the top and bottom decile of size (measured by market value of equity) on the NYSE and AMEX over the period 1963–79

	Monday	Tuesday	Wednesday	Thursday	Friday	Mean daily return over all days
January	0.742	0.698	0.607	0.645	0.821	0.702
	(6.51)	(5.47)	(4.80)	(5.54)	(7.07)	(13.01)
February	0.288	0.150	0.181	0.217	0.240	0.212
	(2.80)	(1.78)	(2.15)	(2.41)	(2.46)	(5.18)
March	0.091	−0.006	0.171	0.175	0.127	0.112
	(1.31)	(−0.08)	(2.99)	(3.14)	(1.97)	(3.81)
April	−0.010	−0.096	0.008	0.047	0.159	0.018
	(−0.14)	(−1.64)	(0.10)	(0.81)	(3.00)	(0.62)
May	0.196	−0.093	0.052	−0.007	0.153	0.057
	(2.57)	(−1.21)	(1.00)	(−0.08)	(2.23)	(1.74)
June	−0.038	−0.135	0.081	0.011	0.171	0.018
	(−0.46)	(−1.80)	(1.71)	(0.17)	(2.62)	(0.57)
July	−0.027	0.151	−0.106	0.152	0.242	0.084
	(−0.38)	(2.35)	(−1.33)	(2.24)	(3.62)	(2.61)
August	0.034	−0.020	0.018	0.130	0.162	0.065
	(0.47)	(−0.28)	(0.27)	(1.68)	(2.28)	(2.00)
September	0.156	0.108	0.043	0.044	0.210	0.111
	(1.50)	(1.84)	(0.71)	(0.52)	(3.68)	(3.37)
October	−0.241	−0.159	−0.080	0.043	0.050	−0.077
	(−2.16)	(−1.90)	(−0.76)	(0.66)	(0.60)	(−1.87)
November	−0.110	−0.158	−0.069	−0.007	0.247	−0.016
	(−1.52)	(−1.61)	(−0.89)	(−0.07)	(4.41)	(−0.44)
December	−0.155	−0.182	−0.023	0.068	0.402	0.022
	(−1.81)	(−1.87)	(−0.20)	(0.90)	(5.44)	(0.52)
Mean return over all months	0.069	0.021	0.075	0.128	0.249	0.109
	(2.60)	(0.85)	(3.08)	(5.43)	(10.98)	(9.84)

The abnormal return opportunities presented by smaller firm stocks do not seem to be confined to the US. Analysis of stock returns on four major stock exchanges – Australia, Canada, Japan and United Kingdom – has revealed a distinct size–return relation.[4] The results are summarized in table 3. It is difficult to draw comparisons about the relative magnitude of the size effect across the four countries because of differing time periods and research design (e.g. some studies use size quintiles, others use deciles). Nevertheless, in each country there is an inverse relation between stock returns and market capitalization.

Much of the subsequent research on the US size effect has attempted to provide a more complete characterization of the phenomenon. For example, we know that among the firms that academic researchers consider 'small,'[5] those small firms with the largest abnormal returns tend to be firms that have recently become small (or that have recently declined in price), that do not pay a dividend or that have high dividend yields (Keim, 1986a) that have low prices (Stoll and Whaley, 1983; Blume and Stambaugh, 1983) and that have low P/E ratios (Reinganum, 1981; Basu, 1983).

Others have examined the time-related patterns of portfolio returns stratified by market capitalization. Brown *et al.* (1983a) find that when averaged over all months the size effect reverses itself for sustained periods: in many periods there is a consistent premium for small size, in (fewer) other periods there is a discount. In other words, there have been periods (one, for example, was 1969–73) when a small-capitalization strategy would have underperformed a large-capitalization strategy on a risk-adjusted basis.

The magnitude of the size effect also seems to differ across days of the week and months of the year. Keim and Stambaugh (1984) find that the size effect becomes more pronounced as the week progresses and is most pronounced on Friday. These tendencies are evident as you scan across the rows of table 4. Reported in table 4 is the average magnitude of the size effect as measured by the difference in returns between the smallest and largest deciles of firms on the NYSE and AMEX, cross classified by day of the week and month of the year over the period 1963–79. The bottom row which measures the average effect by day of the week, demonstrates the tendency for the size effect to increase as the week draws to a close.

The most dramatic seasonal pattern in the size effect is found at the turn of the year. Keim (1983) finds that the size effect is concentrated in January: approximately 50 per cent of the return difference between small and large firm stocks found by Reinganum (1981) is concentrated in January. The January seasonal in the size effect is evident in the rightmost column of table 4. Keim further reports that 50 percent of this January effect is concentrated in the first five trading days of the year. This turn-of-the-year return behavior is also found by Roll (1983a) who notes that, in addition, small firms have abnormally large returns on the last trading day in December.

The price/earnings effect

Earnings-related strategies have a long tradition in the investment community. The most popular of such strategies, buying stocks that sell at low multiples of earnings, can be traced at least to Graham and Dodd

(1940, p. 533) who proposed that 'a necessary but not a sufficient condition' for investing in a common stock is 'a reasonable ratio of market price to average earnings.' They advocated that a prudent investor should never pay as much as 20 times earnings and a suitable multiplier should be 12 or less.

Nicholson (1960) published the first extensive study of the relation between P/E multiples and subsequent total returns showing that low P/E stocks consistently provided returns greater than the average stock. Basu (1977) introduced the notion that P/E ratios may explain violations of the CAPM and found that, for his sample of NYSE firms, there was a distinct negative relation between P/E ratios and average returns in excess of those predicted by the CAPM. If one had followed his strategy of buying the quintile of smallest P/E stocks and selling short the quintile of largest P/E stocks, based on annual ranking, the average annual abnormal return would have been 6.75 percent (before commissions and other transaction costs) over the 1957 to 1971 period. Reinganum (1981), analyzing both NYSE and AMEX firms, confirmed and extended Basu's findings using returns data to 1975.

Some have argued that because firms in the same industry tend to have similar P/E ratios, a portfolio strategy that concentrates on low P/E stocks may indeed benefit from higher than average returns, but at a cost of reduced diversification. These arguments also suggest that the P/E effect may in fact be an industry effect. Peavy and Goodman (1983) address this potential bias and examine the P/E ratio of a stock relative to its industry P/E (PER). They find a distinct negative relation between PERs and abnormal returns over the 1970–80 period. A portfolio strategy that bought the quintile of lowest PER stocks and sold short the stocks in the highest PER quintile would have yielded an annualized abnormal return of 20.80 percent over the period. These results, in conjunction with the findings of Basu and Reinganum, suggest that the P/E ratio – or an underlying and perhaps more fundamental variable for which P/E is a proxy – is capable of explaining a considerable portion of the variation in cross-sectional security returns.

The Value Line enigma

Investment advisory services often base their recommendations on earnings-related information. The largest and most consistently success-ful advisory service is the Value Line Investor Survey. Value Line forecasts the prospective performance of approximately 1700 common stocks on a weekly basis. Value Line separates these stocks into five categories of expected return based on historical and forecast infor-mation such as earnings momentum and P/E ratios.

Table 5 *Average values of price to book (P/B), market value, earnings to price (E/P) and price for ten portfolios of NYSE firms constructed on the basis of increasing price to book values^a (1964–82)*

Price/book portfolio	Average P/B	Average market value ($ million)	Average E/P	Average price ($)
Lowest	0.52	217.1	0.06	20.09
2	0.83	402.5	0.11	22.97
3	1.00	498.6	0.11	25.08
4	1.14	604.7	0.11	27.79
5	1.29	680.2	0.10	28.97
6	1.47	695.6	0.10	31.55
7	1.71	888.9	0.09	36.07
8	2.07	872.6	0.09	37.84
9	2.80	1099.2	0.07	44.80
Highest	7.01	1964.3	0.05	60.09

Note: ^{a}Portfolios are rebalanced at March 31. Prices and number of shares outstanding are March 31 values. Book values and earnings are year-end values. Only December fiscal closers are included in the portfolios.

The success of the Value Line system has been borne out by several academic studies. Black (1973), Holloway (1981) and Copeland and Mayers (1982) all find that, after adjusting for beta risk, investors can obtain abnormal performance by, for example, buying group 1 securities and selling short group 5 securities. Stickel (1985) finds that investors can earn abnormal returns by devising strategies based on rank changes (e.g. buying stocks upgraded from group 2 to group 1).

Value Line's successful performance is puzzling for the same reasons that the size and P/E effects are puzzling – predetermined variables are used to construct portfolios that have abnormal returns relative to the CAPM. It is possible that there is a high degree of association between a ranking produced by Value Line's system and a simple ranking based on P/E or size. Indeed, the evidence of Stickel suggests that much of Value Line's abnormal performance might be attributable to small firms. More research is necessary to sort out these issues.

Interrelation between the effects

The literature discussed in the preceding sections documents a strong cross-sectional relation between abnormal returns and market capitalization, P/E ratios and dividend yields. Other effects have also been documented in the literature, perhaps most notably the relation between risk-adjusted returns and the ratio of price per share to book value per share (P/B) discussed most recently by Rosenberg *et al.* (1985). Few

Table 6 *The P/E, P/B and price effects*

Average monthly returns (standard deviations) for portfolios of NYSE firms over the 1964–1982 period

Decile of ranking variable	Price/earnings effect[a]		Price/book effect[a]		Price effect[b]	
	January	Feb–Dec	January	Feb–Dec	January	Feb–Dec
Lowest	6.65 (9.39)	1.04 (5.34)	9.14 (10.32)	0.87 (5.64)	12.02 (14.07)	0.96 (7.15)
2	6.34 (8.62)	0.98 (4.88)	7.34 (8.99)	0.83 (5.30)	8.08 (10.38)	0.89 (5.70)
3	5.06 (7.44)	0.95 (4.49)	5.96 (7.81)	0.87 (4.78)	6.00 (9.06)	0.83 (5.17)
4	4.22 (7.85)	0.95 (4.49)	4.64 (7.99)	0.81 (4.48)	4.98 (8.62)	0.85 (4.85)
5	4.01 (7.49)	0.62 (4.53)	3.97 (7.49)	0.67 (4.30)	3.93 (7.70)	0.78 (4.70)
6	3.60 (7.60)	0.63 (4.68)	3.28 (7.09)	0.67 (4.62)	3.22 (7.85)	0.79 (5.00)
7	3.32 (7.18)	0.48 (4.67)	3.21 (7.13)	0.79 (4.84)	2.69 (7.29)	0.83 (4.70)
8	3.25 (8.14)	0.75 (5.19)	2.64 (7.67)	0.69 (5.17)	2.24 (6.39)	0.77 (4.89)
9	2.39 (7.07)	0.89 (5.15)	2.93 (7.39)	0.87 (5.37)	1.27 (6.59)	0.85 (5.02)
Largest	2.77 (6.96)	0.90 (5.82)	1.43 (6.55)	1.05 (5.51)	0.83 (6.09)	0.90 (4.93)

Notes: [a]Portfolios are rebalanced at March 31 of each year. The P/E and P/B ratios used to create deciles are computed using the previous year-end earnings and book values and March 31 prices. Only December fiscal closers are included in the portfolios. [b]Portfolios are rebalanced annually at year-end. Year-end prices are used to create deciles.

would argue that these separate findings are entirely independent phenomena, since market capitalization, P/E and P/B are computed using a common variable – price per share of the common stock. Further, results in Blume and Husic (1973), Stoll and Whaley (1983) and Blume and Stambaugh (1983) reveal a cross-sectional association between price per share and average returns.

To demonstrate the association among these variables, table 5 reports average values of P/B, market capitalization, E/P and price for ten portfolios constructed of NYSE firms on the basis of increasing values of P/B. Portfolios are rebalanced annually over the 1964–82 period. It is apparent from table 5 that the higher is the average P/B of the firms in a portfolio, the higher are the corresponding average values of market capitalization, P/E and stock price.[6]

Perhaps more direct evidence that the effects are associated with some common underlying factor lies in the finding that there are significant January seasonals in the dividend yield effect (Keim, 1985), P/E effect (Cooke and Rozeff, 1984) and price and P/B effects. Evidence on the last three effects is reported in table 6 which contains average January and non-January returns for portfolios based on annual rankings on P/B, E/P and price over the 1964–82 period. The three time series of portfolio returns are created in a manner analogous to many previous studies. At annual intervals during the period, NYSE firms are ranked separately according to their P/E ratio, P/B ratio or price and sorted into ten portfolios. These portfolios are held for the next twelve months and equal-weighted portfolio returns are computed in each month. This process is repeated for each year of the sample period. The results are basically the same for each separate experiment. There is a strong inverse relation between the ranking variable and average returns in January, and not much of a relation in the other months.

From a practical perspective, the investor's objective is to isolate and use in a portfolio strategy the characteristic(s) that will result in the highest risk-adjusted returns for the portfolio. That is, the typical investor is less interested in the conjecture that all these effects are somehow related than he is in finding the ranking characteristic that works best. Recent studies have addressed this issue by trying to answer the following question: If an investor screens first on characteristic X, say P/E, can he further improve portfolio performance (on a beta risk-adjusted basis) by adding an additional screen based on characteristic Y, say market capitalization (or vice versa)?

Most of the studies in this area (Reinganum, 1981; Peavy and Goodman, 1982; Basu, 1983; Cooke and Rozeff, 1984) address the interrelation between the P/E and market capitalization effects. The results are less than conclusive: Reinganum argues that the size effect subsumes the P/E effect (i.e. there is no marginal value to P/E after first ranking on size); Basu argues just the opposite. Peavy and Goodman and Cooke and Rozeff, after performing meticulous replications of and extensions to the methodologies of Basu and Reinganum reach surprisingly different conclusions. Peavy and Goodman's results agree with those of Basu, but Cooke and Rozeff (1984, p. 464) conclude, 'it does not appear that either market value subsumes earnings/price ratio or the earnings/price ratio subsumes market value as has been claimed.'

The upshot of these studies is that if one constructs a portfolio based on high E/P stocks, there may still be some value added by considering the additional dimension of firm size, and vice versa. In a similar vein, Keim (1985, 1986a) analyzes the interrelation between the dividend yield and size effects and finds that the two effects are not mutually exclusive and that, over and above the benefits from discriminating along the size dimension, it may be beneficial to discriminate those firms that pay no dividends or that have high dividend yields. One interpretation is that market capitalization, E/P and dividend yield (as well as the other variables mentioned above) may be imperfect surrogates for an underlying and more fundamental 'factor' that is missing from the CAPM (see, for example, Ball, 1978).

4 Can we explain the size effect?

The lion's share of the effort expended in attempts to explain the above phenomena has been directed to the size effect. Some have argued that alternative asset pricing models may explain the cross-sectional association between risk-adjusted returns and size. For example, Chen (1983) and Chan *et al.* (1983) argue that most of the abnormal returns associated with the size effect are explained by additional risk factors in the context of the arbitrage pricing theory of Ross (1976). Others maintain that market imperfections assumed away by the CAPM are responsible. In this vein Stoll and Whaley (1983) argue that round-trip transactions costs are sufficient to offset the abnormal returns associated with the size effect. Schultz (1983) points out, however, that transactions costs would have to be larger in January than in other months to explain the January seasonal in abnormal returns, but he finds no evidence of seasonally varying transaction costs.

Others have addressed the possibility that the size effect is merely a statistical artifact. Roll (1981) suggests that large abnormal returns of small firms could be due to systematic biases (due to infrequent or nonsynchronous trading) in the beta estimates for these firms, but Reinganum (1982) demonstrates that this bias cannot explain the anomaly. Christie and Hertzel (1981) argue that the size effect could be due to non-stationarity of beta. A firm whose common stock price has recently declined – i.e. a firm that is becoming 'small' – has effectively experienced, other things equal, an increase in leverage and a concomitant increase in the risk of its equity. Thus, historical estimates of beta that assume such risk is constant over time are 'stale' and understate (overstate) the risk and overstate (understate) average risk-adjusted returns of stocks whose market capitalization has fallen (risen). Christie and Hertzel adjust for this bias, but the adjustment does not eliminate the size effect. Chan (1983) makes a similar adjustment and finds that 'the size effect is reduced to a magnitude whose economic significance is debatable.' Unfortunately, neither study differentiates between January and non-January returns. Finally, Blume and Stambaugh (1983) demonstrate that the portfolio strategies implicit in papers such as Reinganum (1982) and Keim (1983), which require daily rebalancing of the portfolio to equal weights, yield upward-biased estimates of small-firm portfolio returns due to a 'bid-ask bias' that is inversely related to market capitalization. Roll (1983b) presents similar arguments. The idea is that such strategies sometimes implicitly buy at the bid price and sell at the ask price. Blume and Stambaugh show that for portfolio strategies that avoid this bias, the size effect is substantially reduced and is significant only in January.

In light of these last findings, attempts to explain the size phenomenon have focused primarily on January. Rather than exploring alternative equilibrium models that may accommodate the seasonal, most explanations have instead focused on frictions in the market that represent violations of the CAPM assumptions. The most popular hypothesis attributes the effect to year-end tax-loss selling. The tax-loss hypothesis can be summarized as follows:

The hypothesis maintains that tax laws influence investors' portfolio decisions by encouraging the sale of securities that have experienced recent price declines so that the (short-term) capital loss can be offset against taxable income. Small firm stocks are likely candidates for tax-loss selling since these stocks typically have higher variances of price changes and, therefore, larger probabilities of large price declines. Importantly, the tax-loss argument relies on the assumption that investors wait until the tax year-end to sell their common stock 'losers.' For example, in the U.S., a combination of liquidity requirements and eagerness to realize capital losses before the new tax year may dictate sale of such securities at year-end. The heavy selling pressure during this period supposedly depresses the prices of small firm stocks. After the tax year-end, the price pressure disappears and prices rebound to equilibrium levels. Hence small firm stocks display large returns in the beginning of the new tax year. (Brown *et al.*, 1983b, p.107)

Although popular on Wall Street, support for the tax-loss selling hypothesis has been less than overwhelming (on a priori grounds) in the academic community. Roll (1983b) has called the argument 'ridiculous' and Brown *et al.* (1983b) maintain that the tax laws in the US do not unambiguously induce the year-end price behavior of small stocks as predicted by the hypothesis. Further, Constantinides (1984) claims that optimal tax trading of common stocks should produce a January seasonal pattern in stock prices only if investors behave irrationally.

The evidence on the tax-loss hypothesis is less than conclusive. Reinganum (1983) and Roll (1983b) both examine the hypothesis and their tests suggest that part, but not all, of the abnormal returns in January is related to tax-related trading. On the other hand, Schultz (1985) finds that prior to 1917 – before the US income tax as we know it today created incentives for tax-loss selling – there was no evidence of a January effect.

The tax-loss selling hypothesis predicts a price rebound in the month of January immediately following price declines but makes no predictions regarding price movements for these stocks in subsequent turn-of-the-year periods. Chan (1985) and DeBondt and Thaler (1985) present evidence that the January abnormal returns of such 'loser' firms persist for as long as five years after the loser firms are identified. For example, Chan identifies 'losers' and 'winners' and constructs an 'arbitrage' portfolio (long losers, short winners) within each decile of market value for NYSE firms at December 31 of year t and tracks January abnormal returns in each of the following four years ($t + 1$ to $t + 4$). His results demonstrate a persistent January effect in each of the subsequent three years. Based on such evidence, both Chan and DeBondt and Thaler conclude that the January seasonal in stock returns may have little to do with tax-loss selling.

Others have tested the hypothesis by examining the month-to-month behavior of abnormal returns in countries with tax codes similar to the US code but with different tax year-ends. The tax-loss selling hypothesis predicts that, in the month immediately following the tax year-end, abnormal returns of small firms will be large relative to both other months and larger firms. The hypothesis makes no predictions regarding the time series behavior of abnormal returns during other months. The studies that examine returns in countries with similar tax codes to the US but different tax year-ends (Brown *et al.* (1983b) examine Australia (which has a June tax year-end); Reinganum and Shapiro (1983) examine the UK (which has an April tax year-end)) find seasonals after the tax year-end, but also find seasonals in January that are not predicted by the hypothesis. Further, Berges *et al.* (1984) find a January seasonal in Canadian stock returns prior to 1972, a period when Canada had no taxes on capital gains.

The inconsistent evidence regarding the tax-loss selling hypothesis argues for investigating other possibilities. One such possibility that has received attention on Wall Street is the notion that liquidity constraints of market participants may influence security returns, and these effects may have seasonal patterns. For example, periodic infusions of cash into the market as a result of, say, institutional transfers for pension accounts or proceeds from bonuses or profit-sharing plans, may impact the market. In fact, some evidence can be interpreted as supporting this idea. For example, Kato and Schallheim (1985), in an examination of the size effect in Japan, find January *and* June seasonals in small firm returns that coincide with traditional Japanese bonuses paid at the end of December and in June. Further, Rozeff (1985) finds a substantial *upward* shift in the ratio of sales to purchases of common stock by investors (who are not members of the NYSE) at the turn of the year that coincides with the dramatic increase in small firm returns in January (but Rozeff interprets this as evidence of a tax-loss selling effect). Ritter (1985) documents a similar pattern in the daily sale to purchase ratio for the retail customers of a large brokerage firm. Finally, Ariel (see chapter 8) finds a pattern in daily stock returns in *every month* but February that parallels precisely the pattern that occurs at the turn of the year. It would be easier to interpret such monthly patterns as liquidity or payroll effects than as tax effects.

5 Other 'seasonal' patterns in stock returns

In addition to the January effect, recent studies have documented additional empirical regularities that are related to the day of the week or the time of the month. Research on the so-called 'weekend effect' finds that average stock returns tend to be higher on Fridays and negative on Mondays. Cross (1973) and French (1980) document the effect using the S&P Composite Index beginning in 1953 and Gibbons and Hess (1981) document it for the Dow Jones Industrial Index of 30 stocks (1962–78). Keim and Stambaugh (1984) extend the findings for the S&P Composite to include the period 1928 to 1982 and also find the effect in actively traded OTC stocks. Jaffe and Westerfield (1985) find the effect on several foreign stock exchanges. The average returns associated with this intra-weekly phenomena in the US are shown in figure 1 for the 1928 to 1982 period.

All of the above studies document negative Monday returns using Friday-close-to-Monday-close returns and thus cannot ascertain whether the negative returns are due to the week-end non-trading period or to active trading on Monday. The findings of authors who have investigated this appear to be period-specific. Harris (see chapter 7), for all NYSE stocks for the period 1981 to 1983, and Smirlock and Starks (1984), for the Dow Jones 30 for the period 1963 to 1973, examine intra-daily returns

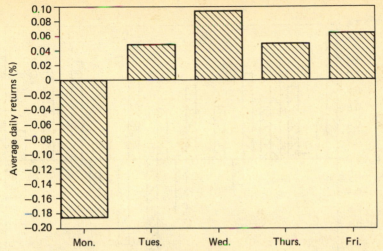

Figure 1   Day of the week effect, S & P Composite, 1928–1982
Source: Keim and Stambaugh (1984)

and show that negative Monday returns accrue from Friday close to
Monday open, as well as during trading on Monday. On the other hand,
Rogalski (1985) examines intra-daily data from 1974 to 1984 and finds
that negative Monday returns accrue entirely during the weekend
non-trading period.

Keim and Stambaugh (1984), noting results in Gibbons and Hess that
suggest Friday returns vary cross-sectionally with market value, find that
the return differential between small and large firms increases as the
week progresses, and is largest on Friday (see table 4). In addition, Keim
(1986b) demonstrates that, controlling for the large average returns in
January, the 'Friday effect' and the 'Monday effect' are no different in
January than in the other months.

Although we do not yet have an explanation of the weekend effect, we
do know that the effect is not likely to be a result of measurement error in
recorded prices (Gibbons and Hess, 1981; Keim and Stambaugh, 1984;
Smirlock and Starks, 1984), the delay between trading and settlement
due to check clearing (Gibbons and Hess, 1981; Lakonishok and Levi,
1982) or specialist trading activity (Keim and Stambaugh, 1984).

The monthly effect was found by Ariel (see chapter 8) who showed
that for the period 1963 to 1981 the average returns for common stocks
on the NYSE and AMEX are positive only for the last day of the month
and for days during the first half of the month. During the latter half of
the month returns are indistinguishable from zero. Ariel (chapter 8, p.
109) concludes that during his sample period '*all* of the market's cumulative advance occurred around the first half of the month, the second half

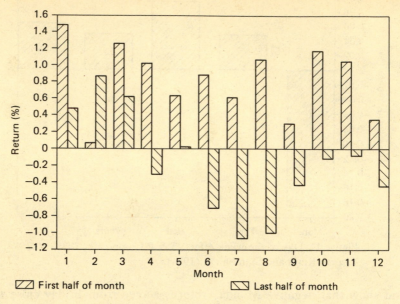

Figure 2   Monthly effect in stock returns, value-weighted CRSP
index, 1963–1981
Source: Ariel (chapter 8)

contributing nothing to the cumulative increase.' Figure 2, which is
drawn from table 3 in chapter 8, illustrates the phenomenon for the total
returns for the CRSP value-weighted index of NYSE and AMEX stocks.
The figure clearly demonstrates that returns in the first half of the month
are consistently larger than second-half returns (except for February); in
fact, negative average returns occur only in the second half. The results
given by Ariel (chapter 8) also suggest that, with the exception of
January, the difference between first-half returns of small firms and the
first-half returns of large firms is not substantial. Although Ariel is
unable to explain the effect, one potential explanation involves liquidity
constraints of investors as discussed above.

6 Concluding remarks

This chapter has presented a summary of evidence on empirical regularities that have persisted for quite a long time – in some instances for as
long as fifty years. Many of these findings are inconsistent with an
investment environment where the CAPM is descriptive of reality and
argue for consideration of alternative models of asset pricing. Other
findings, such as the day-of-the-week effect, do not necessarily represent

violations of any particular asset pricing model, yet are still interesting for their regularity.

Of course, the bottom line for investors is the extent to which this information can be translated into improved portfolio performance. That strategies based on the evidence here can improve performance has, in fact, been borne out in actual 'real world' experiments. In addition, I have attempted in the above discussion to convey (whenever possible) some sense of the practical magnitude of these effects. However, several caveats regarding implementation of such strategies might form a fitting conclusion. First, that some effects have persisted for as many as fifty years in no way guarantees their persistence into the future. In other words, there is no sure thing. Second, even if the effects were to persist, the costs of implementing strategies designed to capture these phenomena may be prohibitive. For example, illiquidity of the market and transactions costs may render a small stock strategy infeasible. Day-of-the-week and other seasonal effects may have practical value only for those investors who were planning to trade (and pay transactions costs) anyway and, thereby, incur only the costs of timing the trade. Finally, one must be cautious when interpreting the magnitudes of the 'abnormal' returns reported in these studies. To the extent that alternative models of asset pricing may be more appropriate than the CAPM, studies that use the CAPM as a benchmark may not be adjusting for the relevant risks and costs in a complete way. In that case, superior performance relative to the CAPM may not be superior once these other costs and risks are considered.

Notes

* This is a substantially revised and expanded version of a paper that appeared in the *Financial Analysts Journal*. I would like to thank Wayne Ferson, Allan Kleidon, Craig MacKinlay, Terry Marsh, Krishna Ramaswamy and Jay Ritter for helpful comments and suggestions at various stages of this project. Of course, any remaining errors are my responsibility.

1 The assumptions for the one-period CAPM are: (1) investors are risk averse and choose 'efficient' portfolios by maximizing expected return for a given level of risk; (2) no taxes or transactions costs; (3) identical borrowing and lending rates; (4) investors are in complete agreement with regard to expectations about individual securities; and (5) security returns have a multivariate normal distribution.

2 Such persistent departures are often referred to as 'anomalies.' The term anomaly, in this context, can be traced to Thomas Kuhn (1970) in his classic book, *The Structure of Scientific Revolutions*. Kuhn maintains that research activity in any normal science will revolve around a central paradigm and that experiments are conducted to test the predictions of the underlying paradigm and to extend the range of the phenomena it explains. Although research most often supports the underlying paradigm, eventually results are found that don't conform. Kuhn (1970, pp. 52–3) terms this stage 'discovery': 'Discovery commences with the awareness of *anomaly*, i.e., with the recognition that nature has somehow violated the paradigm-induced expectations that govern normal science' (emphasis added).

3 The S&P 500, being a value-weighted index of primarily high-capitalization firms, behaves like a portfolio of very large firms (e.g. portfolios 9 and 10 in table 2).

4 Nakamura and Terada (1984) also document a P/E effect on the Tokyo stock exchange.
5 For example, in 1980 the firms that comprised the smallest quintile of size for the NYSE had market capitalization of less than about $50 million.
6 One exception is the lowest P/B portfolio whose stocks on average have a low average E/P. This is due to the negative earnings firms that tend to be concentrated there. Note that firms with negative book values are excluded from the sample.

References

Ball, R. (1978) 'Anomalies in Relationships between Securities' Yields and Yield-Surrogates,' *Journal of Financial Economics*, 6, 103–26.

Banz, R.W. (1981) 'The Relationship Between Return and Market Value of Common Stock,' *Journal of Financial Economics*, 9, 3–18.

Barone-Adesi, G. and Tinic, S. (1983) 'Seasonality in Stock Prices: A Test of the "Tax-Loss-Selling" Hypothesis,' manuscript, University of Alberta.

Basu, S. (1977) 'Investment Performance of Common Stocks in Relation to their Price/Earnings Ratios: A Test of the Efficient Market Hypothesis,' *Journal of Finance*, 32, 3, June 663–82.

Basu, S. (1983) 'The Relationship Between Earnings' Yields, Market Value and the Returns for NYSE Stocks: Further Evidence,' *Journal of Financial Economics*, June, 129–56.

Berges, A., McConnell, J. and Schlarbaum, G. (1984) 'The Turn-of-the-Year in Canada,' *Journal of Finance*, March, 185–92.

Black, F. (1972) 'Yes, Virginia, There is Hope: Tests of the Value Line Ranking System,' *Financial Analysts Journal*, September/October, 10–14.

Black, F. and Scholes, M. (1974) 'The Effects of Dividend Yield and Dividend Policy as Common Stock Prices and Returns,' *Journal of Financial Economics*, 2, 1–22.

Black, F., Jensen, M.C. and Scholes, M. (1972) 'The Capital Asset Pricing Model: Some Empirical Tests.' In M.C. Jensen (ed.) *Studies in the Theory of Capital Markets*, New York: Praeger.

Blume, M.E. (1980) 'Stock Returns and Dividend Yields: Some More Evidence,' *Review of Economics and Statistics*, 62, 567–77.

Blume, M. and Friend, I. (1973) 'A New Look at the Capital Asset Pricing Model,' *Journal of Finance*, March, 19–33.

Blume, M.E. and Husic, F. (1973) 'Price, Beta and Exchange Listing,' *Journal of Finance*, 28, 283–99.

Blume, M.E. and Stambaugh, R.F. (1983) 'Biases in Computed Returns: An Application to the Size Effect,' *Journal of Financial Economics*, November, 387–404.

Brennan, M. (1970) 'Taxes, Market Valuation and Corporate Financial Policy,' *National Tax Journal*, 417–27.

Brown, P., Kleidon, A.W. and Marsh, T.A. (1983a) 'New Evidence on the Nature of Size-Related Anomalies in Stock Prices,' *Journal of Financial Economics*, June, 33–56.

Brown, P., Keim, D.B., Kleidon, A.W. and Marsh, T.A. (1983b) 'Stock Return Seasonalities and the Tax-Loss Selling Hypothesis: Analysis of the Arguments and Australian Evidence,' *Journal of Financial Economics*, June, 105–28.

Chan, K.C. (1983) 'Leverage Changes and Size-Related Anomalies,' manuscript, University of Chicago, December.

Chan, K.C. (1985) 'Can Tax-Loss Selling Explain the January Seasonal in Stock Returns?' manuscript, Ohio State University, August.

Chan, K.C., Chen, N. and Hsieh, D. (1983) 'An Exploratory Investigation of the Firm Size Effect,' manuscript, University of Chicago, April.

Chen, N. (1983) 'Some Empirical tests of the theory of Arbitrage Pricing,' *Journal of Finance*, December, 1393–1414.

Christie, A. and Hertzel, M. (1981) 'Capital Asset Pricing Anomalies', University of Rochester Working Paper.

Constantinides, G.M. (1984) 'Optimal Stock Trading with Personal Taxes: Implications for Prices and the Abnormal January Returns,' *Journal of Financial Economics*, March, 65–90.

Cooke, T.J. and Rozeff, M.S. (1984) 'Size and Earnings/Price Ratio Anomalies: One Effect or Two?' *Journal of Financial and Quantitative Analysis*, 13, 449–66.

Copeland, T.E. and Mayers, D. (1982) 'The Value Line Enigma (1965–1978): A Case Study of Performance Evaluation Issues,' *Journal of Financial Economics*, November, 289–321.

Cross, F. (1975) 'The Behavior of Stock Prices on Fridays and Mondays,' *Financial Analysts Journal*, November-December, 67–9.

DeBondt, W.F.M. and Thaler, R. (1985) 'Does the Stock Market Overreact?' *Journal of Finance*, July, 793–806.

Dimson, E. (1979) 'Risk Measurement when Shares are Subject to Infrequent Trading,' *Journal of Financial Economics*, 7, 197–226.

Fama, E. (1970) 'Efficient Capital Markets: A Review of Theory and Empirical Work,' *Journal of Finance*, May, 383–417.

Fama, E. and MacBeth, J. (1973) 'Risk, Return and Equilibrium: Empirical Tests,' *Journal of Political Economy*, May/June, 607–36.

French, K. (1980) 'Stock Returns and the Weekend Effect,' *Journal of Financial Economics*, March, 55–69.

Gibbons, M. (1982) 'Multivariate Tests of Financial Models: A New Approach,' *Journal of Financial Economics*, 10, 1, March 3–27.

Gibbons, M. and Hess, P. (1981) 'Day of the Week Effects and Asset Returns,' *Journal of Business*, October, 579–96.

Gordon, R.H. and Bradford, D.F. (1980) 'Taxation and the Stock Market Valuation on Capital Gains and Dividends: Theory and Empirical Results,' *Journal of Public Economics*, 109–36.

Graham, B. and Dodd, D. (1940) *Security Analysis*, New York: McGraw-Hill.

Gultekin, M.N. and Gultekin, N.B. (1983) 'Stock Market Seasonality: International Evidence,' *Journal of Financial Economics*, December, 469–82.

Hess, P. (1983) 'Test for Tax Effects in the Pricing of Financial Assets,' *Journal of Business*, 56, 537–54.

Holloway, C. (1981) 'A Note on Testing an Aggressive Investment Strategy Using Value Line Ranks,' *Journal of Finance*, June, 711–19.

Jaffe, J. and Westerfield, R. (1985) 'The Week-end Effect in Common Stock Returns: The International Evidence,' *Journal of Finance*, 40, 2, June.

Kato, K. and Schallheim, J.S. (1985) 'Seasonal and Size Anomalies in the Japanese Stock Market,' *Journal of Financial and Quantitative Analysis*, 20, 107–18.

Keim, D.B. (1983) 'Size-Related Anomalies and Stock Return Seasonality: Further Empirical Evidence,' *Journal of Financial Economics*, March, 13–32.

Keim, D.B. (1985) 'Dividend Yields and Stock Returns: Implications of Abnormal January Returns,' *Journal of Financial Economics*, 14, September, 473–89.

Keim, D.B. (1986a) 'Dividend Yields and the January Effect,' *Journal of Portfolio Management*, 12, December, 54–60.

Keim, D.B. (1986b) 'The Relation Between Day of the Week Effects and Size Effects,' *Journal of Portfolio Management*, forthcoming.

Keim, D.B. and Stambaugh, R.F. (1984) 'A Further Investigation of the Weekend Effect in Stock Returns,' *Journal of Finance*, July, 819–35.

Kuhn, T.S. (1970) *The Structure of Scientific Revolutions*, Chicago: University of Chicago Press.

Lakonishok, J. and Levi, M. (1982) 'Weekend Effects on Stock Returns: A Note,' *Journal of Finance*, June, 883–9.

Lintner, J. (1965) 'The Valuation of Risk Assets and the Selection of Risky Investments in Stock Portfolios and Capital Budgets,' *Review of Economics and Statistics*, February, 13–37.

Litzenberger, R. and Ramaswamy, K. (1979) 'The Effects of Personal Taxes and Dividends on Capital Asset Prices: Theory and Empirical Evidence,' *Journal of Financial Economics*, 7, 163–95.

Litzenberger, R. and Ramaswamy, K. (1980) 'Dividends, Short Selling Restrictions, Tax-Induced Investor Clienteles and Market Equilibrium,' *Journal of Finance*, 35, 2, May, 469–82.

Litzenberger, R. and Ramaswamy, K. (1982) 'The Effects of Dividends on Common Stock

Prices: Tax Effects or Information Effects, *Journal of Finance*, 37, 2, May 429–33.

Mayers, D. (1972) 'Nonmarketable Assets and Capital Market Equilibrium under Uncertainty.' In M.C. Jensen (ed.) *Studies in Theory of Capital Markets*, New York: Praeger.

Miller, M. and Scholes, M. (1978) 'Dividends and Taxes: Some Empirical Evidence,' *Journal of Financial Economics*, 90, 6, December, 333–64.

Morgan, I.G. (1982) 'Dividends and Capital Asset Prices,' *Journal of Finance*, 37, 4, September, 1071–86.

Nakamura, T. and Terada, N. (1984) 'The Size Effect and Seasonality in Japanese Stock Returns,' manuscript, Nomura Research Institute.

Nicholson, S.F. (1960) 'Price-Earnings Ratios,' *Financial Analysts Journal*, July/August, 43–50.

Peavy, J.W. and Goodman, D.A. (1982) 'A Further Inquiry into the Market Value and Earnings Yield Anomalies,' manuscript, Southern Methodist University.

Peavy, J.W. and Goodman, D.A. (1983) 'Industry-Relative Price-Earnings Ratios as Indicators of Investment Returns,' *Financial Analysts Journal*, July/August.

Reinganum, M.R. (1981) 'Misspecification of Capital Asset Pricing: Empirical Anomalies Based on Earnings' Yields and Market Values,' *Journal of Financial Economics*, 19–46.

Reinganum, M.R. (1982) 'A Direct Test of Roll's Conjecture on the Firm Size Effect,' *Journal of Finance*, 37, 27–35.

Reinganum, M.R. (1983) 'The Anomalous Stock Market Behavior of Small Firms in January: Empirical Tests for Tax-Loss Selling Effects,' *Journal of Financial Economics*, June, 89–104.

Reinganum, M.R. and Shapiro, A. (1983) 'Taxes and Stock Return Seasonality: Evidence from the London Stock Exchange,' manuscript, University of Southern California.

Ritter, J.R. (1985) 'The Buying and Selling Behavior of Individual Investors at the Turn of the Year: Evidence of Price Pressure Effects,' manuscript, University of Michigan, November.

Rogalski, R. (1984) 'New Findings Regarding Day of the Week Returns over Trading and Non-trading Periods: A Note,' *Journal of Finance*, December, 1603–14.

Roll, R. (1977) 'A Critique of the Asset Pricing Theory's Tests; Part I: On Past and Potential Testability of the Theory,' *Journal of Financial Economics*, March, 129–76.

Roll, R. (1981) 'A Possible Explanation of the Small Firm Effect,' *Journal of Finance*, 36, 879–88.

Roll, R. (1983a) 'Vas ist das? The Turn of the Year Effect and the Return Premium of Small Firms,' *Journal of Portfolio Management*, 9, 1, 18–28.

Roll, R. (1983b) 'On Computing Mean Returns and the Small Firm Premium,' *Journal of Financial Economics*, November, 371–86.

Rosenberg, B. and Marathe, V. (1979) 'Tests of Capital Asset Pricing Hypotheses.' In Haim Levy (ed.) *Research in Finance*, Greenwich, CT: JAI Press.

Rosenberg, B., Reid, K. and Lanstein, R. (1985) 'Persuasive Evidence of Market Inefficiency,' *Journal of Portfolio Management*.

Ross, S. (1976) 'The Arbitrage Theory of Capital Asset Pricing,' *Journal of Economic Theory*, 13, 3, December.

Rozeff, M.S. (1985) 'The Tax-Loss Selling Hypothesis: New Evidence from Share Shifts,' manuscript, University of Iowa, April.

Scholes, M. and Williams, J. (1977) 'Estimating Betas from Non-synchronous Data,' *Journal of Financial Economics*, 5, 309–27.

Schultz, P. (1983) 'Transactions Costs and the Small Firm Effect: A Comment,' *Journal of Financial Economics*, June, 81–8.

Schultz, P. (1985) 'Personal Income Taxes and the January Effect: Small Firm Stock Returns Before the War Revenue Act of 1917: A Note,' *Journal of Finance*, March, 333–43.

Sharpe, W.F. (1964) 'Capital Asset Prices: A Theory of Market Equilibrium under Conditions of Risk,' *Journal of Finance*, 19, 3, September, 425–42.

Smirlock, M. and Starks, L. (1984) 'Day of the Week Effects in Stock Returns: Some Intraday Evidence,' manuscript, University of Pennsylvania.

Stambaugh, R. (1982) 'On the Exclusion of Assets from the Two-Parameter Model: A Sensitivity Analysis,' *Journal of Financial Economics*, 10, 3, November, 237–68.

Stickel, S.E. (1985) 'The Effect of *Value Line Investment Survey* Rank Changes on Common Stock Prices,' *Journal of Financial Economics*, 14, 121–44.

Stoll, H.R., and Whaley, R.E. (1983) 'Transactions Costs and the Small Firm Effect,' *Journal of Financial Economics*, June, 57–80.

Stone, B.K. and Barter, B.J. (1979) 'The Effect of Dividend Yields on Stock Returns: Empirical Evidence on the Relevance of Dividends' manuscript, Georgia Institute of Technology.

Treynor, J.L. 'Toward a Theory of Market Value of Risky Assets,' (unpublished manuscript, undated).

II
SEASONALITIES IN DAILY
RETURNS

3   Weekend effects in stock market returns: an overview

*MAURICE LEVI**

This part of the book contains five chapters which focus on short-term seasonalities in security returns. The first three chapters, which were presented at the EIASM symposium, deal with day-of-the-week seasonalities in security returns. These papers are by Condoyanni, O'Hanlon and Ward, Saunders and Urich, and Ball and Bowers. The next chapter, by Harris, turns to intra-day stock return patterns. The last of the five contributions examines intra-month regularities in daily returns.

As the chapters on the study of daily returns presented here make so clear, we can no longer limit our attention to apparent anomalies connected solely with weekends or with the stock market. Daily regularities have been claimed for other days and for other markets, necessitating a new title for what was until recently referred to as 'the weekend-effect in stock returns'. However, it is not clear that the extension of the claims of daily return anomalies to other days and other markets has expanded the range of regularities we might attempt to explain. Rather, the irregularity of the evidence itself suggests that there may not be any troublesome daily return regularities at all. Instead, the variety of anomalies and the sensitivity of each to the period being reviewed and to the country being studied suggests a danger that researchers have been drawn by their prior expectations into finding what really isn't there.

We must consider what it was that first drew the attention of empirical researchers into studying the behaviour of stock prices from Friday to Monday. As Cross (1973) and French (1980) point out, they were attracted to the question of returns around the weekend by claims of those involved in the markets that stock prices tended to fall on Mondays. It can hardly be said that the researchers were drawn into examining the data without what Baysians call 'priors', based on readings of the data. It was not a new theory that was to be put to the test. It was the data at the time Cross wrote that led him, and subsequently others, to examine that very same data.

It is notoriously difficult to establish appropriate levels of statistical significance in cases where the study of data leads to the study of data, but even if we overlook this problem and stick with the traditional 5 percent, the papers being presented here make us wonder whether we may be committing a classical Type I error. In the context of the day-of-the-week effect, the Type I error is the rejection of the null-hypothesis that returns are independent of the day of the week when in fact they really are independent of the day of the week. Condoyanni, O'Hanlon and Ward (see chapter 4) provide an excellent starting point to see whether a Type I error may have been committed by earlier researchers. This is because they give considerable evidence covering different time periods and countries, thereby showing the sensitivity of any anomalies in daily returns to our choice of time and location.

Condoyanni *et al.* must be complimented for taking a broad sweep to the question of daily return regularities. In the spirit of Gultekin and Gultekin (1983) who studied the international evidence for turn-of-the-year regularities, and Jaffe and Westerfield (1985) who performed a parallel study of daily returns in numerous countries, Condoyanni *et al.* offer us a chance to see if a pattern in daily returns is limited to the US. The countries examined in chapter 4 are Australia, Canada, the UK, France, Japan and Singapore, thereby giving us evidence that covers a variety of institutional settings and time zones. By studying the lengthy period 1969–84 (except in the case of Australia where analysis is limited to 1981–4) and by looking at subperiods, we have substantial evidence on which to judge the stability of regularities in daily stock returns.

In order to check their procedures, Condoyanni *et al.* begin by comparing their results for the US with the published results of Rogalski (1984). These are shown in table 1 (chapter 4) and immediately highlight the problem of Type I error and of looking for what the researcher thinks the data may show.

Cross's paper was published in 1973, just after the period over which we can identify a negative weekend – or Monday – effect, namely 1969–72. This subperiod would appear to have considerable responsibility for the observation of a negative weekend effect over the period 1969–84, studied in chapter 4, and indeed, results by Rogalski (1984) suggests this is so. With a data period that just happened to start with October 1, 1974 and end in 1984, Rogalski found no Monday effect. Calculating returns as the rate of change in the Dow-Jones Industrial Index closing values, Rogalski obtained a t-value for the Monday effect of -0.62 compared with the -3.82 found in chapter 4 when including the years before 1974.

The importance of the years 1969–72 for finding a weekend effect in the US can be seen by the lack of significant F-statistics in the subsequent subperiods, and by the lack of significant individual day effects in the first row of table 2 (chapter 4) where we find only one significant estimate once 1969–72 is omitted. As we know from the design of the hypothesis test, we would expect significance at the 5 percent level to be found in one in twenty instances when the null hypothesis of no effect is really true, and in table 2 (chapter 4) we find one in fifteen, not a proportion to inspire confidence.

In fact, the case for a weekend effect in US stock returns is a little stronger than is apparent from the analysis in chapter 4 of US data. In an effort to see whether the negative return from Friday's market close to Monday's market close occurred on the weekend itself or during Monday's trading, Rogalski looked at close-to-close and close-to-open returns, and found a significant negative return from Friday's close to Monday's open. His *t*-value for the weekend period was −3.46 over the same period for which his close-to-close data showed a Monday effect *t*-value of −0.62. The close-to-open returns for the selection of other countries in chapter 4 are not studied and we are therefore unable to determine whether the US daily returns behaviour is unusual or part of an international phenomenon.[1] This is a shame since there is such a large difference in results for the US from switching between these two ways of calculating returns.

It would be useful to know whether countries other than the US have regularities in daily returns from market closing to opening because it would help provide evidence on the potential relevance of settlement lags for the pattern of daily returns on stocks calculated correctly, from the settlement rather than order date. Countries differ in their settlement periods and in the time cheques take to clear. The discovery that the weekend effect is from Friday's close to Monday's opening in the US market supports the settlement lag argument as a partial explanation of the weekend effect.[2] This is because the benefit of Friday purchases stemming from two extra days before having to make payment – ten days against eight days for purchases made on other days of the week – is a benefit that can be enjoyed up to the point the market closes on Friday. It would be useful to compare the daily patterns in other countries to their settlement practices.

The evidence that is generated on the daily pattern of stock returns that is summarized by table 1 (chapter 4) reveals that it is not just in the US that results for the full period 1969–84 show clearer day-of-the-week effects than do subperiod results. However, the results outside the US do tend to be more robust than those for the US, with data periods subsequent to 1969–72 showing significant overall effects, and a number of significant effects for individual days. On its own this would support the view that there are daily return regularities, but doubt is introduced by the variety of regularities for different countries – negative Tuesdays for France, Japan and Singapore, but positive Tuesdays for the UK, positive Thursdays for Canada, France and Singapore, negative Mondays for Canada, and so on. Given the number of daily effects in the various subperiods over various countries which are not statistically significant it is unclear whether we may be making the error of rejecting the null hypothesis incorrectly.

The notion that Tuesday effects in, for example, Australia, Japan and Singapore are the result of time zone differences from New York – these countries are all one day ahead of New York, being the other side of the date line – is an interesting hypothesis. The test results looking at the correlations between returns in different markets as shown in table 3 (chapter 4) do reveal lots of significant correlations, and in particular show the US returns as being significant with a one-day lag for every market studied. This is an interesting finding, and may well go beyond an explanation based on differential time zones. The significant one-day lag appears to be as strong for the UK, Canada, France, and so on, as for countries ahead of the US in their local time.

One problem in comparing results for different countries in chapter 4 is the use of indices of different breadth, with the rather narrow Dow-Jones Industrial Index used for the US, and broader market indices used for the other countries. This presents a difficulty because it has been documented by Rogalski that the size of firms may influence the pattern of daily stock returns – as well as risk premiums. Another problem with chapter 4, as with much of the work that preceded it, is the exclusion of dividends from stock returns. If stocks tend to go ex-dividend on Mondays there is a good reason for expecting an average negative return on Mondays in data that exclude dividends.

The results generated in chapter 4 on variability of returns are interesting, but without adding evidence on variances and covariances cannot be related to regularities in mean returns. The results on indigenous daily effects are also of interest because they are stronger than those found with raw data, the opposite result to that we might expect if a pattern in US returns caused the patterns elsewhere.

Something that comes out of the pattern of daily returns found in the studies that spawned much of the interest in daily return regularities is a tendency to observe a large Wednesday and Friday return in the US. Indeed, judging by the size of coefficients rather than by *t*-values, the results of French (1980), Rogalski (1984), Gibbons and Hess (1981) and Lakoniskok and Levi (1982) suggest Wednesdays and Fridays are the abnormally high return days offsetting weekends. This is seen, for example, in Condoyanni's data for the 1969–72 period, and provides an introduction to chapter 5 by Saunders and Urich. This chapter studies the Federal funds market, the market in which reserves at the US Federal

Reserve Banks are traded between commercial banks. The case is made, and the evidence examined, for regularities being found on Wednesdays and Fridays.

Until 1984, the US Fed calculated member bank reserves on a weekly cycle that ran from Thursday to the following Wednesday. Banks' required reserves were based on average deposits on a lagged basis, with the required minimum reserve being stated in terms of a daily average. This meant that by Wednesday the banks had only one day to make their average reserves correct. With no guarantee that the aggregate supply of Fed funds was sufficient, there was a frantic exchange of funds between surplus and deficit reserve holders each Wednesday that resulted in Fed funds rates being volatile. This is the Wednesday anomaly that Saunders and Urich look for in volatility data based on high and low values of Fed funds rates during each day's trading.

Friday's anomaly has to do with the mean of the Fed funds rate rather than volatility. The method of calculating average daily reserves used by the Fed includes Friday holdings as counting for Friday, Saturday and Sunday. This on its own made Friday funds extremely useful, even without the additional benefits derived from playing the Thursday–Friday and Friday–Monday games. Because of the value of Friday funds we would expect higher Fed funds rates on Fridays than on other days of the week. We would also expect to find net purchases of Fed funds by the member banks from the non-member banks. These are the Friday phenomena for which Saunders and Urich are searching.

The time period studied is much shorter than that in chapter 4, being limited to January 1978 to September 1981. The end point of this period is attributed to the shift in the settlement lag at CHIPS, which changed to same-day settlement on October 1, 1981, and the starting point of the period is attributed to availability of Fed supplied data.

Because the coverage of the Fed's data was increased from 46 to 122 banks on February 27, 1980, and because the Fed switched its target from interest rates to monetary aggregates on October 6, 1979, Saunders and Urich split their already limited data into two subperiods, namely

(i) Jan 3, 1978 – October 5, 1979
and (ii) Mar 1, 1980 – September 1, 1981

Each period covers a small number of weeks. This is a potentially serious drawback when looking for an empirical regularity because a pattern for a little over one year would trouble us far less than a pattern sustained for many years.

The results show very little effect of the day of the week on the Fed funds rate during the first period, but do show the expected effect on Fridays of net purchases of Fed funds. In the second time period we do find a Friday Fed funds rate above that for other days, but with such a short period of time covered, the *t*-values are not surprisingly insufficient to infer significance.

The variability of the Fed funds rate on Wednesdays is substantially greater than the variability on other days during both subperiods, just as we would expect. This confirms what has long been known to those directly involved in Fed funds market.

Chapter 6 by Ball and Bowers looks at both daily stock returns and daily interest rates in Australia, thereby combining the concerns of the other two chapters. Where chapter 6 differs from the others is in providing hypotheses for daily regularities, although as it turns out, the pattern Ball and Bowers predict does not conform to that which researchers think they have observed. Starting out by assuming equilibrium in the capital market so that the present values of all capital assets equal their replacement values, it is claimed that there is reason for the return on capital to fall or even be negative on weekends. This is because of the tendency for capital to be idle at that time, and depending on the holding cost, the marginal efficiency of investment over the weekend could be negative. It is noted that nothing ensures adjustment of prices to always give positive returns because there is no naturally positive opportunity cost of capital with which to discount. Of course, this requires that the idle weekend capital is universal. It is perhaps for this reason that it is observed that interest rates are positive during the weekend. We should therefore find a pattern of daily returns on those stocks for which capital is idle that is opposite to that posited in the paper – lowest value on Friday and the highest on Monday.

Having honestly and frankly used positive weekend interest rates to counter their own claims, Ball and Bowers move on to an alternative explanation for a daily pattern in returns that is based on the relation of risk over short versus long periods. It is argued that if investors' horizons are long, the risk that is contributed by holding assets over any short period is the risk that is contributed to the full horizon, with this depending on variances and on covariances between the short period and the full horizon, and potentially causing a daily 'seasonal'.

Other hypotheses for daily regularities are offered with perhaps the most plausible being a concentration on a particular day of the week for stocks going ex-dividend. Given the nature of indices used in most studies it is unlikely that discontinuous trading has been a cause of the observed anomalies, and we should not attribute a pattern of returns in one country to being the pattern of another country, shifted by the difference in time zones, because this merely attributes one anomaly to another. Ball and Bowers also talk of a money seasonal and perhaps too readily discount their own idea of payment practices as the cause of day-of-the-week effects. While some payments are transfers between firms included in the same market index, others are not. There may also be a daily pattern in interest rates due to the sale of government bills or bonds on a particular day, with greater value being placed on liquidity when bids are made for the new issues.

Ball and Bowers must be complimented for their meticulous work in constructing their two series of daily stock returns for Australia. Using these data for a ten-year period, 1975–85, they find a daily seasonal, but with a pattern that differs from that found for the US. Perhaps their most interesting finding is a negative Tuesday, which because of the one-day calendar advance of Sydney over New York, may be a reflection of New York's negative return over the weekend. Interest rates are found to exhibit relatively little seasonal in their means.

The results of Ball and Bowers are very difficult to relate back to their original hypotheses about the possible causes of regularities in daily returns, and because they find positive returns on Thursday and Friday, and negative returns for the rest of the days when combined, the authors do not support their 'idle capital' explanation. This may be because other factors obscure the effect, such as a seasonal due to dividends or to settlement. A test of the idle capital hypothesis would be to compare daily return seasonals for firms continuing to operate on weekends and those that do not. An interesting extension of this would be to consider the monthly pattern of returns of firms likely to suffer from being inactive in December against those that are busy to see if the turn-of-the-year effect is due to December frivolity and holiday shut downs.

Chapter 7 by Harris turns from analysing daily data to the time-ordered record of individual stock transactions on the New York Stock Exchange. Using some sixteen million trades spanning about 300 business days, Harris confirms Rogalski's finding that for large firms the negative Monday returns accrue before the market opens. For smaller firms, Harris notes that the negative Monday return appears to occur throughout the day, but this may be attributable to infrequent trading in these securities.

Splitting the transactions record into fifteen-minute intra-day subperiods, it appears that on Monday mornings prices tend to fall, while the reverse is true for other weekday mornings. There is also an unexplained tendency for prices to rise on the last trade of the day. However, given Harris' evidence, it is unlikely that the low return observed over weekends is attributable to spuriously high Friday closing prices: neither data errors, nor the bid–ask spread, nor forms of price manipulation can explain negative weekend returns.

The final contribution in this section of the book is by Ariel (chapter 8), who documents another form of seasonality in daily data. Examining daily stock returns from 1963 to 1981, he finds that all of the market's accumulated advances occurred between the month-end and the middle of the month. The second half of the month contributes nothing to the cumulative increase in the level of the market. Ariel can offer no wholly satisfactory explanation of this phenomenon. But his favoured conjecture is that it arises from liquidity constraints on investors, and he too sees the US Fed's financing cycle as a possible explanation for the observed intra-month seasonalities.

A question that must be asked of all apparent regularities that have been identified in daily returns is whether they are a challenge to market efficiency. To answer this question we must look for the reasons there are daily patterns. This means finding the size of effects of settlement lags, stocks going ex-dividend, the inactivity of capital on weekends, the sale of government bills on particular days, and so on, and seeing how much these rational explanations can explain. Only if we can be sure there is no reason for observed regularities should we be concerned that markets are behaving inefficiently. Of course, there is no need to look for explanations if there are no clear-cut regularities. Given the variety of results over different subperiods we might save energy looking for explanations until the evidence shows somewhat more consistency.

Those tempted to continue looking for daily or other patterns in returns for which they do not have a theory would do well to recall the fate of William Stanley Jevons. Mr Jevons made a fundamental contribution to microeconomics via his use of marginal reasoning, but is better remembered for his attribution of cycles in the economy to sun spots. Jevon's explanation was basically empirically based, being supported only by casual reference to effects of sun spots on weather and on crop yields. The reduction in the importance of agriculture, and the lack of any solid foundations for his ideas, resulted in considerable discredit for Mr Jevons. With their large computer budgets and keenness to find some irregularity, empirical researchers in finance had better think carefully before reading too much into their results.

Notes

* This overview was written and presented while the author was on a study leave made possible by the Social Sciences and Humanities Research Council of Canada. Their help is most gratefully acknowledged.
1 Our ability to judge the stability of the effect in the US is also hampered by the fact that Rogalski did not publish his results for any subperiods.
2 The details of the settlement lag argument are described in Lakoniskok and Levi (1982).

References

Cross, F. (1973) 'The Behaviour of Stock Prices on Fridays and Mondays', *Financial Analysts Journal*, 29, November–December, 67–9.
French, K. (1980) 'Stock Returns and the Weekend Effect', *Journal of Financial Economics*, 8, March, 55–69.

Gibbons, M. and Hess, P. (1981) 'Day of the Week Effects and Asset Returns', *Journal of Business*, October, 579–96.

Gultekin, M. and Gultekin, N. (1983) 'Stock Market Seasonality: International Evidence', *Journal of Financial Economics*, 12, December, 469–82.

Jaffe, J. and Westerfield, R. (1985) 'The Weekend Effect in Common Stock Returns: The International Evidence', *Journal of Finance*, 40, June, 433–54.

Lakonishok, J. and Levi, M. (1982) 'Weekend Effects on Stock Returns: A Note', *Journal of Finance*, 37, June, 883–9.

Rogalski, R. (1984) 'New Findings Regarding Day-of-the-Week Returns over Trading and Non-Trading Periods: A Note', *Journal of Finance*, December, 1603–14.

4   Weekend effects in stock market returns: international evidence

*L. CONDOYANNI, J. O'HANLON and C.W.R. WARD**

Much interest has been aroused by the revelation of a weekend effect in US stock returns. Recent studies have examined the effect of company size (Rogalski, 1984) and settlement procedures (Lakonishok and Levi, 1982; Dyl and Martin, 1985). Other possible factors investigated include the role of the specialist (Keim and Stambaugh, 1984) and the seasonality effects caused by abnormally large returns observed in January (Rogalski, 1984). French (1980) found that the effect was a 'weekend effect' rather than a more general 'closed market effect'. In this paper, we investigate the phenomenon through an analysis of the daily returns in capital markets in a number of different countries.

We find that weekend effects are the norm rather than being US-specific and, to some extent, our conclusions match those of an independent study by Jaffe and Westerfield (1985). Furthermore we establish that the inclusion of a January factor does not significantly alter the pattern of day-of-the-week effects and provide evidence to suggest that the influence of the US market disguises the weekend effect in other markets.

The first section deals with the sample construction and the methods of identifying confounding factors such as days on which the exchanges were closed and missing observations. In the second section we conduct an analysis of returns drawn from seven national equity markets, namely, New York, Sydney, Toronto, London, Tokyo, Paris and Singapore. Section 3 briefly examines the markets for a January effect and finally we discuss the implications of our findings for future researchers of this phenomenon.

1 Sample selection and construction

The sample was chosen to reflect three main geographical areas: North America, Europe and the Far East including Australia. Indices were collated from DataStream on a daily basis for all weekdays

(Monday to Friday) falling in the period 01/01/69 to 31/12/84. In the case of the Australian market, daily data were only available for part of the period, and the index was therefore only collated for the subperiod 01/01/81 to 31/12/84. Indices were selected on the basis of availability and of the need to reflect a broad industrial base. They consist of: Dow Jones Industrial, Australian Stock Exchanges' All Ordinaries Share Price Index, Toronto Composite, Paris CAC Industrial, FT All-Share, Tokyo New Stock Exchange and the *Straits Times* (Singapore). For each index a series of daily logarithmic returns was calculated.

Since the periods were adjusted to begin and end with complete weeks, there were, in principle, 4170 daily return observations for each exchange (1040 in the case of Australia). Days upon which the exchanges were closed, and missing observations, reduced these numbers to between 3139 (Paris) and 3931 (London) (955 in the case of Australia). In the database source, days for which no index value was available were explicitly shown for the period 1982–4 but required identification in the earlier periods. Since the index values were commonly presented to two decimal places, we inferred missing data if two consecutive days were shown to have exactly the same value and eliminated the return calculated for the missing day and the day following. This procedure might conceivably eliminate days in which trading took place but in which no aggregate price movement could be detected. It is important to note that due to Saturday trading on the Tokyo Stock Exchange, our 'Monday' return is normally the sum of the Friday to Saturday return and the Saturday to Monday return.

2 International capital market analysis

Following the methodology used by several researchers of the phenomenon in the US market, we regressed the returns of each stock market on five dummy variables representing Monday through Friday (intercept term suppressed) for the full sixteen-year period (four years in the case of Australia). For all markets except Australia we repeated the test for four subperiods covering (a) 1969–72, (b) 1973–6, (c) 1977–80, (d) 1981–4. The comparative results for the overall period are presented in table 1. Clearly from examination of the F-statistics there is a strong and general day-of-the-week effect. Also, significant negative parameter estimates for Monday are observed in the Canadian and UK markets.

In table 2 we summarize the results of the repetition of the analysis for four subperiods of four years each (one period of four years in the case of Australia). Here we present for each market the proportion of negative and significantly negative (5 per cent level) subperiod parameter estimates. To establish the numbers in a given cell, we simply divided the

Table 1 *Test for weekend effect – national markets 1969–1984 (printed parameter estimates are multiplied by 10^3)*

Country	Mon.	Tues.	Wed.	Thurs.	Fri.	F
US	−1.34	0.13	0.57	0.21	0.58	4.16[b]
	(−3.82)[b]	(0.39)	(1.69)	(0.62)	(1.68)	[5;3814]
						$R^2 = 0.005$
Canada	−1.57	−0.03	0.73	0.75	0.94	9.97[b]
	(−5.11)[b]	(−0.08)	(2.55)[a]	(2.60)[b]	(3.24)[b]	[5;3765]
						$R^2 = 0.011$
UK	−0.95	1.06	0.90	0.11	0.44	3.75[b]
	(−2.32)[a]	(2.61)[b]	(2.30)[a]	(0.28)	(1.10)	[5;3926]
						$R^2 = 0.005$
France	−0.50	−1.57	1.00	1.52	0.87	7.68[b]
	(−1.18)	(−3.68)[b]	(2.42)[a]	(3.64)[b]	(2.08)[a]	[5;3134]
						$R^2 = 0.012$
Australia	−0.49	−2.00	0.40	0.17	1.63	3.25[a]
(1980–84)	(−0.73)	(−2.97)[b]	(0.62)	(0.27)	(2.54)[a]	[5;950]
						$R^2 = 0.017$
Japan	0.90	−0.95	1.39	0.25	0.39	10.72[b]
	(3.33)[b]	(−3.51)[b]	(5.21)[b]	(0.93)	(1.46)	[5;3690]
						$R^2 = 0.015$
Singapore	−0.36	−1.07	0.79	1.21	1.00	5.47[b]
	(−0.90)	(−2.65)[b]	(2.01)[a]	(3.05)[b]	(2.48)[a]	[5;3704]
						$R^2 = 0.007$

Notes: [a]Significant at 0.05 level.
[b]Significant at 0.01 level.
The *t*-statistic is given in parentheses.
Degrees of freedom is given in square brackets.

number of negative (and significantly negative) parameter estimates for the relevant day and country/geographical zone by the number of subperiods. Thus for example, the 0.75 for Japan (Tuesday) reflects three negative parameter estimates for the four subperiods. Various points are brought out by this subperiod analysis. For example we note from table 1 that Canada exhibits negative returns on both the weekend and Tuesday, although the Tuesday estimate is not significantly different from zero. Before disregarding this sign as unimportant, one should note that table 2 reveals that, in three of the four subperiods, the negative sign persists albeit insignificantly. The market in Canada therefore seems to exhibit both a weekend and possibly a Tuesday effect. The UK presents a picture similar to that in the US and, as table 2 illustrates, the weekend effect persists in all four subperiods. However, for three of the four subperiods, no statistical significance can be attached to the estimates.

The UK case has been investigated for a shorter time period (01/06/75–31/05/81) by Theobald and Price (1984) who found significant differences

Table 2 *Sub-period analysis*

(a) Proportion of negative (and significantly negative) parameter estimates for each day/country

	Mon.	Tues.	Wed.	Thurs.	Fri.
US	1.00[a]	0.50	0.00	0.25	0.25
	(0.50)	(0.00)	(0.00)	(0.00)	(0.00)
Canada	1.00	0.75	0.00	0.25	0.00
	(1.00)	(0.00)	(0.00)	(0.00)	(0.00)
UK	1.00	0.00	0.00	0.50	0.00
	(0.25)	(0.00)	(0.00)	(0.00)	(0.00)
France	0.50	1.00	0.00	0.00	0.25
	(0.25)	(0.75)	(0.00)	(0.00)	(0.00)
Japan	0.25	0.75	0.00	0.50	0.50
	(0.00)	(0.50)	(0.00)	(0.00)	(0.00)
Singapore	0.50	0.75	0.00	0.00	0.25
	(0.25)	(0.25)	(0.00)	(0.00)	(0.00)
Australia	1.00	1.00	0.00	0.00	0.00
	(0.00)	(1.00)	(0.00)	(0.00)	(0.00)

Note: [a] In each case the number quoted first represents the proportion of negative sub-period parameter estimates. The figure quoted below in brackets represents the proportion of significantly (5 per cent level) negative parameter estimates.

(b) Proportion of significant (5 per cent level) negative parameter estimates for each day/geographical zone

	Mon.	Tues.	Wed.	Thurs.	Fri.
North America	0.75	0.00	0.00	0.00	0.00
Europe	0.25	0.375	0.00	0.00	0.00
Far East[b]	0.11	0.44	0.00	0.00	0.00

Note: [b] Including Australia, for which only one subperiod is included.

for Monday returns. They pointed out that analysis of Monday returns in the UK would be confounded by two factors associated with the stock exchange account period system. Stocks usually go ex-div on the first day (normally a Monday) of the trading 'account' (normally of two weeks' duration). 'First Monday of the account' returns calculated on the basis of the FT All-Share-Index will not have been corrected for the downward bias caused by this. Furthermore, a settlement factor is at work. A transaction taking place on the first Monday of an account will be settled twenty-one days after the event, as against eleven days in the case of the previous Friday. Since there is more interest built in to the Monday price, the effect of this factor would be to cause share prices to rise on the first

Monday of an account. A transaction taking place on a non-account Monday will be settled fourteen days after the event, as against seventeen days for the previous Friday. One might thus expect a smaller but opposite effect on non-account Mondays because of the settlement factor.

We examined the effects of these factors in our UK data by segregating the first Mondays of stock exchange accounts and the other Mondays. We then subjected the two sets of Mondays to a difference of means test and found, for the whole sixteen-year period and for each of the four-year long subperiods, that the mean return was positive on first Mondays of an account and negative on other Mondays. With the exception of the 1977–80 subperiod, the two means were in each case significantly different from each other at the 1 per cent level.

Strongly positive returns on account Mondays indicated that the settlement effect was the dominant of the two confounding factors and that it appeared to mask the strength of the underlying negative weekend effect in the UK.

The results of our analysis of the French exchange data appear anomalous since in all four subperiods there is a negative (normally significant) Tuesday return. In the period as a whole, the weekend return is negative but not significantly so, while the Tuesday returns are strongly negative. In fact the French index follows more closely the behaviour of markets from the Far Eastern time zone (see below) than it does the behaviour of the UK market.

In the case of the Japanese, Singapore and Australian markets, both Mondays and Tuesdays exhibit negative returns. Out of the nine sets of subperiods for the three countries, four negative estimates for Mondays were observed against seven negative Tuesdays. In the total period (for Singapore and Japan), the Tuesday effect was stronger, being significant in both cases at the 1 per cent level.

The existence of a worldwide weekend effect is suggested by table 2(b), which focuses on significant (5 per cent level) parameters only. We note that:

(a)   all zones have significant negative Monday parameter estimates in some subperiods

(b)   the European and Far Eastern zones both have some significant negative Tuesday parameter estimates whilst the North American zone does not;

(c)   no zone has any significant negative parameter estimates for Wednesday, Thursday or Friday.

One must point out here that tables 1 and 2(b) show that significant parameter estimates in the sixteen-year data set are sometimes caused by the presence of significant estimates in only one or two of the four-year

Table 3 *Cross-correlations for 0, 1, 2, 3 days between six countries (coefficients significant at 0.1 per cent level only)*

	Number of days' lag			
	0	1	2	3
France				
France		0.198	−0.101	
US		0.324		
UK	0.190	0.123		
Canada	0.164	0.234		
Japan	0.146			
Singapore	0.106			
US				
US		0.133		
UK	0.140			
Canada	0.610			
UK				
France	0.190			
US	0.140	0.254		
UK		0.210		
Canada	0.224	0.164		0.061
Japan	0.099			
Singapore	0.110			
Canada				
France	0.164			
US	0.610	0.294		
UK	0.224	0.063		
Canada		0.189		
Japan	0.122			
Singapore	0.106			
Japan				
France	0.146			
US		0.166	0.077	
UK	0.099	0.101		
Canada	0.122	0.165		
Japan		0.108		0.087
Singapore	0.098			
Singapore				
France	0.106	0.092		
US	0.065	0.205	0.123	
UK	0.110	0.166	0.079	
Canada	0.106	0.185	0.076	
Japan	0.098			
Singapore		0.209		0.113

subperiods. In this context it is worthwhile to remind ourselves that, although all the sixteen-year regressions summarized in table 1 produce F-statistics which are significant at the conventionally quoted 1 per cent confidence level, the explanatory power of the day of the week effect, as measured by the R^2, does not exceed 1.7 per cent for any country.

Tables 2(a) and (b) highlight the similarities between, say, Canada and the US on the one hand and between Japan and Singapore on the other. There appears to be some diminution of the Monday effect and increase of the Tuesday factor as one moves from North America to Europe to the Far East, in a way which suggests that the markets in neighbouring countries might be reacting to a common set of information. This raises the question of whether the weekend and Tuesday effects in non-US markets are due more to a repercussion of the US weekend effect than to indigenous factors. In an attempt to answer this question we carried out a number of lagged and unlagged cross correlations between the various markets. Table 3 summarizes our findings. For each country, we lagged the daily observations by one, two and three days and then calculated the correlations between each series for all countries (except Australia). The correlation coefficients will be significant (at the 0.1 per cent level) if they exceed 0.06. In order to simplify matters we present in table 3 only the coefficients which are significant at this level.

Three points are brought out by this table. Firstly, the pattern of correlation is strongly related to the different time zones in which markets are located. Far Eastern markets tend to be more strongly correlated with the behaviour of non-Far Eastern markets of previous days than with the behaviour of those non-Far Eastern markets on the same day. This is particularly striking in the relationship between the Far Eastern markets and the US market. An exception to this tendency is the 'same day' relationship between Japan and France. On the other hand Canada tends to follow other markets on the same day. (The only non-North American market with which Canada is lag correlated is the UK and this coefficient is much lower than the same day correlation coefficient). This contrast between the Far East and Canada is consistent with the fact that Far Eastern markets are the earliest to trade and North American markets are the latest. The UK market is 'same day' corre-lated with Far Eastern markets but both 'same day' and 'previous day' correlated with North American markets. This result would be expected because European markets can impound all information from Far Eastern markets on the same day but can impound only part of the information from North American markets which remain open after the European markets close.

The fact that the French market appears to behave as though it were a Far Eastern rather than a European market can easily be explained by the fact that the index used to reflect stock prices on the Paris Bourse is compiled at 1.30 p.m. (local time). The index for any day will therefore be compiled before the US markets open.

Secondly, all indices exhibit significant serial correlation. Whilst in most cases the coefficients are consistent with a weak and auto-regressive series of order one, France, Japan and Singapore exhibit more complex processes suggesting moving average or higher-order auto-regressive processes.

Thirdly, the table brings out the dominant influence of the US market. Both Far Eastern markets are significantly correlated with the US market of the previous two days, Singapore also being to a lesser extent 'same day' correlated. Canada and the UK are both 'previous day' correlated with the US. France is the only country not significantly affected by US returns over at least two days. On the other hand, the returns on the US market are not lag correlated with the previous day's returns of any market other than itself.

Thus our review of this correlation structure supported the suspicion that the pattern of effects in non-US markets could be partially attributed to the reaction of those markets to the behaviour of the US market. It was possible that the weekend effect in the US was either generating or disguising the weekend effect in other markets. In order to eliminate the US effect from the data of other markets we used a simple two-stage scheme. We first ran the following regression for Canada, UK, France, Japan and Singapore for the full period and the four subperiods:

$$R_t = \alpha + \beta_1 R_{US(t)} + \beta_2 R_{US(t-1)} + e_t$$

where

R_t is the return on the market index for day t

$R_{US(t)}$ is the return on the US market index for day t

$R_{US(t-1)}$ is the return on the US market index for day $t-1$

For each of the five countries we then regressed the residuals of the above regression on the five dummy variables for Monday through Friday for the sixteen-year period and the four subperiods. The results of the sixteen-year regressions are given in table 4(a). Table 4(b) gives the proportion of significant (5 per cent level) negative parameter estimates for each day/geographical zone on the basis of the subperiod analysis of the 'US purged' data. These tables should be compared with table 1 and table 2(b) respectively.

The removal of the US factor from the data has a noticeable effect on the three markets (France, Japan and Singapore) which did not originally exhibit significantly negative Monday parameter estimates. In the case of Singapore and France *insignificantly* negative Monday parameter

Table 4 *Results of tests on residuals obtained from regressing national market returns on US returns for day t and day* $t-1$

(a) Tests for weekend effect – national markets 1969–1984

	Mon.	Tues.	Wed.	Thurs.	Fri.	*F*-statistic
Canada	−0.20019	0.00123	0.07593	0.05080	0.04471	6.53[b]
	(−5.02)[b]	(0.03)	(2.02)[a]	(1.39)	(1.21)	[5;3428]
UK	−0.11538	0.08370	0.05814	−0.01394	−0.01607	3.30[b]
	(−2.98)[b]	(2.19)[a]	(1.56)	(−0.38)	(−0.44)	[5;3564]
France	−0.10851	−0.15678	0.08766	0.11393	0.04305	6.62[b]
	(−2.52)[a]	(−3.66)[b]	(2.10)[a]	(2.79)[b]	(1.04)	[5;2818]
Japan	0.4750	−0.15716	0.13237	−0.02917	0.00438	5.95[b]
	(1.20)	(−3.99)[b]	(3.43)[b]	(0.78)	(0.12)	[5;3336]
Singapore	−0.08220	−0.10311	0.04695	0.07364	0.04767	3.58[b]
	(−2.05)[a]	(−2.61)[b]	(1.23)	(1.96)[a]	(1.25)	[5;3319]

Notes: [a]Significant at 0.05 level.
[b]Significant at 0.01 level.
t-statistics are given in parentheses.
Degrees of freedom are given in square brackets.

(b) Proportion of significant (5 per cent level) negative parameter estimates for each day/geographical zone

	Mon.	Tues.	Wed.	Thurs.	Fri.
N. America[c]	0.625	0.00	0.00	0.00	0.00
Europe	0.375	0.375	0.00	0.00	0.00
Far East[d]	0.111	0.444	0.00	0.00	0.00

Notes: [c]Including US results included in table 2(b).
[d]Including Australia, for which only 1 subperiod is included.

estimates are converted into *significantly* negative Monday parameter estimates. In the case of Japan, a *significantly* positive Monday parameter estimate is converted into an *insignificantly* positive estimate. (The Japanese market's unique failure to exhibit a significantly negative 'Monday' parameter estimate in its US purged returns must be seen in the light of the fact that most of our 'Monday' returns for that market also incorporate the returns of the last trading day (Saturday) of the previous week. Since this study (see table 1) and others (for example, Keim and Stambaugh, 1984) have indicated a tendency towards significantly positive parameter estimates on the last trading day of the week, it is probable that this apparent anomaly can be explained by this factor.)

In conclusion on this point, we find that returns in the US do indeed appear to influence returns on other markets. In most cases, the effects

Table 5 *Proportion of significant (5 per cent level) negative parameter estimates for each day/geographical zone (dummy variable for January added)*

	Mon.	Tues.	Wed.	Thurs.	Fri.
North America	0.625	0.00	0.00	0.00	0.00
Europe	0.25	0.375	0.00	0.00	0.00
Far East[a]	0.22	0.56	0.00	0.00	0.00

Note: [a]Including Australia, for which only 1 subperiod is included.

are incorporated over two days, with the first day depending on the time zone of the market concerned. This 'US effect' appears to mask the indigenous negative Monday effect in those markets which are lag correlated with the US.

3 The January effect in international markets

Gultekin and Gultekin (1983) found abnormal January returns in most countries when using monthly returns over the period 1959 to 1979. The present study is not designed to be a detailed analysis of the January effect but we investigated whether the effect of January would be sufficient to swamp the weekend effects in the raw data (unadjusted for US effect). Accordingly we repeated the regressions reported in tables 1 and 2 but with another dummy variable which took the value 1 for any day in January and 0 otherwise. The results established a January effect consistently only for the 1973–6 subperiod. Of course, this subperiod covered years in which there were very substantial changes in the behaviour of many investment markets. The 1974–5 period (including January) can hardly be examined for results which would be interpreted as typical of the long term. In some cases the inclusion of the dummy variable for January altered the signs of the parameter estimates for days of the week. However, the summarized results of the regressions presented in table 5 indicate, when compared with table 2(b), that the pattern of effects remains broadly unchanged.

4 Conclusions

The results of this study demonstrate that the weekend effect is a pervasive feature of capital markets around the world, there being some evidence to suggest that the influence of the US market disguises the indigenous weekend effect in some markets. Whilst the use of daily data allows researchers to investigate the speed with which effects are

Table 6 *Times when stock exchanges are open*

	Local time when GMT = 1200	Trading hours (local time)
North America		
New York	0700	1000–1600
Toronto	0700	1000–1600
Europe		
Greenwich mean time	1200	0930–1530
Paris	1300	1230–1430[a]
Far East and Australia		
Tokyo	2100	0900–1500
Singapore	1930	1000–1600
Sydney	2200	1000–1530

Notes: [a]Index compilation time: 1330.
Other indices are based on closing prices or on prices taken soon after close.

systematically transmitted from one exchange to another, it pinpoints the need for more research on institutional factors such as settlement and dividend payment arrangements around the world. Also, analysis of the construction of different national equity market indices, the precise time at which trades are executed and the opportunities for arbitrage await fuller investigation. On the analytical side, it can be seen that the various capital markets form a system which has both associative and causal links. Thus, information about a macro-economic (international) event will simultaneously (associatively) affect all those capital markets which are open for trading. In contrast, domestic (US) information may be expected to affect the US markets which will then (causally) affect stock prices in other capital markets (see Table 6).

The results of this study suggest that whilst it makes sense to continue to search for specific domestic effects which might cause the US weekend effect, researchers investigating non-US capital markets are advised to seek means of purging their data of US-driven effects before investigating whether or not an indigenous weekend effect is present. On the basis of this study, we would tentatively suggest that persistent weekend effects do appear to be the norm rather than the exception in a range of capital markets around the world.

Note

* The results presented in this paper are substantially the same as those reported in greater detail in L. Condoyanni, J. O'Hanlon and C.W.R. Ward: 'Day of the Week Effects: International Evidence', Unpublished Working Paper, University of Lancaster, 1986. Whilst retaining responsibility for any remaining errors, the authors would like to acknowledge the helpful and clarifying comments of Professor K.V. Peasnell of the

University of Lancaster and of Mr Paul Hannon of the *Financial Times* together with those of Professor Maurice Levi and other participants in the EIASM Symposium. We should also like to thank Miss Alice Choy for assistance in considering the effect of the stock exchange account system in the UK and Mr Panos Papaspirou for providing information regarding the times at which non-UK stock exchanges trade.

References

Dyl, E.A. and Martin, S.A. (1985) 'Weekend Effects on Stock Returns: A Comment', *Journal of Finance*, 40, 1, March, 347–52.

French, K.R. (1980) 'Stock Returns and the Weekend Effect', *Journal of Financial Economics*, 8, 55–69.

Gultekin, M.N. and Gultekin, N.B. (1983) 'Stock Market Seasonality', *Journal of Financial Economics*, 12, 469–81.

Jaffe, J. and Westerfield, R. (1985) 'The Week-End Effect in Common Stock Returns: The International Evidence', *Journal of Finance*, 40, 2, June, 433–54.

Keim, D.B. and Stambaugh, R.F. (1984) 'A Further Investigation of the Weekend Effect in Stock Returns', *Journal of Finance*, 39, 1, July, 819–40.

Lakonishok, J. and Levi, M. 'Weekend Effects on Stock Returns: A Note', *Journal of Finance*, 37, June, 883–9.

Rogalski, R.J. (1984) 'New Findings Regarding Day-of-the-Week Returns over Trading and Non-Trading Periods: A Note', *Journal of Finance*, 39, 5, December, 1603–14.

Theobald, M. and Price, V. (1984) 'Seasonality Estimation in Thin Markets', *Journal of Finance*, 39, June, 377–92.

5 Weekly variation in the Federal funds market: the weekend game and other effects

ANTHONY SAUNDERS and THOMAS URICH

1 Introduction

The Federal funds market plays a pivotal role in the US financial system. Not only is it the largest domestic financial market (measured in terms of volume) but also the main market through which banks adjust their day-to-day reserve positions. Although a good deal of attention has been paid to the pricing efficiency of the stock market,[1] little attention has been paid to pricing behavior on the money markets and in particular Fed funds.

There are two major reasons why one might expect pricing 'inefficiencies' to exist and not be arbitraged away in the Fed funds market while, by comparison, such inefficiencies are viewed as anomalies in the context of stock market studies. The first reason is that the number of participants in the market is restricted. Specifically, participation is limited to banks, S&Ls and certain government security dealers. Potential participants from outside this set of institutions (e.g. non-financial corporations) are restricted by the fact that any Fed funds transaction, in which they take part, would be subject to reserve requirements (which are not imposed on participating institutions). Moreover, they do not have direct access to the Fed wire.

The second reason concerns the calculation of reserve requirements. Under the pre-February 2, 1984 system, which is the concern of this paper, the reserve week ran from Thursday to Wednesday and reserves held to meet the weekly reserve *target* were calculated as a *daily* average – which included both Saturday and Sunday.[2] Any excess reserves over 2 percent of required reserves could not be carried over to the following week while banks with deficient reserves faced the possible penalty costs (both explicit and implicit) of using the Federal Reserve discount window to borrow funds. Thus, for the purposes of reserve requirements, Fed funds became a perishable asset (see Garbade *et al.*, 1982). Hence on a Wednesday, banks with excess reserves had faced increased incentives (compared to other days) to dispose of reserves (sell Fed funds) while those with deficient reserves had increased incentives to buy reserves (buy Fed funds). Given the aggregate supply of non-borrowed reserves in the system that week, the Wednesday effect is likely to have resulted in an abnormally high variance, or range of rates, with rates being higher (or lower) than on other days in the week according to whether or not aggregate non-borrowed reserves were in short (excess) supply. Consequently, a Wednesday effect may be observable in both the price and variance of Fed funds.

A further 'permanent' anomaly is likely to have been introduced by the counting of both Saturday and Sunday as full days for the purposes of reserve requirement calculation, so that deposits held by a bank at the close of business on a Friday counted three times (or three-sevenths) towards the calculation of the average daily reserve requirements. As has been discussed by Levi (1978) and Coats(1981), this gave rise to Thursday–Friday and Friday–Monday (or weekend Euro-dollar) games played by large member banks and nonmember banks in order to lower required reserves for future weeks. This game relied on the fact that Fed funds provided immediate (same day settlement) while Euro-dollar transactions through CHIPS (Clearing House Interbank Payments System) provided next day settlement. It might be noted that the ability of large banks to use this mechanism to reduce future required reserves effectively ended on October 1, 1981 when the CHIPS system initiated same day settlement for Euro-dollar transactions.[3]

Under the Thursday–Friday game a member bank would lend clearing house funds to a nonmember (via CHIPS) on Thursday, thereby raising net deposits for one day.[4] When the funds were 'delivered' the next day (Friday) the member bank would cover the loan by purchasing Fed funds.[5] On the same day (Friday), the nonmember bank would initiate repayment of the loan, again using CHIPS. However, because of 'next day settlement', this loan repayment was not collectable until Monday. Thus, the member bank includes this repayment as an item 'in the process of collection' from the nonmember bank. This lowers the member bank's net deposits for Friday and therefore for Saturday and Sunday as well – reducing its net demand deposits for two days (on a net basis). On Monday, when the (loan) repayments (CHIPS funds) are actually received, the member bank then reverses its transaction in Fed funds (i.e. repays Fed funds borrowed on Friday).[6]

The Friday–Monday (or weekend) game occurs when a member bank borrows CHIPS funds from a nonmember bank on a Friday and repays the loan on a Monday. Since the Friday borrowed funds are not actually delivered until the 'next day', or Monday, the member bank adds 'a cash item in the process of collection' on Friday which counts three times for reserve purposes (Friday, Saturday and Sunday). On Monday, when the funds are actually delivered, the member bank can repay the loan immediately with Fed funds without causing an increase in reservable deposits to offset Friday's decrease. This effectively produces three days of savings in reserves (net deposits are reduced for three days). Alternatively, the member bank could repay the nonmember bank by CHIPS (rather than Fed funds) in which case net deposits would rise on the Monday when the loan was received and be removed from the books on Tuesday when the CHIPS repayment becomes good funds. However, this mechanism would only produce two days of reserve savings, since Monday's increase in net deposits would offset Friday, Saturday and Sunday's fall.

The Thursday–Friday game requires Fed funds to be purchased by large banks on Fridays, while Friday–Monday (CHIPS version) requires Fed funds to be sold on Mondays. To the extent that the weekend game was large relative to transactions volume in the Fed funds market, these games may have affected rates abnormally on those days. Indeed, Coats (1981) estimated the size of these games at $20 billion, in June 1979, with 30 percent of this volume accounted for by the Thursday–Friday version of the game and 70 percent by the Friday–Monday version. In the same month, June 1979, the daily average (gross) transactions of all forty-six money center banks on the Fed funds market was equal to $27.7 billion (Federal Reserve *Bulletin*). Thus, given the size of the market relative to the size of these games, one might expect some additional price pressure on those days associated with these games. Specifically, under the Thursday–Friday version there might have been *ceteris paribus* a larger net demand pressure for Fed funds on Fridays, pushing the rate abnormally higher, while for the Friday–Monday game (CHIPS version) there should have been additional selling pressure on Mondays pushing the rate 'abnormally' lower.[7] Furthermore, Levi (1978), in his examination of the weekend games effect on US–Canadian exchange rates, found evidence to support the existence of the Friday–Monday version of the game.

Given these 'permanent' anomalies, the objective of this chapter is to examine the extent to which they were reflected in the data. The period analyzed ran from January 1978 through to September 1981 (ending one month before CHIPS switched to same day settlement). This time period was also divided into two subperiods, the first subperiod ending one day before October 6, 1979, when the Fed announced its switch to non-borrowed reserves from interest rates as its short-run operating target for monetary policy.

In section 2 the data and testing methodology is described and outlined. In section 3, the empirical results are discussed. Finally, section 4 is a summary and conclusion.

2 Data and methodology

Data on Fed funds rates were extracted from the Money Market memo published by Garvin Guy Butler, the Fed funds brokers. These data consist of daily high, low and effective Fed funds rates. The effective Fed funds rate is a transactions weighted average of lending rates over the day and is the rate used to measure the daily 'price' of Fed funds (R_t). We are also interested in the inter-day behavior of the daily variance of Fed funds rates. Usually the variance of interest rates is calculated on a close-to-close basis. However, recent research by Parkinson (1980), Garman and Klass (1980) and Beckers (1983) has shown that estimation based on daily highs and lows can produce estimates of the true daily variance that are over five times more efficient than the close-to-close measure. In this study, we use a measure of daily variance (σ^2) suggested by Parkinson (1980), and used elsewhere by Dothan (1978) and others, that is based on daily highs and lows. That is, $\sigma^2 = [(H-L)^2 \pi]/8$, where $H(L)$ is the high (low) rate. (Note that $H-L$ gives the daily range of Fed fund rates.) An additional interest rate examined is the overnight repurchase agreement rate (RP) since it is closely associated with the Fed funds rate.

If Fed fund rates do exhibit daily anomalies and these anomalies are due to the net purchase (selling) pressure of the largest money center banks, we would also expect to see this behavior reflected in the daily pattern of money center Fed fund net purchases. Thus we would expect to see net purchases abnormally high on Fridays (under the Thursday–Friday version) and abnormally low on Mondays (under the Friday–Monday CHIPS version). Data on *daily* purchases (P) and sales (S) of Fed funds by large banks were supplied by the Federal Reserve Board of Governors. These data list for each day the aggregate dollar volume of Fed funds purchased and sold by the largest banks. The variable net purchases (NP) is simply the difference between the aggregate purchases and sales of these banks. One problem that arose was that the Fed increased its survey of large bank Fed fund transactions from 46 banks to 122 on February 27, 1980. As a result the two subperiods compared in section 3 are January 3, 1978 to October 5, 1979 (the interest-rate target regime) and March 1, 1980 to September 1, 1981 (the reserve target regime).

Letting DEP_t define the dependent variable under consideration (for example, R_t) the methodology for testing for day-of-the-week effects is specified in equation (1) below (see Gibbons and Hess, 1981):

$$DEP_t = \beta_1 D_{1t} + \beta_2 D_{2t} + \beta_3 D_{3t} + \beta_4 D_{4t} + \beta_5 D_{5t} + u_t \qquad (1)$$

where the D_{it} are the dummy variables for Monday ($i=1$) through Friday ($i=5$)

Table 1 *Weekly variation in the Fed funds and RP markets*

1/3/78–10/5/79 $n = 448$

	Thursday	Friday	Monday	Tuesday	Wednesday	F
R	9.02	9.05	9.06	9.05	9.04	52.04[a]
	(0.96)	(0.96)	(0.97)	(0.97)	(0.94)	
σ_R^2	0.03	0.45	0.28	0.75	10.17	4.69[a]
	(0.01)	(0.17)	(0.13)	(0.24)	(1.35)	
$H-L$	0.20	0.58	0.48	0.75	4.05	13.34[a]
	(0.02)	(0.09)	(0.07)	(0.12)	(0.32)	
RP	8.62	8.67	8.61	8.63	8.62	52.43[a]
	(3.31)	(3.34)	(3.29)	(3.31)	(3.31)	
$(R-RP)$	0.39	0.38	0.45	0.41	0.42	2.35
	(0.04)	(0.04)	(0.05)	(0.05)	(0.05)	
P	24,273	25,889	23,783	25,340	25,029	89.61[a]
	(511)	(529)	(518)	(572)	(515)	
S	7,626	7,180	10,292	7,822	7,182	212.32[a]
	(133)	(128)	(138)	(156)	(114)	
NP	16,647	18,709	13,490	17,518	17,816	235.78[a]
	(434)	(440)	(428)	(478)	(420)	

Note: [a] Significant at 1 percent level.
Standard errors are in parentheses and have been adjusted for heteroscedasticity and for autocorrelated errors.
The F-test is for the null hypotheses that all the intra-week means are equal, $H_0(\beta_1 = \beta_2 = \beta_3 = \beta_4 = \beta_5)$.

For each day-of-the-week regression there are four important questions which need to be addressed: (a) are the day of the week dummies statistically significant, and if so, on which days? (b) does the data reject the null hypothesis that the coefficients on the daily dummies are equal, i.e. H_0: $\beta_1 = \beta_2 = \beta_3 = \beta_4 = \beta_5$? (c) if it does, is there evidence of a weekend game and a reserve perishability effect? and (d) is there any evidence of structural shifts in the pattern of daily Fed funds variation between the interest rate target regime (January 3, 1978 – October 5, 1979) and the reserve targeting regime (March 1, 1980 – September 1, 1981)?

3 Empirical results

The results of estimating equation (1) over the first subperiod (January 3, 1978 – October 5, 1979) are presented in table 1, along with F-statistics to test the null hypothesis that the day-of-the-week coefficients are equal. The day-of-the-week coefficients reported are those from the (unadjusted) OLS regression and are equivalent to the mean daily values of the variable under consideration. The standard errors and F-tests reported in the tables are those from regressions adjusted for heteroscedasticity and autocorrelation.[8]

In the first subperiod, the Fed was pursuing a target Fed funds rate which it believed was consistent with its short-run monetary (M1) growth targets. As a result, 'toleration' limits were set as to the range within which the Fed funds rate could fluctuate without corrective open market operations by the Fed – these limits were usually set at 0.5 percent either side of the target. Because of these limits, observed inter-day differences in effective funds rates are very small, with approximately four basis points separating the high and low days.[9] In this period, effective rates (R_t) appeared to increase marginally over the early part of the reserve calculation period, peaking on Mondays, then falling until Wednesdays. This pattern appears to be counter to that expected from participation in Euro-dollar games, i.e. higher rates on Fridays than Mondays.

However, because of the Federal Reserve's rate targeting policy and the extremely small differences in mean rates (prices) between days, e.g. one basis point between Fridays and Mondays, better insights into the importance of these games may be derived by looking at the net quantities of Fed funds purchased on these days. In particular, we would expect to see abnormally large net purchases of Fed funds (NP) by large money center banks on Fridays and sales (or lower net purchases) on Mondays. Interestingly, such a pattern is clearly apparent.

On Fridays, large bank net purchases exceeded those on the next highest day by 4.8 percent, while Mondays net purchases are lower than on any other day by 23 percent. Further, Friday's net purchases exceeded Monday's net purchases by 38.7 percent. Thus the pattern of purchasing behavior is clearly consistent with large bank participation in Euro-dollar games. One inference which can be drawn from these results is that the Fed's targeting policy prevented Friday's (Monday's) net demand (sales) pressures from being reflected fully in market rates. It is also interesting to note that the daily pattern in RP rates closely mimics that observed for Fed funds, so that it is not possible to reject the null hypothesis of *no* weekly variation in Fed fund – RP rate spreads $(R_t - RP_t)$, at the 5 percent level. This suggests that pricing in the two markets was closely interlinked over this period.[10] Finally, Fed fund rate targeting notwithstanding, the daily variance of Fed funds rates (σ^2), and the range of rates $(H-L)$, were considerably larger on Wednesdays than on any other day. For example, σ^2 on a Wednesday was more than five times greater than on other days in the reserve period (week). This result is consistent with Wednesday reserve perishability, leading to anomalous rate behavior in the funds market. Moreover, the size of the observed variance implies that the Fed's toleration limits on

Table 2 *Weekly variation in the Fed funds and RP markets*

3/1/80–9/1/81 $n = 384$

	Thursday	Friday	Monday	Tuesday	Wednesday	F
R	15.09 (1.81)	15.38 (1.76)	15.33 (1.69)	15.18 (1.80)	14.79 (1.82)	62.03[a]
σ_R^2	1.98 (1.17)	3.09 (0.59)	3.51 (1.39)	4.60 (1.63)	35.11 (4.38)	386.60[a]
$H-L$	1.38 (0.21)	2.15 (0.21)	1.87 (0.27)	2.17 (0.30)	7.99 (0.58)	15.23[a]
RP	13.87 (2.16)	14.30 (2.05)	14.19 (1.96)	14.14 (2.10)	13.80 (2.06)	104.38[a]
$(R-RP)$	1.21 (0.13)	1.08 (0.16)	1.14 (0.14)	1.04 (0.13)	0.99 (0.17)	18.92[a]
P	107,810 (1604)	110,601 (1343)	107,075 (1693)	109,650 (1623)	109,225 (1665)	4941.07[a]
S	16,500 (218)	16,769 (243)	19,729 (295)	17,638 (247)	17,864 (223)	39.24[a]
NP	91,310 (1165)	93,832 (1011)	87,347 (1323)	92,011 (1188)	91,362 (1206)	2356.32[a]

Note: [a] Significant at 1 percent level.
Standard errors are in parentheses and have been adjusted for heteroscedasticity and for autocorrelated errors.
The F-test is for the null hypotheses that all the intra-week means are equal, $H_0 (\beta_1 = \beta_2 = \beta_3 = \beta_4 = \beta_5)$.

Fed fund rate variability had to be relaxed quite frequently on Wednesdays.

On October 6, 1979 the Fed announced that its short-run monetary policy operating target had been switched from Fed fund rates to the quantity of nonborrowed reserves – with the long-run target remaining the rate of growth of the money supply. This regime change implied a greater willingness on the part of the Fed to accept high interest rates and increased interest rate volatility in return for enhanced control or leverage over the reserve base. In practice, the FOMC continued to specify a maximum range or tolerance band within which it was prepared to allow the Fed funds rate to vary before stabilizing open market operations or RP transactions by the Fed. This range was set at 4 percent in the early months of the new policy – rising later to 8.5 percent.

To the extent that reserve perishability and the Euro-dollar game created abnormal demand/supply pressures in the Fed funds market, these should be more readily evident in the observed behavior of rates over this reserve-target subperiod (compared to the rate-target subperiod). The results of estimating equation (1) in the second sub-period (March 1, 1980 – September 1, 1981) are presented in table 2.

First, it can be seen that there is now far greater variability in the effective Fed funds rate (R_t) over the reserve week, with fifty-nine basis points separating the high from the low days (while the average rate is more than 600 basis points greater than under rate targets). Second, the behavior of these rates is clearly consistent with that implied by participation in Euro-dollar games. That is, Friday's rate is not only higher than Monday's rate (by five basis points), but it is also the highest of all days in the reserve week. Moreover, the behavior of rates is also consistent with large bank net purchase (NP) behavior. Specifically, Friday's net purchases of Fed funds were the largest over the reserve week, while those on Monday were the lowest – with Friday's net purchases exceeding Monday's by 7.4 percent.

It can also be seen that the effective Fed funds rate on Wednesday was lower than on any other day (by thirty basis points). It may seem puzzling as to why, the Euro-dollar game notwithstanding, large banks did not leave the bulk of their net purchases to the last day of the reserve week, i.e. Wednesdays. To gain some insights into why large banks did not exploit this apparently profitable arbitrage opportunity consider the $H-L$ and σ^2 rows in tables 1 and 2. As can be seen, reserve targeting led to much greater variability in the daily variance of the Fed funds rate than rate targeting (as might be expected). Further, Wednesday's rate variability (σ^2) and high–low range were respectively 7.6 and 3.68 times greater than on the next highest day in the reserve week. This high variance of Fed funds on Wednesdays, along with binding reserve commitments would have discouraged strategies such as waiting until Wednesdays to purchase Fed funds for all but the least risk averse banks.[11] Hence the results for the second subperiod are consistent with permanent anomalies in the funds market due to the 'perishability' of reserves and binding reserve commitments. Finally, it is interesting to note that RP rate variation continued to broadly mirror the day of the week behavior of Fed fund rates with the highest rate remaining Friday's and the lowest Wednesday's.[12] These results suggest that both markets continued to be closely tied together, irrespective of the Fed's monetary policy targeting regime. However, it can also be seen that the *spread* between the two rates increased substantially in the second subperiod from an average of forty-one basis points under rate targets to an average of 109 basis points under reserve targets. This increase was possibly due to the greater variability of interest rates in the second subperiod, and the resulting impact of this higher rate volatility on the perceived riskiness of uncollateralized Fed funds relative to collateralized RPs.[13]

4 Summary and conclusion

This chapter examined weekly variations in the Federal funds market. The major result was that weekly variation was clearly present over the period studied (1978/1 – 1981/9). Specifically, there was evidence of week-end Euro-dollar games in both the interest rate and reserve target subperiods. Moreover, reserve perishability led to considerably more volatile rates on Wednesday's than on other days. This volatility, combined with binding reserve commitments (and associated penalty costs), appeared to deter the major money-center banks from arbitraging away 'apparently' profitable anomalies in Wednesday's effective rates.

Notes

1 See, for example, Gibbons and Hess (1981).
2 For a good comparison of lagged versus contemporaneous reserve accounting see Gilbert (1980).
3 This does not mean to imply that member banks did not search for new mechanisms to reduce their 'reservable' deposits on Fridays (and, therefore, for the weekend).
4 The Clearing House Interbank Payments System (CHIPS) is the primary vehicle for clearing Euro-dollar and other transactions between domestic and foreign banks.
5 This presumes it does not have excess reserves.
6 Because good CHIPS funds are used to repay the Fed fund loan this transaction does not generate a net increase in demand for Fed funds on the Monday.
7 Coats' (1981) calculation of member bank profits from these games was equal to the saving in reserve times the return on these funds invested in the next but one calculation period (i.e. two weeks in the future, due to lagged reserves) minus the cost of participation which equaled the overnight rate on Euro-dollars minus the Fed funds rate on Friday (for the Thursday–Friday game) and Monday (for the Friday–Monday game). Although Coats (1981) never discussed the implications of weekly variations in Fed funds rates (see Coats, 1981, footnote 12, p. 654), his calculus nevertheless implies that the greater the abnormal upward (downward) pressure placed on Fed funds rates on Fridays (Mondays) the *less* profitable these games were to member banks (and nonmember banks) – i.e. the cost to the member banks from participating increased relative to the benefits. This may well have been one reason for the observed finite size of these games.
8 Each data series was individually corrected for heteroscedasticity by weighting the data by the appropriate standard deviation for that day of the week. The Cochrane–Orcutt method was then used to correct for autocorrelation in the equation residuals.
9 Despite these small differences in the unadjusted data, the F-test rejects the null hypothesis of coefficient equality.
10 One possibility is that the Fed funds market acted as the dominant market with the RP market acting as its satellite, with the latter setting similar pricing bounds to those established or tolerated by the Fed in the funds market.
11 Why we might expect banks to be risk averse in their reserve management can be explained as follows. First, waiting until the last moment on Wednesday's to buy Fed funds over the Fed wire occasionally results in 'failed transactions.' That is, the wire closes before a transaction is completed because of traffic on the wire. In this case a bank would be forced to borrow at 'penalty prices' from the discount window (explicit plus implicit costs) – (see Ho and Saunders, 1985). Second, even if over a long length of time each day's reserve position is independent, there is still a finite possibility of a run of negative reserve positions. Thus, a bank on a Wednesday may face the (small) probability of having to buy a large amount of reserves at a high (rather than low) rate. (This has an analogy to the gambler's risk of ruin.)

12 However, we no longer can reject the hypothesis of no weekly variation in their spreads $(R-RP)$.
13 This period ends before the failure of Drysdale Securities in 1982 which raised doubts as to whether RPs were swaps or loans and therefore who had rights to the underlying collateral. See Ho and Saunders (1985) for a theoretical discussion of the risk-premium spread between Fed funds and RPs.

References

Beckers, S. (1983) 'Variances of Security Price Returns Based on High, Low, and Closing Prices.' *Journal of Finance*, 56, January, 97–112.

Coats, W.L. (1981) 'The Weekend Eurodollar Game.' *Journal of Finance*, 36, June, 649–59.

Dothan, U.L. (1978) 'On the Term Structure of Interest Rates.' *Journal of Financial Economics*, 6, January 59–69.

Eisemann, P. and Timme, S. (1982) 'Intraweek Seasonality in the Federal Funds Market.' Mimeograph.

Garbade, K., Lopez-Brito, J. and Melton, W. (1982) 'Federal Funds: Efficiency of a Market for a "Perishable" Asset.' Salomon Brothers Center for the Study of Financial Institutions, New York University, October.

Garman, M.B. and Klass, M.J. (1980) 'On the Estimation of Security Price Volatilities from Historical Data.' *Journal of Business*, 53, January, 67–78.

Gibbons, M. and Hess. P. (1981) 'Day of the Week Effects and Asset Returns.' *Journal of Business*, 54, October, 579–96.

Gilbert, R.A. (1980) 'Lagged Reserve Requirements: Implications for Monetary Control and Bank Reserve Management.' *Federal Reserve Bank of St. Louis Review*, May, 7–20.

Ho, T.S.Y. and Saunders, A. (1985) 'A Micro Model of the Federal Funds Market.' *Journal of Finance*, 40, 977–90.

Levi, M.D. (1978) 'The Weekend Game: Clearinghouse vs Federal Funds.' *Canadian Journal of Economics*, 4, November, 750–7.

Melton, W. (1982) 'Fedwatching and The Federal Funds Market.' Mimeograph.

Parkinson, M. (1980) 'The Extreme Value Method for Estimating the Variance of the Rate of Return.' *Journal of Business*, 53, January, 61–6.

Sellon, G. and Serbert, D. (1982) 'The Discount Rate: Experience Under Reserve Targeting.' *Economic Review*, September–October, 3–18.

6   Daily seasonals in equity and fixed-interest returns: Australian evidence and tests of plausible hypotheses

*RAY BALL and JOHN BOWERS**

The objectives of this paper are to present new evidence on the day-of-the-week seasonal in Australian equity returns, to extend the evidence to daily interest rates and to evaluate several plausible hypotheses concerning the seasonal. It is offered as a preliminary study aimed at stimulating discussion.

The first section of the paper discusses the nature of the anomaly arising from a daily return seasonal and proposes that it can only be understood by analyzing seasonals in supply parameters and in investor preferences. Section 2 describes alternative hypotheses. Sections 3 and 4 describe the Australian data and our results. The final section draws conclusions from this preliminary work.

1 Anomaly and hypotheses

The day-of-the-week seasonal was first documented by Osborne (1962, tables IV and V). Subsequent work by Cross (1973), French (1980), Gibbons and Hess (1981), Lakonishok and Levi (1982), Smirlock and Starks (1983), Keim and Stambaugh (1983), Rogalski (1984), Jaffe and Westerfield (1985) and others has confirmed the existence of a seasonal, in that equity return distributions are not independent of the day of the week or of the time of the day. One result that researchers have found to be particularly anomalous is that sample mean returns over weekends are negative.

The existence of seasonals in equity returns is not *in itself* surprising, since there is no theoretical reason to preclude seasonals in either supply or demand parameters. For example, in a simple Fisherian world, the rate of interest reflects both the marginal efficiency of investment and the marginal rate of intertemporal consumption preferences (see Hirshleifer, 1970, ch. 6). There is no reason to believe that the ratio of marginal utilities of present and future consumption is identical on weekends and weekdays, during daytime and during nighttime. Nor is there reason to believe that the marginal efficiency of investment is a constant, independent of time of day and day of week. Indeed, casual observation suggests the existence of seasonals in consumption patterns and returns on investment.

Seasonal variation in the expected value of returns from real investments is likely, particularly on weekends. If weekends are universal times of leisure, then it is likely that the marginal efficiency of investment (MEI) is lower on weekends than during the week. A proportion of the capital stock lies idle and incurs positive real holding costs on weekends (deterioration, insurance, security costs, etc.). Note that we are dealing with the *marginal* expected return on real investment: the expected return on the market-clearing marginal investment. The argument does not address the expected return on the *average* real investment. On weekends (when much of the real capital stock is idle across the world), it is plausible that at least the *marginal* expected return on real assets is lower than on weekdays, and perhaps it is negative. Note also that a similar point can be made about overnight returns. A complete treatment of these issues requires modelling the real investment market; we offer an incomplete analysis.

It is not sufficient to argue that systematic seasonals in returns are inconsistent with rational expectations. When both supply and demand for real assets are considered jointly (as they must be, to explain a seasonal in the price of capital), the equilibrium expected return on real assets is endogenous. Prices can be present values and still yield equilibrium expected returns that display seasonals.

Nor is it sufficient to argue entirely in terms of pure-exchange models. While modern finance concentrates on pure exchange, a source of explanations of seasonals in prices is likely to be seasonals in supply parameters. Nevertheless, pure-exchange models can provide insight. In particular, the anomalous feature of the negative mean returns over weekends on the NYSE is that the *ex-post* risk premium is negative over a prolonged period. We therefore investigate daily interest rates, in the hope of finding clues about the 'weekend effect'.

The above argument presumes that equity returns are riskier than the interest rate, over weekends. This presumption is worth checking. The second parameter of interest therefore is risk. Here we repeat the distinction between short- and long-term effects in real asset markets and again make a simple observation, without providing an articulated supporting model. The observation is that, in a security market where the marginal investor has a long-term horizon, the risk arising from holding investments over a short interval depends upon the contribution of that interval to risk over the complete horizon, not simply the short term. Consider a world where the security markets trade at discrete intervals and the marginal investor evaluates risk over a T-period horizon. The return over this horizon is

$$R_{0,T} = \sum_{t=0}^{T} r_t,$$

where $R_{0,T}$ is return over the interval $(0,T)$, r_t is return over the discrete interval t lying in $(0,T)$ and returns are continuously compounded. Risk over this horizon is:

$$\text{var}(R_{0,T}) = \sum_t \sum_\tau \text{covar}(r_t r_\tau)$$

where var and covar denote variance and covariance respectively. The contribution of any single period to risk over the complete horizon depends upon that period's own return variance and its covariance with returns in other periods. A seasonal in risk is feasible. Furthermore, there is the intriguing possibility that short-term periods could have negative risk (this could occur if a period's own variance was more than offset by negative covariance with returns in other periods). We therefore investigate seasonals in the day-of-the-week covariances, as well as in the day-of-the-week means, of security returns.

2 Other hypotheses

In the previous section, we hypothesized that seasonals in security returns could reflect underlying seasonals in returns from real assets. This section outlines several alternative hypotheses.

Dividend seasonal

Institutional practices could cause seasonals in dividend payment and ex-dividend days. Any effect of tax on pre-tax yields (including both dividends and price changes) and error in recording dividends in the index then would induce seasonals in observed security returns. We therefore test for a day-of-the-week seasonal in dividends and its effect on equity return seasonals.

Money seasonal

Institutional practices in money management (e.g. payment of wages near the weekend) could cause seasonals in security returns. While we are sceptical of this argument, because most of these practices suggest seasonals in zero-sum flows rather than stocks of real assets, we test for the day-of-the-week seasonal in interest rates and its effect on equity return seasonals.

International capital market

Sydney time on average (i.e. ignoring daylight saving time in both countries) is 15 hours ahead of New York time and 18 hours ahead of Pacific Coast time. It is 10 hours ahead of GMT. The Sydney Stock Exchange claims to be the first exchange in the world to open for the week. If capital markets strike international equilibria, then it is possible that 'weekend effects' on the international market would carry over into 'Tuesday effects' in Sydney.

Discontinuous trading

It is not possible to observe security returns over precisely daily intervals, because securities are not traded continuously in time. If there is a seasonal in trading volume, then a spurious seasonal could be observed in daily returns. We therefore investigate whether the day-of-the-week seasonal can be attributed in part to serial correlation arising from discontinuous trading.

Weekend float

Lakonishok and Levi (1982) observe that the time interval, between contracting to purchase and delivering cash for stocks, is two days longer in the case of contracts written on Fridays. Because the buyer obtains an extra two-day 'float' on Friday trades, Friday closing prices would incorporate the present value of the float, whereas Monday opening prices would not. This implies lower apparent returns on equities over weekends. The practice on the Sydney exchange is to effect invoicing and settlement in terms of elapsed business days after trading, so that an additional two-day float is provided on weekends. We test this hypothesis in two ways: (a) by comparing the difference in weekend and Friday returns with the interest rate over the weekend; and (b) by comparing weekend and holiday returns (holidays provide additional float).

3 Data

Equities

The equity data consist of 2759 observations of the daily closing values of two Sydney Stock Exchange indexes, the Statex-Actuaries Price and

Accumulation Indexes. The Sydney data are interesting because of the opportunity to replicate US results and because the difference in timing of the weekends in Sydney and New York might provide insights into the 'weekend effect'. Data are available for the eleven years from 2 January 1974 until 28 December 1984. The price index does not include dividends, whereas the accumulation index does. It therefore is possible to derive a daily dividend yield variable for the index stocks.

The indexes are based upon an annually rebalanced portfolio of fifty stocks. The stocks are chosen annually on the basis of capitalization, volatility and turnover: from the set of stocks that have 'consistently been in the top 250 by market capitalisation for the prior two years,' the fifty highest-turnover stocks in the immediately preceding year are selected. The indexes thus are comprised of relatively actively traded stocks. They are equal weighted at the beginning of each year. There is no 'small firm effect' in the indexes.

We found considerable error in reported values of the indexes. Some error arose from typographical mistakes in publication. Other errors arose from problems that the Sydney Stock Exchange experiences in computing an index in real time. These had been corrected in subsequent output from the Sydney Stock Exchange Research Service, which we obtained. Each observation was cross-checked against newspaper reports, the *Sydney Stock Exchange Daily Official List*, the *Australian Stock Exchange Journal* and (finally) the Exchange's hand-written copy supplied to the printer of the *Journal*. We now believe that we have a clean data series.

A further source of error was found in the construction of the index. Daily dividends are not reinvested in the index portfolios until the annual rebalance data. Instead, the accumulation index is valued at the simple sum of the daily closing prices of the index stocks, plus the accumulated dividends on the index for the year to date. This introduces error in measuring rates of return on the index, because the index observation and the preceding observation are displaced by a constant, the accumulated dividend to date. We discovered the error when we observed that the price index had a higher rate of return than the accumulation index on slightly more than 40 percent of all trading days. (The difference exceeded rounding error.) We were able to develop an algorithm to correct for the error, because the daily dividend yield on the index portfolio can be inferred from the two indexes. Corrected copies of the indexes are provided in Ball and Bowers (1986), which is available on request.

Interest rates

Clues concerning the source of seasonals in daily equity returns possibly lie in daily interest rates. Unfortunately, the rates available to us are

Table 1 *Summary statistics, excluding days immediately following holidays, 2 January 1974–28 December 1984*

	$\bar{x}$	σ	Skew	Kurt	ϱ_1	$B-P$	N
Accumulation index							
Mon.	−0.00007	0.01150	1.15	11.79	0.07	18.9	499
Tue.	−0.00152	0.00942	0.01	2.80	0.05	28.9	498
Wed.	0.00053	0.01009	1.19	9.83	−0.07	28.6	554
Thu.	0.00191	0.00950	−0.15	1.75	0.02	20.1	560
Fri.	0.00161	0.00918	−0.55	4.97	−0.07	26.7	545
			$F = 8.6, p < 0.01$				
Price index							
Mon.	−0.00048	0.01157	1.11	11.45	0.07	17.3	499
Tue.	−0.00160	0.00942	0.01	2.79	0.05	29.9	498
Wed.	0.00043	0.01009	1.13	9.28	−0.07	29.1	554
Thu.	0.00172	0.00951	−0.17	1.78	0.02	19.3	560
Fri.	0.00136	0.00925	−0.60	5.09	−0.08	28.1	545
			$F = 8.4, p < 0.01$				

Note: Columns describe sample mean, standard deviation, standardized skewness and kurtosis statistics, first-order serial correlation in the sequence of returns for the denominated day of the week, the Box–Pierce statistic for the first fifteen serial correlation statistics and sample size. Returns on holidays and days immediately following holidays are replaced by sample day-of-the-week means for purposes of calculating ϱ and $B-P$. The F-statistic and associated probability are offered as a test of the null hypotheses that the day-of-the-week means are equal.

averages: the dollar-weighted average rate on all transactions for the day. While this is not necessarily a market-clearing rate, we are led to believe that there is little cross-sectional variation in rates within each day. Further, the average rates should capture any daily seasonal in the fixed-interest market: the averaging occurs within (but not across) days.

The data cover the period 15 April, 1975 to 28 December, 1985. They were made available in clean form by the Reserve Bank of Australia.

4 Results

All rates of return are expressed as logarithms of price relatives. Returns are measured from close of trading to close of trading on the next day that the Exchange is open. Thus, returns labelled 'Monday' cover the three-day period from Friday closing to Monday closing, in the absence of holidays, and have *not* been expressed as daily average equivalents. Returns on the first trading day after a holiday (or holidays) cover more than one calendar day.

Order	Auto-corr.	S.E. random model	−1 −.75 −.50 −.25 0 .25 .50 .75 +1
			:-------:-------:-------:-------:-------:-------:-------:-------:
1	0.020	0.042	+ * +
2	0.089	0.042	+ : *
3	0.037	0.042	+ :*+
4	−0.019	0.042	+ * +
5	−0.075	0.042	* : +
6	−0.024	0.041	+ * +
7	−0.025	0.041	+ * +
8	0.062	0.041	+ :*+
9	0.006	0.041	+ * +
10	0.037	0.041	+ :*+
11	0.066	0.041	+ :*+
12	0.001	0.041	+ * +
13	0.075	0.041	+ : *
14	−0.028	0.041	+*: +
15	0.017	0.041	+ * +

```
                :-------:-------:-------:-------:-------:-------:-------:-------:
                -1 -.75 -.50 -.25  0    .25    .50   .75   +1
```

*   Autocorrelations
\+   2 standard error limits (approx.)

Figure 1   Autocorrelation in sequence of 560 Thursday accumulation index returns: 2 January, 1974–28 December, 1984

Descriptive statistics: equity returns

Table 1 reports sample statistics by day of the week for the accumulation and prices indices. The sample of 2656 observations covers the entire period for which we have data, excluding holidays (for which there are no data) and the 102 days immediately following holidays. Following days are included in other analyses below, but they distort the day-of-the-week seasonal because there is a daily seasonal in holidays. The following conclusions are drawn from the table:

1.   The five separate day-of-the-week samples are 'well behaved' relative to the pooled sample of returns across all days. There is no evidence of skewness: the individual day-of-the-week skewness statistics range from −0.55 to +1.15 for the accumulation index, in contrast with +6.90 for all days pooled together. There is some leptokurtosis, though it is not stationary (compare table 2, for a subsample of these days) and the leptokurtosis in the individual day-of-the-week series does not approach the degree of leptokurtosis for the pooled daily returns sequence (96.4 for the accumulation and 98.7 for the price index). This suggests that a major source of leptokurtosis in pooled daily equity returns is the seasonal across days of the week.

2.   The significant Box–Pierce statistics imply autocorrelation in each of the day-of-the-week sequences. However, the coefficients for lags up to fifteen seldom exceed one standard deviation, as shown in figure 1.
3.   There is a significant day-of-the-week seasonal in both indices. The F-statistics of 8.6 and 8.4 for the accumulation index and the price index suggest that the null hypothesis (time-invariant mean returns) can be rejected at conventional significance levels. The sample mean returns are positive on Thursday and Friday: univariate t-statistics for the accumulation index are $+4.76$ and $+4.09$ for these days. In contrast, the mean return over the other five days of the week, taken as a whole, is negative.

The sample mean return for the weekend (designated 'Monday') has the same sign as in the NYSE studies, but it is not significantly different from zero. It changes sign for a subsample of this period, reported in table 2.

The surprises in the data, given the NYSE results, are the sample means for Tuesday and Wednesday. On a univariate basis, the Tuesday mean is negative and significant ($t = -3.60$ for the accumulation index); and the Wednesday mean is positive but small and insignificant ($t = 1.24$). An interpretation of this result is provided below.

4.   While the seasonal is significant, it explains little of the variation in daily returns. This can be seen from the low explanatory power of the regression reported in table 3.
5.   The day-of-the-week standard deviations also exhibit a seasonal. While the weekdays differ insignificantly in volatility, the weekend variance is not in the order of three times the average weekday variance, implying either lower variances on weekend days or negative covariance among weekend returns.
6.   There is a day-of-the-week seasonal in dividends, as shown by the difference in means of the accumulation and price indices. Approximately 40 percent of dividends are recorded in the accumulation index on Mondays, 25 percent on Fridays and 20 percent on Thursdays.

The preliminary evidence thus confirms a day of the week seasonal on the Sydney Stock Exchange, though it appears to take a different form than the NYSE seasonal.

Descriptive statistics: interest rates

Table 2 reports equivalent sample statistics over the period for which

Table 2 *Summary statistics, excluding days immediately following holidays, 15 April 1975–28 December 1984*

	$\bar{x}$	σ	Skew	Kurt	ϱ_1	$B-P$	N
Accumulation index							
Mon.	0.00044	0.01012	1.24	9.69	0.11	22.4	442
Tue.	−0.00116	0.00883	0.28	2.34	0.06	27.3	446
Wed.	0.00045	0.00838	−0.01	1.60	−0.02	17.9	496
Thu.	0.00198	0.00863	−0.19	1.19	0.03	16.1	499
Fri.	0.00157	0.00800	−0.48	2.32	−0.02	25.6	490
			$F = 8.7, p < 0.01$				
Price index							
Mon.	0.00006	0.01015	1.18	9.13	0.11	22.6	442
Tue.	−0.00123	0.00883	0.28	2.36	0.07	28.4	446
Wed.	0.00037	0.00839	−0.01	1.62	−0.02	17.8	496
Thu.	0.00180	0.00863	−0.19	1.14	0.02	15.7	499
Fri.	0.00134	0.00800	−0.49	2.31	−0.02	26.6	490
			$F = 8.5, p < 0.01$				
Interest rates							
Mon.	0.00081	0.00024	0.27	−0.28	0.64	2551	442
Tue.	0.00026	0.00008	0.45	−0.27	0.57	2118	446
Wed.	0.00024	0.00008	0.68	−0.17	0.46	1565	496
Thu.	0.00027	0.00008	0.54	−0.17	0.57	2186	499
Fri.	0.00029	0.00008	0.33	0.07	0.66	2651	490
			$F = 752.1, p < 0.01^a$				

Note: $^a F = 29.0$ ($p < 0.01$) when 'Monday' rates (i.e. from 3 p.m. Friday to 3 p.m. Monday) are expressed as daily averages, rather than three-day rates.
Columns describe sample mean, standard deviation, standardized skewness and kurtosis statistics, first-order serial correlation in the sequence of returns for the denominated day of the week, the Box–Pierce statistic for the first fifteen serial correlation statistics and sample size. Returns on holidays and days immediately following holidays are replaced by sample day-of-the-week means for purposes of calculating ϱ and $B-P$. The F-statistic and associated probability are offered as a test of the null hypotheses that the day-of-the-week means are equal.

interest rate data are available. Again, days immediately following holidays are excluded. The data suggest the following:

7.   There is little skewness or kurtosis in daily interest rates.

8.   There is considerable serial correlation in each of the five day-of-the-week sequences. Figure 2 graphs the autocorrelation function for Thursdays, which is representative of the days. This result implies significant non-stationarity in the interest rate series. Note that observations are spaced seven calendar days apart and that the result is not due to the seasonal in the means.

Order	Auto-corr.	S.E. random model	−1 −.75 −.50 −.25 0 .25 .50 .75 +1
			:-------:------:------:------:------:------:------:------:--------:
1	0.565	0.044	+:+ *
2	0.610	0.044	+:+ *
3	0.541	0.044	+:+ *
4	0.610	0.044	+:+ *
5	0.550	0.044	+:+ *
6	0.614	0.044	+:+ *
7	0.544	0.044	+:+ *
8	0.493	0.044	+:+ *
9	0.562	0.044	+:+ *
10	0.493	0.044	+:+ *
11	0.480	0.044	+:+ *
12	0.450	0.044	+:+ *
13	0.513	0.044	+:+ *
14	0.438	0.044	+:+ *
15	0.466	0.044	+:+ *

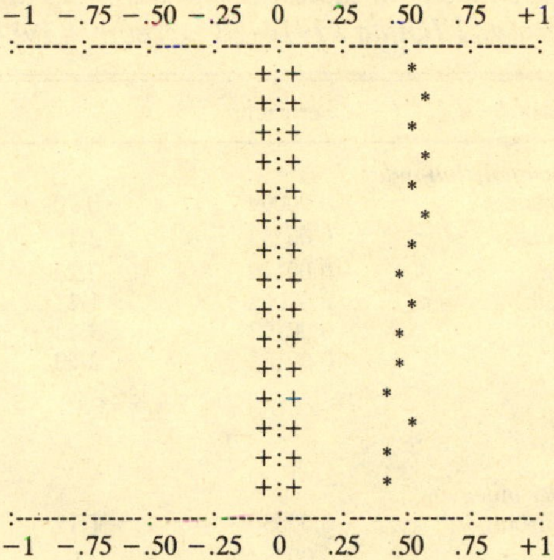

```
:--------:------:------:------:------:------:------:------:--------:
 −1  −.75 −.50 −.25  0   .25  .50  .75  +1
```

*   Autocorrelations
\+   2 standard error limits (approx.)

Figure 2   Autocorrelation in sequence of 499 Thursday interest rates:
15 April, 1975–28 December, 1984

9.   Compared with equity returns, interest rates exhibit little seasonal variation in means. The F-statistic and the Monday (i.e. weekend) mean are misleading, because the latter is a three-day rate. When the weekend rate is transformed into a daily average, the weekend mean is 0.027 percent per day and the F-statistic falls to 29.0. Because of the large sample sizes, the small differences in means either are significant or border on significance: for example, a univariate t-statistic for the difference in Tuesday and Wednesday mean interest rates (0.002 of 1 percent) is 1.25, taking into account the sample covariance between Tuesday and Wednesday rates (refer to table 7). The absence of a daily seasonal in interest rates is consistent with the regulatory policy of the Reserve Bank of Australia. Regulation of banks' balance sheets is conducted on the second Wednesday of each month, based upon the average position of the bank over the entire month. Consequently, there is no reason for the banks to vary their trading systematically with the day of the week.

10.   The behavior of the day-of-the-week interest rate standard deviations is intriguing. Whereas weekday sample standard deviations are almost identical, the weekend standard deviation is within rounding error of three times the weekday equivalent.

Table 3 *Dependent variable: return on index*
Independent variables: DOW dummies and holiday dummy
Period: 2 January 1974–28 December 1984, N = 2758

Variable	Coefficient	t	$p<$
Accumulation index			
Constant	−0.00009	−0.20	0.84
Holiday	0.00253	2.15	0.03
Tue.	−0.00140	−2.25	0.03
Wed.	0.00068	1.11	0.27
Thu.	0.00192	3.14	0.01
Fri.	0.00162	2.63	0.01
	$F = 7.8, p<0.01$		
	$\bar{R}^2 = 0.01$		
Price index			
Constant	−0.00050	−1.12	0.27
Holiday	0.00237	2.02	0.05
Tue.	−0.00108	−1.73	0.09
Wed.	0.00099	1.62	0.11
Thu.	0.00214	3.49	0.01
Fri.	0.00178	2.88	0.01
	$F = 7.6, p<0.01$		
	$\bar{R}^2 = 0.01$		

Note that 'weekends' here cover exactly three days (since holidays are excluded) and that independence of daily weekend interest rates would imply a scaling by $\sqrt{3}$. The evidence suggests a mechanism such as perfect positive correlation of interest rates across the three days. This is consistent with the high serial correlation observed in the data, particularly for adjacent days (table 7).

Descriptive statistics: risk premia

The anomalous nature of these results can be highlighted by calculating day-of-the-week risk premia, for equities relative to the fixed-interest contract. The sample mean risk premium is negative.

The interest rate data allow a test of the 'weekend float' hypothesis, which predicts that the weekend return is a three-day equity return, net of the value of a two-day float. The float value can be approximated by twice the daily average weekend interest rate and the daily equity return can be approximated by the Friday average. Thus, the hypothesis predicts a 'Monday' return (using table 2 accumulation index) of $0.00417 = 3 \times 0.00157 - 2 \times 0.00027$. This hypothesis is rejected by the data.

The preliminary evidence thus reveals little day-of-the-week seasonal behavior in interest rates, significant serial correlation and an intriguing behavior in the dispersion of weekend rates.

Regression analysis

There are several reasons for not taking the descriptive statistics at face value. These reasons, and our attempts to correct for them, are outlined in this section.

First, we are not satisfied with treating holidays by excluding the immediately following day. Table 3 reports a regression which includes these data and with five (0,1) independent variables representing normal days of the week and holiday-affected returns. The 'holiday' dummy variable is set to unity for days following holidays and to zero otherwise. The other four dummy variables denote Tuesday through Friday. The constant term therefore captures the mean return on those Mondays that do not follow Fridays on which the exchange was closed. The 'holiday' coefficient captures the marginal mean effect of a holiday. For example, the regression prediction of the accumulation index return on a Wednesday following a Tuesday holiday is 0.00312 ($= -0.00009 + 0.00253 + 0.00068$).

The 'holiday' coefficient is positive and significant, suggesting that the 'weekend effect' does not carry over into holidays, as observed on the NYSE. This result is surprising when one considers that: (a) most of the holidays include weekends; and (b) the size of the coefficient is in the order of an average *weekly* return. Addition of the holiday 'dummy' variable does not increase the significance of the regression. However, it slightly alters the pattern of the daily seasonal, by bringing the Tuesday and Wednesday means closer to those of the other days. All coefficients show higher *t*-statistics than for an (unreported) regression without the holiday variable.

Second, there is considerable positive serial correlation in index returns on successive trading days, as shown in table 7. First-order coefficients are in the order of $+0.30$. This result holds for the entire time series and for each day of the week, except for Friday/Monday – a result we are pursuing. While the Statex-Actuaries Indices comprise only high-turnover stocks, there is not continuous trading in these stocks and it is essentially an equally-weighted index. Thus, it is possible that measured returns are being attributed incorrectly to the days of the week. The regression reported in table 4 attempts to deal with this problem by introducing lagged values of the index return as independent variables.

The adjusted R^2 and *F*-statistic increase, largely due to the first-order

Table 4 *Dependent variable: return on index*
Independent variables: table 3 plus lagged dependent variable
Period: 2 January 1974–28 December 1984, N = 2758

Variable	Coefficient	t	$p<$
Accumulation index			
Constant	−0.00055	−1.33	0.18
Holiday	0.00193	1.77	0.08
Lag 1	0.39351	20.66	0.01
Lag 2	−0.09552	−4.67	0.01
Lag 3	0.05667	2.77	0.06
Lag 4	−0.02067	−1.09	0.28
Tue.	−0.00088	−1.52	0.13
Wed.	0.00156	2.73	0.01
Thu.	0.00205	3.57	0.01
Fri.	0.00150	2.62	0.09

$$F = 54.2, p<0.01$$
$$\bar{R}^2 = 0.15$$

Price index			
Constant	−0.00088	−2.11	0.04
Holiday	0.00178	1.62	0.11
Lag 1	0.39421	20.69	0.01
Lag 2	−0.09845	−4.81	0.01
Lag 3	0.06089	2.98	0.01
Lag 4	−0.02497	−1.31	0.19
Tue.	−0.00049	−0.85	0.40
Wed.	0.00181	3.15	0.01
Thu.	0.00223	3.89	0.01
Fri.	0.00165	2.87	0.01

$$F = 54.1, p<0.01$$
$$\bar{R}^2 = 0.15$$

lag variable. The first three lags have significant coefficients. The 'holiday' coefficient falls but remains significant at $p = 0.07$. The important result is that the Tuesday mean now looks more like the Monday (i.e. weekend) mean and the Wednesday mean now looks like Thursday and Friday. Presumably, the positive first-order serial correlation in the stock returns confounds the descriptive statistics reported in tables 1 and 2. One cannot be sure that this first-order serial correlation is due to discontinuous trading, as distinct from dependence in the unobserved true returns, but the increased sharpness of the day-of-the-week seasonal suggests that it is.

Third, the daily seasonal in dividends could present an explanation of the return seasonal if either: (a) there is a 'tax effect'; or (b) the index does not record dividends at the correct time. Table 5 therefore repeats

Table 5 *Dependent variable: return on index*
Independent variables: table 4 plus dividend yield
Period: 2 January 1974–28 December 1984, N = 2758

Variable	Coefficient	t	$p<$
Accumulation index			
Constant	−0.00052	−1.15	0.26
Holiday	0.00202	1.85	0.07
Lag 1	0.39467	20.71	0.01
Lag 2	−0.09625	−4.70	0.01
Lag 3	0.05749	2.81	0.01
Lag 4	−0.02132	−1.12	0.27
Div(t)	−0.34835	−1.01	0.32
Div($t-1$)	−0.47541	−1.37	0.17
Div($t-2$)	0.90510	2.62	0.01
Div($t-3$)	−0.12416	−0.36	0.73
Div($t-4$)	0.49117	1.42	0.16
Tue.	−0.00093	−1.57	0.12
Wed.	0.00118	2.00	0.05
Thu.	0.00194	3.28	0.01
Fri.	0.00135	2.31	0.03

$F = 35.7\ p<0.01$
$\bar{R}^2 = 0.15$

Variable	Coefficient	t	$p<$
Price index			
Constant	−0.00051	−1.13	0.26
Holiday	0.00203	1.86	0.07
Lag 1	0.39462	20.70	0.01
Lag 2	−0.09559	−4.67	0.01
Lag 3	0.05779	2.82	0.01
Lag 4	−0.02238	−1.18	0.24
Div(t)	−1.40557	−4.07	0.01
Div($t-1$)	0.14180	0.41	0.69
Div($t-2$)	0.70903	2.05	0.05
Div($t-3$)	−0.03354	−0.10	0.93
Div($t-4$)	0.44298	1.28	0.21
Tue.	−0.00097	−1.63	0.11
Wed.	0.00120	2.02	0.05
Thu.	0.00195	3.29	0.01
Fri.	0.00134	2.29	0.03

$F = 36.5,\ p<0.01$
$\bar{R}^2 = 0.15$

the regression reported in table 4, with the addition of the contemporaneous dividend yield on the index as one variable and its four lagged values as others. (The lagged variables correspond to the four lags of the dependent variable.) The explanatory power of the regression is not altered by introducing the dividend variables. The coefficients on the day-of-the-week 'dummies' all fall slightly in absolute value, but the seasonal pattern of table 4 is not disturbed. The coefficients of the dividend variables flip-flop, suggesting multicollinearity.

Fourth, research by Ariel (see chapter 8) on returns before and after the midpoints of months and various papers on 'month-of-the-year effects' suggests the addition of twelve further 'dummy' variables to the regression: one for position within the month and eleven to distinguish among months. In this (unreported) regression, the adjusted R^2, the seasonal pattern and the marginal effect of the lagged returns and dividend variables do not change noticeably. The coefficient on the 'holiday' variable falls to 0.00166, the coefficient on the 'first-half-of-the-month' variable is 0.000498 ($t = 1.39$), and the eleven month-of-the-year coefficients are all negative (implying a positive 'January effect'). Only the March coefficient is significant at $p = 0.05$.

Finally, we attempt to determine whether the equity seasonal is related to interest rates, by adding five interest rates to the above regression: the contemporaneous rate, two leads and two lags. We found no relation between daily equity returns and interest rates over the period April 1975 to December 1985.

Correlation matrices

Table 6 reports the correlation matrix for the five day-of-the-week sequences. Except for Friday, equity returns are significantly positively correlated with returns on the immediately following day. There is no evidence of weekend returns being negatively correlated with returns on other days of the week, thus ruling out the negative-risk hypothesis as an explanation of negative weekend returns. However, we noted above that the weekend variance is 'low' relative to weekday variances. Note also that the seasonal in covariances among adjacent-day returns (i.e. the low Friday/weekend covariance) implies that the regressions reported in tables 4 and 5 are misspecified.

In contrast, table 7 reveals that the positive autocorrelation in day-of-the-week interest rates (reported above) also is observed across days: adjacent days exhibit correlation coefficients in excess of +0.8. As in the case of equity returns, the Friday/Monday correlation is lower, suggesting that not all of the positive serial correlation in equity returns is due to discontinuous trading.

5 Conclusions

Equity returns on the Sydney Stock Exchange exhibit a significant day-of-the-week seasonal. Some of the seasonal is due to a 'weekend effect' in which mean returns from close of trading on Friday to close of

Table 6 *Correlation matrices, 453 weeks without holidays 2 January 1974–29 December 1984*

	Mon.	Tue.	Wed.	Thu.
Accumulation index				
Tue.	0.340			
Wed.	−0.186	0.264		
Thu.	−0.024	0.055	0.312	
Fri.	0.007	0.008	−0.025	0.409
Price index				
Tue.	0.344			
Wed.	−0.189	0.265		
Thu.	−0.023	0.055	0.315	
Fri.	0.003	0.017	−0.025	0.409

Table 7 *Correlation matrices, 405 weeks without holidays 15 April 1975–28 December 1984*

	Mon.	Tue.	Wed.	Thu.
Accumulation index				
Tue.	0.303			
Wed.	−0.082	0.326		
Thu.	0.052	0.058	0.358	
Fri.	0.027	0.009	0.053	0.306
Price index				
Tue.	0.307			
Wed.	−0.082	0.326		
Thu.	0.055	0.057	0.358	
Fri.	0.025	0.012	0.053	0.307
Interest rates				
Mon.				
Tue.	0.883			
Wed.	0.688	0.858		
Thu.	0.671	0.758	0.866	
Fri.	0.713	0.702	0.652	0.812

trading on Monday are negative but not significantly different from zero. This suggests an explanation in terms of a negative *marginal* efficiency of investment on weekends, due to idle capacity. This explanation is difficult to reconcile with the other conclusion from the data, that the seasonal does not extend to daily interest rates: the weekend average interest rate is almost exactly the weekday rate on a daily average basis. Several other hypotheses are not consistent with the data.

Much of the daily seasonal is due to a significant, negative mean return on Tuesdays. This covers the period 3 p.m. Monday to 3 p.m. Tuesday,

Sydney time. This is midnight Sunday/Monday to midnight Monday/
Tuesday, New York time. The possibility of an international effect
cannot be ruled out, since the Sydney seasonal looks like the NYSE
seasonal, lagged in calendar time. The lag in trading hours, however, is
not precisely one day, so we are not convinced by this explanation.

   Other puzzling regularities are observed, particularly in the weekend
standard deviations. For equities, weekend volatility seems 'low' and for
interest rates it seems 'high', relative to weekdays. The latter appears to
be related to the high serial correlation in daily interest rates, which
suggests a similar explanation for the 'low' weekend equity variance: that
is, negative correlation among the three implicit weekend-day returns.
While the covariance matrix across days of the week provides no
additional clues, it is possible that the patterns in standard deviation are
related to the seasonals in the mean returns.

Notes

* We are indebted to Maurice Levi for comments on an earlier draft. The Centre for
  Research in Finance, AGSM, provided financial support and the Reserve Bank of
  Australia provided valuable daily interest rate data.

References

Ball, R. and Bowers, J. (1986) 'A Corrected Statex-Actuaries Daily Accumulation Index,'
   manuscript, Australian Graduate School of Management.
Cross, F. (1973) 'The Behavior of Stock Prices on Fridays and Mondays', *Financial
   Analysts Journal*, 29, November–December 67–9.
Fama, E.F. (1965) 'The Behavior of Stock Market Prices', *Journal of Business*, 38,
   January, 34–105.
Fisher, I. (1930) *The Theory of Interest*, New York: Macmillan, reprinted by Augustus M.
   Kelley (1970, New York).
French, K. (1980) 'Stock Returns and The Weekend Effect', *Journal of Financial
   Economics*, 8, March, 55–69.
Gibbons, M. and Hess, P. (1981) 'Day of the Week Effects and Asset Returns', *Journal of
   Business*, 54, October, 579–96.
Hirshleifer, J. (1970) *Investment, Interest and Capital*, Englewood Cliffs, NJ: Prentice-
   Hall.
Jaffe, J. and Westerfield, R. (1985) 'The Week-end Effect in Common Stock Returns: The
   International Evidence', manuscript, University of Pennsylvania.
Keim, D. and Stambaugh, R. (1984) 'A Further Investigation of the Weekend Effect in
   Stock Returns', *Journal of Finance*, 39, May.
Lakonishok, J. and Levi, M. (1982) 'Weekend Effects on Stock Returns – A Note', *Journal
   of Finance*, 37, June, 883–9.
Osborne, M.F.M. (1962) 'Periodic Structure in the Brownian Motion of Stock Prices',
   Operations Research, 10, 345–79.
Rogalski, R. (1984) 'New Findings Regarding Day of the Week Returns over Trading and
   Non-Trading Periods', manuscript, Dartmouth College.
Smirlock, M. and Starks, L. (1983) 'Day of the Week Effects in Stock Returns: Some
   Intraday Evidence', manuscript, University of Pennsylvania and Washington University.

7   Intra-day stock return patterns

*LAWRENCE HARRIS**

1 Introduction

Research on the day-of-the-week effect has proceeded in a number of
directions since the effect was first identified by Cross (1973), French
(1980) and Gibbons and Hess (1981) in their studies of daily close-to-
close returns in US common stock indices. It is now known that
weekday patterns are found in other national markets (see chapters 4
and 6), that they are present to varying degrees in the returns of firms of
all sizes (Keim, 1984; Keim and Stambaugh, 1984; Rogalski, 1984), that
they may be partially, but not completely related to settlement effects
(Lakonishok and Levi, 1982; see also chapter 5), and that the weekday
differences in close-to-close returns in value-weighted indexes are more
likely due to weekday differences in close-to-open returns than in open-
to-close returns (Rogalski, 1984).

Although these studies of international data, of firm-disaggregated
data, and of time-disaggregated data are unable to provide a satisfactory
explanation of the day-of-the-week effect, they are important because
they provide a more complete characterization of the day-of-the-week
phenomenon. Results from these studies help focus the search for a
complete explanation of the day-of-the-week effect.

This chapter reports on research conducted using transaction-by-
transaction data for NYSE stocks. These data make possible simultaneous analyses of both cross-sectional and intra-temporal characteristics of the day-of-the-week effect. Previous studies have established the
value of both types of analyses yet none has determined whether cross-
sectional and intra-temporal effects interact. This research shows that
patterns in time-decomposed returns vary by firm size. Perhaps more
importantly, the transaction data also allow a more precise characterization of the timing of systematic return patterns within the trading day.
This chapter characterizes patterns in intra-day returns measured over
15-minute intervals and demonstrates how they differ by weekday.

Several new observations emerge. Decomposition of close-to-close returns into trading- and nontrading-period returns indicates that for large firms, the negative Monday close-to-close return accrues before the market opens, while for smaller firms most of it accrues during the day on Monday. Further decomposition of the trading-period return into a series of 15-minute intra-day returns reveals that there are only significant differences among weekdays during the first 45 minutes of trading. On Monday mornings, prices tend to drop, while on the other weekday mornings, they rise. Otherwise, price patterns are similar on all weekdays. The most striking similarity is a strong, and as yet unexplained, tendency for prices to rise on the last trade of the day.

The remainder of this chapter is organized into six sections. Section 2 briefly describes the data set and shows that previous results are replicated. Section 3 describes the cross-sectional analysis of the decomposition of the daily close-to-close return into trading- and nontrading-period returns. Sections 4 and 5 discuss weekday differences and similarities in 15-minute intra-day returns respectively. Section 6 presents new evidence from the transaction data concerning the Friday-closing-price hypothesis while section 7 presents evidence concerning end-of-day regularities. Finally, a summary is provided in section 8.

2 Replication of previous results

The stock transaction data, obtained from Francis Emory Fitch Inc., consist of a time-ordered record of every common stock transaction made at the NYSE for the fourteen months between December 1, 1981, and January 31, 1983. For each of the approximately sixteen million transactions, the date, time, price and number of shares traded are available.

There are 296 different trading days in the sample period. Data for the nine days which followed trading holidays are excluded from the analyses to insure that no post-holiday trading effects influence the results. When necessary, daily and overnight returns are adjusted for splits and dividends.[1]

The weekday pattern of close-to-close returns in this sample period is similar to that observed in all previous studies (such as French, 1980; Gibbons and Hess, 1981). The mean Monday close-to-close return of the equal-weighted NYSE portfolio is negative, in contrast to the other mean weekday returns, which are positive (table 1 (a) line 1). Although an F-test of the equivalence of the weekday means (F_5) cannot reject equivalence at the 5 percent significance level ($F(4;281) = 1.86$), an F-test of whether the Monday mean is equal to the average of the other weekday means (F_{Mon}) does reject equality at this level

Table 1 *Mean portfolio close-to-close, close-to-open and open-to-close returns by weekday and market value capitalization.*[a]

(a) Close-to-close returns

Market value decile	Means in percent							
	Mon. (1)	Tue. (2)	Wed. (3)	Thu. (4)	Fri. (5)	F_5 (6)	F_{Mon} (7)	F_4 (8)
All firms[b]	−0.202	0.138	0.146	0.170	0.195	1.86	7.30^d	0.06
(STDERR)	(0.154)	(0.117)	(0.118)	(0.095)	(0.100)			
Smallest	−0.117	0.177	0.096	0.136	0.304	1.95^c	5.74^d	0.82
2	−0.211	0.085	0.211	0.175	0.262	3.23^d	11.33^d	0.62
3	−0.227	0.112	0.174	0.223	0.234	2.79^d	10.41^d	0.29
4	−0.220	0.137	0.197	0.155	0.208	2.30^c	8.91^d	0.10
5	−0.202	0.130	0.203	0.166	0.250	2.19^c	8.19^d	0.21
6	−0.208	0.125	0.166	0.194	0.160	1.96^c	7.62^d	0.07
7	−0.205	0.138	0.167	0.191	0.150	1.51	5.92^d	0.04
8	−0.204	0.131	0.115	0.143	0.144	1.28	5.11^d	0.01
9	−0.229	0.191	0.070	0.166	0.118	1.48	5.46^d	0.18
Largest	−0.196	0.156	0.060	0.149	0.124	0.82	3.05^c	0.09
F_{MV}	0.48	0.53	2.16^d	0.55	2.12^d			
N	53	56	61	60	56			

(b) Previous close-to-open returns

Market value decile	Means in percent							
	Mon. (1)	Tue. (2)	Wed. (3)	Thu. (4)	Fri. (5)	F_5 (6)	F_{Mon} (7)	F_4 (8)
All firms[b]	−0.095	0.001	0.052	0.018	0.066	1.63	5.40^d	0.44
(STDERR)	(0.065)	(0.049)	(0.045)	(0.041)	(0.040)			
Smallest	−0.029	−0.045	−0.054	−0.027	0.042	0.46	0.02	0.66
2	−0.074	−0.032	0.037	0.005	0.056	1.31	3.08^c	0.82
3	−0.029	−0.040	0.061	0.061	0.081	0.83	2.87^c	0.18
4	−0.096	−0.001	0.051	0.011	0.047	1.61	5.42^d	0.36
5	−0.108	−0.018	0.060	0.026	0.076	2.15^c	6.47^d	0.81
6	−0.072	0.015	0.064	0.001	0.045	1.36	4.13^d	0.50
7	−0.101	0.005	0.073	0.029	0.066	1.70	5.66^d	0.42
8	−0.139	−0.008	0.048	0.015	0.047	2.22^c	7.97^d	0.34
9	−0.121	0.023	0.072	0.027	0.084	2.09^c	7.41^d	0.37
Largest	−0.177	0.034	0.105	0.047	0.144	2.87^d	10.39^d	0.44
F_{MV}	4.09^d	2.47^d	5.85^d	1.43	1.43			
N	53	56	61	60	56			

Table 1 (*cont.*)

(c) Open-to-close returns

Market value decile	Means in percent							
	Mon. (1)	Tue. (2)	Wed. (3)	Thu. (4)	Fri. (5)	F_5 (6)	F_{Mon} (7)	F_4 (8)
All firms[b]	−0.105	0.140	0.098	0.157	0.136	1.12	4.29^d	0.07
(STDERR)	(0.124)	(0.106)	(0.105)	(0.080)	(0.081)			
Smallest	−0.064	0.249	0.173	0.193	0.288	2.26^c	8.06^d	0.38
2	−0.144	0.119	0.182	0.182	0.218	2.85^d	10.70^d	0.27
3	−0.205	0.074	0.111	0.175	0.158	2.55^d	9.49^d	0.27
4	−0.123	0.139	0.153	0.147	0.167	1.55	6.16^d	0.02
5	−0.090	0.138	0.145	0.143	0.177	1.16	4.57^d	0.03
6	−0.135	0.111	0.103	0.197	0.117	1.59	5.72^d	0.23
7	−0.102	0.134	0.095	0.164	0.085	0.81	2.89^c	0.12
8	−0.063	0.136	0.067	0.131	0.100	0.50	1.76	0.09
9	−0.110	0.167	−0.000	0.141	0.037	0.84	2.01	0.50
Largest	−0.018	0.122	−0.045	0.101	0.012	0.27	0.16	0.34
F_{MV}	1.39	1.39	3.83^d	0.92	5.34^d			
N	53	57	61	60	56			

Notes: [a]*F*-tests of whether the five weekday means are equal (F_5), of whether the Monday mean is equal to the other weekday means (F_{Mon}), of whether the Tuesday through Friday means are equal (F_4). *F*-tests of whether the mean returns on a given weekday are equal for all market value decile portfolios (F_{MV}). All 1616 NYSE common stocks, all 296 trading days, Dec. 1, 1981–Jan. 31, 1983, except nine days which followed a holiday.

The *F*-statistics are obtained from analysis of variance regressions on dummies. F_5 and F_{Mon} are obtained from the regression of the returns on five weekday dummies. F_4 is obtained from the regression of only the Tuesday through Friday returns on four weekday dummies. The degrees of freedom associated with these *F*-statistics are F_5, 4,281; F_{Mon}, 1,281; and F_4, 3,229. The corresponding 10 percent, 5 percent and 1 percent points are 1.94, 2.37, 3.32; 2.71, 3.84, 6.63; and 2.08, 2.60, 3.78.

F_{MV} is obtained from the regression of the returns for a given weekday on dummies for each of the market value decile portfolios and on dummies for each of the dates in the sample corresponding to that weekday. The latter set of dummies are used to control for the cross-sectional covariation among the various size portfolio returns on a given day. The degrees of freedom associated with these *F*-tests are 9,468 on Monday; 9,495 on Tuesday; 9,450 on Wednesday; 9,531 on Thursday; and 9,495 on Friday. The corresponding 10 percent, 5 percent and 1 percent points of these *F*-statistics are all 1.63, 1.88 and 2.41.
[b]The NYSE equal-weighted portfolio.
[c]*F*-statistics with corresponding tail areas between 0.10 and 0.05.
[d]*F*-statistics with corresponding tail areas of less than 0.05.

($F(1;281) = 7.30$).[2] These results are qualitatively and quantitatively similar to all previous results concerning close-to-close returns; the failure to reject equivalence of the weekday means is a consequence of the short time-series sample.

Keim (1984), Keim and Stambaugh (1984) and Rogalski (1984) all observe that stocks of all sizes have negative Monday close-to-close returns. The evidence from this sample is very similar. Each of the ten size decile portfolios of the NYSE sample (based on market value capitalization) exhibit the same weekday pattern of returns as does the market as a whole (table 1 (a)). In this short time-series sample, the Monday mean is significantly different at the 5 percent level from the other weekday means for all but the largest of the size portfolios (table 1 (a) column 7).

The cross-sectional distribution of close-to-close returns displays a pattern similar to that observed by Keim (1984) and by Keim and Stambaugh (1984). Smaller firms have greater mean returns on Friday than do larger firms. To test rigorously whether this cross-sectional difference is statistically significant, an analysis of variance was conducted. Friday returns for the various portfolios were regressed on a set of size dummies and on a set of date dummies. The latter set consists of a dummy for each different date in the sample on which a Friday fell. These dummies are included to control for the substantial cross-sectional covariation which exists among the portfolio returns on any given day. The results (table 1 (a) last row) indicate that Friday mean close-to-close returns are significantly different in cross-section. Similar tests for the other weekdays indicate that Wednesday returns are also significantly different. The cross-sectional pattern of returns on Friday appears to be related to the well-known small firm effect identified by Banz (1981) and Reinganum (1981). The pattern on Wednesday is not immediately identifiable.

Rogalski (1984) analyzed the decomposition of daily close-to-close returns in the S&P 500 and Dow Jones Industrial Average (DJIA) indexes into a previous close-to-open return and an open-to-close return. In his sample the negative Monday close-to-close return accrues primarily between the Friday close and the Monday open. He was unable to reject equality of the weekday open-to-close returns and therefore did not reject the hypothesis that stock prices evolve at uniform rates in chronological time during the trading day. In this sample, the same analysis for the equal-weighted NYSE portfolio yields somewhat different results (table 1 (b) and (c) line 1, column 5). Only half of the negative Monday close-to-close return accrues between the Friday close and the Monday open, while the rest accrues during the Monday trading period. Although F-tests of the equivalence of the weekday means cannot reject equivalence at the 5 percent significance level for either the close-to-open weekday means ($F(4;281) = 1.63$) or the open-to-close weekday means ($F(4;281) = 1.12$), F-tests of whether the Monday mean is equal to the average of the other weekday means do reject equality in both cases ($F(1;281) = 5.4$, 4.29, respectively). The next section shows that Rogalski's results may differ from these because of cross-sectional differences in the day-of-the-week effect.

3 Cross-sectional differences in trading- and nontrading-period returns

Unlike previous research, this research analyzes trading- and non-trading-period returns by firm size. The results (table 1 (b) and (c)) show that although the mean Monday close-to-open return and the mean Monday open-to-close return are both negative for all size decile portfolios, their magnitudes vary by firm size. For large firms, the close-to-open return is greater in absolute value than the open-to-close return, and for small firms, just the opposite. This cross-sectional difference in Monday returns is clearly identified in tests of the equivalence of the mean Monday return with the average of the other weekday means. These F-tests (table 1 (b) and (c) column 7) reject equivalence at the 5 percent significance level for all size portfolios larger than the third when the nontrading-period returns are examined and they reject for all size portfolios smaller than the seventh when the trading-period returns are examined.

To test rigorously for cross-sectional differences among the various portfolio trading- and nontrading-period mean returns, an analysis of variance, similar to that used to analyze the close-to-close returns, was conducted. The F-tests (table 1 (b) and (c) last row) indicate that the Monday close-to-open means are significantly different in cross-section ($F(9;468) = 4.09$) but that the open-to-close means are not ($F(9;468) = 1.39$). The cross-section differences in the time of accrual of the negative Monday close-to-close return are due primarily to significant differences in the nontrading-period returns and only to a lesser extent to differences in the open-to-close returns.

The size differences in the decomposition of the Monday close-to-close returns can explain the differences noted above among Rogalski's results (concerning the S&P 500 and DJIA indices) and those presented in this study (concerning the NYSE equal-weighted portfolio). Since Rogalski analyzes indexes that are heavily weighted towards large firms, his results are very similar to the results presented here for the largest decile portfolio. The S&P 500, the DJIA and the largest NYSE size decile portfolio all have Monday open-to-close returns which are positive, or in the case of the largest size portfolio, nearly zero. The equal-weighted NYSE portfolio is more heavily weighted towards small firms. It has significantly negative Monday open-to-close returns because small firms have large negative Monday open-to-close returns.

Size differences in the decomposition of the negative Monday close-to-close return may have implications for theories which try to relate negative Monday returns to macroeconomic information. If macroeconomic information generated over the weekend were the cause of the negative Monday close-to-close returns, why would that information be fully incorporated into the prices of large firms when they open trading on Monday, but not fully incorporated into the opening prices of small firms (especially since small firms typically first trade after large firm prices are observed)? If markets were not completely efficient, perhaps there could be a lagged reaction to macroeconomic information among small firms. However, if small and large firm markets are informationally efficient, it appears unlikely that the day-of-the-week effect would be related to macroeconomic information. Further research will be necessary before strong conclusions can be made.

Tests for cross-sectional differences among the various portfolio trading- and nontrading-period mean returns also were conducted for the other weekdays. The results (table 1 (b) and (c) last row) indicate that the close-to-open means are also significantly different in cross-section on Tuesday and Wednesday and that the open-to-close means are significantly different on Wednesdays and Fridays. An examination of the mean returns, by size decile, reveals that the Monday close-to-open returns and the Wednesday and Friday open-to-close returns may be related to the small-firm effect (small firms have greater returns than large firms). No easily identifiable pattern characterizes the close-to-open returns on Tuesday or Wednesday. These cross-sectional results show that the large Friday close-to-close returns observed in small firms portfolios by Keim (1984) and by Keim and Stambaugh (1984) accrue primarily during the trading day.

4 Weekday differences in intra-day price patterns

To further investigate systematic weekday differences in open-to-close returns, means were computed, by 15-minute intervals, of the returns which accrue within the trading day. These means estimate the average rate of return accrual in a given 15-minute interval rather than the average realization of returns within that interval. An accrual method is used because it is less sensitive to problems associated with nonsynchronous trading. These problems are very serious in transaction data because most securities do not trade within each 15-minute interval on every day (and therefore returns are not realized in each interval for all stocks), and when securities do trade, in general the trade is not at the end of each interval.[3] The results are plotted by weekday in figure 1.

There is a striking difference between Monday and the other weekdays in the first 45 minutes of trading. The mean return in this interval for the NYSE equal-weighted portfolio is negative on Monday (-0.13 percent), while on the other weekdays it is positive (0.09, 0.14, 0.12 and 0.10 percent). The difference is significant. An F-test of the equivalence of the weekday means and an F-test of the equivalence of the Monday mean to

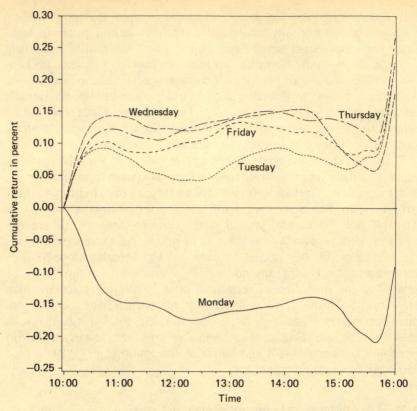

Figure 1　Cumulated mean fifteen-minute intra-day returns, by weekday, in percent
Note: The accrued return is the average rate of return experienced by common stocks in the NYSE equal-weighted portfolio within a given fifteen-minute interval. All 1616 NYSE common stocks, all 296 trading days, December 1, 1981 – January 31, 1983, except nine days which followed a holiday.

the average of the other weekday means both reject equality at the 5 percent significance level in each of the first three 15-minute intervals but in none of the following twenty-one intervals. Only after the Monday returns are removed from the sample can equivalence of the remaining weekday means not be rejected in all the intra-day intervals.

The weekday pattern of returns observed in the first 45 minutes of trading is pervasive both through time and throughout the cross-section. In eleven of the fourteen months in the sample, the mean return realized by the NYSE equal-weighted portfolio over the first 45 minutes on Monday is negative while in thirty-nine of the fifty-six (4×14) other

Table 2 *The cumulated sum of the first three 15-minute mean accrued returns, by month and weekday, in percent*[a]

Month	Mon.	Tue.	Wed.	Thu.	Fri.
All months	−0.133	0.092	0.142	0.121	0.103
(STDERR)	(0.066)	(0.044)	(0.045)	(0.039)	(0.041)
N	53	57	61	60	56
December, 1981	−0.230	−0.075	−0.003	0.071	0.178
January, 1982	−0.306	−0.051	0.088	0.258	0.233
February	−0.219	0.091	0.241	0.193	0.133
March	0.182	0.185	−0.052	0.157	−0.079
April	0.058	−0.094	0.005	0.097	0.235
May	−0.216	0.144	−0.016	0.091	0.125
June	−0.086	0.033	0.186	−0.003	0.086
July	0.132	−0.006	−0.021	−0.065	0.026
August	−0.011	0.354	0.370	0.348	−0.000
September	−0.216	0.282	0.163	−0.015	0.123
October	−0.052	0.114	0.299	0.414	0.017
November	−0.501	0.051	0.753	−0.023	0.146
December	−0.076	0.275	−0.032	−0.041	0.232
January, 1983	−0.279	−0.030	0.114	0.320	0.052

[a] These means are of the average rate of return experienced by common stocks in the NYSE equal-weighted portfolio between 10.00 and 10.45. All 1616 NYSE common stocks, all 296 trading days, December 1, 1981–January 31, 1983, except nine days which followed a holiday.

weekday months, the mean return is positive (table 2). If positive and negative values were equally likely, the probability of observing eleven or more negative values in a sample of fourteen months would be 0.0287 and the probability of observing thirty-nine or more positive values in a sample of fifty-six would be 0.0016. Similar results (not presented) are obtained for each of the decile portfolios. These statistics indicate that the beginning-of-day differences among weekday mean returns are common; they are not caused by a few large returns in only a few months or only a few firms.

To summarize, there are weekday differences in the pattern of intra-day returns within the first 45 minutes of trading only. Later in the day, no such weekday differences are apparent. The latter results might suggest that the chronological trading time hypothesis may be an adequate description of the evolution of returns after the market opening. The next section, however, shows that even this limited form of the hypothesis is not supported by the data. There are systematic patterns in the time-series of intra-day returns which are common to all of the weekdays.

5 Time-series patterns in intra-day prices

A cursory examination of intra-day cumulative means (figure 1) for the equal-weighted NYSE portfolio reveals that the evolution of prices during the trading day is not uniform on any of the weekdays. Mean intra-day returns at the beginning and end of trading day are five to ten times larger in absolute value than the returns which accrue in the middle of the day. These casual observations are confirmed in *F*-tests of the equivalence of the twenty-four 15-minute intra-day return means, of the equivalence of the first three 15-minute means to the average of the following fifteen means, and of the equivalence of the last 15-minute mean to the average of the preceding twenty-three means. On every weekday, these tests all can reject their respective null hypotheses at significance levels of less than 5 percent. Similar results are found for each of the size decile portfolios. Equivalence among the intra-day means is accepted only for the inner twenty (10.45–15.35) 15-minute means.

Transaction-by-transaction returns were examined to determine whether the large beginning-of-day returns and end-of-day returns observed in the 15-minute interval returns are related to the first and last transactions only. At the beginning of the day, the results do not support this view. The mean returns accruing between the first and second and between the second and third transactions are both large relative to later mean transaction returns (table 3 (a)). These two means rank first and second in absolute value among the first ten mean transaction returns on all weekdays. At the end of the day, however, only the return accruing between the penultimate and last transactions is large (table 3 (b)). The mean of this transaction return is positive and approximately five to ten times larger in absolute value than each of the nine preceding mean transaction returns. The end-of-day phenomenon is pervasive through time – the mean of the last transaction return is positive in 292 out of the 296 trading days in the sample, and it is pervasive in cross-section – all market-value groups experience end-of-day returns which are positive and significantly larger than earlier returns (results not shown). Apparently, the return-generating processes for the first few transactions and for the last transaction are different from those which generate the mid-day transaction returns.

In addition to the large returns at the beginning and end of the trading day, there are other time-series patterns in the 15-minute intra-day returns which are common to all weekdays and therefore worthy of note. These patterns appear to include a rise in prices between 12.30 and 1.30 and a fall between 2.30 and 3.15. To measure whether these observations are statistically significant, Spearman correlations were computed among

Table 3 *Mean transaction returns (percentage change in price from one transaction to the next) at the beginning and end of the trading day, by weekday.*[a]

(a) The first ten transaction returns

Transaction	Mon.	Tue.	Wed.	Thu.	Fri.	All days
2[b]	−0.0313	0.0155	0.0254	0.0189	0.0271	0.0114
3	−0.0284	0.0071	0.0131	0.0194	0.0210	0.0066
4	−0.0222	0.0047	0.0093	0.0069	0.0075	0.0014
5	−0.0160	0.0026	0.0082	0.0175	0.0152	0.0055
6	−0.0063	0.0001	0.0084	0.0133	0.0067	0.0045
7	−0.0164	0.0073	0.0111	0.0181	0.0106	0.0062
8	−0.0094	0.0033	0.0052	0.0105	0.0103	0.0040
9	−0.0090	0.0033	0.0040	0.0097	0.0165	0.0048
10	−0.0034	0.0019	0.0112	0.0079	0.0050	0.0046
11	0.0017	0.0077	0.0063	0.0069	0.0087	0.0063

(b) The last ten transaction returns

Transaction	Mon.	Tue.	Wed.	Thu.	Fri.	All days
Last	0.0371	0.0527	0.0342	0.0574	0.0568	0.0476
2	−0.0091	0.0051	−0.0059	0.0038	0.0047	−0.0002
3	−0.0135	−0.0054	−0.0076	−0.0036	0.0038	−0.0053
4	−0.0186	−0.0023	−0.0131	−0.0043	−0.0022	−0.0081
5	−0.0062	−0.0003	−0.0064	0.0002	−0.0041	−0.0033
6	−0.0091	−0.0010	−0.0054	−0.0032	0.0106	−0.0018
7	−0.0069	0.0009	−0.0085	−0.0031	−0.0013	−0.0038
8	−0.0054	−0.0015	0.0011	0.0012	0.0041	−0.0001
9	−0.0048	0.0057	−0.0069	0.0034	−0.0011	−0.0007
10	−0.0037	0.0034	0.0012	−0.0006	0.0052	0.0011

Note: [a]All 1616 NYSE common stocks, all 296 trading days, December 1, 1981–January 31, 1983, except nine days which followed a holiday. The standard errors of these means range between 0.0030 and 0.0033.

Since many securities did not trade twenty-one times each day, some transaction returns contribute to means found in both panels of this table.

[b]The transaction return associated with the first transaction of the day is the previous close-to-open return. Means for this return can be found in table 1.

all ten pairs of the five weekday time series of mean 15-minute accrued returns. Since it is already known that there are weekday similarities at the beginning and end of the trading day, only the twenty mean 15-minute returns which accrued between 10.45 and 3.45 are used to compute the correlations. The results obtained for the equal-weighted NYSE portfolio tend to confirm the casual observations. All ten of the correlations are positive (range 0.209 to 0.651) with four of them significantly different from zero at the 5 percent level and three others significantly different at the 10 percent level.[4]

The results indicate that there are systematic time-series patterns in mean intra-day returns which are common to all of the weekdays. Even within weekday trading periods, prices do not evolve at equal rates. Further research will be necessary to identify the origin of these patterns and to determine whether traders can profit by considering time-of-day effects when planning their transactions.

6 New transaction data evidence concerning high Friday closing prices

Several authors (Gibbons and Hess, 1981; Smirlock and Starks, 1983; Keim and Stambaugh, 1984) have suggested that abnormally high closing prices on Friday could account for high Friday close-to-close returns and negative Monday returns. These same studies, however, are able to reject this hypothesis using an *F*-test of whether the sum of the Friday and Monday mean close-to-close returns is equal to the average of the other weekday means. Using transaction data, at least three new tests of the high Friday closing price hypothesis are possible. These tests also reject the high closing price hypothesis.

If high closing prices on Friday were the result only of errors in the measurement of the last transaction price, then the mean of the last transaction return of the day would be greater on Friday than on the other weekdays, and the last Friday transaction return would be negatively correlated with the Friday-close-to-Monday-open return. The data, however, do not support either prediction. For all market value decile portfolios but the smallest, the mean Friday last transaction return is not significantly larger than the average of the other weekday means.[5] For six of the portfolios, the Friday mean is not even the maximum of the weekday means.

Two issues make the second prediction somewhat more difficult to test. Portfolio returns will not display negative serial autocorrelation due to measurement errors in security prices if those errors are nonsystematic. Correlations must therefore be computed for each security separately. Secondly, normal price jumps from bid to ask can also cause the last Friday transaction return to be correlated with the weekend non-trading-period return. Therefore that correlation must be compared to similar correlations obtained for the other weekdays – there is no obvious reason why the bid–ask induced correlation should be any larger on Friday than on the other weekdays. If it is found that the correlation on Fridays is greater (in absolute value) than on the other weekdays, this would be evidence in favor of the high Friday closing price hypothesis.

The data, however do not favor this hypothesis. The mean across all securities of the Friday correlation is not significantly greater (at the 5 percent level, one-sided test) than the average of the other weekday means ($F(6627;1) = 3.12$).[6] To determine whether there might be cross-sectional differences in this result, the means were compared separately for the securities in each market value decile. The results are the same for all deciles.

The third transaction data test of the high Friday closing price hypothesis is based on the assumption that high Friday closing prices are artificially created by traders wishing to overstate stock prices over the weekend period. If so, it is likely that the price would be established in a small transaction as late as possible in the day in order to minimize the costs of trading at and maintaining an above-market price. The data, however, offer little evidence of such behavior. Not only is there little variance across weekdays in the end-of-day transaction return, there is also little weekday variance in the number of shares traded in the last transaction, or in the time of that transaction. Mean shares traded, by weekday, are 1016, 1135, 1192, 1113 and 1066 shares; mean times are 3.34, 3.33, 3.33, 3.32 and 3.33. For all size portfolios, F-tests (results not shown) reject the hypothesis that the Friday means of these variables are significantly different from the average of the other weekday means. It is unlikely that the weekend effect seen in this sample is the result of manipulated Friday closing prices.

7 The end-of-day effect

The large end-of-day transaction return is surprising and merits further attention. Several questions are of immediate interest. Is the end-of-day effect simply a consequence of the sample selection? Is it related to the bid–ask spread? Can it be explained by errors in the data? The evidence presented in this section suggests that none of these explanations is likely.

End-of-day transaction returns would be higher than previous transaction returns if the period typically spanned by the end-of-day return is longer than that spanned by earlier transactions and if the market is generally rising. Although both conditions are true in this sample, the evidence from the 15-minute mean accrued returns contradicts this simple sample selection argument. Recall that the end-of-day mean 15-minute accrued return is much greater than all earlier mean accrued returns. Since the accrual method of computing mean returns averages rates of return accrual within each interval, it is not sensitive to the sample selection problem mentioned above. If accrual rates were equal throughout the day, the last 15-minute mean accrued return would be approximately equal to the previous mean returns.

Table 4 *Mean percentage returns for the last daily transaction, cross-classified by the times of the last and penultimate transactions.*[a]

Mean return
(standard error of mean)
[mean sign of return]
N

Time of penultimate trade	Time of last trade						All trades
	10:00 -1:00	1:01 -3:00	3:01 -3:45	3:46 -3:55	3:56 -3:59	4.00	
10:00–1:00	-0.026 (0.011) [-0.035] 12306	-0.014 (0.010) [-0.029] 15322	-0.052 (0.014) [-0.059] 8004	-0.055 (0.028) [-0.056] 2536	0.043 (0.039) [-0.019] 1504	0.045 (0.033) [0.005] 1744	-0.023 (0.006) [-0.036] 41416
1:01–3:00		-0.009 (0.006) [-0.025] 29623	-0.025 (0.006) [-0.043] 35147	-0.024 (0.012) [-0.052] 9797	0.086 (0.016) [0.023] 5722	0.160 (0.017) [0.079] 5649	0.000 (0.004) [-0.025] 85938
3:01–3:45			0.005 (0.004) [-0.014] 61390	0.012 (0.005) [-0.011] 41346	0.086 (0.007) [0.050] 20866	0.207 (0.008) [0.153] 18367	0.045 (0.003) [0.018] 141969
3:46–3:55				0.021 (0.004) [0.010] 32320	0.077 (0.005) [0.053] 30365	0.191 (0.006) [0.180] 22766	0.086 (0.003) [0.071] 85451
3:56–3:59					0.061 (0.004) [0.059] 25809	0.153 (0.005) [0.168] 31636	0.112 (0.003) [0.119] 57445
4:00						0.096 (0.005) [0.118] 20860	0.096 (0.005) [0.118] 20860
All trades	-0.026 (0.011) [-0.035] 12306	-0.011 (0.005) [-0.026] 44945	-0.010 (0.003) [-0.027] 104541	0.009 (0.003) [-0.009] 85999	0.075 (0.003) [0.051] 84266	0.158 (0.003) [0.150] 101022	0.049 (0.002) [0.033] 433079

[a] All NYSE common stocks, December 1, 1981–January 31, 1983. For comparison, the average transaction return for the last ten transactions, excluding the last, is −0.0024 percent.

Mean end-of-day transactions returns, cross-classified by the times of the penultimate and ultimate transactions (table 4) provide more direct evidence contradicting the sample selection argument. End-of-day returns are greatest the later is the last transaction, and, surprisingly, the later is the penultimate transaction. Although the sample selection hypothesis can predict the first result, it is contradicted by the second result. This evidence strongly suggests that large end-of-day returns are somehow related to the close of the market trading period.

One possible explanation of the end-of-day effect is that it might be related to the bid–ask spread. Assuming that the bid and ask prices do not change, it may be that, relative to previous transaction prices, the end-of-day transaction price is more likely an ask price than a bid price. Unfortunately, since the Fitch tape does not classify transaction prices by who initiated the trade, it is difficult to test this hypothesis directly. However, by examining reversal and continuation frequencies, an indirect test can be undertaken against the following alternative: All prices, both bid and ask, increase at the end of the day.

Both hypotheses predict that returns computed from end-of-day prices will be positive. Their predictions differ concerning the conditional probability of an uptick, given that the previous transaction return was an uptick. The bid–ask hypothesis predicts that this probability should be no different at the end of the day than earlier in the day. The alternative predicts that it should be greater. In all other respects, the two hypotheses have identical or indeterminant predictions.

These two alternatives were examined by computing frequency transition matrices of the signs of adjacent transaction returns. Since the end-of-day effect is strongest when the penultimate transaction occurs in the last 15 minutes of the day, only data for these transactions are studied. The evidence does not support the bid–ask argument hypothesis. Transition frequency matrices for all adjacent returns from tenth-to-last to second-to-last are nearly identical to each other. The last transition matrix differs, but not entirely as expected. Although the unconditional frequency of an uptick is greater for the last trade than for the earlier trades, the conditional frequency of an uptick, given a previous uptick is significantly greater than that found in earlier matrices. In the last matrix, this frequency is 0.2137 (41698 trials) while in the previous ones it averaged 0.1611. If 0.1611 is assumed to be the population conditional probability of an uptick given a previous uptick under the bid–ask hypothesis, it is extremely unlikely that the process generating the last matrix was the same as that which generated the earlier ones. (The approximate standard error of the frequency estimate is 0.0018.)

The fact that large end-of-day returns are found for all firm size portfolios and on almost every day in the sample strongly suggests that the phenomenon is not simply caused by miscoded data. However, to be more certain, the means were computed of the sign of the transaction returns (shown in table 4), of the transaction price changes (not shown), and of the transaction returns, truncated at ±12.5 percent (not shown). Large end-of-day means were found for each of these variables. If miscoded data were the cause of the end-of-day effect, the process generating it would have to be very subtle and pervasive.

One such process can be imagined: it may be that the transactions reported on the Fitch tape as the last one of the day are often transactions which for some reason were not reported earlier in the day or for which corrected prices are reported. Both cases are supposed to be identified on the Fitch tape and all analyses reported above have excluded these rare reported events. It is interesting to note, however, that since the market tended to rise within the trading day during this sample period, if the closing reports were of unreported earlier transactions, end-of-day returns would have been negative, not positive.

8 Summary

Fourteen months of the complete transaction record of the NYSE were examined to further characterize systematic weekly and intra-daily price patterns. Several results were found:

1.   There are cross-sectional differences in weekday patterns found in both trading-period and nontrading-period returns. For large firms the negative Monday close-to-close return accrues between the Friday close and the Monday open. For small firms it accrues during the Monday trading day.
2.   There are significant weekday differences in intra-day trading returns in the first 45 minutes of trading. On Monday, returns are negative while on the other weekdays, returns in this interval are positive.
3.   There are systematic intra-day return patterns which are common to all of the weekdays. Returns are very large at the beginning and end of the trading day. The beginning-of-day returns accrue over several transactions. The large positive end-of-day returns accrue only on the last transaction of the day and do not appear to be related to the bid–ask spread.
4.   These patterns are pervasive over time and over market value groups.
5.   It is unlikely that the weekend effect in this sample is caused entirely by high Friday closing prices, caused either by systematic errors in the data or by deliberate price manipulation.

Trading strategies based only on these weekly and intra-daily patterns would not be profitable because of transaction costs. However, profits may be made when there are other reasons to trade. Purchasers of stock may wish to avoid transacting early on Monday morning and sellers may wish to avoid early transactions on Tuesday through Friday.

This study does not solve the day-of-the-week anomaly. It does, however, provide a more complete and detailed characterization of the effect and it is hoped that these results will help others to develop new hypotheses.

Notes

1 Some additional details concerning the sample:
  Although the Fitch data are relatively free of errors, some do exist. To ensure that the results are not severely biased by errors in the data, only data for which returns (transaction, open-to-close, close-to-open, or close-to-close) are less than 25 percent in absolute value are analyzed. This filter is narrow enough to exclude large errors in the prices but not so wide that it excludes large percentage changes that often result from trading low-priced stocks on discrete 'ticks.'
  Multiday returns are excluded from the analyses of close-to-close returns.
  If a security traded only once on a given day, both the opening price and the closing price were set equal to the one transaction price and that day was excluded from the analyses of the open-to-close returns.
  Split and dividend adjustments were made using the same procedure used by the Center for Research in Security Prices. The distributions data were obtained from the CRSP Daily Master File.
2 All F-tests in this study are computed from analysis of variance regressions. Returns are regressed on a set of dummies, one for each level of a classification variable (for example, weekday). The equality of means test determines whether the regression coefficients associated with the set of dummies are equal. The equality of the Monday mean with the average of the other weekday means test determines whether that linear restriction on the parameter estimates can be rejected.
3 A full description of how the accrual means are computed can be found in Harris (1985).
4 The statistical tests are one-sided tests for positive correlation. Pearson correlations were also computed with similar results. The Spearman correlations are reported because they are more robust. Correlations were also computed for each market value decile separately. The results for each group are very similar to those reported for the equal-weighted NYSE index.
5 The mean returns on the last transaction of the day for the smallest firms by weekday, are 0.073 percent for Monday, and 0.133, 0.092, 0.138, 0.185 percent for the other weekdays. The Friday mean return is significantly different from the average of the other weekday means $(F(1;281) = 5.42, p\text{-value} = 0.0207)$. Large Friday returns at the end of the day for small firms may cause the large Friday open-to-close returns noted for these same firms.
6 The cross-security mean correlation of the last Friday transaction return with the following nontrading-period return is -0.144. The means for Monday through Thursday are $-0.130, -0.134, -0.130$ and -0.150.

References

Banz, R.W. (1981) 'The Relationship between Return and Market Value of Common Stock', *Journal of Financial Economics*, 9, 3–18.
Cross, F. (1973) 'The Behavior of Stock Price on Fridays and Mondays', *Financial Analysts Journal*, November–December 67–9.
French, K.R. (1980) 'Stock Returns and the Weekend Effect', *Journal of Financial Economics*, 8, 55–69.
Gibbons, M.R. and Hess, P. (1981) 'Day of the Week Effects and Asset Returns', *Journal of Business*, 54, 579–96.
Harris, L.E. (1985) 'Transaction Data Tests of the Mixture of Distributions Hypothesis', Working paper, University of Southern California.
Keim, D.B. (1984) 'The Relation between Day of the Week Effects and Size Effects', Working paper, The Wharton School, University of Pennsylvania.
Keim, D.B. and Stambaugh, R. (1984) 'A Further Investigation of the Weekend Effect in Stock Returns', *Journal of Finance*, 39, 819–40.
Lakonishok, J. and Levi, M. (1982) 'Weekend Effects on Stock Returns: A Note', *Journal of Finance*, 37, 883–9.

Reinganum, M.R. (1981) 'Misspecification of Capital Asset Pricing: Empirical Anomalies based on Earning Yields and Market Values', *Journal of Financial Economics*, 9, 19–46.

Rogalski, R. (1984) 'New Findings Regarding Day of the Week Returns over Trading and Non-trading Periods', *Journal of Finance*, 39, 1603–14.

Smirlock, M. and Starks, L. (1983) 'Day of the Week Effects in Stock Returns: Some Intraday Evidence', Working Paper, The Wharton School, University of Pennsylvania.

8 Evidence on intra-month seasonality in stock returns

*ROBERT A. ARIEL**

1 Introduction

A distinct monthly seasonal exists in the daily returns accruing to United States traded equities. In essence, the mean return for stocks is positive only for days immediately before and during the first half of calendar months, and indistinguishable from zero for days during the last half of the month. During the 1963–81 period, all of the market's cumulative advance occurred just before and during the first half of months, with the last half contributing nothing to the cumulative increase. This 'monthly effect' is not simply a manifestation of other known calendar anomalies such as the January effect (Rozeff and Kinney, 1976; Roll, 1983a; Keim, 1983; Reinganum, 1983) and appears to be caused by a shift in the mean of the daily return distribution in the first half of the month relative to the last half.

Section 2 describes this monthly seasonal in stock returns.[1] In section 3, several biases that might explain the monthly effect are examined and ruled out, while a possible economic rationale for its occurrence is discussed.

2 The monthly seasonal in stock returns

Throughout this study the University of Chicago's Center for Research in Security Prices (CRSP) equally-weighted and value-weighted daily stock index returns are used to proxy for the returns accruing to US 'stocks.' Both indexes are 'dividend reinvestment' indexes and hence capture both the capital gains and dividend components of the total return accruing to stocks.

Figure 1 contains histograms of the arithmetic mean returns across the nine trading days before and after the start of each month for both the value-weighted and the equally-weighted CRSP indexes from January 1, 1963 through December 31, 1981;[2] each daily mean is estimated from 228

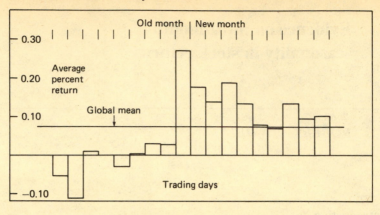

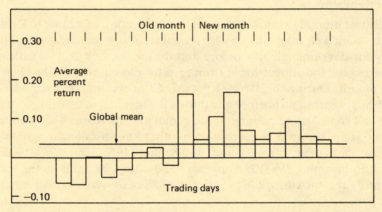

Figure 1   Histograms of daily arithmetic mean returns for trading days surrounding the turn of calendar months for the CRSP equally weighted (top) and value-weighted (bottom) indexes.

daily observations (i.e. nineteen years times twelve months). The global mean is estimated from the returns across all trading days in this nineteen-year period.

It is clear from figure 1 that positive mean returns predominate on the last trading day of each calendar month and on the trading days in the first half of calendar months. Low or negative returns predominate following the midpoint of the month.

Since the last day of the month shares the high returns common to the early days of the following month, it is convenient to define a 'trading month' as extending from the last trading day (inclusive) of each calendar month to the last trading day (exclusive) of the following calendar month, i.e. the last trading day of each calendar month is defined as the first day of a 'trading month.'

Table 1 *The mean cumulative return from the first nine trading days of each trading month in the sample, the mean cumulative return from the last nine trading days of each trading month in the sample, and t-statistics for the difference of these two means for the full period and four subperiods*

	1963–1981 (228 months)	1963–1966 (48 months)	1967–1971 (60 months)	1972–1976 (60 months)	1977–1981 (60 months)
Equally-weighted index					
Mean of first					
nine-day returns (%)	1.411	1.295	1.445	1.256	1.627
(standard deviation (%))	(3.71)	(2.45)	(3.36)	(5.16)	(3.07)
Mean of last					
nine-day returns (%)	−0.021	−0.0125	−0.002	−0.148	0.079
(standard deviation (%))	(3.51)	(2.25)	(4.10)	(3.94)	(3.23)
t-statistic	4.23	2.70	2.10	1.66	2.70
(implied *p*)	(0.00003)	(0.007)	(0.034)	(0.095)	(0.007)
Value-weighted index					
Mean of first					
nine-day returns (%)	0.826	0.969	0.866	0.546	0.950
(standard deviation (%))	(2.70)	(1.71)	(2.40)	(3.30)	(2.95)
Mean of last					
nine-day returns (%)	−0.182	−0.290	−0.177	−0.094	−0.188
(standard deviation (%))	(2.65)	(1.86)	(2.95)	(3.07)	(2.39)
t-statistic	4.01	3.41	2.11	1.09	2.30
(implied *p*)	(0.0007)	(0.0006)	(0.035)	(0.28)	(0.021)

A formal test of the hypothesis that the mean return for days in the first half of trading months exceeds that of days in the last half can be performed by dividing each trading month evenly in half (discarding the odd day, if any, in the middle of the month) and calculating relevant statistics for the two daily subpopulations: for the equally-weighted index, the means (standard deviations) of days in the first and last halves of trading months are 0.144 percent (0.787 percent) and 0.004 percent (0.782 percent) respectively, yielding a *t*-statistic for the difference in the daily means of 6.07, based on the 2325 observations in each subpopulation. Comparable figures for the value-weighted index are 0.085 percent (0.770 percent) and −0.013 percent (0.756 percent) respectively with a *t*-statistic of 4.34. For both indexes, the mean return from days in the first half of trading months significantly exceeds the mean return from days in the last half.[3] It is interesting to note that the estimated standard deviations are virtually identical for daily returns in the first and last halves of trading months. Further, the mean daily return during the last half of trading months is indistinguishable from zero ($t = 0.25$ and -0.83 for the equally- and value-weighted indexes respectively); during this nineteen-year period, stocks advanced only during the first half of trading months.

While the arithmetic mean return on days in the first half of trading months significantly exceeds the arithmetic mean return on days in the last half, individuals do not typically have one-day investment horizons. Since the high-return and low-return days cluster in the first and last halves of trading months respectively, the *cumulative* returns over these half-months constitute an economically more relevant measure of the monthly effect. Table 1 reports a standard difference-of-the-means test comparing the mean *cumulative* return over the first nine trading days of trading months with the mean cumulative return over the last nine trading days of trading months, both for the entire 1963–81 period and for four subperiods.

The following conclusions can be drawn from table 1: first, for the entire 1963–81 period, for both indexes, the *t*-statistic for the difference of the mean cumulative returns is statistically significant. Second, the monthly effect is present in all four subperiods, and is statistically significant at conventional confidence levels in three of the four subperiods. Third, the estimated variance of cumulative returns from the first nine days and the last nine days of trading months are roughly equal; indeed, the hypothesis that the first half-month and last half-month cumulative return variances are equal cannot be rejected by an *F*-test at the 5 percent level. The significantly higher average return earned during the first half of trading months is not accompanied by comparably higher risk.

The difference-of-the-half-month-means test reported above assumes that the distribution of returns accruing to the market indexes over the nineteen-year test period does not shift. Unfortunately, the available empirical evidence suggests that the market return distribution is not stable over such a time span (see, for example, Rosenberg, 1972). Even if the distribution of returns accruing to stocks is not constant, it is possible that the *incremental* return earned by stocks during the first half over the last half of trading months is constant over the test period. Define the 'first half of trading month premium' for each trading month as the difference between the cumulative return earned during the first nine and the last nine trading days of that trading month. The mean of these 228 monthly first half premia for the equally-weighted and value-weighted indexes respectively are 1.433 percent (standard deviation: 4.518 percent) and 1.008 percent (standard deviation: 3.755 percent). The associated *t*-statistics are 4.78 and 4.04. Interestingly, pairwise comparisons of the means of the first half premia accruing in each of the four

Table 2 *Tabulation of the number of times the first half of a trading month had a higher return than the last half of that same trading month for the full period and four subperiods, and a χ^2 statistic for the difference between realized and expected frequency of superior first half of trading month returns*

	1963–1981 (228 months)	1963–1966 (48 months)	1967–1971 (60 months)	1972–1976 (60 months)	1977–1981 (60 months)
Equally-weighted index					
Frequency of higher first-half returns	155	36	38	38	43
χ^2	29.48	12.00	4.27	4.27	11.27
(implied p)	(<0.00001)	(0.0005)	(0.04)	(0.04)	(0.0008)
Value-weighted index					
Frequency of higher first-half returns	150	38	38	37	37
χ^2	22.74	16.33	4.27	3.27	3.27
(implied p)	(<0.00001)	(0.00006)	(0.04)	(0.07)	(0.07)

previously examined subperiods did not lead to rejecting the hypothesis that those mean premia are equal. In sum, both the difference-of-the-means test and the related first-half-premium test show that, on average, stocks earn significantly more during the first half of trading months compared with the last half.

Is the higher mean first-half cumulative return due to chance high returns during the first half of only a few months? To check this possibility a nonparametric χ^2 test can be performed in which each trading month is divided evenly in half (with the odd middle day, if any, discarded) and the cumulative return over the first half of the trading month compared with the cumulative return over the last half of that same trading month. In the absence of a monthly seasonal in stock returns, the first half of a trading month should outperform the last half 50 percent of the time. As table 2 shows, the observed frequency of superior first-half performance is in fact closer to two-thirds. The resulting χ^2 statistic for testing equality between the expected and observed frequencies of superior first half of trading month performance for the full nineteen years of data results in a rejection of the null hypothesis of no monthly seasonal for all confidence levels. Moreover, in each of the four subperiods previously examined, the monthly effect is present in both indexes; in six of the eight comparisons the test is significant at the 0.05 level. The statistically significant results obtained

Table 3 *Tabulation of the mean cumulative returns from the first and from the last nine trading days of each trading month of the year, for both CRSP indexes, for the years 1963–1981; and t-statistic for significance of first half of trading month premium*

Trading month		Equally-weighted index		Value-weighted index	
		Mean return[a] (%)	t-statistic[b]	Mean return[a] (%)	t-statistic[b]
January	Beg.	5.97	3.77	1.49	1.46
	End	1.83		0.48	
February	Beg.	0.23	−0.61	0.07	−0.77
	End	0.92		0.87	
March	Beg.	1.22	0.76	1.26	0.90
	End	0.53		0.62	
April	Beg.	0.94	1.68	1.02	1.34
	End	−1.29		−0.31	
May	Beg.	1.19	0.62	1.63	0.70
	End	0.53		0.02	
June	Beg.	0.85	1.08	0.88	1.46
	End	−0.47		−0.71	
July	Beg.	1.28	1.96	0.61	1.24
	End	−0.89		−1.07	
August	Beg.	1.23	2.68	1.07	2.49
	End	−1.26		−1.00	
September	Beg.	0.26	0.58	0.30	0.79
	End	−0.30		−0.43	
October	Beg.	1.40	2.02	1.17	1.83
	End	0.00		−0.12	
November	Beg.	1.51	1.73	1.05	1.66
	End	0.14		−0.09	
December	Beg.	0.95	0.91	0.35	0.80
	End	0.02		−0.45	

Notes: [a]Each reported return represents the mean of the nineteen observations of the cumulative returns from the first or last nine trading days of the indicated trading month. [b] t-statistic for significance of the mean first half of trading month premium (defined for each month as the first nine days minus last nine days cumulative return) based on the nineteen premia for each month.

from the nonparametric χ^2 test, which is insensitive to a handful of outliers, shows that they are not responsible for the monthly effect.

Is the monthly effect being induced by consistently high returns during the first half of only several trading months of the year (e.g. the high return months of January and July (Rozeff and Kinney; 1976))? Table 3 tabulates the mean of the cumulative returns for the first and last nine trading days of each trading month of the year, along with a t-statistic for the significance of the mean first half of trading month premium for each of these months. In only the one month of February does the point

Table 4 *Cumulative returns for both CRSP indexes, 1963–1981*

Nineteen-year cumulative return	Equally-weighted index (%)	Value-weighted index (%)
First-half of trading month cumulative return	2552.40	565.40
Last-half of trading month cumulative return	−0.25	−33.80
Overall cumulative return	2545.90	339.90

estimate of the average cumulative return from the last half of that trading month exceed that in the first half, and this February reversal is statistically insignificant. For all the remaining months, the difference of the first half–last half relative performance is in the direction established earlier; for several of the months for both indexes the *t*-statistic is significant at the 0.10 level (two-tailed) based on that month's nineteen observations alone. Thus we can conclude that the overall monthly effect does not result from unusually high returns during the beginning of only a few months.

Finally, the cumulative impact of the higher first half of trading months stock returns is substantial. The nineteen-year cumulative returns from investing in stocks only during the first half of all trading months (and the comparable returns from the last half of all trading months) are tabulated in table 4.

In any trading month with an odd number of trading days, the odd day in the middle of the month is included in the last-half cumulative return, and hence about 5 percent more days are included in the latter. Even so, during these nineteen years, all of the market's cumulative advance occurred during the first half of trading months, with the last half of trading months contributing nothing.

3 Possible causes of the monthly effect

Several possible reasons for the observed monthly seasonal in stock returns readily suggest themselves, but can as readily be eliminated.[4]

The monthly effect is not being driven solely by high stock returns during the first half of January (the 'January effect'). As table 3 shows, the monthly seasonal has been present not just in January, but in most months of the year during the sample period. Moreover, if the difference-in-means test reported in table 1 is repeated after excluding January from the sample, statistically significant differences are still found (*t*-statistics for the difference of the means after excluding January: $t = 3.68$ (implied p: 0.0003) and $t = 3.93$ (implied p: 0.0001) for the CRSP equally- and value-weighted indexes respectively).

Nor is the monthly effect being induced by the concentration of dividend payments in the first or last halves of months. The CRSP indexes are total return (or 'dividend reinvestment') indexes so preferential dividend payments in the first or last half of trading months will not bias the temporal pattern of total return, at least to a first approximation. It could be argued that different taxation of dividends and capital gains results in earnings retained in the corporation being valued differently than earnings paid out as dividend. If so, stock prices could fall on the ex-dividend dates by more or less than the dividend payment, and thus a concentration of dividend payments in the first or last half of trading months could still induce a monthly seasonal in a total return stock series. However, a simple order of magnitude argument suffices to show that the monthly seasonal cannot arise from this tax effect. The statistics presented earlier show in essence that during the nineteen years examined, the total return earned by stocks accrues solely during the first half of trading months; on average, the last-half returns are virtually indistinguishable from zero. It is difficult to imagine any mechanism whereby a monthly asymmetry in the payment of the dividend *component* of this total return could induce the entire return to accrue during the first half of trading months, especially in a dividend-reinvestment index. For example, suppose the dividend yield on the CRSP value-weighted index had averaged 6 percent per year, or 0.5 percent per month. The observed first half of trading month premium has been 1.008 percent per month (as reported in section 2) or *twice* the monthly dividend payment. Hence, even if all dividend payments were concentrated in the same half of trading months, the ex-dividend tax effect would have to be twice as large as the dividend payment itself in order to induce the observed monthly effect. Such a change in stock prices on ex-dividend dates is not observed.

Finally, the observed monthly effect in stock returns cannot be explained as a chance pattern found by extensive 'mining' of the data. The difficulties associated with allegations of data mining can be overcome by employing a hold-out sample; one 'mines' some of the data and then tests resulting conclusions on the remainder. There is an implicit hold-out sample in the present study. Stock market 'technical' analysts have long known of the existence of a monthly seasonal (see, for example, Fosback, 1976). The last of the four subperiods examined in the empirical tests of section 2 correspond to the five years since the 1976 publication date of Fosback's report; the statistically significant results from this subperiod alone show that 'data mining' cannot be the foundation of the monthly effect. Moreover, the monthly effect has shown remarkable persistence over time: in a tabulation of the frequency of advances in the Dow-Jones Industrial Averages on different days of the calendar month from 1896 to 1965, another technician (Merrill, 1966) reports a pattern of frequency of up-days similar to that shown in figure 1. The presence of a monthly pattern during this pre-test period again suggests that data mining to discover a chance pattern is not responsible for the reported monthly seasonal.

It is easier to offer the above catalog of factors which are not inducing the monthly effect than to offer suggestions for its possible cause. Roughly speaking, there are three classes of potential factors which can move aggregate stock prices: new information concerning future corporate cash flows, riskless rate changes, or changes in preferences causing variations in aggregate demand for stocks not offset by supply adjustments.

It is unlikely that the monthly effect can be explained in terms of information release: the starting of a month is a deterministic event. The selective release of corporate or economic news, whether expected or unexpected, during one or another half of trading months cannot explain the observed monthly seasonal. *Expected* economic or corporate news cannot explain the monthly seasonal in returns; if good news is regularly expected to predominate in the first half of trading months, given any reasonable definition of market efficiency, stock prices will not fluctuate in response to such expected good news. Only the unexpected component of information release will influence prices and this unexpected component should itself have an expected zero mean impact on stock prices.

If unexpected releases of good *and* bad news is concentrated in the first half of trading months, stocks might be riskier during the first half, thus justifying higher first-half returns. However, stocks are *not* riskier during the first half of trading months; as reported in section 2, the variance of aggregate stock returns is virtually identical during the first and last halves. Hence, at least in straightforward models which identify portfolio variance with risk, the risk (and *a fortiori* information release) is *constant* over the month, and thus cannot explain the observed monthly pattern in stock returns. Since information-related variations in risk do not suffice to explain the observed monthly effect, its genesis might be sought in supply and demand factors.

Theoretical work on market microstructure shows that market makers have incentives to change the price at which transactions occur in response to order flows (Glosten and Milgrom, 1985; Gammill, 1985).

Empirical evidence shows that listing and delisting from the S&P 500 index impacts market valuation of the affected stock and hints at price pressure from buying and selling by index funds (Harris and Gurel, 1985; Jain, 1985). Perhaps most relevant to the present discussion, Ritter (1985) finds that immediately after the New Year, retail brokerage accounts (which tend to be intensive in small capitalization, low priced stocks) abruptly switch from net selling to net buying of stocks. Moreover, variations in the magnitude of the switch in any given year can explain a significant portion of the variation in the magnitude of that year's January returns in these small-capitalization, low-priced stocks, thereby suggesting retail volume is associated with the January effect. And while the available empirical evidence suggests that individual stocks have highly elastic demand curves, it is less likely that risky assets in aggregate, or the subset of traded risky assets, have equally elastic demand curves.

Shifts in market-wide demand curves for equities might be induced by monthly buying programs by large investors or periodic contributions to pension plans by corporations. If such is the case, then since the quantities of stocks are fixed over the short term, stock prices must adjust. A possible scenario is one in which some investors (e.g. corporations which make pension fund contributions at the end of each month) sell short-term interest-bearing instruments and buy stocks, pushing up the price of risky assets. In such a scenario, one might also expect to observe a monthly seasonal in the prices of short-term debt instruments (i.e. in interest rates), even though the very large volume of debt instruments outstanding and Federal Reserve policies designed to cushion interest rate fluctuations may tend to damp such monthly swings. In this connection, it is interesting to note that Park and Reinganum (1985) find that t-bills which mature just after the start of calendar months have higher yields (lower prices) than those that mature just before the start of calendar months.[5] Possible interdependencies between the monthly seasonals in stock returns and t-bills yields and their connections to fund flows seem to merit further exploration.

Notes

* I would like to thank Terry Marsh for comments and suggestions and also seminar participants at the Wharton School; Baruch College, CUNY; Boston University; Boston College; and the University of Southern California.
1 A more complete description of the statistical tests used to establish the existence of the monthly effect may be found in Ariel (1983) and Ariel (1987).
2 The starting and ending dates of the test period were determined, respectively, by the start of the first full year of CRSP daily return data, and by the last full year of data available at the time this research was initiated.
3 Daily stock index returns are strongly autocorrelated, which is typically attributed to non-synchronous trading of the component securities. As a check on the possible bias in the t-statistics induced by this autocorrelation these index returns were regressed against

a first half of trading month dummy variable using the Hildreth–Lu autocorrelation correction procedure. This model in essence performs a difference-of-the-means test corrected for autocorrelation. For both indexes, the resulting F- and t-statistics on the dummy are significant at the 0.0001 level, thereby showing that autocorrelation in the index returns has not induced the significance of the above reported difference-of-the-means t-statistics.

4 The cumulative returns are derived by chaining together daily index returns. For the equally-weighted index, this procedure requires daily rebalancing of portfolio weights and hence is not representative of realistically attainable investment results (Roll, 1983b; Blume and Stambaugh, 1983). No such limitations apply to the cumulative returns quoted for the value-weighted index.

5 See also chapters 5 and 6 of this volume.

References

Ariel, R.A. (1983) 'A Monthly Effect in Stock Returns', Working paper no. 1624–84, Sloan School of Management, Massachusetts Institute of Technology, Cambridge, MA.

Ariel, R.A. (1987) 'A Monthly Effect in Stock Returns', *Journal of Financial Economics*, 18, 1–14.

Blume, M.E. and Stambaugh, R.F. (1983) 'Biases in Computing Returns: An Application to the Size Effect', *Journal of Financial Economics*, 12, 387–404.

Fosback, Norman, 1976, Stock market logic (The Institute for Econometric Research, Fort Lauderdale, FL).

Gammill, J. (1985) 'The Design of Financial Markets', unpublished Ph.D. dissertation, Sloan School of Management, Massachusetts Institute of Technology, Cambridge, MA.

Glosten, L.R. and Milgrom, P.R. (1985) 'Bid, Ask, and Transaction Prices in a Specialist Market with Heterogenously Informal Traders', *Journal of Financial Economics*, 14, 71–100.

Harris, L. and Gurel, E. (1985) 'Price and Volume Effects Associated with Changes in the S&P 500 List: New Evidence for the Existence of Price Pressure', unpublished working paper, University of Southern California.

Jain, P.C. (1985) 'The Effects of Changes in Standard and Poor's Indexes on Common Stock Prices', unpublished working paper, University of Pennsylvania.

Keim, D.R. (1983) 'Size Related Anomalies and Stock Return Seasonality: Further Empirical Evidence', *Journal of Financial Economics*, 12, 13–32.

Merrill, A.A. (1966) *Behavior of prices on Wall Street*, Chappaqua, NY: The Analysis Press.

Park, S.Y. and Reinganum, M.R. (1985) 'The Puzzling Behavior of Treasury Bills that Mature at the Turn of Calendar Months', unpublished working paper, University of Southern California.

Reinganum, M.R. (1983) 'The Anomalous Stock Market Behavior of Small Firms in January: Empirical Tests for Tax-loss Effects', *Journal of Financial Economics*, 12, 89–104.

Ritter, J. R. (1985) 'The Buying and Selling Behavior of Individual Investors at the Turn of the Year: Evidence of Price Pressure Effects', unpublished working paper, University of Michigan.

Roll, R. (1983a) 'Vas ist das?', *Journal of Portfolio Management*, Winter, 18–28.

Roll, R. (1983b) 'On Computing Mean Returns and the Small Firm Premium', *Journal of Financial Economics*, 12, 371–86.

Rosenberg, B. (1972) 'The Behavior of Random Variables with Non-stationary Variances and the Distribution of Security Prices', Graduate School of Business Administration Working paper no. 11, University of California, Berkeley, CA.

Rozeff, M.S. and Kinney, W.R. Jr. (1976) 'Capital Market Seasonality: The Case of Stock Returns', *Journal of Financial Economics*, 3, 379–402.

III
THE SMALL FIRM,
TURN-OF-THE-YEAR
AND OTHER ANOMALIES

9   Comments on stock return seasonality

*GEORGE M. CONSTANTINIDES**

As far back as 1942, Wachtel (1942) reported 'Certain Observations in Seasonal Movements in Stock Prices'. In the 1970s, Officer (1975) reported stock return seasonality in Australian capital markets, Rozeff and Kinney (1976) in US capital markets, and Richards (1978) in UK and other European markets. In his 1973 Ph.D. thesis, Dyl reported empirical evidence on stock return and trading volume seasonality and interpreted it as year-end, tax-induced trading. Dyl (1977) and Branch (1977) reported further empirical evidence which they interpreted as tax induced.

At the time, anomalies were not in fashion and this evidence attracted little attention. It was the firm size anomaly, reported in Banz (1981), that attracted attention first. Then Keim (1983) reported that nearly 50 percent of the size effect is due to January abnormal returns. Further, more than 50 percent of the January premium is attributable to the first week of January. The work of Roll (1983) and Keim (1983) revived the tax-loss-selling hypotheses and from that time on there has been an explosion of interest in the January effect and in the relation between the January effect and the small firm effect.

Some of the best research on the January anomaly is reported in the 1983 special issue of the Journal of Financial Economics, in the chapters included in this volume, and in the references provided therein. Therefore it is unnecessary for me to provide a review of this literature. Rather, I present a conceptual framework for the chapters included in this volume.

First, we have three chapters (chapters 10, 11 and 12) which test the implications of tax-motivated trading on the seasonal pattern of prices and trading volume on stocks in general, and in particular on stocks classified as winners or losers based on their past performance. In my work on 'Optimal Stock Trading with Personal Taxes' (Constantinides, 1984) I have demonstrated on both theoretical and empirical grounds that there are strong economic reasons – quantified and named tax-timing options – for taxable investors to take into consideration the holding period status (i.e. long term or short term) of their stocks and the time relative to the end of their tax year in deciding on the realization of their capital gains and losses. We may name this hypothesis and its variants as the tax-trading hypothesis on the volume of trade. I also stated that we need to further assume some irrationality or ignorance on behalf of investors if we want to claim that the trading volume seasonality maps into a seasonal pattern in stock returns. We may name the second hypothesis as the tax-trading hypothesis on stock returns. It is the second hypothesis that is commonly referred to as the tax-loss-selling hypothesis. I find the first hypothesis plausible but I find the second one objectionable. But we should turn to the evidence.

Chapters 10 and 11 test the tax-trading hypothesis on stock returns, and in particular the January seasonal. Chapter 12 tests the related hypothesis that relative stock returns are influenced by the overall volume of institutional buying and selling of equities.

At the risk of oversimplifying, I would summarize the evidence as follows: tax trading may very well contribute to a seasonal pattern of stock returns and the volume of trade around January; but it cannot be the sole reason or even the most important reason for these seasonals. De Bondt and Thaler (1985) and Chan (1986) find that portfolios of losers experience larger January returns than portfolios of winners, for as long as five years following the classification, casting some doubts on tax-related explanations. Also Poterba (1985) examines the evidence on capital gain realizations from the 1982 IRS individual tax model and finds that for about one-fifth of the investors who realize gains, the ordinary income loss-offset limitations are binding constraints; another significant group escapes taxation by not reporting realized gains.

A clever way to test the tax-loss-selling hypothesis is to look at countries other than the US in which the tax laws may differ. In chapter 10 Seha Tinic and Giovanni Barone-Adesi re-examine the Canadian evidence focusing on the imposition of capital gains tax in 1973. After carefully controlling for the possible influence of US taxable investors trading Canadian stocks, they conclude that tax-related trading by Canadian investors cannot account for all of the observed seasonality in returns. Furthermore, there is strong evidence that those Canadians who were subject to taxation prior to 1973 behaved in such a way that their transactions could not account for the seasonality.

In chapter 11 Willem van den Bergh, Roberto Wessels and Roel Wijmenga test the implications of the tax-loss-selling hypothesis on the Amsterdam Stock Exchange. What is novel about this study is that individual investors in The Netherlands are not subject to capital gains tax. If we can ignore the trading by Dutch corporations and by foreign investors, both of which are subject to capital gains tax, then their finding of a January seasonal means that there is some factor at work other than tax-related trading. In a related paper (which was presented at the EIASM symposium but is not included here) Lakonishok and Smidt (1986) find that winning stocks have higher abnormal volume of trade than losing stocks, contrary to the predictions of the tax-trading hypothesis on volume of trade and in line with the Kahneman and Tversky theory, recently put forth in Shefrin and Statman (1985). The second conclusion of the Lakonishok and Smidt paper is that, as predicted by the tax-trading theory, the abnormal volume of winners is higher than usual in January and the abnormal volume of losers is higher than normal in December.

In chapter 12, Mario Levis examines the conjecture that the small firm premium is related to the volume of trading by institutional investors. He finds that there is no contemporaneous relationship, though there appears to be a response by institutions to stock price movements in the preceding quarter. Despite some difficulties in interpreting these results (see Theo Vermaelen's discussion in chapter 13), the message from Levis' chapter is that in the UK trading volume seasonality appears to be correlated to stock return regularities.

There are also several chapters which have a broader scope than the stock return seasonality. I focus on a subset of issues addressed by these, that of the stock return seasonality. A more detailed discussion is provided in chapter 14 by Nai-fu Chen. Unlike the tax-trading hypothesis addressed earlier, we now pose the question whether the seasonality in the mean return is due to some seasonality in some equilibrium factor pricing model.

In an equilibrium factor pricing theory Keim and Stambaugh (1986) put forth the hypothesis that changes in the expected rate of return of assets over time are driven primarily by changes in the factor premia, that is the price of risk associated with the various factors. In this paper (also presented at the EIASM symposium), they use three *ex-ante* variables to predict the time-varying factor premia. One of their *ex-ante* variables is the small-firm price variable and in the post-1953 period this explains 40 percent of the variance of the difference between returns on stocks of small and large firms in January. They interpret this evidence as possibly saying that January returns were high because rare negative outcomes, whose risk was perceived *ex ante*, were unrealized *ex post*.

In a closely related earlier paper, Chan *et al.* (1985) use some macroeconomic variables as instrumental variables for APT factors. They find that a measure of the changing risk premium explains a large portion of the size effect. They also find that their economic variables explain all but 1½ percent of the January seasonal.

In a third related paper, also presented at the symposium, Huberman and Kandel (1985) generalize the market model to one that has three factors proxied by three portfolios of small, medium and large stocks. What is novel in this paper is that the factor loadings are not asset specific, but instead are size specific. Since the January effect is pronounced in small stocks, this model is consistent with the view that the risk premium of a factor proxied by size is primarily responsible for the January effect.

It is, of course, possible that risk is seasonal and is highest in January, and that conventional estimation of beta underestimates systematic risk in January. That begs the question as to what fraction of the January seasonal is explained away by the corrected beta estimates. In connection with this, we also have some evidence in Chan and Chen (1987) that once we allow for non-stationary betas, the instrumental variable 'firm size' does not have marginal explanatory power.

Finally, chapter 15 is by Albert Corhay, Gabriel Hawawini and Pierre Michel. They measure the stock return seasonality and the CAPM-based risk premium on the NYSE, London, Paris and Brussels stock exchanges. In the NYSE the pattern of risk-premium seasonality coincides with the pattern of stock return seasonality, both being positive and significant only in January. However on the European exchanges the pattern of the risk premium seasonality does not coincide with the pattern of stock return seasonality. Future research will tell whether this phenomenon is due to some missing factor or non-stationarity.

The way I summarized these chapters reflects my frame of mind in thinking about these issues. I think that tax-related trading may contribute to a seasonal pattern of stock returns and volume of trade around January; but it cannot be the whole story or even the most important story. We have to re-examine the equilibrium factor pricing models and look for seasonals either in the factors or in the factor premia. As the chapters included in this volume testify, this endeavour is well under way, and may shed some light on the economic forces which seem to act in a different way in the month of January than they do in the rest of the year.

That the month of January is different, is well known and is disturbing. For example Tinic and West (1984) find in the context of the CAPM that, for the eleven months excluding January the risk premium is not reliably different from zero. Similarly Gultekin and Gultekin (1985) conclude that the APT can explain the risk-return relation in January only. The disturbing conclusion is that our pricing models have something to say or become irrelevant depending on whether we include January or not. Whereas some people would object to the idea of excluding January returns as a statistically meaningless procedure, I do find it worrisome that our equilibrium models depend so much on the month of January.

Thus the problem is deeper than just explaining away the January seasonality. The problem is why January should play such an important role in equilibrium pricing models. This is an important question which should be addressed in the future.

Notes

* I am particularly indebted to Elroy Dimson for detailed and incisive comments on an earlier draft of this chapter.

References

Banz, R.W. (1981) 'The Relationship between Return and Market Value of Common Stocks', *Journal of Financial Economics*, 9, 3–18.

Branch, B. (1977) 'A Tax Loss Trading Rule', *Journal of Business*, 50, 198–207.

Chan, K.C. (1986) 'Can Tax-loss Selling Explain the January Seasonals in Stock Returns?' *Journal of Finance*, 41, 1115–28.

Chan, K.C. and Chen, N. (1987). 'An Unconditional Asset Pricing Test and the Role of Firm Size as an Instrumental Variable for Risk.' Unpublished, University of Chicago.

Chan, K.C., Chen, N. and Hsieh, D.A. (1985) 'An Exploratory Investigation of the Firm Size Effect', *Journal of Financial Economics*, 14, September, 451–71.

Constantinides, G.M. (1984) 'Optimal Stock Trading with Personal Taxes', *Journal of Financial Economics*, 13, 65–89.

Corhay, A., Hawanini, G. and Michel, P. (1987) 'Seasonality in the Risk–Return Relationship: Some International Evidence', *Journal of Finance*, 42, 49–68.

De Bondt, W.F.M. and Thaler, R. (1985) 'Does the Stock Market Overreact?', *Journal of Finance*, 40, July, 793–805.

Dyl, E.A. (1973) 'The Effect of Capital Gains Taxation on the Stock Market', unpublished doctoral dissertation, Graduate School of Business, Stanford University, Stanford, CA.

Dyl, E.A. (1977) 'Capital Gains Taxation and Year-end Stock Market Behavior', *Journal of Finance*, 32, 165–75.

Gultekin, M.N. and Gultekin, N.B. (1985) 'Stock Return Anomalies and the Asset Pricing Tests: The Case of the Arbitrage Pricing Theory', unpublished, University of North Carolina.

Huberman, G. and Kandel, S. (1985) 'A Size Based Stock Returns Model', unpublished, University of Chicago.

Keim, D.B. (1983) 'Size-related Anomalies and Stock Return Seasonality: Further Empirical Evidence', *Journal of Financial Economics*, 12, June, 13–32.

Keim, D.B. and Stambaugh, R.F. (1986) 'Predicting Returns in the Stock and Bond Markets', *Journal of Financial Economics*, 17, 357–90.

Kryzanowski, L., Rahman, A., Singh, B. and Chau To, M. (1985) 'Bootstrapping the Measure of Systematic Risk in the SFM Model', unpublished, Concordia University.

Lakonishok, J. and Smidt, S. (1986) 'Volume for Winners and Losers: Taxation and Other Motives for Stock Trading', *Journal of Finance* 41, 951–974.

Officer, R.R. (1975) 'Seasonality in the Australian Capital Markets: Market Efficiency and Empirical Issues', *Journal of Financial Economics*, 2, 29–52.

Poterba, J.M. (1985) 'How Burdensome are Capital Gains Taxes?', unpublished, MIT and NBER.

Richards, P. (1978) 'Sharpe Performance among Pension Funds?', *Investment Analyst*, 51, September, 9–14.

Roll, R. (1983) 'Vas ist das? The Turn of the Year Effect and the Return Premium of Small Firms', *Journal of Portfolio Management*, 9, 18–28.

Rozeff, M.S. and Kinney, W.R. Jr. (1976) 'Capital Market Seasonality: The Case of Stock Returns', *Journal of Financial Economics*, 3, 379–402.

Shefrin, H. and Statman, M. (1985) 'The Disposition to Sell Winners too Early and Ride Losers too Long: Theory and Evidence', *Journal of Finance, Papers and Proceedings*, 40, July, 777–90.

Tinic, S.M. and West, R.R. (1984) 'Risk and Returns: January vs the Rest of the Year', *Journal of Financial Economics*, 13, 561–74.

Van den Bergh, W.M. and Wessels, R.E. (1984) 'Stock Market Seasonality and Taxes. An Examination of the Tax Loss Selling Hypothesis', unpublished, Erasmus University Rotterdam.

Wachtel, S.B. (1942) 'Certain Observations on Seasonal Movements in Stock Prices, *Journal of Business*, 15, 184–93.

10 Stock return seasonality and the tests of asset pricing models: Canadian evidence

SEHA M. TINIC and GIOVANNI BARONE-ADESI*

1 Introduction

Over the past several years, a plethora of empirical studies have documented that the returns on small firm stocks tend to exhibit pronounced seasonality in the month of January.[1] First Keim (1983) and then Roll (1983) demonstrated that a very large percentage of the abnormally high returns of small firm stocks in the US occurs during the first few days in January. The causes of large abnormal returns generated by small firm stocks at the turn of the year are not fully understood. Neither the year-end tax-loss-selling pressure nor the high transaction cost associated with the stocks of smaller firms seems to provide persuasive explanations for the anomalous empirical regularity.

While the explanation of observed seasonality in stock returns remains an important unresolved issue, more recently Tinic and West (1984, 1986) have produced empirical results which show quite clearly that the return seasonalities have profound implications for the tests of equilibrium asset pricing models. Specifically, Tinic and West (1984) reported that when the two-parameter tests of the capital asset pricing model (CAPM) with data on US stock returns are analyzed for seasonality, the relationship between returns and systematic risk is consistently positive only in January. When the data for the month of January are withheld from the analysis of the risk–return tradeoff, the estimated monthly risk premia are not significantly different from zero. However, after additional tests Tinic and West (1986) discovered that the observed relationship between stock returns and systematic risk appears to exhibit much more perplexing patterns than just a simple January seasonal in risk premia. Their results reveal that the risk–return relationship in the US stock market contains important nonlinearities that cannot be ascribed solely to the anomalies related to firm size or the turn-of-the-year seasonality in stock returns.

In view of Tinic and West's findings in the US stock market and the growing body of literature on stock market anomalies, it is appropriate to look more deeply into the behavior of risk premia estimated from CAPM in Canada. The purpose of this chapter is to report on tests of the CAPM using Canadian stock returns from February, 1963 through December, 1983. While the turn-of-the-year seasonality in the returns of Canadian stocks has already been documented by Berges *et al.* (1984) and Tinic *et al.* (1987), its impact on the basic relationship between risk and expected return in the Canadian stock market was left unexplored. For completeness, however, we start by documenting the January seasonal in Canadian stock returns in the next section. In section 3, we describe the methodology and the data used in testing the major implications of CAPM in Canada. Section 4 reports the results of our tests. Finally, the summary and conclusions are presented in section 5.

2 Seasonality in the returns of Canadian stocks

It is generally well known that the returns on Canadian stocks exhibit a significant January seasonal. For purposes of completeness, we present some evidence on the seasonality in the returns of the Toronto Stock Exchange 300 index (TSE 300). The TSE 300 index is widely accepted as the barometer of the Canadian stock market. It is a value-weighted portfolio of 300 Canadian common stocks that are traded on the Toronto and the Montreal Stock Exchanges. Some of the stocks in the index are also listed either on the NYSE or the AMEX. The monthly returns of the TSE 300 index were available from February, 1956 through August, 1981. The returns included actual dividends paid during the month as well as changes in the values of the stocks.

To test the seasonality in the returns of the TSE 300 index, both before and after the introduction of the capital gains tax in Canada, the following regression equation was estimated with monthly returns during the periods 1956–72 and 1973–81:

$$\bar{R}_{1t} = \beta_1 + \beta_2 D_{2t} + \beta_3 D_{3t} + \beta_4 D_{4t} + \ldots + \beta_{12} D_{12t} + \bar{e}_t \qquad (1)$$

In the regression equation, R_{1t} is the return on the TSE 300 index during month t, and $D_{2t}, D_{3t}, \ldots, D_{12t}$ are the dummy variables corresponding to the months of February to December. Equation (1) corresponds to analysis of variance where the return on the Index in January is captured by the intercept β_1. Other regression coefficients, $\beta_2, \ldots, \beta_{12}$, measure the difference between January returns and the average returns during each of the remaining months.

The estimated coefficients of equation (1) are reported in table 1. The intercept, which measures the average return of the TSE 300 index in January, is positive and statistically significant in both periods. During

Table 1 *Seasonality in the returns of the TSE 300 index*[a]

(1) $R_{1t} = \beta_1 + \beta_2 D_{2t} + \beta_3 D_{3t} + \beta_4 D_{4t} + \beta_5 D_{5t} + \beta_6 D_{6t} + \beta_7 D_{7t} + \beta_8 D_{8t} + \beta_9 D_{9t} + \beta_{10} D_{10t} + \beta_{11} D_{11t} + \beta_{12} D_{12t} + e_t$

(2) $R_{1t} = \beta_0 + \beta_1 D_{1t} + \beta_{12} D_{12t} + u_t$

Time period	β_0	β_1	β_2	β_3	β_4	β_5	β_6	β_7
1956–1972 (1)	—	00253 (2.7734)	-0.0292 (-0.2939)	-0.0069 (-0.5418)	-0.0116 (-0.9096)	-0.0312 (-2.4558)	-0.0340 (-2.6712)	-0.0139 (-1.0957)
1956–1972 (2)	0.0032 (1.1465)	0.0221 (2.2814)	—	—	—	—	—	—
1973–1981 (1)	—	0.0396 (2.1804)	-0.0178 (-0.6944)	-0.0423 (-1.6470)	-0.0449 (-1.7471)	-0.0318 (-1.2379)	-0.0181 (-0.7044)	-0.0246 (-0.9593)
1973–1981 (2)	0.0046 (0.8085)	0.0350 (1.8823)	—	—	—	—	—	—

Table 1 (*Continued*)

Time period	β_8	β_9	β_{10}	β_{11}	β_{12}	R^2	F-statistic	Durbin–Watson statistic
1956–1972 (1)	-0.228 (-1.7958)	-0.0304 (-2.3948)	-0.0335 (-2.6384)	-0.0070 (-0.5517)	0.0020 (0.1596)	0.1169	3.9767[b]	1.6269
1956–1972 (2)	—	—	—	—	0.0241 (2.5611)	0.0513	10.8961[b]	1.6862
1973–1981 (1)	-0.0456 (-1.7772)	-0.0411 (-1.5540)	-0.0532 (-2.0093)	-0.0329 (-1.2423)	-0.0148 (-0.5601)	0.0800	1.4050	2.1864
1973–1981 (2)	—	—	—	—	0.0202 (1.0280)	0.0407	4.5405[b]	2.1676

Note: [a]The *t*-statistics of the coefficients are presented in parentheses.
[b]Significant beyond $\alpha = 0.01$.

1956–72, prior to the introduction of the capital gains tax in Canada, the regression coefficients of all months except December are negative. However, statistically speaking, the average returns in March, April, July, November and December are not significantly lower than January returns. Nevertheless, the regression equation (1) reveals that the returns of the TSE 300 index have been substantially larger in January. The average monthly return of the index was 0.70 percent per month during 1956–72. The average return in January was more than 3.6 times the average monthly return.

The results of the post-capital gains tax period are essentially the same. Probably due to paucity of observations during 1973–81, a smaller subset of the coefficients are statistically significant. Nevertheless, the estimated coefficients are negative for all months. The average return in January was about 4.3 times as large as the average monthly return of 0.92 percent during 1973–81.

Since our primary concern is with the seasonality of stock returns during the turn of the year, equation (1) can be reformulated parsimoniously by using only two dummy variables, D_1 and D_{12}, for January and December respectively. In this case, the intercept measures the average return of the TSE 300 index in all months except January and December. The regression coefficients β_1 and β_{12} capture the difference in average returns of January and December respectively from the average returns during the rest of the year. The estimated coefficients of this equation

$$R_{1t} = \beta_0 + \beta_1 D_{1t} + \beta_{12} D_{12t} + u_t \qquad (2)$$

are also presented in table 1.

During 1956–72, January returns of the TSE 300 index averaged around 2.5 percent. Similarly, the average December return was 2.7 percent. In contrast, the average return during the remaining months was 0.32 percent. In other words, the TSE 300 index exhibited substantially large returns at the turn of the year even before capital gains taxes were introduced into Canada. The estimated coefficients of equation (2) tell a very similar story during 1973–81, but the t-statistics are smaller. Indeed, the regression coefficient for December is not statistically significant. The small t-value can be attributed to slightly larger error variance during 1973–81 when return variability of stocks in general was greater than the pre-1973 period. More importantly, the 1973–81 period includes only nine Januaries and eight Decembers. That is, the number of January and December returns used to estimate the regression coefficients is virtually one-half the number used during 1956–72.

While these results demonstrate the January seasonal in the Canadian stock market, they also suggest that the large turn-of-the-year (December and January) returns of the Canadian stocks cannot be attributed to tax-related trading. Indeed, the results of more comprehensive tests conducted by Tinic *et al.* (1987) fail to support the proposition that tax-induced trading is the sole cause of the seasonality in Canadian stock returns.

In any event, while perplexing in their own right, these results do not tell us how the seasonal in stock returns affects the tests of the asset pricing model in Canada. Nor do they provide information about the extent to which the functional form of the relationship between risk and return varies over calendar months or is sensitive to the composition of the proxy used for the Canadian market portfolio. It is to these subjects that the remainder of the paper is devoted.

3 Test methodology and the data

To test the implications that flow from the CAPM's proposition of a positively sloped linear relationship between expected returns and systematic risk of Canadian common stocks, we used the two-stage test methodology that was pioneered by Fama and MacBeth (1973). It should be recalled that to alleviate the inevitable 'errors-in-the-variables' problem and to guard against the 'regression tendency' in betas, the Fama and MacBeth methodology uses a grouping procedure and requires three non-overlapping subperiods for (a) portfolio formation; (b) estimation; and (c) testing. In the portfolio formation subperiod, stocks are allocated into twenty portfolios on the basis of the ranked values of their beta coefficients. Then, in a subsequent time period (initial estimation period) the betas of the individual securities are re-estimated and averaged across all stocks in each portfolio. Finally, a third subperiod (testing period) is utilized to generate the monthly returns on the portfolios and to estimate the following cross-sectional relationships between portfolio returns and risk:

$$\tilde{R}_{pt} = \tilde{\gamma}_{0t} + \tilde{\gamma}_{1t}\beta_{pt-1} + \tilde{e}_{pt} \tag{3}$$

and

$$\tilde{R}_{pt} = \tilde{\gamma}_{0t} + \tilde{\gamma}_{1t}\beta_{pt-1} + \tilde{\gamma}_{2t}\beta_{pt-1}^2 + \tilde{\gamma}_{3t}S(e_{pt-1}) + \tilde{\gamma}_{4t}\log S_p + \tilde{u}_{pt} \tag{4}$$

where

$\tilde{R}_{pt}$ = the return on portfolio p in month t (measured in percent per month);

β_{pt-1} = the average of the estimated beta coefficients of the stocks in the pth portfolio as of the beginning of the month for which the return is calculated;

Table 2 *Portfolio formation, estimation, and testing periods*

	Periods				
	1	2	3	4	5
Portfolio formation period	1963–1965	1966–1968	1969–1971	1972–1974	1975–1977
Initial estimation period	1966–1968	1969–1971	1972–1974	1975–1977	1978–1980
Testing period	1969–1971	1972–1974	1975–1977	1978–1980	1981–1983
Number of securities	321	358	407	461	435

β^2_{pt-1} = the average of the squared values of the beta coefficients of the securities in portfolio p at the beginning of the month t;
$S(e_{pt-1})$ = the average of the estimated unsystematic risks of the securities in portfolio p as of the beginning of month t;
$\log S_p$ = the logarithm of the average equity capitalization of the firms in portfolio p;
$\tilde{e}_{pt}, \tilde{u}_{pt}$ = random error terms; and
$\tilde{\gamma}_{0t}, \tilde{\gamma}_{1t}, \tilde{\gamma}_{2t}, \tilde{\gamma}_{3t}, \tilde{\gamma}_{4t}$ = partial regression coefficients in month t.

Based on the two-parameter asset pricing model, $E(\tilde{\gamma}_{2t})$, $E(\tilde{\gamma}_{3t})$ and $E(\tilde{\gamma}_{4t})$ in equation (4) should all be zero and $E(\tilde{\gamma}_{1t})$, the expected monthly risk premium associated with non-diversifiable risk, should be positive. On the other hand, nonzero $\tilde{\gamma}_2$, $\tilde{\gamma}_3$ and $\tilde{\gamma}_4$ would imply that either the proxy used for the market portfolio is not mean-variance efficient or the equilibrium risk–return relationship is misspecified (see Roll, 1977).

The data used in testing the implications of the CAPM were obtained from the file developed at the Laval University. The file contains monthly returns on Canadian stocks that were traded on the Toronto Stock Exchange from February, 1963 through December, 1983. The returns include dividends, and the price changes were adjusted for stock dividends and splits. Unfortunately, however, the data on Canadian stocks do not span as many years as the data on the NYSE listed securities. Unlike Fama and MacBeth (1973) and Tinic and West (1984, 1986), we were forced to use shorter time intervals for portfolio formation, estimation and the testing periods. Only three years of monthly data were used to form twenty portfolios and to compute the initial values of the regressors in equations (3) and (4). Thus, we have 180 months to test the major implications of the asset pricing model. The five different portfolio formation, initial estimation and testing periods are presented in table 2 together with the number of stocks that were included in the twenty portfolios.

4 Results

Based on Tinic and West's findings in the US and the large body of data indicating that the stock market's behavior in January is significantly different from the rest of the year, we analyzed the estimated coefficients, $\bar{\gamma}_0$, $\bar{\gamma}_1$, $\bar{\gamma}_2$, $\bar{\gamma}_3$ and $\bar{\gamma}_4$ separately for January and the remaining eleven months of the year. The results of our tests, based on three different proxies for the market portfolio, demonstrate very clearly that the Canadian evidence does not support the major implications of the two-parameter asset pricing model. Moreover, they confirm Tinic and West's (1986) findings that the results of the tests are highly sensitive to the composition of the proxy used for the market portfolio.

Tests based on an equally weighted index

Allocation of the stocks to portfolios and the calculation of β_{pt-1}, β_{pt-1}^2 and $S(e_{pt-1})$ are based on estimates obtained from the market model, which requires identification of a proxy for the market portfolio. We started our tests by using the equally weighted portfolio of all the Canadian stocks in our sample as the proxy for the market portfolio. That is, the proxy market portfolio contained 321, 358, 407 and 435 stocks respectively in the five different portfolio formation and estimation periods. The estimated coefficients of the monthly cross-sectional regressions (3) and (4) based on the equally weighted index were averaged over 180 months spanned from January, 1969 through December, 1983, and over 15 Januaries separately. The results are presented in table 3. Focusing first on the results obtained from the two-parameter cross-sectional regression for the whole period, we observe that the average monthly risk premium associated with systematic risk is not significantly different from zero.[2] In fact, the coefficient has the wrong sign and the average coefficient of determination for the regression is virtually zero. On the other hand, returns are positively related to systematic risk in January. Despite the small number of observations, the t-statistic for $\bar{\gamma}_1$ is 2.38 which is significantly different from zero beyond the 0.025 probability level. These results are remarkably similar to those reported by Tinic and West (1984, p. 568). Their results for the January, 1969–December, 1982 subperiod in the US stock market show a highly significant, 6.08 percent, average risk premium in January and virtually nothing in the remaining months of the year. Taken at face value, our estimates imply that investors would have reaped the rewards from shouldering systematic risk only if they maintained long positions in Canadian stocks in the first month of the year!

The reasons for these puzzling results become somewhat more

Table 3 Average values of the estimated coefficients of the two- and five-parameter regression models (estimated with monthly data and based on the equally-weighted index) January, 1969–December, 1983[a]

Average over	Sample size	$\bar{\gamma}_0$	$\bar{\gamma}_1$	$\bar{\gamma}_2$	$\bar{\gamma}_3$	$\bar{\gamma}_4$	Average adjusted R^2
			$\bar{R}_{pt} = \bar{\gamma}_{0t} + \bar{\gamma}_{1t}\beta_{pt-1} + \bar{e}_{pt}$				
January only	15	0.0081 (0.82)	0.0495[b] (2.38)				0.1172
Rest of the year	165	0.0146[b] (4.57)	−0.0053 (−1.40)				0.0377
All months	180	0.0140[b] (4.63)	−0.0008 (−0.19)				0.0443
			$\bar{R}_{pt} = \bar{\gamma}_{0t} + \bar{\gamma}_{1t}\beta_{pt-1} + \bar{\gamma}_{2t}\beta_{pt-1}^2 + \bar{\gamma}_{3t} S(e_{pt-1}) + \bar{\gamma}_{4t} \log S_p + \bar{u}_{pt}$				
January only	15	0.1360[b] (2.28)	−0.0009 (−0.01)	0.0229 (0.44)	0.2133 (1.39)	−0.0065[b] (−4.13)	0.2339
Rest of the year	165	0.0155 (0.81)	−0.0052 (−0.30)	−0.0015 (−0.16)	0.0771 (1.40)	−0.0004 (−0.43)	0.1403
All months	180	0.0255 (1.39)	−0.0048 (−0.28)	0.0005 (0.05)	0.0885[b] (1.71)	−0.0009 (−1.12)	0.1481

Note: [a] t-statistics are presented in parentheses.
[b] Significant at the 0.05 level.

transparent when we examine the estimated coefficients of the five-parameter regression model that are also reported in table 3. When firm size and unsystematic risk are included in the cross-sectional regressions, the anomalous January risk premium vanishes. Instead, we observe a highly significant negative coefficient for firm size, and a positive coefficient with a *t*-statistic of 1.39 for unsystematic risk, which is significantly different from zero beyond the 0.10 probability level.[3] In other words, the results indicate that residual risk is the only measure of risk that approaches statistical significance at the conventional probability levels if returns in January are adjusted for the ubiquitous 'size effect'. The data for the whole period (180 months) also show that the residual risk is the only measure of risk that has exhibited a significant positive association with returns in the Canadian stock market during the fifteen years we were able to analyze. Thus, we cannot accept the propositions that (a) there is a positive linear relationship between returns and systematic risk, and (b) beta is the only measure of risk that is priced in the Canadian stock market.

Tests based on a value weighted index

It is generally recognized that an equally weighted index is not a particularly good proxy for the market portfolio. Therefore, we replicated our tests using twenty equally weighted portfolios of Canadian stocks formed on the basis of ranking security betas relative to a value weighted index. The index included all the stocks in our sample during each of the five portfolio formation and estimation periods. The weights for the stocks in the index were recalculated monthly. The average values for the coefficients estimated from the monthly cross-sectional regressions that are based on the value weighted index are presented in table 4. The average monthly risk premia estimated from the two-parameter regression model are statistically indistinguishable from zero. Although the average risk premium in the month of January has the correct sign, and appears large relative to other months, its *t*-statistic is only 0.84. In contrast to Tinic and West's (1984) findings in the US stock market, the anomalous risk premium in January estimated from the two-parameter regression model appears to be highly sensitive to the composition of the proxy used for the market portfolio in Canada.

The results obtained from the five-parameter regression model are qualitatively similar to those reported in table 3. However, there is one major quantitative difference. The average value of the monthly regression coefficients for residual risk, $\bar{\gamma}_3$, is considerably larger in January than in other months when a value weighted index is used as the proxy for the market portfolio. The *t*-statistics of the coefficients are also large.

Table 4 *Average values of the estimated coefficients of the two- and five-parameter regression models (estimated with monthly data and based on the value-weighted index) January, 1969–December, 1983[a]*

Average over	Sample size	$\tilde{\gamma}_0$	$\tilde{\gamma}_1$	$\tilde{\gamma}_2$	$\tilde{\gamma}_3$	$\tilde{\gamma}_4$	Average adjusted R^2
				$\tilde{R}_{pt} = \tilde{\gamma}_{0t} + \tilde{\gamma}_{1t}\tilde{\beta}_{pt-1} + \tilde{e}_{pt}$			
January only	15	0.0383[b] (2.82)	0.0176 (0.84)				0.0917
Rest of the year	165	0.0129[b] (3.46)	−0.0034 (−0.72)				0.0394
All months	180	0.0150[b] (4.14)	−0.0017 (−0.36)				0.0438
			$\tilde{R}_{pt} = \tilde{\gamma}_{0t} + \tilde{\gamma}_{1t}\tilde{\beta}_{pt-1} + \tilde{\gamma}_{2t}\tilde{\beta}^2_{pt-1} + \tilde{\gamma}_{3t}S(e_{pt-1}) + \tilde{\gamma}_{4t}\log S_p + \tilde{u}_{pt}$			
January only	15	0.1216[b] (2.56)	0.0950 (0.87)	−0.0549 (−0.89)	0.3748[b] (2.34)	−0.0077[b] (−3.19)	0.1584
Rest of the year	165	−0.0093 (−0.53)	−0.0174 (−0.46)	0.0072 (0.31)	0.1157[b] (2.42)	0.0009 (1.11)	0.1660
All months	180	0.0016 (0.10)	−0.0081 (−0.23)	0.0020 (0.09)	0.1373[b] (2.98)	0.0002 (0.24)	0.1654

Note: [a]t-statistics are presented in parentheses.
[b]Significant at the 0.05 level.

Table 5 Average values of the estimated coefficients of the two- and five-parameter regression models (estimated with monthly data and based on the TSE 300 index) January, 1969–December, 1983[a]

Average over	Sample size	$\bar{\gamma}_0$	$\bar{\gamma}_1$	$\bar{\gamma}_2$	$\bar{\gamma}_3$	$\bar{\gamma}_4$	Average adjusted R^2
				$\bar{R}_{pt} = \gamma_{0t} + \gamma_{1t}\beta_{pt-1} + \bar{e}_{pt}$			
January only	15	0.0337[b] (2.59)	0.0243 (1.07)				0.1030
Rest of the year	165	0.0130[b] (3.79)	−0.0039 (−0.89)				0.0499
All months	180	0.0147[b] (4.41)	−0.0015 (−0.34)				0.0544
				$\bar{R}_{pt} = \gamma_{0t} + \gamma_{1t}\beta_{pt-1} + \bar{\gamma}_{2t}\beta^2_{pt-1} + \bar{\gamma}_{3t}S(\bar{e}_{pt-1}) + \bar{\gamma}_{4t}\log S_p + \bar{u}_{pt}$			
January only	15	−0.0248 (−0.34)	0.1573[b] (1.86)	−0.0757 (−1.74)	0.2406 (1.09)	−0.0013 (−0.33)	0.1948
Rest of the year	165	0.0177 (1.10)	−0.0395 (−1.58)	0.0216 (1.43)	−0.0189 (−0.44)	0.0006 (0.65)	0.1591
All months	180	0.0141 (0.89)	−0.0231 (−0.95)	0.0135 (0.93)	0.0028 (0.06)	0.0004 (0.48)	0.1621

Note: [a]t-statistics are presented in parentheses.
[b]Significant at the 0.05 level.

Contrary to the implications of the CAPM, $\bar{\gamma}_1$, is positive but insignificant in January, and has the wrong sign during the remaining months of the year. Needless to say, the Canadian data do not provide any support for a linear relationship between returns and systematic risk even when a value weighted index is used as the market proxy.

Tests based on the TSE 300 index

The TSE 300 index is widely used as a benchmark in evaluating investment performances of mutual funds, pension plan portfolios, and in obtaining estimates of the cost of equity capital for regulated and unregulated firms in Canada. Because of its widespread use as the proxy for the market portfolio we decided to replicate our tests of the asset pricing model once again using the TSE 300 index. The results, presented in table 5, should not provide any comfort for the aficionados of the CAPM. The averaged values of the coefficients that are estimated from the two-parameter regression model show quite clearly that $\bar{\gamma}_1$ is not significantly different from zero during the 180 months covered by the data. In fact, they have the wrong sign in all months except January. Their average value in January is much larger, but is not statistically significant at the conventional probability levels.

When we examine the coefficients obtained from the five-parameter regression model in table 5, we observe that there is a statistically significant linear relationship between returns and systematic risk. But the relationship holds only in the month of January. During the rest of the year, none of the risk measures exhibit large t-statistics that would distinguish their individual coefficients from zero. Somewhat surprisingly, even the 'small-firm effect' in January is not statistically significant when the TSE 300 index is used as the proxy for the Canadian market portfolio. In short, although the test results seem to change when the TSE 300 index is used, fifteen years of data do not provide support for a statistically significant linear relationship between returns and systematic risk.

Sensitivity of the monthly coefficients to the choice of market proxies

Our findings in tables 3, 4 and 5 show that the results of the tests on the asset pricing model are quite sensitive to the composition of the proxy used for the true market portfolio. To examine the sensitivity of the seasonals in the monthly coefficients to the choice of the proxy for the market portfolio in more detail, we estimated the following regression, for the entire period covered by the data, separately for each set of coefficients that are based on the three market proxies:

Table 6 *Sensitivity of the estimated seasonals in the monthly coefficients of the cross-sectional risk–return relationships to different proxies for the market portfolio*

Proxy market portfolio	Two-parameter regression model		Five-parameter regression model				
	$\bar{\gamma}_0$	$\bar{\gamma}_1$	$\bar{\gamma}_0$	$\bar{\gamma}_1$	$\bar{\gamma}_2$	$\bar{\gamma}_3$	$\bar{\gamma}_4$
Equally weighted index	None are significantly different from January	All except December are significantly smaller than January	February, March, September, December are significantly smaller than January	None are significantly different from January	Only February is significantly smaller than January	Only April is significantly smaller than January	February, March, June, September, December are significantly larger than January
Value weighted index	April, May, September are significantly smaller than January	None are significantly different from January	February, March, June, September, October, December are significantly smaller than January	Only April is significantly smaller than January	Only April is significantly larger than January	Only November is significantly smaller than January	February, March, April, June, August, September are significantly larger than January
TSE 300 index	March, April, May, June, July, September, October are significantly smaller than January	None are significantly different from January	May, July, August, September, December are significantly smaller than January	Only September is significantly larger than January	None are significantly different from January	None are significantly different from January	Only August is significantly larger than January

$$\bar{\gamma}_{jt} = \alpha_1 + \sum_{i=2}^{12} \alpha_i D_i + \bar{e}_{jt} \tag{5}$$

where $j = 0$ to 4 and D_2 through D_{12} are dummy variables representing the months of the year from February through December. In this equation, α_1 captures the average values of $\bar{\gamma}_{jt}$ in January and the coefficients for α_2 through α_{12} measure the difference between the means in January and the other months.

The results, summarized in table 6, quickly lead to the conclusion that there are significant seasonalities in the behavior of all of the coefficients, and that these seasonals are highly sensitive to the choice of the proxy used for the market portfolio. For example, in the case of $\bar{\gamma}_0$ obtained from the two-parameter regression model, its average values are virtually constant across all months when the estimates are based on an equally weighted index. When a value weighted index is used, however, the averages for April, May and September are significantly smaller than the average in January. With the TSE 300 index as the market proxy, on the other hand, March, April, June, July, September and October exhibit significantly smaller $\bar{\gamma}_0$ than January. In the case of $\bar{\gamma}_1$, its values in other months are not significantly different from January's $\bar{\gamma}_1$ when the TSE 300 index or the value weighted index are used. With the equally weighted market proxy, on the other hand, the values of $\bar{\gamma}_1$ for all months except December are significantly smaller than the $\bar{\gamma}_1$ in January.

The differences in the average values of the monthly coefficients obtained from the five-parameter regression model appear to be even more sensitive to the choice of the proxy for the market portfolio. For example, January's $\bar{\gamma}_1$ is not significantly different from the values of $\bar{\gamma}_1$ in other months when they are based on the equally weighted index. With the value weighted index, the $\bar{\gamma}_1$ for April is significantly smaller than the $\bar{\gamma}_1$ for January, while September's $\bar{\gamma}_1$ is the only one that is significantly smaller than January's when the TSE 300 index is used as the proxy for the market portfolio. The other three coefficients also exhibit non-stationarities across months and these non-stationarities appear to be highly sensitive to the choice of the index used for the Canadian market portfolio.

5 Summary and some concluding observations

We documented the January seasonal in Canadian stock returns and examined the implications of the anomalous behavior of stock returns on the tests of the capital asset pricing model in Canada. In contrast to the earlier results of Brennan and Schwartz (1982) and Calvet and Lefoll (1982 and 1983), our results for the period from January, 1969 through December, 1983 do not provide support for the major propositions of the asset pricing model. At the risk of oversimplifying our findings, we can conclude that the data do not show a statistically meaningful relationship between stock returns and systematic risk when the latter is estimated from the conventional market model, which assumes that betas are stationary over calendar months and over a period of years. Contrary to the implications of the CAPM, we found a somewhat more consistent association between returns and unsystematic risk. Lest the reader should wonder whether this perplexing result primarily reflects the effects of the anomalous January seasonal, we would point out the data in table 4. They show that even when the January returns are excluded from the analysis and firm size is explicitly recognized, residual risk is the only measure of risk that exhibits a significant positive association with stock returns.

Like Tinic and West (1986), our findings also indicate that the results of the CAPM tests are sensitive to the composition of the proxy used for the true market portfolio. Indeed, the Canadian results appear to be much more sensitive to the choice of the index used in the tests. Even the minor differences in the compositions of two value weighted market proxies, the TSE 300 index and the value weighted portfolio of all the stocks in our sample, had a significant impact on the results of our tests. These findings seem to provide substantial empirical support for Roll's (1977) theoretical arguments regarding the difficulties in conducting completely unambiguous tests of the CAPM without having a knowledge of the composition of the true wealth portfolio, which in theory contains all risky assets in proportion to their outstanding values.[4]

For the past score of years the CAPM has constituted the cornerstone of the modern theory of finance. The model continues to be used by both academics and practitioners in numerous financial applications that range from evaluating capital investment projects to estimating cost of equity capital for regulated utilities. At this stage, it seems legitimate to ask: where do these results leave us? Some researchers would answer this question by suggesting the use of the arbitrage pricing model (APT) of Ross (1976) as a superior alternative to the CAPM.[5] Before discarding the two-parameter asset pricing model, and jumping on the APT bandwagon, however, we must entertain the possibility that implementation of the APT may also be plagued by the anomalous behavior of securities returns over the calendar. Indeed, Tinic and West (1984, p. 573) have conjectured that 'Based on what we have found it is conceivable that the factors (in the APT) are priced only in January.' More recently, their conjecture received some empirical support in the work of Gultekin and Gultekin (1985), who reported that the APT explains the return–risk relationship in the US stock market only in the month of January.[6] Thus much more work remains before the CAPM can be discarded completely, and replaced by the APT.

Obviously, first we need to understand the economic causes of the January seasonal in the stock returns of firms with low market capitalizations. One possible explanation is that the risks of stocks – in particular the risk of small-firm stocks – may exhibit seasonals over the calendar. In fact, Rogalski and Tinic (1984) reported that the beta coefficients of small-firm stocks in the US experience a pronounced increase at the beginning of the calendar. They found that the betas of these stocks in January tend to be 30 to 60 percent larger than their average betas in other months depending on the method used in estimating the betas. All of our and others' tests of the CAPM, however, are built on the assumption that the beta coefficients remain unchanged over calendar months.[7] If betas do indeed change in January, the testing methodologies that ignore these changes are bound to produce erroneous conclusions. For example, the statistically significant large risk premium associated with systematic risk in January (in the first row of table 3) disappears (in the first rows of tables 4 and 5) when the equally weighted index is replaced by a value weighted index as the proxy for the market portfolio. It is conceivable that this finding and some of the other results, e.g. the statistically significant relationship between stock returns and residual risk or firm size, may turn out to be merely the artifacts of test methodologies that ignore potential seasonalities in systematic risk.

In any event, until we discover the fundamental economic forces that shape the anomalous behavior of stock returns in Canada, we have to rely on the test results of the kind described in this paper and view the existing empirical support for the CAPM with more than a modicum of skepticism.

Notes

* We are indebted to Berry Hsu for his assistance with the computations. Financial support of the College of Business Administration Foundation at the University of Texas for Tinic is gratefully acknowledged.

1 See the papers in the special issue 'Symposium on Size and Stock Returns, and Other Empirical Regularities,' *Journal of Financial Economics*, 12 (June 1983) and Berges *et al.* (1984), Gultekin and Gultekin (1983), Roll (1983), Reinganum (1983) and Lakonishok and Smidt (1984).

2 The tests involved in determining the significance of the various regression coefficients are t-tests which require that $\bar{\gamma}_j$ ($j = 0,2,\ldots,4$) follow a Gaussian distribution. Fama and MacBeth (1973, p. 624) and Officer (1971) have claimed that the distribution of *monthly* stock returns is symmetric stable. The distribution of the means of monthly $\bar{\gamma}_{jt}$ (regression coefficients from the two- or five-parameter model) should be symmetric but fat-tailed. Ratcliffe (1968, p. 46) has demonstrated that moderate kurtosis in the distributions of $\bar{\gamma}_{jt}$ does not have an effect on the probability levels associated with calculated t-statistics when the sample size exceeds fifteen.

Unless $\bar{\gamma}_j$ exhibit extremely skewed distributions (e.g. an exponential distribution) the approximate increase in the calculated t-values at any given probability level is relatively small even in samples as small as fifteen (see Ratcliffe, 1968, p. 47). Since $\bar{\gamma}_{jt}$ in each month are linear combinations of twenty portfolio returns, their distributions would be less skewed than the individual residuals. When the distributions of $\bar{\gamma}_j$ are only

Stock return seasonality 145

moderately skewed, the assumption of normality for $\bar{\gamma}_j$ would introduce very small bias to the probability values of the calculated t-statistics even in samples as small as fifteen. For example, Ratcliffe (1968, p. 47) found that when the distribution is moderately skewed (e.g. skewed bell-shaped) the calculated t-statistic of 2.75 from a sample of fifteen observations corresponds to the same probability level as the t-value of 2.12 when the distribution is exactly normal.

But since the t-test is fairly robust to even extreme skewness for sample sizes over eighty, this caveat is only relevant to the results of the analyses for the month of January.

3 It is important to note that the 5 percent significance levels for the t-tests in tables 3, 4 and 5 are based on the following null and alternative hypotheses for examining the individual regression coefficients:

$$H_0: E(\bar{\gamma}_{0t}) = 0 \qquad H_A: E(\bar{\gamma}_{0t}) > 0$$
$$E(\bar{\gamma}_{1t}) = 0 \qquad E(\bar{\gamma}_{1t}) > 0$$
$$E(\bar{\gamma}_{2t}) = 0 \qquad E(\bar{\gamma}_{2t}) \neq 0$$
$$E(\bar{\gamma}_{3t}) = 0 \qquad E(\bar{\gamma}_{3t}) > 0$$
$$E(\bar{\gamma}_{4t}) = 0 \qquad E(\bar{\gamma}_{4t}) < 0$$

The CAPM posits that $E(\bar{\gamma}_{0t})$ and $E(\bar{\gamma}_{1t})$ should be positive. While there is no reason to expect $E(\bar{\gamma}_{2t})$ to be either positive or negative, the signs of the alternative hypotheses for $E(\bar{\gamma}_{3t})$ and $E(\bar{\gamma}_{4t})$ are based on previous findings (e.g. see Miller and Scholes, 1972; Keim, 1983 respectively).

Since the individual confidence intervals for $E(\bar{\gamma}_{jt})$ are not necessarily independent, the probability that all four or five confidence intervals are exactly 95 percent may not be true simultaneously. A rigorous treatment of simultaneous confidence intervals, permitting inferences on all linear combinations of the regression coefficients that are at the 95 percent level, was not made.

4 Roll (1977) claimed that statistically significant coefficients for such non-linearities as β_{pt-1}^2 and $S(e_{pt-1})$ are consistent with the explanation that the market proxy was not exactly mean-variance efficient during the test period.

5 For example, see Roll and Ross (1983).

6 Gultekin and Gultekin reported that when the returns for January and December are excluded from their analysis, the risk premia vector was virtually null (1985, p. 9).

7 The major assumptions underlying the tests used by Fama and MacBeth (1973), Gibbons (1982) and Stambaugh (1982) are identical. They all require that the monthly returns of common stocks follow a multivariate normal distribution and the parameters of the distribution remain unchanged over the time interval used in estimating the betas. Fama (1976) concluded that monthly returns of common stocks are approximately normal, and Fama and MacBeth (1973) assumed that the parameters of the distribution remain constant over five-to-eight years. Similarly, Stambaugh (1982) reported that the stationarity assumption holds well over the six-year period used in his study. However, none of these studies examined the seasonalities in β over calendar months. Rogalksi and Tinic (1984) presented evidence that betas exhibit seasonals over calendar months. The betas of small firms, in particular, change dramatically over calendar months.

References

Banz, R. (1981) 'The Relationship between Return and Market Value of Common Stocks', *Journal of Financial Economics*, 9, 3–18.
Berges, A., McConnell, J. and Schlarbaum, G. (1984) 'The Turn-of-the-year in Canada', *Journal of Finance*, 39, 185–92.
Black, F. (1972) 'Capital Market Equilibrium with Restricted Borrowing', *Journal of Business*, 45, 444–54.
Brennan, M. and Schwartz, E. (1982) 'Canadian Estimates of the Capital Asset Pricing Model', unpublished report, Corporate Finance Division, Department of Finance, Ottawa, Canada.
Calvet, A. and Lefoll, J. (1982) 'Le Medaf avec ou sans Inflation et les Marches Financiers Canadiens', Analyse Financière 4E trimestre.

Calvet, A. and Lefoll, J. (1983) 'Acquisition Activity on Canadian Capital Markets', unpublished report, Corporate Finance Division, Department of Finance.

Fama, E. (1976) *Foundations of Finance*, New York: Basic Books.

Fama, E. and MacBeth, J. (1973) 'Risk, Return, and Equilibrium: Empirical Tests', *Journal of Political Economy*, 71, 607–36.

Gibbons, M. (1982) 'Multivariate Tests of Financial Models: A New Approach', *Journal of Financial Economics*, 10, 3–27.

Gultekin, M. and Gultekin, B. (1983) 'Stock Market Seasonality: International Evidence', *Journal of Financial Economics*, 12, 469–81.

Gultekin, M. and Gultekin, B. (1985) 'Stock Return Anomalies and the Asset Pricing Tests', unpublished working paper, University of Pennsylvania.

Keim, D. (1983) 'Size Related Anomalies and Stock Return Seasonality: Further Empirical Evidence', *Journal of Financial Economics*, 12, 12–32.

Lakonishok, J. and Smidt, S. (1984) 'Volume, Price, and Rate of Return for Active and Inactive Stocks with Applications to Turn-of-the-year Behavior', *Journal of Financial Economics*, 13, 435–55.

Miller, M. and Scholes, M. (1972) 'Rates of Return in Relation to Risk: A Re-examination of Some Recent Findings.' In M.C. Jensen, ed. *Studies in the Theory of Capital Markets*, New York: Praeger Publishers, pp. 47–78.

Officer, R. (1971) 'A Time Series Examination of the Market Factor of the New York Stock Exchange', Ph.D. dissertation, University of Chicago.

Ratcliffe, J. (1968) 'The Effects on the *t* distribution of non-normality in the Sampled Populations', *Applied Statistics*, 17, 1, 42–8.

Reinganum, M. (1983) 'The Anomalous Stock Market Behavior of Small Firms in January: Empirical Tests for Tax-loss Selling Effects', *Journal of Financial Economics*, 12, 89–104.

Rogalski, R. and Tinic, S. (1984) 'The January Size Effect: Anomaly or Risk Mismeasurement?', unpublished working paper, Dartmouth College.

Roll, R. (1977) 'A Critique of the Asset Pricing Theory's Tests', *Journal of Financial Economics*, 4, 129–76.

Roll, R. (1983) 'Vas ist das? The Turn of the Year Effect and the Return Premium of Small Firms', *Journal of Portfolio Management*, 9, Winter, 18–28.

Roll, R. and Ross, S. (1983) 'Regulation, the Capital Asset Pricing Model, and the Arbitrage Pricing Theory', *Public Utilities Fortnightly*, May, 22–8.

Ross, S. (1976) 'The Arbitrage Theory of Capital Asset Pricing', *Journal of Economic Theory*, 343–62.

Rozeff, M. and Kinney, W. (1976) 'Capital Market Seasonality: The Case of Stock Returns', *Journal of Financial Economics*, 3, 379–402.

Schwert, W. (1983) 'Size and Stock Returns, and Other Empirical Regularities', *Journal of Financial Economics*, 12, 3–12.

Sharpe, W. (1964) 'Capital Asset Prices: A Theory of Market Equilibrium under Conditions of Risk', *Journal of Finance*, 19, 425–42.

Stambaugh, R. (1982) 'On The Exclusion of Assets from Tests of the Two-parameter Model', *Journal of Financial Economics*, 10, 237–68.

Tinic, S. and West, R. (1984) 'Risk and Return: January vs. the Rest of the Year', *Journal of Financial Economics*, 13, 561–74.

Tinic, S. and West, R. (1986) 'Risk, Return, and Equilibrium: A Revisit', *Journal of Political Economy*, 94, 126–47.

Tinic, S., Barone-Adesi, G. and West, R. (1987) 'Seasonality in Canadian Stock Prices: A Test of the "Tax-loss-selling" Hypothesis', *Journal of Financial and Quantitative Analysis*, 22, 1.

11   Two tests of the tax-loss selling hypothesis

*WILLEM MAX VAN DEN BERGH, ROBERTO E.
WESSELS and ROEL T. WIJMENGA**

1 Introduction

The turn-of-the-year effect, also known as the January effect, has been
extensively studied in the literature. See for a review, Van den Bergh and
Wessels (1985). In this chapter we examine the relation between a stock's
turn-of-the-year effect and that stock's previous return. Several
researchers have documented a negative relation between these two
returns. This result is generally interpreted as providing support for the
hypothesis that the January effect is caused by tax-loss selling, which
depresses stock prices – temporarily – at the end of the fiscal year. Once
selling pressure abates, prices rebound to their 'normal' level. The
rebound is what is recorded as the turn-of-the-year effect.

A problem with tests of this kind is that we do not know what the
relevant holding period is for an investor selling stock in December for
tax reasons. Ideally, we would want to know for each investor selling at
the end of the year, the date on which the stock was acquired and weigh
each holding period with a function of the number of investors for which
this holding period applies. Under the tax-loss selling hypothesis, the
relation between a stock's January effect and that stock's previous return
will be stronger as this weight increases. Unfortunately, no such data are
available.

In this paper, we try to deal with this problem by introducing the
concept of all possible holding periods. Using weekly data, we calculate
the return on a portfolio of stocks to a hypothetical stockholder who held
the portfolio for the one-week period prior to the turn-of-the-year, the
two-week period, etc. We then analyse the relation between these
returns and the subsequent January effect.

2 Measuring the turn-of-the-year effect

The data used in our tests are described in the appendix. The tests are conducted using unexpected January returns rather than actual or raw returns. These returns are derived as the prediction errors from the following regression model:

$$R_{it} = \alpha_i + \beta_i R_{mt} + \theta_{it} \qquad [i = 1,(max)145] \tag{1}$$

where

R_{it} = the return on the ith stock in period t;
R_{mt} = the return on an index (m) portfolio in period t;
α_i, β_i = regression coefficients;
θ_{it} = a disturbance term satisfying the usual assumptions.

The advantage of using unexpected, rather than actual returns are twofold. First, results can be pooled over time. Second, stocks which have a negative return in January might still be subject to a January effect through tax-loss selling, namely when the stock's price decline is less than expected. One would not be able to take this into account if actual returns are used.

In our tests, we use two measures of unexpected returns. The reason for doing this is that first, the values of β need not be stable within the year (possible seasonality of risk) and second, the return on the index portfolio during the turn of the year, is contaminated by the very effect we are trying to isolate. As a result the return on the index portfolio during the turn of year cannot be used to generate predictions of unexpected returns for individual stocks during that same interval of time.

In order to gauge the sensitivity of our results to these problems the parameters of equation (1) were estimated twice: including and excluding the contaminated periods. First, we estimated the equation on a year by year basis, including the contaminated period and used the contaminated return on the index portfolio to generate the predictions. Then, we re-estimated the equation, excluding the contaminated periods, and used a 'clean' return on the index portfolio to generate a second set of predicted returns. The 'clean' index is defined as a linear interpolation, over the turn of the year, of the return on the index.

3 Description of the tests

Our first test seeks to identify the pattern of holding periods for which the turn-of-the-year effect is most marked. If tax-loss selling takes place, one would expect to find a distribution of holding periods for which the January effect is strongest. For instance, one could imagine finding that a six-month holding period has the strongest effect, with a five- and seven-month period having the same qualitative effect but of reduced magnitude. This would imply that a majority of investors selling in December have, on average, held their stocks for a six-month period.

For this test, previous returns are measured over all possible holding periods using weekly returns. This is done as follows. Using weekly data we calculated the previous returns for all the stocks in the sample taking the end of the second week of December as the end date and extending our holding period backwards by one week at a time until the third week of the previous January was reached. The five weeks surrounding the turn of the year were thus deleted. In this manner, forty-six holding periods of increasing length are defined. Stocks can then be allocated to forty-seven portfolios depending on the number of holding periods when the stock experienced a negative return during the previous year. In the first portfolio we include those stocks which had negative previous returns for the one-week holding period prior to the end of the year. In the second portfolio we include stocks with negative returns for a two-week holding period prior to the end of the year. In the forty-seventh portfolio we include the stocks not included in any of the other portfolios. This method of allocating stocks to portfolios implies that each stock in the sample can end up being allocated to more than one portfolio.

These portfolios, finally, were used to define a vector of dummy variables, each of which represents the length of a possible holding period during which the stocks in the portfolio experienced a negative previous return. In equation form, the first test is a regression of unexpected turn-of-the-year returns on dummy variables:

$$\theta_{it} = \phi_0 + \phi(k)H(k,i)_t + e_{it} \qquad [k = 1,46] \qquad (2)$$

where

> θ_{it} = the prediction error of the ith stock during the first week of January;
> $H(k,i)$ = a dummy variable which equals 1 if the ith stock had a negative previous return during k-week holding period, and is zero otherwise;
> ϕ = regression coefficients;
> e_{it} = a disturbance term satisfying the usual assumptions.

In this regression, the intercept measures the mean of the turn-of-the-year effect for stocks with no negative previous returns. The estimated ϕ coefficients measure the differential impact on the January return to an investor who selects stocks on the basis of the length of the period during which the stock experienced a negative return prior to the end of the year. The total expected return of selecting stocks on the basis of the length of a period of negative previous returns, is given by the sum of the intercept and the $\phi(k)$ coefficient for that period.

Unless investors carry their losses randomly before selling in December, we would expect a plot of the $\phi(k)$ coefficients to reflect the relative weights attached by investors to the different holding periods when deciding whether or not to realize their losses at the end of the year. By looking at the pattern of coefficients, we could infer which holding periods are most closely associated with the January effect.

If the distribution is flat this would suggest that there is no particular holding period for which the implications of the TLS hypothesis hold. However, this finding does not imply a rejection of the hypothesis: it could very well be that the flat pattern is caused by the fact that stocks held by investors at the end of the year were acquired uniformly during the year.

But then, if the TLS hypothesis is correct, the number of investors for which a stock is a tax-loss selling candidate, should increase as a function of the *number* of holding periods during which the stock experienced a negative return. The more holding periods over which the stock's return was negative, the more likely it is – under the TLS hypothesis – that the stocks will be sold at the end of the year for tax purposes. This suggests conducting a test based on a regression of the following form:

$$\theta_{it} = \delta_0 + \delta(k)D(k,i)_t + e_{it} \qquad [k = 0,45] \qquad (3)$$

where

θ_{it} = the prediction error of the ith stock during the first week of January;

$D(k,i)$ = a dummy variable which equals 1 when the previous return over a number of k weeks was negative and zero otherwise;

δ = regression coefficients;

e_{it} = a disturbance term satisfying the usual assumptions.

Here, the intercept term measures the effect of the *largest* number of holding periods with a negative return.

4 Results

The results of the tests are presented in figure form. The regression results and summary statistics are available on request. In these figures, we have plotted the effects captured by the dummy variables, i.e. the sum of the intercept and the estimated regression coefficient of each dummy. There are two plots for each test, i.e. figures 1(a) and (b) and figures 2(a) and (b), corresponding to the two measures of unexpected January returns used in the regressions.

In the first test we are trying to identify a distribution of holding periods which is consistent with tax-loss selling. As can be seen from the

(a) Index and beta contaminated

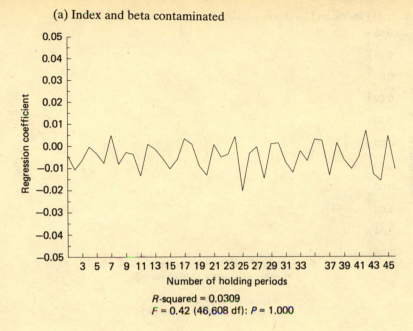

R-squared = 0.0309
F = 0.42 (46,608 df): P = 1.000

(b) Index and beta clean

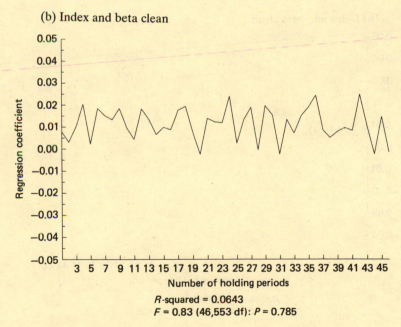

R-squared = 0.0643
F = 0.83 (46,553 df): P = 0.785

Figure 1   Regression results for equation 2

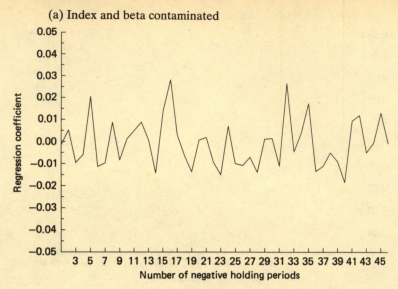

(a) Index and beta contaminated

R-squared = 0.0472
F = 0.65 (46,608 df): P = 0.962

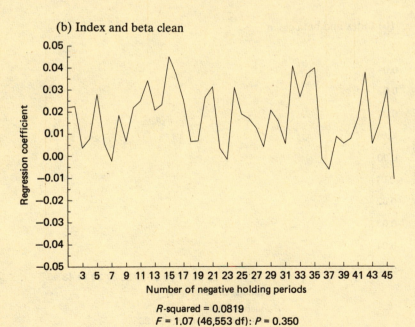

(b) Index and beta clean

R-squared = 0.0819
F = 1.07 (46,553 df): P = 0.350

Figure 2   Regression results for equation 3

plots (see figures 1(a) and (b)), no such holding period is revealed by the data. This is the case for both our measures of unexpected returns.

However, it is noteworthy that in the regression which uses uncontaminated prediction errors as the dependent variable, the intercept term is positive and statistically significant.

It should be noted though, that in the regression, the length of the period of previous negative returns has no explanatory power. This means that we are not able to replicate the results of previous studies which document a strong negative relation between a stock's (negative) previous return and its January return, even though there is a marked January seasonal in our sample data.

Nevertheless, the cause for this result could be traced to the uniform distribution of the weights attached to the holding periods. In that case, however, the second test should indicate that the more periods over which a stock experienced negative previous returns, the more likely it becomes that the stock will have been sold for tax reasons. In figures 2(a) and (b) the estimated effects are given in ascending order, the first data point corresponding to the effect of the portfolio of stocks that had no negative previous returns; the last data point corresponding to the portfolio of stocks which experienced losses in all forty-six holding periods. Thus, if the hypothesis is not to be rejected, the effects should be in descending order of magnitude, the largest negative effect shown last.

As visual inspection clearly shows, that is not the case for our sample data. Thus the results of the second test confirm our previous findings: a rejection of the tax-loss selling hypothesis.

Notes

* This is a revised version of the paper presented at the symposium on Capital Market Regularities held at EIASM, Brussels, December 5–7, 1985. We wish to thank Hersh Shefrin and the participants in the symposium for their comments.

Data appendix

In this appendix we describe the data used in our tests. For the pertinent institutional background, we refer the reader to our earlier paper, Van den Bergh and Wessels (1985). The stocks in our sample were selected from a comprehensive file of stocks listed on the Amsterdam Stock Exchange during the period January 1, 1978 up to December 31, 1983. This master file covers circa 95 per cent of the market value (excluding mutual funds) of the stocks traded on the exchange. The file lists a maximum of 145 stocks and includes stocks which were either delisted or newly listed during the sample period. Thus, the data are not subject to survivorship bias.

From this file, we selected stocks for our tests as follows. For each January in the sample, we checked if the ith stock had been listed during the whole previous year. If so, it was added to our sample. If not, it was dropped.

We then calculated weekly returns for each stock, using the closing price on Wednesday as our point of reference. If no trade took place on Wednesday (e.g. if the exchange was closed), the nearest day following that Wednesday was used.

as our point of reference. If no trade took place on Wednesday (e.g. if the exchange was closed), the nearest day following that Wednesday was used.

Finally, the return on the index (R_m) was calculated, on a week-by-week basis, as the equally weighted return on all the stocks in the sample during that period.

Reference

Van den Bergh, W.M. and Wessels, R.E. (1985) 'Stock Market Seasonalities and Taxes: An Examination of the Tax-Loss Selling Hypothesis', *Journal of Business Finance and Accounting*, 12, 515–30.

12 Size related anomalies and trading activity of UK institutional investors

MARIO LEVIS

1 Introduction

The increasing ownership of quoted companies by financial institutions during the last two decades has been one of the most significant features of the financial markets on both sides of the Atlantic. Moreover, the evidence from surveys of institutional portfolio holdings suggests a marked concentration on larger companies. The implications of these developments in general and the effect of institutional investment strategies on share prices in particular has attracted considerable attention by both academics and governmental departments, but still remains a matter of considerable controversy. The recent evidence on the small firm effect provides an additional and largely unexplored dimension to the role played by institutional investors in determining share prices. Given the well-documented preference for larger firms and the substantial empirical support for the market impact hypothesis, it is conceivable that the small size premium, observed in all main national stock exchanges, is directly associated with the pattern of institutional trading. Buying/selling imbalances may have a significant effect on the long-term return of the traded securities.

The purpose of this chapter is to examine the implications of institutional trading on the share prices of various market size portfolios. Besides being the first study to look explicitly at institutional activity in relation to company size, the 'transfer functions' methodology used in this analysis is a considerable improvement over previous studies, as it allows an in-depth exploration of the direction and nature of the relationships under consideration. The study also provides interesting insight on the differences in trading behaviour between the four types of institutional investors considered in this paper. Section 2 provides a review of the relevant literature while section 3 describes the adopted methodology; sections 4, 5 and 6 present the empirical evidence. Finally, section 7 outlines the main conclusions of the study.

2 Institutional activity and share prices

The controversy regarding the institutional shareholders' investment behaviour has evolved around two main interrelated issues: first, whether institutional investors have any ability to predict or influence subsequent price changes or are influenced by price movements; second, whether institutional activity stabilizes or induces further instability into the market.

The study of Friend *et al.* (1970) for the US market concludes that the bulk of the evidence favours the market impact hypothesis rather than the predictive hypothesis. The *Institutional Investor Study* (Securities and Exchange Commission, 1971) has also provided some evidence of a systematic positive relationship between the net trading imbalance, in a given month, and the percentage price change in that month; net buying was associated with an average price increase and net selling with an average price decline. Kraus and Stoll's (1972a, 1972b) results suggest not only a significant effect on share prices as a result of institutional trading pressure, but also indicate that when parallel trading occurs it tends to be price aggressive rather than price responsive. Klemkosky's (1977) findings are also consistent with the market impact hypothesis, but in addition provide some evidence of the possibility of market leadership on the part of certain institutions. Dobbins and Witt (1980) also conclude that 'the equity activities of financial institutions do influence the general level of prices in the UK stock market' (p. 272). However, as their study only focuses on the contemporaneous relationship between various aspects of institutional activity and market index changes the conclusions about the market impact hypothesis have to be treated with caution.

The market stabilization hypothesis refers to the ability of institutional investors to iron out the peaks or troughs in market behaviour. Dobbins and Greenwood (1975) hypothesize that 'the most obvious way in which institutions could iron out market extremes would be by disposing of shares at the peaks and being net purchasers at market troughs' (p. 263). They test the hypothesis by examining the correlations between the market index and net acquisitions. Their empirical evidence as a whole does not support the hypothesis. On the issue of whether institutional activity induces further volatility on the stock market, the *Institutional Investor Study* (SEC, 1971) is adamant that institutional trading has not impaired price stability in the US market. Moreover, Reilly and Wright (1984) assert that not only does institutional trading not increase stock price volatility but on the contrary the evidence indicates that greater institutional trading in an individual stock or in stocks in general is associated with a lower level of stock price volatility. Essentially similar results have been obtained by Lee and Ward (1980) and Brealey *et al.*

(1978) for the UK market. On the other hand, the US Senate (1974) took the view that the investment decisions of bank trust departments, insurance companies and pension funds can indeed alter the stability of the market and individual companies.

Recent empirical evidence first by Banz (1981) and Reinganum (1981) for the US market, Brown *et al.* (1983) for the Australian market, Berges *et al.* (1984) for the Canadian stock exchange, Kato and Schallheim (1985) for the Japanese market and Levis (1985) for the London Stock Exchange suggests distinct differences in the return distributions of large and small companies. In an attempt to understand the sources of this apparent 'anomaly' a number of possible explanations have been suggested. Roll (1981), for example, conjectures that the small firm premium might be attributed to the misestimation of the risk characteristics of smaller firms, while Blume and Stambaugh (1983) questioned the methodology used for estimating the actual rates of return. Stoll and Whaley (1983) and Schultz (1983), on the other hand, present evidence indicating that the size effect may be substantially reduced when the higher transaction costs involved in trading with smaller firms are taken into account. The explanation, however, that attracted most attention relates to the observed seasonal pattern of the small size premium. The concentration of abnormal returns for small companies on one single month, January, gave rise to the tax loss selling (TLS) hypothesis. While, however, Reinganum (1983), Roll (1983a) and Schultz (1985) present evidence in support of the TLS hypothesis, the results of Givoly and Ovadia (1983) and Lakonishok and Smidt (1984) cast doubts on the efficacy of the hypothesis to account for the entire January effect. Even more interesting is probably the evidence from other countries with different tax year-ends and/or different tax regimes. The findings of Brown *et al.* (1983) for Australia, Berges *et al.* (1984) and Tinic *et al.* (1984) for Canada and van den Bergh and Wessels (1985) for The Netherlands suggest that the TLS hypothesis, on its own, is not a sufficient explanation for the small size effect. Moreover, Constantinides (1984), on a theoretical level, has shown that rational investors would realize losses as they occur during the year, rather than wait till the end of the year; thus, studies that provide empirical support for tax induced behaviour, towards the tax year-end, should also be indicative of some sort of market inefficiency.

The seasonal pattern of the small firm premium could also be related to possible seasonal liquidity constraints evident in capital markets. For example, significant periodic infusions of funds into the market may have an impact on share prices. Kato and Schallheim (1985), for example, provide evidence suggesting that the January and June seasonals observed in the Japanese market may be related to the traditional bonuses paid at the end of December and June. The findings of Rozeff (1985) and Ariel (see chapter 8) could also be interpreted as evidence in support of the liquidity hypothesis.

Parallel trading by institutional investors is another source of liquidity constraints with potential effects on share prices. The impact may be temporary if a seasonal pattern to such activity is evident or longer lasting depending on the form, intensity and information content of institutional behaviour as well as the efficiency of the capital market. The information content dimension, for example, has been explored by Arbel and Strebel (1983) who argue that the small size effect is just a special case of the 'neglect effect'. They provide evidence for the US market suggesting that firms that were relatively neglected by security analysts exhibited superior market performance compared with those that were intensively researched. They reason that 'intensive analyst coverage raises stock prices and the corresponding returns to investors are lower' (Arbel and Strebel, 1983, p. 41). On the issue of form and intensity of parallel trading, it is interesting to note that careful examination of Klemkosky's (1977) findings indicates that the impact of parallel trading on share prices is not necessarily symmetrical; while the gains caused by large net buying imbalances were effectively eliminated in the subsequent twelve months, negative abnormal returns persisted during and long after net selling imbalances.

3 Methodology

The rates of return data is drawn from the London Share Price Database (LSPD) monthly returns file. The sample of firms used in this study changes yearly. To qualify for inclusion in a given calendar year a firm need only possess data on market capitalization at the beginning of the year and a valid rate of return for January. Thus, firms included in the sample for, say, 1966 are selected at the beginning of this year and retained in the sample, for this particular year, for as long as they have valid rates of return. This process is repeated for each year, thus no survival requirements are imposed on the sample. The number of firms included in the sample ranges from around 1500 in the mid-sixties to 2400 in the mid-seventies.[1] Portfolios are created by ranking all firms in the sample according to their market value at the beginning of each year and placing them in one of the ten portfolios depending on their relative market position. Firms in the bottom ten percent of this ranking comprise the smallest portfolio, while the top ten percent comprise the largest portfolio. The monthly rates of return of firms within each portfolio are added with equal weights to form the monthly return of the portfolio. For each calendar year under consideration the ranking and portfolio process is repeated. In this study the process is repeated seventeen times to cover the period January 1966 to December 1982.

The data on institutional activity is only available on a quarterly basis. Thus, the monthly series of returns, for each of the ten portfolios, are converted to quarterly rates of return. The data for institutional trading is derived from *Financial Statistics* and covers the activities of unit trusts, investment trusts, insurance companies and pension funds.[2]

For the purpose of this study the important variable is the quarterly net acquisitions over turnover of UK ordinary shares by financial institutions, i.e. (purchases−sales) over (purchases+sales). Thus, as a starting model of the analysis, the Dobbins and Witt (1980) specification is adopted:

$$R_t = b(A_t) + u_t \qquad (1)$$

where:

R_t = quarterly rates of return;
A_t = ratio of quarterly changes in net acquisitions over turnover.

According to Dobbins and Witt a positive and significant coefficient supports the hypothesis that financial institutions influence share prices. However, as this is not the only plausible specification, the following alternative model is also investigated:

$$A_t = b(R_t) + e_t \qquad (2)$$

Analysis of these models is based on transfer function methodology. Box and Jenkins (1970) propose a rich set of transfer functions models for time series data. In a very general form, for example, specification (1) can be written as the following discrete linear process:

$$R_t = v_0 A_t + v_1 A_{t-1} + v_2 A_{t-2} + \ldots + u_t \qquad (3)$$

or using the backshift operator B:

$$R_t = v(B)A_t + u_t \qquad (4)$$

The polynomial operator $v(B)$ represents the transfer function relating rates of return to institutional net acquisitions and it summarizes the dynamic structure of the effect transferred from the net acquisition sequence to the returns sequence. To find the best model of $v(B)$, the transfer function technique utilizes the fact that any distributed lag polynomial can be approximated as a ratio of two polynomials of lower order. The general form of the transfer function can be written as:

$$v(B) = \frac{\omega(B)}{\delta(B)} B^b \qquad (5)$$

$\omega(B)$ = an sth order polynomial operator;
$\delta(B)$ = an rth order polynomial operator;

Table 1 *Mean quarterly returns, standard deviations, OLS beta estimates, autocorrelations and partials for the ten market value portfolios over the period 1966 to 1982*

	Average rate of return[a]	Standard deviation	OLS beta	Autocorrelations and partials for the quarterly returns[b]								$P-B$[c]
				ρ1	ρ2	ρ3	ρ4	ρ5	ρ8	ρ9	ρ10	
Smallest	3.901 (3.30)	9.66	0.509 (6.98)	0.357 / 0.357	0.308 / 0.206	0.201 / 0.049	−0.031 / −0.121	−0.074 / −0.131	−0.247 / −0.182	−0.184 / −0.031	−0.357 / −0.236	62.4
2	3.352 (2.60)	10.57	0.663 (10.03)	0.308 / 0.308	0.204 / 0.121	0.219 / 0.141	−0.008 / −0.142	−0.113 / −0.145	−0.186 / −0.101	−0.148 / −0.088	−0.313 / −0.233	47.8
3	3.365 (2.52)	10.95	0.742 (12.57)	0.286 / 0.286	0.163 / 0.089	0.172 / 0.114	−0.088 / −0.193	−0.190 / −0.172	−0.186 / −0.087	−0.128 / −0.082	−0.248 / −0.215	37.6
4	3.029 (2.22)	11.16	0.782 (14.29)	0.266 / 0.266	0.150 / 0.086	0.159 / 0.108	−0.073 / −0.161	−0.192 / −0.185	−0.121 / −0.036	−0.091 / −0.085	−0.245 / −0.240	28.5
5	2.949 (1.95)	12.38	0.911 (18.19)	0.233 / 0.233	0.089 / 0.036	0.155 / 0.134	−0.094 / −0.172	−0.199 / −0.170	−0.077 / 0.000	−0.054 / −0.067	−0.194 / −0.220	27.3
6	2.864 (1.84)	12.70	0.943 (19.37)	0.233 / 0.223	0.070 / 0.021	0.148 / 0.135	−0.080 / −0.151	−0.204 / −0.177	−0.100 / −0.026	−0.045 / −0.055	−0.175 / −0.194	24.6
7	2.889 (1.78)	13.25	1.013 (24.56)	0.180 / 0.180	0.059 / 0.038	0.101 / 0.085	−0.076 / −0.115	−0.237 / −0.224	−0.062 / −0.018	−0.056 / −0.082	−0.162 / −0.218	24.2
8	2.911 (1.80)	13.25	1.017 (25.67)	0.176 / 0.176	0.052 / 0.022	0.077 / 0.066	−0.077 / −0.107	−0.247 / −0.231	−0.029 / 0.014	−0.037 / −0.070	−0.148 / −0.210	25.6
9	2.978 (1.83)	13.29	1.045 (37.41)	0.144 / 0.144	0.010 / −0.011	0.083 / 0.085	−0.130 / −0.159	−0.273 / −0.241	−0.015 / 0.022	−0.010 / −0.085	−0.135 / −0.212	30.8
Largest	2.497 (1.61)	12.68	1.007 (48.19)	0.153 / 0.153	−0.003 / −0.027	0.070 / 0.076	−0.133 / −0.161	−0.251 / −0.212	−0.007 / 0.010	0.000 / −0.066	−0.144 / −0.214	31.0
FTA	3.266 (2.12)	12.43		0.159 / 0.159	0.022 / −0.003	0.085 / 0.084	−0.192 / −0.226	−0.250 / −0.197	−0.065 / −0.084	0.010 / −0.064	−0.132 / −0.224	34.5
(S−L)	1.403 (1.22)	9.40		0.220 / 0.220	−0.002 / −0.053	0.047 / 0.063	−0.089 / −0.121	−0.150 / −0.105	0.009 / −0.005	−0.081 / −0.130	−0.047 / −0.009	30.5

Notes: [a]Mean quarterly returns are calculated using sixty-seven observations; *t*-statistics in parenthesis.
[b]The standard error of these autocorrelations and partials is approximately 0.12.

B^b = a bth order 'dead time' of periods before any effect is discernible.

Here (r,s,b) are integers greater than or equal to zero. Basically $\omega(B)$ describes the magnitude of the more immediate effects of net acquisitions, $\delta(B)$ describes the duration and pattern of their decay. The choice of the model is based entirely on empirical grounds.

4 Average return, risk and autocorrelations

Table 1 provides summary statistics about various attributes for each of the ten market-value portfolios, the difference return series between the two extreme portfolios $(S-L)$ and the FTA value weighted index, over the period 1966 to 1982. The market value ranking procedure produced some interesting results.

First, the quarterly average rates of return for the ten portfolios provide some evidence of a size effect on the London Stock Exchange. The smallest portfolio seems to outperform its largest counterpart by about 6 per cent per annum. The t-statistics indicate that the mean average returns, for all but portfolios 7, 8 and the largest, are statistically significant. It is worth noticing that while the return for the largest portfolio is roughly the same as the return of equivalent US portfolios over similar periods, the lowest decile of British firms appears to earn, according to Reinganum's (1983) findings based on daily data, only half the return of its US equivalent. On the other hand, the premium observed in this study is very similar to the premia reported by Blume and Stambaugh (1983) and Roll (1983b) using a 'buy-and-hold' method for estimating portfolio returns.[3]

Second, contrary to conventional wisdom, smaller companies in our study appear to be less risky than the larger ones both in terms of total and systematic risk. The standard deviations of quarterly returns and OLS betas and portfolio size is reported for the US market by Keim (1983) and Reinganum (1982). However, Scholes and Williams (1977) and Dimson (1979) have demonstrated that in the case of infrequently traded shares, as small companies are likely to be, the last transaction in the month may well have taken place sometime beforehand; but as this study is based on quarterly data, thin trading is unlikely to be of such magnitude as to induce a reversal in the order of beta rankings. While the extent of such a bias is beyond the scope of this study, a possible bias, of a different kind, is of more immediate concern; the tests of significance of the mean portfolio returns have to be interpreted with caution as the estimated variance of these returns, particularly for the smaller portfolios, is likely to be biased downwards because of the autocorrelations in the quarterly rates of return.

Table 2 *Mean quarterly changes of net equity acquisitions over turnover, standard deviations, autocorrelations and partials for various institutional investors over the period 1966 to 1982*

	Average[a] change in acquisition	Standard deviation	Autocorrelations and partials for quarterly changes[b]								$P - B$[c]
			ρ1	ρ2	ρ3	ρ4	ρ5	ρ8	ρ9	ρ10	
Unit trusts	0.0039	0.117	-0.248	-0.244	0.113	0.045	-0.148	0.165	-0.065	-0.129	38.2
			-0.248	-0.304	-0.041	0.002	-0.125	0.034	-0.108	-0.167	
Investment trusts	-0.0097	0.134	-0.241	-0.177	0.147	-0.032	-0.051	-0.043	0.060	-0.096	30.7
			-0.241	-0.250	0.039	-0.025	-0.028	-0.166	-0.064	-0.135	
Insurance companies	0.0013	0.116	-0.173	-0.092	-0.149	0.103	-0.237	0.300	-0.054	-0.172	64.4
			-0.173	-0.126	-0.197	0.023	-0.276	0.235	0.076	-0.192	
Pension funds	0.0080	0.118	-0.110	-0.196	-0.106	-0.095	0.067	-0.018	0.125	0.081	30.2
			-0.110	-0.210	-0.164	-0.192	-0.046	-0.139	-0.013	0.002	
All institutions	0.0033	0.083	-0.032	-0.289	-0.024	-0.014	-0.152	0.062	0.007	-0.018	39.9
			-0.032	-0.290	-0.049	-0.111	-0.200	-0.022	-0.129	-0.091	

Notes: [a]Mean quarterly changes in net equity acquisition are calculated using sixty-seven observations.
[b]The standard error of these autocorrelations and partials is approximately 0.12.
[c]Pierce–Box test for random correlogram; χ^2_{32} (95%) = 46.2.

Third, examination of the ten portfolios' correlograms indicates first-order autocorrelations are also apparent for the smallest portfolio. Note that the autocorrelations of these five series damp out quickly and there is only one nonzero partial autocorrelation. The Box–Pierce statistic suggests that all but the smallest portfolio series are essentially random series. However, it is interesting to note some higher-order correlations apparent in the data. For the four smaller portfolios, for example, we observe significant autocorrelations at the tenth lag while the two larger portfolios and the FTA index exhibit similar autocorrelations at the fifth lag. Such autocorrelations might indicate a cyclical pattern in the data.

5 Transfer function modelling

The transfer function model building methodology utilized herein follows the procedure described in Box and Jenkins (1970), i.e. identification, estimation, diagnostic checking. Although the same analysis has been undertaken for all ten portfolios, for space considerations only the results for the smallest and largest portfolios and the FTA market value index are given. It is important, however, to note that the results for the eight intermediate size portfolios are entirely consistent with the pattern suggested by the two extreme portfolios. Table 2 shows the means, standard deviations, autocorrelations and partials of the natural logarithms of the ratio of changes in net acquisitions over the turnover for each of the four institutional investors under consideration.[4] The mean estimates give some indication of the above mentioned increasing ownership of ordinary shares by financial institutions. It is interesting, however, to note the case of investment trusts which appear to be divesting of UK ordinary shares. This probably reflects the shifting of emphasis by these trusts to overseas equity markets. The correlograms suggest some pattern in the series, but no further transformations are required as the series are stationary in the mean.

So far no decision has been made about the choice between models (1) and (2). The former postulates the changes in net acquisitions as the input series, while the latter regards acquisitions as the output series. The choice of the functional model is based on the cross-correlation coefficients between the two series.

Transfer function methodology requires prewhitening of the input series by an ARMA process and application of the same process to the output series. This requires identification of ARMA models for each one of the series under consideration. On the basis that the autocorrelations for the smallest portfolio damp out after lag 3 and only a single significant partial is observed, an AR(1) model is chosen for this series; on the other hand, the largest portfolio and the FTA market-value index show no

Table 3 Cross-correlations between the prewhitened input series (returns) and the prewhitened output series (acquisitions)[a]

k	−5	−4	−3	−2	−1	0	1	2	3	4	5
Smallest portfolio											
Unit trusts	−0.123	0.078	0.039	−0.004	−0.115	0.465	−0.360	−0.066	0.088	−0.067	−0.074
Investment trusts	0.038	0.032	0.083	0.077	−0.224	0.322	−0.029	−0.264	−0.015	−0.016	−0.099
Insurance companys	0.076	−0.068	0.135	0.051	−0.045	0.042	0.387	−0.191	−0.050	0.019	−0.064
Pension funds	0.138	−0.126	0.053	0.054	−0.116	0.161	0.230	−0.403	0.112	−0.092	−0.185
All institutions	0.087	−0.068	0.127	0.038	−0.148	0.295	0.182	−0.387	0.080	−0.075	−0.167
Largest portfolio											
Unit trusts	−0.137	−0.015	0.053	0.042	−0.052	0.620	−0.147	−0.298	0.014	0.018	−0.166
Investment trusts	−0.048	0.072	0.125	0.077	0.008	0.238	0.141	−0.317	−0.178	0.038	−0.106
Insurance companys	0.056	−0.159	0.040	−0.064	0.040	0.116	0.569	−0.013	−0.172	−0.024	−0.058
Pension funds	0.150	−0.106	−0.096	−0.000	0.043	0.278	0.436	−0.346	−0.173	−0.078	−0.242
All institutions	0.060	−0.100	0.011	−0.013	0.039	0.378	0.456	−0.343	−0.168	−0.036	−0.223
FTA market-value index											
Unit trusts	−0.135	−0.022	0.078	0.040	−0.016	0.598	−0.148	−0.298	0.037	−0.022	−0.163
Investment trusts	−0.066	0.086	0.142	0.066	0.032	0.218	0.131	−0.321	−0.154	0.028	−0.140
Insurance companys	0.048	−0.161	0.024	−0.061	0.043	0.143	0.157	−0.014	−0.175	0.019	−0.123
Pension funds	0.125	−0.100	−0.081	0.023	0.042	0.298	0.392	−0.325	−0.173	−0.069	−0.297
All institutions	0.036	−0.092	0.022	−0.004	0.055	0.396	0.410	−0.331	−0.161	−0.027	−0.283

Note: [a]The standard error of these cross-correlations is approximately 0.13
The k value may be interpreted as 'number of quarters that the returns series leads the acquisition series'.

Table 4 Cross-correlations between the prewhitened input series (acquisitions) and the prewhitened output series (returns)[a]

k	−5	−4	−3	−2	−1	0	1	2	3	4	5
Smallest portfolio											
Unit trusts	−0.158	−0.091	0.007	−0.042	−0.082	0.508	−0.028	−0.046	0.070	0.038	−0.148
Investment trusts	−0.181	−0.149	−0.177	−0.116	0.178	0.363	−0.136	0.148	0.178	0.104	0.063
Insurance companys	−0.080	0.018	0.140	0.053	0.360	0.094	−0.190	0.033	0.055	−0.176	−0.028
Pension funds	−0.274	−0.155	0.124	−0.121	0.324	0.241	−0.084	0.038	0.082	−0.080	0.091
All institutions	−0.126	−0.027	0.225	0.025	0.385	0.388	−0.065	0.012	0.100	−0.116	−0.064
Largest portfolio											
Unit trusts	−0.182	0.023	−0.004	−0.084	0.091	0.638	−0.181	0.042	−0.063	−0.098	−0.176
Investment trusts	−0.119	−0.054	−0.272	−0.134	0.277	0.226	−0.004	0.161	0.148	0.077	−0.018
Insurance companys	−0.132	0.011	−0.083	0.066	0.456	0.028	−0.145	−0.189	−0.040	−0.177	0.054
Pension funds	−0.237	−0.061	0.046	−0.060	0.578	0.163	−0.029	−0.071	−0.077	−0.097	0.143
All institutions	−0.120	0.031	0.141	−0.020	0.581	0.200	−0.088	−0.156	−0.066	−0.214	−0.004
FTA market-value index											
Unit trusts	−0.182	−0.006	0.034	−0.087	0.108	0.633	−0.135	0.030	−0.035	−0.117	−0.171
Investment trusts	−0.153	−0.041	−0.247	−0.145	0.275	0.216	0.016	0.146	0.164	0.081	−0.038
Insurance companys	−0.172	0.038	−0.092	0.073	0.379	0.081	−0.161	−0.194	−0.032	−0.197	0.049
Pension funds	−0.294	−0.022	0.041	−0.026	0.544	0.209	−0.0321	−0.040	−0.075	−0.090	0.117
All institutions	−0.189	0.069	0.132	0.003	0.548	0.223	−0.079	−0.144	−0.067	−0.203	−0.029

Note: [a]The standard error of these cross-correlations is approximately 0.13
The k value may be interpreted as 'number of quarters that acquisition series leads the return series'.

significant pattern, except for the marginally significant autocorrelation at lag 5 which is ignored at the moment; thus no prewhitening for these latter series is necessary. The pattern of the change in net acquisitions series is evidently more complicated. An MA(2) model is applied for the unit trusts, pension funds and all institutions series, while the investment trusts and insurance companies series are modelled as AR(2) and MA(5) respectively. The cross-correlation coefficients for the two alternative models, filtering the output series with the relevant input ARMA model, are shown in tables 3 and 4. Note that all cross-correlations in table 3 for $k = -1$ through $k = -5$, except for investment trusts and the smallest portfolio, are essentially zero. In other words, rates of return in any given quarter do not appear to be related to net acquisitions in any previous quarter. On the other hand, both an instantaneous and a forward relationship between rates of return and changes in net acquisitions is firmly evident. For the FTA market-value index, for example, the cross-correlation with all institutions is 0.396 at lag $k = 0$, 0.410 at $k = 1$ and -0.331 at $k = 2$; from lag 3 onwards the association dies out so that for $k = 3$ through $k = 5$ the cross-correlations are nearly zero.

The cross-correlations in table 4, where the returns output series is prewhitened by the ARMA models of input series (net acquisitions), support the same conclusions. In this case we observe zero correlations at $k = 1$ through $k = 5$, while most of the coefficients at lags $k-1$ through $k = -5$ are significantly different from zero. It is, therefore, apparent that the returns series leads the changes in net equity acquisitions by financial institutions. Furthermore, the lack of non-zero coefficients at lags $k = -1$ through $k = -5$ in table 4, suggests the absence of any 'feedback' effects. On these grounds the following transfer function models are based on specification (2), i.e. the returns series is the input variable while the changes in net equity acquisitions by financial institutions is taken as the output series. On the basis of the impulse response coefficients the appropriate (r,s,b) parameters for the transfer function models are chosen. Given the practical difficulties in selecting the parameters, various alternative models were analyzed; the final selection depends in part on the goodness of fit criterion. Furthermore, checks are made to ensure that the residuals of the model chosen are not autocorrelated. A second diagnostic check is also applied to verify that there is no cross-correlation between the prewhitened returns input series and the residuals. The transfer function results for the various financial institutions and the smallest and largest portfolios and the FTA index presented in tables 5, 6 and 7 respectively, satisfy all the above criteria. Each table shows the transfer function parameters, with their t-statistics in parentheses, the form of the noise process and the mean square error of the selected model; for comparative purposes the mean square errors for the

Table 5 Transfer functions for returns of the smallest portfolio (input) and changes in net equity acquisitions for the period 1966–1982

	ω_0	ω_1	ω_2	δ_1	ARMA	Transfer function MSE	Univariate MSE	Autocorrelations and cross-correlations of residuals[a]				
								1	2	3	4	5
Unit trusts	0.0055 (4.81)	−0.0048 (−3.57)	−0.0015 (−1.33)	—	(0,2)	0.0068	0.0115	−0.025	−0.042	0.036	0.061	−0.043
								0.011	−0.048	0.084	0.069	0.005
Investment trusts	0.0049 (3.43)	−0.0003 (−0.14)	−0.0058 (−4.00)	—	(2,0)	0.0105	0.0155	0.021	−0.061	−0.009	−0.044	0.070
								−0.015	0.092	−0.087	0.031	−0.006
Insurance companies		0.0072 (5.42)	−0.0048 (−3.59)	—	(0,5)	0.0092	0.0106	0.007	0.014	−0.024	−0.027	−0.117
								−0.007	0.166	−0.029	−0.037	−0.014
Pension funds		0.0043 (3.25)	−0.0056 (−4.27)	—	(0,2)	0.0092	0.0121	0.026	0.023	−0.167	−0.044	0.020
								−0.030	0.010	0.055	−0.041	−0.165
All institutions	0.0030 (3.60)	0.0017 (1.74)	−0.0045 (−5.34)	—	(0,2)	0.0038	0.0058	0.012	−0.033	−0.144	0.047	−0.051
								−0.011	0.024	−0.013	−0.001	−0.090

Note: [a]The standard error is approximately 0.12.

Table 6 Transfer functions for returns of the largest portfolio (input) and changes in net equity acquisitions for the period 1966–1982

	ω_0	ω_1	ω_2	δ_1	ARMA	Transfer function MSE	Univariate MSE	Autocorrelations and cross-correlations of residuals[a]				
								1	2	3	4	5
Unit trusts	0.0050 (7.29)	−0.0017 (−2.24)	−0.0023 (−3.45)		(0,1)	0.0047	0.0115	−0.034	−0.029	0.130	0.052	−0.076
								0.030	0.008	−0.017	0.157	0.016
Investment trusts	0.0023 (2.10)	0.0017 (1.31)	−0.0039 (−3.58)		(2,0)	0.0117	0.0155	0.029	−0.015	0.040	−0.057	0.008
								0.000	0.082	−0.141	0.029	0.008
Insurance companies		0.0045 (5.00)			(0,5)	0.0079	0.0106	−0.117	0.033	−0.077	−0.122	0.074
								0.057	−0.048	−0.142	−0.099	−0.036
Pension funds		0.0049 (5.86)	−0.0057 (−7.08)	0.4626 (4.24)	(0,2)	0.0065	0.0121	−0.042	−0.923	−0.097	0.056	0.131
								−0.017	−0.040	0.096	0.037	−0.076
All institutions	0.0017 (3.25)	0.0023 (3.08)	−0.0035 (−6.81)	0.3885 (2.90)	(0,2)	0.00238	0.0058	−0.041	−0.082	0.003	0.032	−0.082
								0.010	−0.032	0.013	0.102	0.010

Note: [a]The standard error is approximately 0.12.

Table 7 *Transfer functions for returns of the FTA market-value index (input) and changes in net equity acquisitions for the period 1966–1982*

	ω_0	ω_1	ω_2	δ_1	ARMA	Transfer function MSE	Univariate MSE	Autocorrelations and cross-correlations of residuals[a]				
								1	2	3	4	5
Unit trusts	0.0051 (7.19)	−0.0018 (−2.22)	−0.0024 (−3.46)		(0,1)	0.0048	0.0115	−0.045	−0.002	0.104	0.080	−0.042
								0.034	−0.011	0.018	0.120	0.016
Investment trusts	0.0021 (1.97)	0.0018 (1.33)	−0.0040 (−3.59)		(2,0)	0.0119	0.0155	0.024	−0.025	0.026	−0.057	0.012
								−0.026	0.001	0.064	−0.122	−0.059
Insurance companies		0.0041 (4.37)			(0,5)	0.0085	0.0106	−0.113	0.028	−0.070	−0.114	0.082
								0.035	−0.044	−0.168	−0.128	−0.057
Pension funds	0.0011 (1.52)	0.0033 (2.77)	−0.0051 (−5.81)	0.4758 (4.24)	(0,2)	0.0068	0.0121	−0.022	−0.048	−0.137	0.033	0.109
								−0.026	−0.054	0.041	0.078	−0.079
All institutions	0.0019 (3.32)	0.0019 (2.40)	−0.0034 (−6.07)	0.3904 (2.70)	(0,2)	0.0030	0.0058	−0.031	−0.070	−0.037	0.044	−0.084
								0.012	−0.033	−0.013	0.156	−0.028

Note: [a]The standard error is approximately 0.12.

best univariate model of the changes in net equity acquisitions series are also displayed. Furthermore, the tables show the residuals' autocorrelations coefficients and the cross-correlations, for the first five lags, between the model's residuals and the input series.

Two basic forms of transfer function models can be identified. Net changes on equity acquisitions by pension funds and all institutions together are related to the returns of the largest portfolio and the FTA market-value index by the model:

$$A_t = \frac{(\omega_0 - \omega_1 B - \omega_2 B^2)}{(1 - \delta_1 B)} \, R_t + (1 - \theta_1 B - \theta_2 B^2) u_t \tag{6}$$

On the other hand, for the returns of the smallest portfolio with each one of the net acquisition series the following basic model is observed:

$$A_t = (\omega_0 - \omega_1 B - \omega_2 B^2) R_t + (\text{noise model}) \tag{7}$$

This same model is also applicable to the returns of the largest portfolio and the FTA index with the acquisitions by unit trusts, investment trusts and insurance companies.

6 Interpretation of the results

Several interesting points are raised by the transfer function results regarding the relationship between changes in net equity acquisitions of financial institutions and the rates of return of the various size portfolios. First, the mean square errors of the residuals for all transfer function models are substantially lower than their univariate equivalents. The ratio of the mean square error to the variance of the output series, gives an indication of the variance explained by the various univariate and transfer function models. For example, the univariate MA(2) model appears to account for 16 per cent of all institutions series' variability; the explained variability increases to 59 per cent when the returns of the largest portfolio are included in the transfer function model. Substantial increases are also observed for all other models.

Second, the reduction in mean square error of the output series residuals, achieved by the transfer function models, is not the same across the various size portfolios. While, for example, the smallest portfolio appears to explain 34 per cent of the variability of the changes in net equity acquisitions by pension funds, the largest portfolio accounts for 53 per cent of this variability. The largest portfolio appears also to account for a higher proportion of the unit trusts', insurance companies' and all institutions' variability. On the other hand, it is interesting to note that the variability of changes in net equity acquisitions by investment trusts is better explained by the returns of the smallest portfolio. Furthermore, as would be expected, given the value weighted nature of the FTA index, the mean square error estimates of models, including this series, lie between the two extreme portfolios but are closer to the larger one. Thus, on the grounds of the mean square errors of the various transfer function models, it is apparent that the trading activity of financial institutions is more closely related to the price behaviour of larger companies.[5] The notable exception is the case of investment trusts; further transfer function results with other size portfolios, not presented in this paper, clearly indicate that their trading activity is better explained by the price behaviour of medium size companies. These findings are consistent with the available evidence from surveys about the nature of equity holdings by various institutional investors. Hills' (1984) study, for example, based on a sample of 240 companies, stratified by market values in 1981, concludes that 'Registered holdings by pension funds are half the size for small companies as they are for large and very large companies. The investment trusts tend to avoid very large companies preferring medium to large ones' (p. 83).

Third, the transfer function results provide no evidence in support of either the market impact or the predictive hypothesis. In fact, the evidence as a whole points to a 'follow the market' hypothesis, i.e. institutional activity follows rather than leads the market. In other words, it seems that institutional investors wait for market signals before they commit themselves to any changes in the pattern of ordinary shares transactions. Within this general framework, however, some significant differences in the investment strategies of the four financial institutions are readily apparent. Notice, for example, that the ω_0 coefficients for unit and investment trusts are positive and significant while the equivalent coefficients for insurance companies and pension funds, in all three relevant tables, are zero or not statistically significant. This indicates that the former two institutions react instantly to any market changes, while the latter appear to wait for a period of up to three months, from the time that a market trend emerges, before any definite action is taken. The positive and statistically significant ω_1 coefficients for insurance companies and pension funds suggest that these two institutions increase (decrease) their net equity acquisitions three months after an increase (decline) in the market. In this context, it should be emphasized that the nature of the available data on institutional activity (quarterly intervals) is a serious constraint for any analysis of this kind. The instantaneous relationship, evident for unit and investment trusts, could also be interpreted as evidence in support of the market impact hypothesis and/or some type of 'follow the leader' type of trading behaviour similar to that found by Friend *et al.* (1970) and Klemkosky (1977); under the latter scenario, investment and unit trusts would be setting the pace followed by insurance companies and pension funds. Considering, however, that the combined ownership of ordinary shares by unit and investment trusts has never exceeded the 10 per cent level, while insurance companies and pension funds, according to the Stock Exchange study (1983), owned 48 per cent of the total amount of UK listed equities at the end of 1981, the ground for a market impact interpretation is rather limited.

Fourth, the overall pattern of the transfer function parameters points to the markedly different behavioural patterns adopted by the four financial institutions. Consider first the case of their combined trading activity. The parameters of table 5 suggest that the response of institutional investors to changes in small firms' prices takes place mainly during the same quarter and to a lesser degree, if at all, extends over the next quarter as well. The negative sign of the ω_2 parameter is of particular interest as it points to a reversal of recent trading activity. While, for example, a given increase in the returns of the smallest portfolio first results in a spree of net buying, spread unevenly over two quarters, suddenly the position is reversed to net selling action over the following quarter. The sum of these three coefficients (0.0002) can be interpreted as the total effect on net equity acquisitions due to price changes of the smallest portfolio. Table 6, on the other hand, suggests that the net buying (selling) activity of all institutional investors, following an increase (decline) in the returns of the largest portfolio, is spread evenly over two quarters; thereafter, the selling (buying) follows an exponential decay pattern. The total gain (0.0008) in this case, is four times higher than that observed for the smaller portfolio, indicating that institutional trading activity is mainly in response to the market behaviour of larger firms. It is also worth noticing some subtle differences in the investment behaviour of individual institutional investors emerging from the overall pattern of transfer function parameters. The reversal in trading activity after one or two quarters seems to be an established feature of investment behaviour for unit trusts, investment trusts and pension funds; they appear to readjust their portfolios after their initial reaction to a given market change. Such readjustment might occur during a single quarter (unit and investment trusts) or be a gradual process over a number of quarters (pension funds). On the other hand, insurance companies demonstrate a more conservative strategy; they are rather slow to react to market changes, but when they eventually do they find no need for further readjustment.

7 Conclusions

The evidence presented in this study fails to support the market impact hypothesis suggested in previous studies and thus the conjecture that the small size premium may be related to institutional investors' trading strategies. Instead the findings point to a 'follow the market' hypothesis, i.e. institutional trading follows market behaviour. This conclusion is consistent with the spirit of the efficient market hypothesis. Furthermore, trading activity of all institutions but investment trusts appears to follow the market behaviour of larger firms. Of course, this finding by itself does not necessarily imply investment concentration on such firms. Nevertheless, given the existing documentation from survey studies, on the relative institutional preference for larger companies, the results of this work probably reflect this preference. On the other hand, however, there is no evidence to suggest that the inferior long-term market performance of larger firms, in comparison to their smaller counterparts, can be attributed to the trading strategies of institutional investors.

The transfer function parameters also suggest readjustment of portfolio positions after the initial response to market changes. This latter result is of particular interest as it could be taken as evidence in support of the stabilizing influence usually attributed to institutional shareholders. Dobbins and Greenwood's (1975) failure to discover evidence in support of the stabilization hypothesis is understandable since they examined only the contemporaneous relationship while the transfer function models of this study indicate a rather more complicated process of investment behaviour. However, it should be emphasized that even the negative and statistically significant parameters obtained in this study are not sufficient to provide unambiguous support of the stabilization hypothesis. If institutional investors do indeed have a stabilizing effect on share prices, one would expect to find some signals of 'feedback' reaction in the transfer function framework. No such evidence has been discovered in this study.

Finally, it is worth considering for a moment some of the wider implications of these findings. For example, given the small firm effect, the immediately arising question is whether the observed preference by investment trusts for medium to smaller companies is reflected in their overall investment performance. Although no systematic comparative evidence is available a number of empirical studies have demonstrated that UK investment trusts have failed over the years to outperform the market. This is undoubtedly an intriguing issue but beyond the scope of this chapter. Along the same lines it would also be interesting to investigate whether the clues of market leadership by unit and investment trusts, discovered in this study, are indicative of superior portfolio management skills.

Notes

1 For the period January 1966 to December 1974 the samples of companies on the LSDP returns file are somewhat biased towards larger firms. From January 1975 onwards the

database has been extended to cover all listed shares on the London Stock Exchange (see Smithers 1979). Thus, the small firm effect reported in this study is likely to be understated during the former period.

2 Data for purchases and sales of ordinary UK shares by the four groups of financial institutions have been collected from various issues of *Financial Statistics*. Quarterly transactions for all institutions are published about three months after the end of the quarter to which they refer. The statistics for unit trusts cover all unit trusts authorized by the Department of Trade. From the first quarter of 1975 responsibility for the collection of these statistics passed from the Unit Trust Association to the Bank of England. The investment trust companies which are included in the statistics are those which are recognized as investment trusts by the Inland Revenue for tax purposes. These are collected and aggregated by the Bank of England. The data for insurance companies covers insurers, members of the British Insurance Association (BIA), and a sample of insurance companies who are not members of BIA; the statistics include pension schemes they operate on behalf of other companies and are collected and compiled by the Department of Industry and Trade. The data for Pension funds covers the transactions by the funded schemes of local authorities, the rest of the public sector (mainly nationalized industries) and the private sector. While statistics for the former two groups are based on the responses of all funds and compiled by CSO the estimates for the latter are based on a sample of self-administered and managed superannuation funds and compiled by the Department of Trade.

3 As the results of this study are based on monthly returns data it seems unlikely that the rebalancing method used here for calculating portfolio returns would have a marked effect on the reported small size effect.

4 The natural logarithm transformation was applied in order to stabilize the variance of the series over time. It was selected on the basis of the roughly linear relationship in the range-mean plot of the series.

5 Note that the returns of the various size portfolios are cross-sectionally dependent and conclusions must be interpreted with this in mind.

References

Arbel, A. and Strebel, F. (1983) 'Pay Attention to Neglected Firms', *The Journal of Portfolio Management*, Winter, 37–41.

Banz, R.W. (1981) 'The Relationship between Return and Market Value of Common Stocks', *Journal of Financial Economics*, 9, 3–18.

Berges, A., McConnell, J.J. and Schlarbaum, G.G. (1984) 'The Turn-of-the-year in Canada', *Journal of Finance*, 39, 185–92.

Blume, M.E. and Stambaugh, R.F. (1983) 'Biases in Computed Returns: An Application to the Size Effect', *Journal of Financial Economics*, 12, 387–404.

Box, G.E.P. and Jenkins, G.M. (1970) *Time Series Analysis*, San Francisco: Holden-Day.

Brealey, R.A., Bryne, J. and Dimson, E. (1978) 'The Variability of Market Returns', *The Investment Analyst*, December, 19–23.

Brown, P. Keim, D.B., Kleidon, A.W. and March, T.A. (1983) 'Stock Return Seasonalities and the Tax-loss Selling Hypothesis: Analysis of the Arguments and Australian Evidence', *Journal of Financial Economics*, 12, 105–27.

Constantinides, G.M. (1984) 'Optimal Stock Trading with Personal Taxes: Implications for Prices and the Abnormal January Returns', *Journal of Financial Economics*, 13, 65–89.

Dimson, E. (1979) 'Risk Measurement when Shares are Subject to Infrequent Trading', *Journal of Financial Economics*, 7, 197–226.

Dobbins, R. and Greenwood, M.J. (1975) 'Institutional Shareholders and Equity Market Stability, *Journal of Business Finance and Accounting*, 2, 257–68.

Dobbins, R. and Witt, S.F. (1980) 'Stock Market Prices and Sector Activity', *Journal of Business Finance and Accounting*, 7, 261–76.

Friend, L., Marshall, B. and Crockett, J. (1970) *Mutual Funds and Other Institutional Investors: A New Perspective*, New York: McGraw-Hill.

Givoly, D. and Ovadia, B. (1983) 'Year-end and tax-induced Sales and Stock Market Seasonality', *Journal of Finance*, 38, 171–86.

Hills, J. (1984) *Savings and fiscal privilege*, London: The Institute of Fiscal Studies.

Kato, K. and Schallheim, J. (1985) 'Seasonal and Size Anomalies in the Japanese Stock Market', *Journal of Financial and Quantitative Analysis*, 20, 243–60.

Keim, D.B. (1983) 'Size Related Anomalies and Stock Market Seasonality: Further Empirical Evidence', *Journal of Financial Economics*, 12, 13–32.

Klemkosky, R.C. (1977) 'The Impact and Efficiency of Institutional Trading Imbalances', *Journal of Finance*, 32, 79–86.

Kraus, A. and Stoll, H. (1972a) 'Price Impacts of Block Trading on the New York Stock Exchange', *Journal of Finance*, 27, 569–88.

Kraus, A. and Stoll, H. (1972b) 'Parallel Trading by Institutional Investors', *Journal of Financial and Quantitative Analysis*, 7, 2107–38.

Lakonishok, J. and Smidt, S. (1984) 'Volume and Turn of the Year Behaviour', *Journal of Financial Economics*, 13, 435–55.

Lee, S.L. and Ward, C.W.R. (1980) 'The Association of Stock Market Volatility and Parallel Trading by UK Institutional Investors', *Journal of Business Finance and Accounting*, 7, 415–26.

Levis, M. (1985) 'Are Small Firms Big Performers?' *The Investment Analyst*, 76, 21–7.

Reilly, F.K. and Wright, D.J. (1984) 'Block Trading and Aggregate Stock Price Volatility', *Financial Analysts Journal*, March–April, 54–60.

Reinganum, M.R. (1981) 'Misspecification of Capital Asset Pricing: Empirical Anomalies based on Earnings Yields and Market Values', *Journal of Financial Economics*, 9, 19–46.

Reinganum, M.R. (1982) 'A Direct Test of Roll's Conjecture on the Firm Size Effect', *Journal of Finance*, 37, 27–35.

Reinganum, M.R. (1983) 'The Anomalous Stock Market Behaviour of Small Firms in January', *Journal of Financial Economics*, 12, 89–104.

Roll, R. (1981) 'A Possible Explanation of the Small Firm Effect', *Journal of Finance*, 36, 879–88.

Roll, R. (1983a) 'Vas ist das? The Turn of the Year Effect and the Return Premium of Small Firms', *Journal of Portfolio Management*, Winter, 18–28.

Roll, R. (1983b) 'On Computing Mean Returns and the Small Firm Premium', *Journal of Financial Economics*, 12, 371–86.

Rozeff, M.S. (1985) 'The Tax-loss Selling Hypothesis: New Evidence from Share Shifts', unpublished manuscript, University of Iowa.

Scholes, M. and Williams, J. (1977) 'Estimation Betas from Non-synchronous Data', *Journal of Financial Economics*, 5, 309–27.

Schultz, P. (1983) 'Transaction Costs and the Small Firm Effect', *Journal of Financial Economics*, 12, 81–8.

Schultz, P. (1985) 'Personal Income Taxes and the January Effect: Small Firm Stock Returns before the War Revenue Act of 1917', *Journal of Finance*, 40, 333–43.

Securities and Exchange Commission (1971) *Institutional Investor Study Report*, Washington DC. US Government Printing Office.

Smithers, P.J. (1979) 'London Share Price Database', unpublished documentation, London Business School, London.

Stock Exchange (1983) *The Stock Exchange Survey of Share Ownership*, London: The Stock Exchange.

Stoll, H.R. and Whaley, R.E. (1983) 'Transaction Costs and the Small Firm Effect', *Journal of Financial Economics*, 12, 57–78.

Tinic, S.M., Barone-Adesi, G. and West, R.R. (1984) 'Seasonality in Canadian Prices: A Test of the Tax-loss-selling Hypothesis', unpublished manuscript, Faculty of Business, University of Alberta.

US Senate Sub-Committees on Intergovernmental Relations and Budgeting Management and Expenditures (1974) *Disclosure of Corporate Ownership*, Washington DC: Government Printing Office.

Van den Bergh, W.M. and Wessels, R.E. (1985) 'Stock Market Seasonality: An Examination of the Tax-loss-selling Hypothesis'. *Journal of Business Finance and Accounting*, 12, 515–30.

13 Discussion of 'Size related anomalies and trading activity of UK institutional investors'

THEO VERMAELEN

Chapter 12 consists of two parts. In the first part the author documents the size anomaly in the UK. Table 1 shows that small firms earn significantly higher returns than large firms: the difference between the smallest and the largest market value portfolio is approximately 1.5 per cent per quarter. The results are even stronger when one considers the difference in beta-adjusted excess returns: betas of large firms are approximately twice as large as betas of small firms. (This is not due to thin trading because the estimates are based on quarterly returns.) Hence, with a risk-premium of, for example, 8 per cent per annum, small firms experienced, in the period from 1966 to 1982, CAPM excess returns (relative to large firms) of approximately 10 per cent per year. I believe this result is quite interesting and deserves further exploration. For example, does the size effect only show up in January? Why are small firms less risky than large firms in the UK, while the opposite is true in the US?

In the second part of the chapter the relationship between stock returns and institutional trading activity is examined. Two hypotheses are proposed. First the market impact-predictive hypothesis which argues that institutional trading actively influences current and future market price changes. The second hypothesis, one may call the 'market leadership' hypothesis which argues that institutional trading follows market behaviour. The linkage between the second and the first part of the paper is explained on page 158: 'Arbel and Strebel (1983) . . . argue that the small size effect is just a special case of "the neglect effect"'; firms that are neglected by security analysts exhibit superior market performance because intensive analyst coverage raises stock prices and therefore lowers returns. And this theory assumes that the market impact hypothesis is true.

I personally find the Arbel–Strebel argument rather poor: explaining the small firm effect requires explaining why *expected* returns per period are systematically higher for small firms than for large firms. It is not because a security is more valuable that it should provide lower expected rates of return. For example, a company with larger expected profits should sell, *ceteris paribus*, at a higher stock price, but there is no reason to assume that expected stock returns are different for highly profitable and less profitable firms. However, a related explanation for the small firm effect has been proposed by Klein and Bawa (1977). They find that if insufficient information is available about a subset of securities, investors will not hold these securities because of estimation risk, i.e. uncertainty about the true parameters of the return distribution. If the amount of information generated on small firms is smaller, many investors will choose not to hold such firms. Banz (1978) shows that securities held by only a subset of the investors have higher risk-adjusted returns than those considered by all investors.

While it is not clear to me that the Klein and Bawa model predicts anything about the relationship between institutional trading activity and stock returns (the so called market impact hypothesis), Levis' paper nevertheless reports on a topic which should be interesting by itself: the relationship between current, past and future stock returns and institutional trading activity. The empirical tests in the paper are a straightforward application of multivariate ARIMA modelling. First, univariate models must be built for the two input variables, i.e. stock returns and changes in net acquisitions (tables 1 and 2). Using these models, each of the series is prewhitened. Next, cross-correlations between prewhitened series are computed, assuming first that the net acquisitions are the causor variable (table 3) and second that the returns are the causor variable (table 4). If we assume that the past must cause the future, then one can infer from tables 3 and 4 that stock returns lead trading activity: as the market leadership hypothesis predicts, institutional purchase activity reacts positively to market movements.

I do have some reservations about the interpretations of results, however. First it seems unlikely that institutions wait a quarter before they react to a stock market change. A shorter reaction period would be more convincing, but, unfortunately, data on institutional purchase activity are only available on a quarterly basis. Second, I do not see how the methodology could distinguish between the *contemporaneous* (i.e. in the same quarter) market impact hypothesis and the market-leadership hypothesis: the results are consistent, for example, with the joint hypothesis that (a) institutional traders react to stock price changes in the previous quarter and (b) they have an impact on the returns of the current quarter. Finally, it may well be that institutions have an impact on stock returns, but there is no reason why this impact should be proportional, as is being assumed in this paper; i.e. in an efficient market there is no reason why stock price changes should be positively related to the amount of (net) purchases of a trader even if this trader is setting the price.

Finally, transfer functions which specify trading activity as a function of current and past stock returns are estimated in tables 5, 6 and 7, for small, large and all firms. Note that the institutional purchases variable (the dependent variable) is the same in all three tables. It is found that the relationship is much less pronounced for small firms. Apart from the comments made above about the possibility of inferring anything about the small firm effect on the basis of this methodology, I have some problems with interpreting these results. Table 5 tells me that net purchases by institutional investors (who are not allowed to invest in small firms) are positively related to stock returns of companies of firms they are not allowed to invest in (small firms)! This result is obviously caused by the positive correlation between small firms and other companies. A more meaningful test could be performed by relating *excess returns* (after adjusting for common factors such as market movements) of small firms with trading activity. In that case, much larger differences between table 5 and table 6 should be observed (i.e. all the coefficients in table 5 should become zero).

In short, I believe there are some interesting, but sometimes difficult to interpret, results in this paper. Because it touches a new data set (institutional trading activity) it is normal that it leaves many questions for further research. I also believe that doing this type of research which explores new data sets from different countries is important if we want to improve our understanding of small firm effects and other anomalies.

References

Arbel, A. and Strebel, F. (1983) 'Pay Attention to Neglected Firms', *Journal of Portfolio Management*, Winter, 37–41.
Banz, R. (1978) 'Limited Diversification and Market Equilibrium: An Empirical Analysis', Ph.D. dissertation, University of Chicago.
Klein, R. and Bawa, V. (1977) 'The Effect of Limited Information and Estimation Risk on Optimal Portfolio Diversification', *Journal of Financial Economics*, 5.

14 Equilibrium asset pricing models and the firm size effect

*NAI-FU CHEN**

1 Introduction

One of the empirical regularities discovered in recent years is that the average return of a small firm portfolio is higher than that of a large firm portfolio when measured over a sufficiently long time period. This in itself is not surprising because intuitively most of us believe that small firms are in some sense 'riskier' than large firms. Therefore, if investors are risk averse, market equilibrium would imply that expected returns of small firms are higher than those of large firms.

In recent empirical studies, Banz (1981) and Reinganum (1981) find that the difference in returns between small and large firms cannot be explained by the capital asset pricing model (CAPM). When portfolios are formed based on past beta and firm size, the instrumental variable firm size has significant explanatory power for the average returns across the portfolios even after controlling for the estimated CAPM betas.

In this chapter, we shall give a brief account of our investigation of the firm size effect, concentrating on the motivation and the intuition underlying the approaches, and the interpretation of the empirical results that we obtain. Since many researchers have also proposed alternative explanations of the size effect, let us first categorize them before describing how our work fits into the general effort.

(i)   The average returns, especially for small firm portfolios, are 'miscalculated.' Roll (1983) demonstrates that the computed average returns of small firm portfolios decline as the length of the interval for rebalancing the portfolio increases, and stabilize when the interval length is a month or longer. Blume and Stambaugh (1983) show that the returns computed over short rebalance intervals may be biased upward due to the bid–ask effect, especially for small firm portfolios. Since the return of a buy-and-hold strategy is best mimicked by the return computed using a rebalance interval of at least one month, returns computed using shorter rebalance intervals may overstate the difference between small and large firms. While this explanation casts doubt on some of the firm size studies using daily rebalance intervals, it does not materially affect the conclusion of the studies by Banz and others who use monthly rebalance intervals.

(ii)   Trading in small firms involves substantially higher transaction costs. There is no doubt that buying and selling small firm stocks results in higher direct and indirect costs as a percentage of the price. See Stoll and Whaley (1983) and Schultz (1983) for some related statistics. The implication of this difference in transaction cost for the observed averaged returns of small and large firms is, however, difficult to determine. For investors who simply want to buy and hold small stocks and do not require immediacy (as opposed to information trades) in executing the orders, the effective bid–ask spread is probably different from the quoted bid–ask spread. Differential transaction costs will probably induce a clientele effect: investment that is anticipated to turn over frequently is more likely to be placed with low transaction cost assets. Thus the implication for the observed averaged returns cannot be fully assessed without knowing the market equilibrium induced by the differential transaction costs.

(iii)   The market betas, especially for smaller firms, are misestimated. Roll (1981) suggests that a partial answer to the observed size effect is that betas for small firms are underestimated due to nonsynchronous trading. Both Roll (1981) and Reinganum (1982) conclude that when betas are estimated 'properly,' the magnitude of the size effect decreases. Recently, Chan and Chen (1985) re-examine this beta misestimation problem in a framework that allows both the market betas and the market premium to change over time. We find that once the betas are estimated with 'sufficient accuracy,' a firm size proxy does not have additional explanatory power for the cross-sectional differences in average returns. We discuss this approach in greater detail in the following section.

(iv)   The capital asset pricing model is misspecified. The equilibrium risk–return relation used in many previous studies is the well-known CAPM pricing relation

$$E(r_i) = \lambda_0 + \lambda_1 \beta_i \qquad (1)$$

It is conceivable that the equilibrium risk–return tradeoff in our economy can be better described by an alternative equilibrium asset pricing model that captures the size effect. An examination of the firm size effect in the framework of the arbitrage pricing theory (APT) of Ross (1976) is reported in Chen (1983). We find that size does not have explanatory power for cross-sectional average returns once the factor loadings (the risk measures of the APT) are controlled for. Since this implementation of APT is purely statistically based, the only conclusion drawn is that firm size is proxying for some risk factor. Other researchers, for example Connor and Korajczyk (1985), Huberman and Kandel (1985) and Lehmann and Modest (1985), have also examined the size effect with different statistical implementations of the APT. To gain further understanding of the risk that size is proxying for, Chan *et al.* (1985) investigate the size effect with a multifactor pricing model using economically identifiable variables (chosen on the basis of the work of Chen *et al.* (1986)). We shall discuss the results of this paper in detail in the following section.

To summarize the research described above, we can safely conclude that the size effect, as measured by the average monthly return difference between small and large firms, is both economically and statistically significant. When measured 'properly,' differences in risk, perhaps jointly with the effect induced by differential trading costs, are sufficient to explain the differences in averaged return between small and large firms. In section 2 we discuss the intuition underlying the two risk-based explanations proposed in Chan *et al.* (1985) and Chan and Chen (1985). Section 3 considers the implications of the observed return seasonal. Section 4 concludes the chapter and considers some future research directions.

2 Risk and return of small firms

Asset pricing theories suggest that one possible explanation of why the observed averaged returns are different for two classes of securities is that their risk characteristics are different. In this section, let us examine the risks of investing in small firms in the framework of asset pricing models.

A multifactor model explanation of the size effect

Chen (1983) shows that the size effect can be captured by the risk exposures (factor loadings) implied by arbitrage pricing theory. In other words, small firms are 'riskier' in terms of certain common factors (pervasive forces) in the economy and consequently have higher averaged returns over time. To further understand the risks affecting both small and large firms, we must identify the relation between common factors extracted from the covariance matrix of stock returns and the macroeconomy. In the study of Chen *et al.* (1986), we match the time series of the factors with variables suggested by financial theory, and find that indeed these macroeconomic variables can explain common co-movements of stock returns. Furthermore, we also find that the risk exposures (factor loadings) are priced in a multifactor asset pricing equation. The selection of these variables follows from the intuition behind the simple valuation formula that the price of a financial asset can be expressed as

$$\rho = \frac{E(\tilde{c})}{k} \tag{2}$$

where $\tilde{c}$ is the future uncertain cash flows and k is the risk-adjusted discount rate. Thus, the return of a financial asset will be affected by common factors influencing the expected cash flows and the risk-adjusted discount rate. Of course, we do not assert that equation (2) is appropriate for all possible distributions of uncertain cash flows, but we hope that the intuition behind equation (2), that leads us to the identification of the common factors, is the same as that behind a more general evaluation equation (for example in Cox *et al.* 1985). The variables that we choose are changes in the long- and short-run growth rates of the economy, changes in the short-run interest rates and inflation rates, changes in the slope of the term structure of interest rates and changes in the risk premium.

In the Chan *et al.* (1985) study, we use this multifactor pricing equation to examine the size effect. However, we replace the long-run economic growth variable by the equally weighted market index since the aggregate growth rate is also reflected in the aggregate market return. The exact model that we use is

$$r_i = \lambda_0 + \lambda_1 b_i(\text{EWNY}) + \lambda_2 b_i(\text{IP1SA}) + \lambda_3 b_i(\text{DEI}) + \lambda_4 b_i(\text{UITB}) \\ + \lambda_5 b_i(\text{PREM}) + \lambda_6 b_i(\text{UTS}) + \varepsilon_i \tag{3}$$

where EWNY is the equally weighted NYSE stock index, IP1SA is the seasonally adjusted monthly industrial production growth rate, DEI is the change in expected inflation rate (which is roughly the change in the T-bill rate), UITB is unanticipated inflation, PREM is the return difference between a low grade bond portfolio and a long-term government bond portfolio, and UTS is the return difference between long-term government bonds and the T-bill rate. We find that the multifactor model risk-adjusted return difference between small and large firms is only about 1–2 percent a year, a drop from about 12 percent per year before risk adjustment.

As we examine the risk–return relation predicted by the multifactor model, we find that the most important return adjustment to the total return corresponds to loadings on the market factor (EWNY) that we use for proxying the aggregate economic growth rate. While the return adjustment corresponding to this market factor affects firms of all sizes, it does not explain much of the return difference between small and large firms. The risk adjustments corresponding to the changing risk premium (PREM) are smaller in absolute magnitude than the market factor adjustments, but they are monotonic; positive for small firms and negative for large firms, and explain close to half of the difference.

This changing risk premium is often regarded as a function of the 'price of risk' and 'risk.' The price of risk here refers to the marginal tradeoff between consumption today and risky return from investment, and this tradeoff is usually dependent on the current and the expected future states of the economy. For example, if the current level of consumption is low, it would take a high expected return to induce us to forego our marginal unit of current consumption. As for risk, both business risk and financial risk are also dependent on current and expected future states of the economy. Therefore, we expect the risk premium to be a function of the business cycle.

The economic reasoning linking the changing risk premium to the size effect is quite straightforward. During economic expansions and contractions, both the aggregate risk premium and the cash flows of many firms fluctuate. Since small firms tend to be marginal firms, they fluctuate more with business cycles and thus have higher risk exposure to the changing aggregate risk premium. When this risk exposure is priced in an equilibrium asset pricing model, small firms would have higher expected returns than large firms to compensate investors for this additional dimension of risk beyond the market factor (aggregate production) risk. Even though both the market factor and the changing risk premium vary with business cycles, their time series fluctuations may not be coincident. For example, conditional on a current lukewarm economic growth rate, the fortunes of many marginal firms can still go either way and the risk premium may well be high. Such a scenario is consistent with the empirical finding that when we regress the returns of small firm portfolios on the market factor and the changing risk premium factor across time, the slope coefficients corresponding to both factors are simultaneously statistically significant in a multiple regression.

To further corroborate our reasoning for the size effect, we use directly a business cycle indicator replacing the changing risk premium variable in the multifactor pricing equation. The indicator we choose is the series net business formation, which is a weighted average of two components: (a) the number of new incorporations minus the number of business failures and (b) the change in the number of business telephone lines. This business cycle indicator yields results similar to those corresponding to the changing risk premium. The evidence is consistent with the interpretation that smaller firms are riskier because they suffer disproportionately a higher rate of failure during economic contractions, and the bearer of such risk is compensated by higher average return.

On the basis of the evidence we have gathered, we conclude that the size effect can be captured by the multifactor model implemented directly with the macroeconomic variables. The small firms have higher averaged returns because of their higher risks.

Estimation error of stock betas and its implication to the observed size effect

While we find that the size effect can be captured by a multifactor pricing equation, it is still interesting to consider whether the size effect can also be captured by a single factor model for several reasons.

(i)   From efficient set mathematics, we know that it is sufficient to use an efficient portfolio on the frontier of our size-ranked portfolios for the pricing relation. It would be interesting if one of the market indices is sufficiently close to the frontier that we no longer observe the size effect after controlling for these market index betas.

(ii)   In an economy with $k+1$ fund separation, the market clearing condition implies that the market portfolio would be a particular linear combination of the k portfolios corresponding to the k common factors. For the purpose of explaining the behavior of the size-ranked portfolios, a particular combination of the common factors can well be approximately sufficient.

(iii)   In an intertemporal setting, if the investment and consumption opportunity set is changing, generally we would have a multifactor model. However, with additional assumptions, this multifactor model can be collapsed into a single factor model (see, for example, Breeden, 1979) with stochastic parameters. Therefore, it is conceivable that the economy is consistent with both a multifactor model and a single factor model.

(iv)   It is also possible that the multifactor betas are merely proxying for the estimation errors of the market betas, and if we can estimate the market betas with higher precision, a one factor asset pricing model is descriptive of the economy. On the other hand, even if the size effect can be captured by a one factor asset pricing model, it is possible that the single factor is proxying for the macroeconomic variables.

In the Chan and Chen (1985) study, we consider the question of how to estimate the market betas more accurately, and whether betas thus estimated can explain the cross-sectional differences in returns of the size-ranked portfolios. We do not require that the betas are constant but we do require that they have a stationary distribution and follow the stochastic process described by

$$\bar{\beta}_{it-1} = \bar{\beta}_i + \bar{\theta}_{t-1}(\bar{\beta}_i - \bar{\bar{\beta}}) + \bar{\eta}_{it-1} \tag{4}$$

where $\bar{\beta}_i$ is the mean of the distribution of $\bar{\beta}_i$, $\bar{\bar{\beta}}$ is the cross-sectional mean of the $\bar{\beta}_i$s (which would be identically equal to 1 if we take an equally weighted index of financial assets as the market), $\bar{\theta}_{t-1}$ has zero mean and reflects some recent findings that the cross-sectional spectrum of β_is tends to expand and contract with the business cycles (see Chan, 1985), and $\bar{\eta}_{it-1}$ is a random noise term independent of all other parameters.

We derive a linear relation between unconditional expected return and the unconditional mean beta $\bar{\beta}_i$ implied by the single factor asset pricing model. We then test the model with the estimated values of $\bar{\beta}_i$.

At first it would appear that improving the accuracy of the stock betas can be accomplished simply by using more observations in the estimation procedure. Unfortunately, if we increase the number of observations by reducing the length of the observation intervals to less than a month, the effect of nonsynchronous trading together with the bid–ask spread produces estimated betas that are worse rather than better. If we increase the number of observations by using a longer estimation period, past empirical studies have shown that estimated betas tend to drift and do not remain constant beyond a five- to seven-year window. The 'trick' we use in this study is to form portfolios based on the instrumental variable firm size and string together portfolios with the same size ranking over different years. We allow the composition of the portfolios to change, maintaining the same relative size ranking (and, we assume, the same risk measure). If size is a good instrumental variable for beta, we are able to use a long time period (thirty years) to estimate the betas with high precision.

We can also view our size-based portfolio formation as a way to create financial assets such that equation (4) holds. As long as equation (4) holds over a long time period, we would be able to estimate $\bar{\beta}_i$ accurately. We examine the estimated values of $\bar{\beta}_i$ over five-year, ten-year and fifteen-year subperiods in addition to the thirty-year sample test period from 1954–83. We find that the pattern of cross-correlations between the estimated betas are not in conflict with equation (4). Therefore, we adopt equation (4) as a reasonable working approximation and test the model accordingly with the equally weighted NYSE stock index as the market proxy.

The most interesting finding is that once the estimated values of $\bar{\beta}_i$ are controlled for, a size proxy, such as the logarithm of the market value of equity, no longer has explanatory power for the cross-sectional return differences among the size-ranked portfolios. In many cases, the estimate of the slope coefficient corresponding to the size proxy becomes insignificantly positive for the overall sample period. These results stand in striking contrast with the negative and statistically significant slope coefficient for the size proxy when the betas are estimated only over a five-year period. We conclude that the previously observed average size effect can at least be partially explained by the estimation error of the market betas.

Summary

We have shown that the average returns across size-ranked portfolios are consistent with both a multifactor model with macroeconomic variables and a single factor model with the equally weighted NYSE stock index. In both cases, the smaller firms are 'riskier' (as measured by the models), and their higher averaged returns are compensation for bearing the higher risk. Both sets of results are consistent with our intuition that smaller firms are more susceptible to fluctuations of the economy.

As we suggest above, the data can be consistent with both a multifactor model and a single factor model specification. Furthermore, even the economy can be consistent with both specifications. We have not performed the necessary work that enables us to distinguish sharply between the two possibilities.

On the question of size effect itself, we regard our results above as efforts to explain the phenomenon rather than an attempt to replace the size variable as an instrumental variable for risk. The size variable is a remarkable instrumental variable because it requires only one observation (the price) and is easily observable. Our beta estimation takes thirty years of data and requires portfolio formation satisfying the distributional assumptions to produce a risk measure that is as good as the size proxy. One obvious way to combine the instrumental ability of the size variable and our interpretation of the size effect would be to assign the betas of stocks based on their size ranking, perhaps with an adjustment conditional on the state of the business cycle. Such an approach would have the empirical support documented above and the benefit of the instant observability of the size proxy. Therefore, for practical considerations, we are not ready to abandon the size proxy even though we have models that can explain the size effect.

3 The observed return seasonality and its implications

Possible explanations of the January seasonal

Monthly stock return seasonality is observed by Officer (1975), Rozeff and Kinney (1976) and Keim (1983), among others. Some of the studies describe the seasonality of the aggregate market return, while others describe the seasonality of the return difference between small and large firms. Proposed explanations of the return seasonality include: (a) the tax-loss selling hypothesis, (b) information release, the conditional risk-expected return hypothesis, (c) the *ex-post* realization hypothesis, and (d) the joint effect of the above hypotheses. We shall briefly discuss the evidence and then consider the implications for tests of equilibrium asset pricing models.

The tax-loss selling hypothesis

The tax-loss selling hypothesis probably receives the most attention among the proposed explanations of the January seasonal. It is not because the hypothesis has the most compelling logical foundation, but because of the amount of data available across countries with different tax years, different tax codes, across different tax regimes over time within a country, and volume data around the end of the tax year. The availability of this huge amount of data should enable us to determine whether tax-loss selling can explain the January seasonal (at least that is what the researchers thought before they began). The number of academic papers on this topic is large and readers are referred to the recent Reinganum and Shapiro (1985) study for an up-to-date bibliography. For the US stock market, Schultz (1985) examines the price change difference between small firms and the Dow-Jones Industrials index around the turn of the year before and after 1917, the year that 'income tax rates [were raised] to levels near those of today.' He found no January seasonal for 1900 to 1917, and a January seasonal for 1918 to 1929 that is similar to the one observed by Keim (1983). Other studies which examine market index monthly return seasonality across countries usually find a January seasonal and another seasonal around the month the tax year ends. Given the evidence, the argument in favor of a tax-loss selling hypothesis is at least as persuasive as the argument against. Conditional on what we know today, very few researchers would take the extreme positions that there is no tax effect or that tax effects can explain the entire January seasonal in the US. Indeed, it is difficult to argue against the proposition that a fraction of the observed January seasonal is due to tax trading.

Expected return seasonality

A possible explanation for the January seasonal is that the expected returns are higher in Januaries. If more information is released in Januaries, then risk is higher because 'more uncertainty' is resolved. An equilibrium risk–return relation may predict higher expected returns in Januaries. While this hypothesis is credible, we do not know of evidence that clearly establishes this as the main reason for the January seasonal.

Nevertheless, we can investigate possible increases in January expected returns by examining a period different from the original seasonality studies. In an unpublished work with Myron Scholes, we look at the return computed from the average monthly wealth index (including dividends) of investing in the aggregate US stock market between 1871 and 1913 (data collected from Cowles Commission for Research in Economics: Common Stock Indexes, by Alfred Cowles third and Associates), and find that the average percentage change is higher from December to January (closely followed by July to August) than the average between any other two consecutive months, lending support to the hypothesis that the expected return around the year end is higher.

If we can observe expectations directly, we can examine seasonality of expected returns. While the risk premium for stocks must be inferred from statistical analysis, the *ex-ante* promised yields on one-month private-issuer instruments are observable. From the quoted rates (provided for us by Robert Stambaugh, computed from data collected by Fama) on commercial paper, banker's acceptances, certificates of deposit (over the T-bill rate), we find that indeed the averaged *ex-ante* yield is highest in January, but it is closely followed by July and August and other months. Indeed, if we were presented with these *ex-ante* measures before knowing of the January seasonality, we might not notice it.

Overall, we believe that the expected returns are higher in January and they are partly responsible for the observed January seasonal. However, from the magnitudes of the *ex-ante* measures as well as out-of-sample evidence collected by Schultz (1985) and us, it is unlikely that the higher expected January returns are the only explanation for the striking January seasonal that we observe in the recent sample period from 1930 to 1980.

The ex-post realization hypothesis

Since the discovery of the January effect was not motivated by any compelling *ex-ante* theoretical considerations, it is quite possible that part of the observed seasonal is simply a result of *ex-post* realization. This is supported by the findings that since 1931 a portfolio of small firms almost always outperforms a portfolio of large firms during January (in contrast with Schultz's (1985) findings of roughly half the times before 1917, which he interprets as evidence in support of a tax-loss selling effect). If indeed the realized distribution since 1931 is truly representative of the perceived *ex-ante* risk, it would imply, in the absence of transaction costs, extreme risk averse behavior around the turn of the year. Perhaps such considerations lead Keim and Stambaugh (1986) to conjecture that the observed January seasonal may be due to the possibility that 'the bad-news whose risk was perceived was not realized ex-post.'

It is also interesting to consider the experience of other markets. In Chan *et al.* (1985), we find that the *ex-post* realized return difference between a portfolio of low grade nonconvertible long-term corporate bonds and long-term government bonds also has a January seasonal. In fact, from 1958 to 1977, the February to December average return difference is statistically insignificant and negative, in contrast with positive and highly significant realized January return difference. Unlike stocks whose risk measures are highly dependent on the models and therefore subject to disagreement, very few people would argue that nonconvertible low grade corporate bonds are not riskier than government bonds from February to December. Comparing these *ex-post* results with the *ex-ante* one month default premiums mentioned above, one would not rule out the negative and insignificant realized risk premium for February to December as partly an *ex-post* sample bias.

Finally, we can examine the period since 1980. The 'small stock premium' (defined as the difference between the lowest quintile and the S&P 500 index) and 'small company stocks: inflation-adjusted total returns' are documented in Ibbotson (1985) for the period 1980–4. The average January small company stock real return is ranked fifth among the twelve months and the average 'small stock premium' for January is ranked second. However, five years is probably too short for us to determine if the realized distribution from 1931 to 1979 is also representative of stock after 1979.

Considering the evidence collectively, it would be difficult to assert that nonzero *ex-ante* risk premiums exist only in Januarys and are zero from February to December. If the January seasonal is uncovered partly because of unusual positive realizations, then it may not be sensible to investigate the risk–return relation just within the eleven months (without January) over the same sample period.

The joint effect hypothesis
This hypothesis is not as empty as one might think, especially when we come to realize that none of the above-mentioned hypotheses can alone

adequately explain the January seasonal. There are other potential candidates, such as liquidity and trade patterns, that we have not discussed. Perhaps trying to advocate one simple explanation for the observed January seasonal is as futile as coming up with one simple explanation why people like chocolate. As long as we do not insist on extreme positions, the January seasonal is not particularly anomalous nor bothersome. In the following sections, we consider implications of the observed January seasonal for tests of equilibrium asset pricing models.

Implications for testing a risk–return relation

Most asset pricing models describe a tradeoff between conditional risk and conditional expected returns. If the conditional expected risk premium is changing but not conditional risk, we can still test the model with the constant risk parameter as long as we allow the estimated risk premiums to be time dependent (such as in the Fama–Macbeth approach or its SURM extension). If both conditional risk premium and conditional risks are changing, then one may use unconditional parameters in the tests only under some restrictive assumptions on the stochastic processes, preferences, or the form of the model. An example of the last case is the model in Chan and Chen (1985).

In this section, we want to consider how the observed January seasonal may or may not affect the empirical design of tests of asset pricing models. Must our interpretation of the existing results necessarily be influenced by the seasonal?

Estimation of conditional risk parameters
If expected returns are different in January, then either the risk premium is different or the risk parameter is different or both. If the risk parameters are different, then we have to estimate them separately. This is not as easy as we might think because to compute the January covariance (which is the type of calculation involved for computing risk parameters for most asset pricing models) we need to know the January expected return. As we discussed in the previous section, the sample January average may be a very poor and biased estimate of the January expected return. The fortunate case would be that the January risk measure is insensitive to the choice of expected returns. While this may be true for risk parameters computed against a stock index, such as the market, it is less likely to be true for risk parameters computed against the macroeconomic variables used in Chen *et al.* (1986) and Chan *et al.* (1985). In fact, Keim and Stambaugh (1986) point out that the January multibetas for the changing risk premium variable are very sensitive to the choice of expected returns.

There are two possible ways to get around this problem. The first is to form mimicking portfolios corresponding to the macroeconomic variables. Chen *et al.* pick economic variables that are outside of the stock market to investigate the relation between these economic variables and the risks borne in the stock market. Since the time-series properties of these economic variables are quite different from those of stock returns, the computed covariance between the extracted innovations and stock returns are bound to be more sensitive than the covariances computed using mimicking stock portfolios. Beyond the straightforward procedure we use to measure these macroeconomic risk parameters, there are bound to be variations of the procedures that will produce parameters with different characteristics. This and other considerations prompt Chan and Chen (1986) to use the same economic intuition underlying the Chen *et al.* study to form mimicking portfolios for the changing risk premium variable. The risk parameters corresponding to this mimicking portfolio exhibit far more stability, and we do not observe the sensitivity that Keim and Stambaugh (1986) find in the risk parameters for the changing risk premium when bond rather than stock returns are used.

Another possibility for getting around the January risk parameter sensitivity problem is if there are reasons to believe that the January risk parameters are close to cross-sectionally perfectly correlated with the February to December risk parameters, then we may simply estimate the risk parameters from February to December. In this case, the estimated risk premium does not have the usual interpretation, but we can still test the model against specific alternatives and examine other cross-sectional restrictions. This assumption of near perfect correlation is an expression of belief much like the stationarity assumptions that are often implicitly made. It cannot be unambiguously tested because we do not have unambiguous January risk parameters to compare to. In the Chan *et al.* study, we re-estimate the risk parameters without Januarys and the model results are similar to those with Januarys included.

We believe that changing risk parameters is a rather difficult issue. If we cannot find an index against which the risk parameters are stable, and we cannot make the assumption that even though the parameters are time varying they are perfectly cross-sectionally correlated, then we are rather pessimistic about the prospect of obtaining a marginal increase in explanatory power from a model resulting from estimating the changes in the conditional risk parameters.

Implications of the realized risk premiums
In this section, we want to consider the question of whether the observed seasonal behavior of the estimated risk premiums is consistent with an equilibrium asset pricing model.

From the *ex-post* seasonal pattern of the realized returns over the past several decades, estimates of risk premiums from February to December are likely to be statistically indistinguishable from zero. Under what conditions is it meaningful to exclude January and consider the realized estimates from February to December as estimates of their *ex-ante* expectations? If we randomly choose and exclude one month out of the twelve in our estimation procedure, the estimates for the remaining eleven months would be unbiased for the expectations. Thus if January is excluded as a result of such a random procedure, then it is meaningful to examine the estimated risk premiums just from February to December. On the other hand, if January is excluded in part because of the observed large realized average returns, then inferences drawn from the February to December estimates may be biased.

A simple example will illustrate this point. Suppose the return distribution is the same for each of the twelve months. If after we compute the realized average returns for the twelve months, we exclude the month with the highest realized average return, the mean estimate for the remaining eleven months will be a downward biased estimate of the true mean. The assumption of identical distribution across months is not critical here, but helps bring across the main point in a simple way. The critical issue here is that if the exclusion decision is at least partially dependent on the *ex-post* observation of the unanticipated returns, then the unexcluded data cannot always be used to produce unbiased estimates. In our case, the true *ex-ante* expected returns could well be higher in January than in any other month. For example, January is the month with the highest *ex-ante* default premium for one-month private-issuer instruments. However, this January default premium is not sufficiently higher than *some* of the other months' premiums that it would have caught our eyes. Thus, even though the expected returns in January might be high, as long as the decisions to exclude Januaries is partly based on the *ex-post* realizations, we cannot draw unambiguous inferences from the remaining data.

There is still another deeper issue involving the observed return seasonality. Can we consider an asset pricing model satisfactory on the basis that the time averaged returns of assets are consistent with their risks?

Let us first take a step back and consider what is involved in testing an asset pricing model. We use a long period of time to measure the averaged realized returns so that they will approximate the unobservable averaged expected returns. We also pick a time unit for the purpose of measuring risk. The time unit of observation is important because the measurement of risk may depend on it. For example, the return on a one month T-bill is riskless in nominal terms only if the observation interval is not shorter than one month. In the case of asset pricing models, the time unit of observation should correspond to how frequently investors revise their investment and consumption decisions. Intuitively, we would guess that this time unit is shorter than one year but probably at least as long as one day in a world with transaction costs. The choice of using a monthly observation interval is a compromise that avoids the measurement difficulty with daily data and the measurement imprecision with yearly data. However, the time unit corresponding to investment and consumption decisions could well be different. In fact, it does not even need to have a regular length, and it is probably endogenous to other external shocks of the economy. Thus the choice of one month is merely an approximation and, just as all non-vacuous models are false, the real meaning of empirical tests of models lies with whether our implementation can help explain some phenomenon in a consistent (over time) way. If our implementation of the model can explain the averaged returns of assets without unexplainable contradictions with the data, then we would regard the model to be satisfactory.

Let us then consider whether the *ex-post* seasonal pattern of returns can be deemed as contradictory evidence. We shall abstract away from issues such as *ex-post* biases, seasonal risk parameters and seasonal price of risk. Suppose the time-averaged returns of assets are consistent with our model, but the time pattern of the *expected* return is not coincident with the time pattern of 'risk' borne, does that contradict our model?

In a perfect capital market, risk and expected returns are likely to be coincident to eliminate profitable across-time substitutions. In a less than perfect capital market the across-time substitution decision becomes a very complicated optimization problem taking into account the timing of tax trades, direct and indirect transaction costs, the cost of speeding up and delaying purchases and sales, and the cost of deviating from investment strategy that has the best risk characteristics for hedging. Let us expand on this point using the following scenario.

Assume that the true expected returns of small firms are in excess of the risks in January. Consider the strategy of an investor trying to exploit this excess. If he follows the simple rule of buying small company stocks in December and selling them after January, the round-trip transaction cost as a percentage of this anticipated 'excess expected return' is going to be very high. If he should concentrate on just a few small company stocks, he is bearing large non-systematic risk for the purpose of gaining the 'excess.' If he should spread his purchases across many small company stocks, his transaction costs will even be higher. If he decides to sell the stocks in February, his entire profit, both the 'normal' and the 'excess,' less transaction cost is subject to ordinary income tax (versus if he buys and holds, he can accumulate tax free until realization). If he waits until the purchases qualify as long-term capital transactions, he is bearing more than just the risk in January. If he creates another hedge portfolio to neutralize the risk until sale, he is incurring yet another cost. Suppose before the trades to capture this 'excess,' the risk characteristics of his investment portfolio are at the optimum. His trades in December will force him to bear the cost of deviating from this optimum. (If he chooses derivative securities that are usually highly levered, this cost is usually even higher.) Thus if we total up all the marginal costs, it is doubtful that the marginal benefit is large enough to induce any across-time substitution (to capture the 'excess').

Let us next consider the case of a long-term investor. He knows that over the time the expected return will justify his risk bearing. Even though he intends to buy and hold, he is still bearing the period-to-period risk because he revises his investment and consumption decisions accordingly. If the revision can be accomplished via either transactions with large or small company stocks, he will choose the large company stocks because of lower transaction costs. As long as the period-to-period return variance is large for small stocks, he may not bear the cost of waiting (after January) and deviating from optimal investment risk characteristics when the optimum calls for liquidating some of the small company stocks. Overall, the seasonal pattern of return affects very little the investment decisions of the long-term investor. In addition, if the higher transaction costs of trading small company stocks induce a clientele effect, that purchases of small stocks are mainly held for long-term investment purposes, the long-run expected returns will be determined by the risks borne, and the time pattern of expected return could well be rather arbitrary for the short run.

What we try to illustrate in the above scenario is that it is not necessarily a contradiction to an asset pricing model for the expected return to have an unexploitable seasonal pattern that is not coincident with the risk borne. Of course, an equilibrium where the risk–return relation holds, not only on the average across time but also at every moment in time, will be more stable. However, if temporary violations of pure arbitrage conditions are not uncommon in low transaction cost markets such as the options and the futures, perhaps requiring a preference based risk–return relation to hold at every moment is not too realistic. As long as the seasonal pattern of returns is not clearly exploitable, we do not find any contradiction in accepting an asset pricing model that explains only the averaged returns.

4 Conclusions

Let us briefly summarize what we know and what we do not know at this stage. We know that the averaged returns of size-ranked portfolios can be captured by either a multiple factor model with macroeconomic variables or a single factor model with time varying parameters. There are several possible scenarios in which both of these models can be consistent with the data, but we have not distinguished among them.

These models do not explain why we observe the January seasonal in the *ex-post* return data. As we argue above, it is not necessary for an asset pricing model that explains the averaged returns of size-ranked port-folios to also explain the January seasonal. In a less than perfect capital market, the existence of the January seasonal does not pose any contradiction to the models.

Even though the question of the January seasonal can be logically disjoint from the question why averaged returns are different across assets, it is still a fascinating challenge to find out why the realized average returns in January have been so high. Perhaps unlocking the mystery of the January seasonal will give us profound insights into many other problems in investments.

Notes

* I am grateful to K.C. Chan, Wayne Ferson, Shmuel Kandel, Marc Reinganum, Rob Stambaugh, Sheridan Titman and Rob Vishny for helpful comments and suggestions.

References

Banz, R. (1981) 'The Relationship between Return and Market Value of Common Stocks', *Journal of Financial Economics*, 9, 3–18.

Blume, M. and Stambaugh, R. (1983) 'Biases in Computed Returns, an Application to the Size Effect', *Journal of Financial Economics*, 12, 387–404.

Breeden, D. (1979) 'An Intertemporal Asset Pricing Model with Stochastic Consumption and Investment Opportunties', *Journal of Financial Economics*, 7, 265–96.

Chan, K.C. (1985) 'Market Value Changes and Time-Varying Risk', unpublished Ph.D. dissertation, University of Chicago.

Chan, K.C. and Chen, N. (1985) 'An Unconditional Asset Pricing Test and the Role of Firm Size as an Instrumental Variable for Risk', working paper, University of Chicago.

Chan, K.C. and Chen, N. (1986) 'Business Cycles and the Returns of Small and Large Firms', manuscript, University of Chicago.

Chan, K.C., Chen, N. and Hsieh, D. (1985) 'An Exploratory Investigation of the Firm Size Effect', *Journal of Financial Economics*, 14, 451–71.

Chen, N. (1983) 'Some Empirical Tests of the Theory of Arbitrage Pricing', *Journal of Finance*, 38, 1393–1414.

Chen, N., Roll, R. and Ross, S. (1986) 'Economic Forces and the Stock Market', *Journal of Business*, 59(3), 383–403.

Connor, G. and Korajczyk, R. (1985) 'Risk and Return in an Equilibrium APT, Theory and Tests', working paper, University of California, Berkeley.

Cox, J., Ingersoll, J. and Ross, S. (1985) 'An Intertemporal General Equilibrium Model of Asset Prices', *Econometrica*, 53, 363–84.

Huberman, G. and Kandel, S. (1985) 'A Size Based Stock Returns Model', working paper, University of Chicago.

Ibbotson, R. (1985) 'Stocks, Bonds, Bills and Inflation', *1985 Yearbook*, Chicago Ibbotson Associates, Capital Market Research Center.

Keim, D. (1983) 'Size-related Anomalies and Stock Market Seasonality: Further Empirical Evidence', *Journal of Financial Economics*, 12, 13–32.

Keim, D. and Stambaugh, R. (1986) 'Predicting Returns in the Stock and Bond Markets', *Journal of Financial Economics*, 17, 357–90.

Lehmann, B. and Modest, D. (1985) 'The Empirical Foundations of the Arbitrage Pricing Theory I: The Empirical Tests', working paper, Columbia University.

Officer, R.R. (1975) 'Seasonality in the Australian Capital Market: Market Efficiency and Empirical Issues', *Journal of Financial Economics*, 2, 29–52.

Reinganum, M. (1981) 'Misspecification of Capital Asset Pricing: Empirical Anomalies based on Earnings' Yields and Market Values', *Journal of Financial Economics*, 9, 19–46.

Reinganum, M. (1982) 'A Direct Test of Roll's Conjecture on the Firm Size Effect', *Journal of Finance*, 37, 27–36.

Reinganum, M. and Shapiro, A. (1985) 'Taxes and Stock Return Seasonality: Evidence from the London Stock Exchange', working paper, University of Southern California.

Roll, R. (1981) 'A Possible Explanation of the Small Firm Effect', *Journal of Finance*, 36, 879–88.

Roll, R. (1983) 'On Computing Mean Returns and the Small Firm Premium', *Journal of Financial Economics*, 12, 371–86.

Ross, S. (1976) 'The Arbitrage Theory of Capital Asset Pricing', *Journal of Economic Theory*, 13, 341–60.

Rozeff, M.S. and Kinney, W.R. Jr. (1976) 'Capital Market Seasonality: The Case of Stock Returns', *Journal of Financial Economics*, 3, 379–402.

Schultz, P. (1983) 'Transaction Costs and the Small Firm Effect: A Comment', *Journal of Financial Economics*, 12, 81–8.

Schultz, P. (1985) 'Personal Income Taxes and the January Effect: Small Firm Stock Returns before the War Revenue Act of 1917, *Journal of Finance*, 40, 333–43.

Stoll, H. and Whaley, R. (1983) 'Transaction Costs and the Small Firm Effect', *Journal of Financial Economics*, 12, 57–79.

15 The pricing of equity on the London Stock Exchange: seasonality and size premium

ALBERT CORHAY, GABRIEL HAWAWINI and PIERRE MICHEL

1 Purpose of the study

In this study we examine the relationship between average monthly returns and risk for portfolios of common stocks traded on the London Stock Exchange (LSE). We test the validity of the capital asset pricing model (Sharpe, 1964; Black, 1972) using a methodology similar to that of Fama and MacBeth (1973). To the best of our knowledge, this is the first empirical test of the CAPM on the LSE that uses the Fama–MacBeth methodology.

Using the LSE data we also investigate two phenomena recently observed on the New York Stock Exchange (NYSE). The first is the size effect discovered by Banz (1981). He showed that small capitalization firms earn, on average, higher risk-adjusted returns than large capitalization firms.[1] The second phenomenon was documented by Tinic and West (1984, 1986). They showed that the estimated slope coefficient (risk premium) of the relationship between average returns and systematic risk on the NYSE is significantly positive only in January. During the rest of the year there is no significant relationship between average returns and systematic risk on the NYSE. In other words, the CAPM is valid only in January on the NYSE.

The rest of this chapter is organized as follows. In section 2 we give a summary of our major findings. In section 3 we look at the evidence from countries other than the United Kingdom. In section 4 we describe the properties of our sample and outline the methodology we employ to perform our analysis. As pointed out earlier, we estimate the coefficient (risk premium) of the relationship between average monthly stock returns and their corresponding risk using a methodology similar to that of Fama and MacBeth (1973). We examine various specifications of the risk–return relationship. In section 5.1 we adopt the two-parameter capital asset pricing model in which the risk measure is systematic risk (beta coefficient), and examine the seasonality of the average estimated monthly *systematic* risk premia. In section 5.3 we examine the seasonality of the average estimated monthly risk premia when the risk measure is total risk (variance of returns), unsystematic risk and skewness. In section 5.4 we look at the seasonality in the average estimated monthly coefficients of the Fama–MacBeth (1973) four-parameter model. In sections 6 and 7 we examine the size effect on the LSE. Concluding remarks are found in section 8.

2 Summary of major findings

1   The relationship between average monthly returns and systematic risk over the entire test period is *not* statistically significant (section 5.1 and table 1).

2   The relationship between average monthly returns and systematic risk is significantly *positive* only in *April* and significantly *negative* in *May* and *November*. An interpretation of this phenomenon is given in section 5.2 and table 1.

3   When risk is measured by either total risk, unsystematic risk or skewness, we found a significantly positive relationship between average monthly returns and risk. These relationships do, however, exhibit monthly seasonality (section 5.3 and table 2).

4   The positive April seasonal in the systematic risk premium remains but the negative May seasonal disappears after controlling for unsystematic risk. It appears that the CAPM is valid on the LSE only in April (section 5.4 and table 3).

5   There is a weak size effect on the LSE. This phenomenon is seasonal. *May* is the *only* month for which the size effect is significant. On the LSE most of the small size premium is earned during the month of May (section 6 and tables 4 and 5).

6   After controlling for systematic risk, the size effect is significant over the entire period as well as over April and May. After controlling for size, the systematic risk premium is significantly positive in April. It is significantly negative in May and June (section 7 and table 6).

3 Evidence from other countries

At the time of this writing the evidence on estimated risk-premia seasonality is limited to the United States, the United Kingdom, France and Belgium. The US evidence was briefly presented in the introductory section. The UK evidence is presented in this chapter. Evidence on

French and Belgian common stocks can be found in Corhay *et al.* (1986, 1987). They report a significantly positive January effect in the systematic risk premium of Belgian common stocks over the fifteen-year period from January 1969 to December 1983. Over that same period, the systematic risk premium of French common stocks is never significant.

4 Methodology

4.1 Data

The rates of return data used in the study are drawn from the London Business School monthly returns file (Smithers, 1977, 1980). Monthly returns are calculated as logarithms of price relatives including dividend payments ($\log(P_t+D_t)/P_{t-1}$). The data begin in January 1955 and end in December 1983. The number of firms in the sample varies from a minimum of 761 to a maximum of 1674.

The market index we employed is an equally weighted portfolio of all the securities in the sample. We have also performed our tests with a value weighted index. Since we found that the choice of the index does not affect the results significantly, we only report our findings based on the equally weighted index.[2]

4.2 Test design

The methodology employed to estimate monthly risk premia and examine the size effect on the LSE is similar to that found in Fama and MacBeth (1973) and Banz (1981). It is carried out in three steps. An initial period of one year of monthly data is used to construct portfolios on the basis of size and risk (construction period). The following year of monthly data is employed to estimate the risk of the portfolios (estimation period). Finally, the estimation of the risk premia and the examination of the size effect are performed over the third year of monthly data (test period). The entire procedure is then repeated after dropping the first year of data. Details are given below.

4.3 Portfolio construction

The first year of monthly data (1955) is used to construct *five* equally weighted portfolios ranked on the basis of the magnitude of their year-end market capitalization (size). Each of those five size-related portfolios are then divided into *four* portfolios ranked on the basis of the magnitude of their beta coefficients.[3] This procedure led to a total of *twenty* equally weighted portfolios constructed on the basis of both market capitalization (size) and systematic risk (beta). The total number of securities with which we constructed the portfolios varied from 761 over the period 1971–76 to 1674 over the period 1979–83.

4.4 Risk estimation

The second year of monthly data (1956) is used to estimate the risk of each stock in the sample. Four measures of risk are considered in this study: systematic risk (beta coefficient), total risk (variance of total returns), unsystematic risk (standard error of the residuals of the single-index market model) and skewness (the ratio of the return distribution's third moment around its mean to the distribution's standard deviation cubed). Portfolios' betas (β_p) are obtained by calculating the arithmetic average of the betas of the individual stocks that make up the portfolio. The same averaging procedure is used to calculate portfolios' total risk or variance (V_p), portfolios' unsystematic risk (U_p) and portfolios' skewness (SK_p).

4.5 Model testing

Finally, the third year of monthly data (1957) is used to estimate the monthly risk premia according to the following set of regressions:

$$R_{pt} = \gamma_{0t} + \gamma_{1t}\beta_{p,t-1} + \mu_{pt} \tag{1}$$

$$R_{pt} = \gamma'_{0t} + \gamma_{2t}V_{p,t-1} + \mu'_{pt} \tag{2}$$

$$R_{pt} = \gamma''_{0t} + \gamma_{3t}U_{p,t-1} + \mu''_{pt} \tag{3}$$

$$R_{pt} = \gamma^*_{0t} + \gamma^*_{1t}\beta_{p,t-1} + \gamma^{**}_{1t}\beta^2_{p,t-1} + \gamma^*_{3t}U_{p,t-1} + \mu^*_{pt} \tag{4}$$

$$R_{pt} = \gamma'''_{0t} + \gamma_{4t}SK_{p,t-1} + \mu'''_{pt} \tag{5}$$

$$R_{pt} = \gamma^{**}_{0t} + \gamma_{5t}\log(SIZE)_{p,t-1} + \epsilon_{pt} \tag{6}$$

$$R_{pt} = \gamma^s_{0t} + \gamma^s_{1t}\beta_{p,t-1} + \gamma^s_{5t}\log(SIZE)_{p,t-1} + \epsilon^s_{pt} \tag{7}$$

in which:

R_{pt} = realized return of portfolio p in month t;
γ_{1t} = systematic risk premium in month t;
γ_{2t} = total risk premium in month t;
γ_{3t} = unsystematic risk premium in month t;
γ_{4t} = skewness premium in month t;
γ_{5t} = size premium in month t;
$\beta_{p,t-1}$ = beta of portfolio p estimated over a twelve-month

estimation period ending in the calendar year preceding month t and updated yearly;

$V_{p,t-1}$ = variance of portfolio p estimated over a twelve-month estimation period ending in the calendar year preceding month t and updated yearly;

$U_{p,t-1}$ = unsystematic risk of portfolio p estimated over a twelve-month estimation period ending in the calendar year preceding month t and updated yearly;

$SK_{p,t-1}$ = skewness coefficient (return distributions' third moment around the mean divided by the standard deviation cubed) of portfolio p estimated over a twelve-month estimation period ending in the calendar year preceding month t and updated yearly;

$\log(SIZE)_{p,t-1}$ = logarithm of the market capitalization of portfolio p (market capitalization is given in units of ½ million pounds) at the end of the calendar year preceding month t and updated yearly.

Regression (1) is the standard two-parameter capital asset pricing model (Sharpe, 1964; Black, 1972; Fama, 1976) according to which security holders are compensated only for bearing systematic risk. Regressions (2) and (3) are run on the theory that investors may not be fully diversified. In this case, both total risk (variance) and unsystematic risk may contribute to the pricing of securities (Levy, 1978).

Regression (4) is the Fama–MacBeth (1973) version of a four-parameter capital asset pricing model. With this specification we test for the linearity of the relationship between average returns and systematic risk (if the relationship is linear γ_{1t}^{**} should be statistically equal to zero) and for the marginal contribution of unsystematic risk to the pricing of securities (if unsystematic risk is diversified away it is not priced in the market and γ_{3t}^{*} should be statistically equal to zero).

Regression (5) is run to determine whether the skewness of return distributions is priced in the market. We should expect a negative relationship between average returns and skewness ($\gamma_{4t}<0$) since investors should be willing to accept lower average returns on portfolios with positively skewed returns (Francis and Archer, 1979, ch. 16).

Regression (6) is run to determine if there is a size premium on the LSE. If portfolios constructed on the basis of market capitalization at the end of the calendar year have different average returns over the following year then γ_{5t} will be different from zero. If portfolios of smaller firms outperform portfolios of larger firms then γ_{5t} will be negative. Finally, regression (7) allows us to examine the combined effect of systematic risk and size on average returns.

Table 1 *Average values of the estimated coefficients of the regression*
$$R_{pt} = \gamma_{0t} + \gamma_{1t}\beta_{p,t-1} + \mu_{pt}$$

based on monthly data from January 1957 to December 1983[a] using the Fama–MacBeth (1973) methodology with an equally weighted market index

Average over	Sample size	$\bar{\gamma}_0$ (intercept)	$\bar{\gamma}_1$ (beta)
All months	324	0.0153 [b] 7.59	−0.0041 −1.51
January	27	0.0282 [b] 3.61	0.0094 0.61
February	27	0.0249 [b] 5.44	−0.0119 −1.45
March	27	0.0087 1.49	0.0006 0.06
April	27	0.0177 [b] 2.28	0.0184 [b] 1.89
May	27	0.0204 [b] 3.00	−0.0207 [b] −2.84
June	27	0.0069 1.05	−0.0148 −1.40
July	27	0.0122 1.53	−0.0106 −1.10
August	27	0.0040 0.57	0.0118 1.64
September	27	0.0083 1.03	−0.0091 −1.35
October	27	0.0194 [b] 3.19	−0.0094 −1.27
November	27	0.0189 [b] 2.16	−0.0153 [b] −1.91
December	27	0.0135 [b] 2.96	0.0026 0.31

Notes: [a]t-statistics are below the average values of the estimated coefficients.
[b]Significant average values at the 0.05 level.

For each *month* of the twelve-month test period we calculate the realized return of each one of the twenty portfolios (R_{pt}). These twenty portfolio returns are then cross-sectionally regressed on beta (regression (1)), variance (regression (2)), unsystematic risk (regression (3)), skewness (regression (5)), size (regression (6)) as well as on beta, beta squared and unsystematic risk (regression (4)) and beta and size (regression (7)). Recall that risk and size are estimated over the preceding calendar year (estimation period) and are updated every year. From the twelve cross-sectional regressions we obtain twelve monthly estimates of the market risk premia $\gamma_1, \gamma_2, \gamma_3, \gamma_4, \gamma_1^*, \gamma_1^{**}, \gamma_3^*$ and γ_1^s, and the coefficients of size γ_5 and γ_5^*.

The entire procedure is then repeated using the second year of monthly data (1956) to construct portfolios, the third year of monthly data (1957) to estimate risk and size and the fourth year of monthly data (1958) to estimate the monthly relationship between realized returns, risk and size. Dropping one year of early data and adding a new one to estimate the risk and size premia, we kept on repeating the entire procedure until we reached the year 1983. This approach provides a total of 324 monthly estimates of the risk and size premia $\gamma_1, \gamma_2, \gamma_3, \gamma_4$ and γ_5; twenty-seven estimates for each of the twelve months of the year (from January 1957 to December 1983). Note that all the tests performed in this study are predictive tests since the set of independent or explanatory variables are estimated over a period that precedes the month over which portfolios' returns are calculated.

5 Evidence of monthly risk-premia seasonality

5.1 *Systematic risk-premium seasonality* (regression (1))

Evidence of seasonality in the monthly estimates of the systematic risk premia is reported in Table 1. First, note that no relationship exists, on average, between monthly portfolio returns and systematic risk over the entire twenty-seven-year period from January 1957 to December 1983. Price behavior on the LSE is not consistent with the standard two-parameter capital asset pricing model.

Turning to the month-to-month results we see that *April* is the *only* month of the year in which the systematic risk premium is *positive*. It is equal to 1.84 percent. This is equivalent to 22 percent on an annual basis. If we remove the month of April from the data, the relationship between return and systematic risk is, on average, negative. This phenomenon is primarily the result of a significantly downward sloping risk–return relationship in the months of May and November (the May risk premium is equal to minus 2.07 percent, that is, minus 24.84 percent on an annual

Table 2 *Average values of the estimated slope coefficient of the regressions*

$$R_{pt} = \gamma'_{0t} + \gamma_{2t}V_{p,t-1} + \mu'_{pt}$$
$$R_{pt} = \gamma''_{0t} + \gamma_{3t}U_{p,t-1} + \mu''_{pt}$$
$$R_{pt} = \gamma'''_{0t} + \gamma_{4t}SK_{p,t-1} + \mu'''_{pt}$$

based on monthly data from January 1957 to December 1983[a] using the Fama–MacBeth (1973) methodology with an equally weighted market index

Average over	Sample size	$\bar{\gamma}_2$ (total risk)	$\bar{\gamma}_3$ (unsystematic risk)	$\bar{\gamma}_4$ (skewness)
All months	324	0.3038 [b] 1.89	0.0896 [b] 2.19	0.0338 [b] 2.36
January	27	1.4429 [b] 2.16	0.1860 1.01	0.1253 1.27
February	27	0.4746 1.09	0.1720 1.31	0.1244 [b] 2.41
March	27	−0.3982 −0.69	−0.1048 −0.73	−0.0393 −0.93
April	27	0.0643 0.14	−0.0036 −0.03	−0.0514 0.94
May	27	0.6266 1.14	0.3338 [b] 2.57	0.0825 [b] 2.61
June	27	0.0300 0.06	0.1178 0.93	0.0104 0.19
July	27	0.9677 1.42	0.1953 1.34	0.0111 0.26
August	27	−0.9614 [b] −2.68	−0.2115 [b] −1.97	−0.0379 −0.96
September	27	0.2961 0.53	0.1376 1.03	0.0248 0.65
October	27	0.8932 1.49	0.2508 1.73	0.0080 0.28
November	27	−0.0543 −0.09	0.1317 0.82	0.0606 1.54
December	27	0.2639 0.52	−0.1298 −1.02	−0.0151 −0.43

Notes: [a]t-statistics are below the average values of the estimated slopes.
[b]Significant average values at the 0.05 level.

basis). Clearly, the negative relationship between return and systematic risk in the months of May and November offsets the positive contribution of the month of April and yields a negative but statistically insignificant risk–return relationship over the entire twenty-seven-year test period.

5.2 Interpretation

The positive April effect reported above *may* be tax-induced. It is consistent with the tax-loss selling hypothesis. According to this hypothesis, as the end of the fiscal year approaches (March in the United Kingdom), investors can reduce their taxes by selling the stocks on which they lost money during the year. In doing so, they realize capital losses that are deductible from their taxable income. The sale of securities at the end of the fiscal year depresses prices which recover at the beginning of the next fiscal year (April) as stocks move back toward their equilibrium value. The linear and positive relationship between average returns and systematic risk in April is therefore consistent with the tax-loss selling hypothesis.

The negative May effect is consistent with the old LSE adage 'sell in May and go away'. According to the *Investors Chronicle* (1986), there is some logic behind this adage since the market winds down for the holiday season. Parliament goes quiet and many companies with March year-ends have published their final results by mid-June.

5.3 Other risk-premia seasonality (regressions (2), (3) and (5))

The estimated risk premia when risk is measured by variance, unsystematic risk and skewness are reported in Table 2. To save space, we do not report the estimated value of the intercepts[4]. Over the twenty-seven-year period, the three risk measures are significantly positively related to average return.

Turning to the month-to-month results, note that the total risk premium (variance) is significantly positive in January and significantly negative in August. Hence, the positive *April* effect in the systematic risk premium is replaced by a positive *January* effect in the total risk premium. The unsystematic risk premium is significantly *positive* in May and significantly negative in August. The skewness premium is significantly positive in February and May.

A comparison of results in table 2 and table 1 indicates that unsystematic risk premia (table 2) and systematic risk premia (table 1) have opposite signs. This observation is consistent with the fact that portfolios' unsystematic risk is negatively correlated with portfolios' systematic risk on the LSE (low beta portfolios have higher unsystematic risk than high beta portfolios).

Table 3 *Average values of the estimated coefficients of the regression*
$$R_{pt} = \gamma^*_{0t} + \gamma^*_{1t}\beta_{p,t-1} + \gamma^{**}_{1t}\beta^2_{p,t-1} + \gamma^*_{3t}U_{p,t-1} + \mu^*_{pt}$$
based on monthly data from January 1957 to December 1983[a] using the Fama–MacBeth (1973) methodology with an equally weighted market index

Average over	Sample size	$\bar{\gamma}^*_0$ (intercept)	$\bar{\gamma}^*_1$ (beta)	$\bar{\gamma}^{**}_1$ (beta^2)	$\bar{\gamma}^*_3$ (unsyst. risk)
All months	324	0.0102 [b] 3.17	−0.0040 −1.05	0.0001 0.10	0.0653 [b] 1.81
January	27	−0.0003 −0.02	0.0176 1.12	−0.0012 −0.28	0.3263 [b] 1.83
February	27	0.0112 0.94	−0.0043 −0.29	−0.0036 −0.58	0.2071 1.58
March	27	0.0136 1.05	−0.0019 −0.15	0.0016 0.29	−0.1121 −0.81
April	27	0.0137 1.35	0.0269 [b] 1.87	−0.0061 −1.24	0.0565 0.64
May	27	0.0079 0.63	−0.0136 −1.02	−0.0026 −0.47	0.1424 1.19
June	27	0.0066 0.81	−0.0159 −0.96	−0.0008 −0.15	0.0143 0.18
July	27	0.0149 1.40	−0.0267 −1.69	0.0076 1.40	0.0428 0.34
August	27	0.0099 1.15	0.0149 1.68	−0.0032 −1.11	−0.0217 −0.23
September	27	0.0060 0.57	−0.0109 −1.10	0.0002 0.61	0.0334 0.25
October	27	−0.0052 −0.43	0.0067 0.56	−0.0061 −1.21	0.2142 1.60
November	27	0.0201 1.54	−0.0267 [b] −2.22	0.0057 1.49	−0.0305 −0.22
December	27	0.0239 [b] 2.74	−0.0147 [b] −1.46	0.0100 [b] 2.34	−0.0893 −0.85

Notes: [a]t-statistics are below the average values of the estimated coefficients.
[b]Significant average values at the 0.05 level.

Table 4 *Average values of the estimated coefficients of the regression*
$$R_{pt} = \gamma_{0t}^{**} + \gamma_{5t} \log(SIZE)_{p,t-1} + \epsilon_{pt}$$
based on monthly data from January 1957 to December 1983[a] using the Fama–MacBeth (1973) methodology with an equally weighted market index

Average over	Sample size	$\bar{\gamma}_0^{**}$ (intercept)	$\bar{\gamma}_5$ (size)
All months	324	0.0244 [b] 3.70	−0.0009 −1.74
January	27	0.0246 0.67	0.0008 0.26
February	27	0.0402 [b] 1.81	−0.0018 −1.05
March	27	0.0025 0.11	0.0005 0.32
April	27	0.0213 0.94	0.0009 0.56
May	27	0.0690 [b] 3.92	−0.0045 [b] −3.51
June	27	0.0249 1.21	−0.0021 −1.31
July	27	0.0363 [b] 2.01	−0.0023 −1.69
August	27	−0.0146 −0.74	0.0020 1.35
September	27	0.0337 [b] 1.88	−0.0022 −1.54
October	27	0.0487 [b] 2.20	−0.0026 −1.56
November	27	0.0267 1.10	−0.0014 −0.82
December	27	−0.0201 −0.87	0.0024 1.54

Notes: [a]t-statistics are below the average values of the estimated coefficients.
[b]Significant average values at the 0.05 level.

Finally, the significantly positive skewness premium reported in table 2 is not consistent with the hypothesis that investors should be willing to accept lower average returns on portfolios with positively skewed returns. A similar positive skewness effect has been observed in US common stock data. See Francis and Archer (1979) for possible explanations of this phenomenon.

5.4 Seasonality in the risk premia of the four-parameter capital asset pricing model (regression (4))

Results are summarized in table 3. For the overall period unsystematic risk dominates with a significantly positive premium. This result is not consistent with security pricing according to the CAPM.

Turning to the month-to-month results we still observe a positive April effect in the systematic risk premium even after controlling for unsystematic risk. This result provides additional support to our earlier conclusion (section 5.1) that stock price behavior on the LSE is consistent with the standard CAPM only in *April*.

6 Evidence of a size effect (regression (6))

The relationship between average portfolio returns and the logarithm of market capitalization is given in table 4. Note first that over the twenty-seven-year period (from 1957 to 1983) the relationship is negative (indicating that small firms outperformed, on average, large firms) but it is not statistically significant.

Turning to the month-to-month results we can see that the size effect is a seasonal phenomenon. Indeed, *May* is the *only* month of the year for which there is a *significant* relationship between average returns and size. The relationship is negative indicating that most of the small size premium is earned during the month of May. These results are consistent with the earlier findings of Levis (1985).

7 The risk-adjusted size effect and risk-premia seasonality (regression (7))

What is the relationship between average returns and size after controlling for systematic risk? If small firms were riskier than large firms the risk differential would explain the difference in returns. This is not the case. On the contrary, the results in table 5 indicate that on the LSE smaller firms have smaller systematic risk than larger firms. Similar findings are also reported by Levis (1985).

The relationship between average returns and size after controlling for

Table 5 *Characteristics of the five size portfolios over the period January 1957 to December 1983[a]*

Portfolio size	Average market value in £ million	Average monthly beta	Average monthly return (all months)	Average return in May
Largest	99.59	1.09	0.0095 $(3.02)^b$	−0.0060 $(−0.67)$
2	14.30	0.97	0.0114 $(3.82)^b$	−0.0002 $(−0.02)$
3	5.14	0.82	0.0110 $(4.06)^b$	−0.0020 $(−0.26)$
4	2.03	0.68	0.0122 $(5.24)^b$	−0.0029 $(−0.46)$
Smallest	0.66	0.51	0.0144 $(7.04)^b$	0.0096 $(1.96)^b$

Notes: [a] t-statistics are below the average returns.
[b] Significant average values at the 0.05 level.

systematic risk can also be examined with the estimated coefficients of regression (7) given in table 6. Over the twenty-seven-year period the size effect is *significantly* negative after controlling for systematic risk. Recall that the size effect without risk adjustment was found negative but not statistically significant (regression (6)).

Turning to the month-to-month results we note the following: (a) after adjusting for size, the systematic risk premium is significantly positive only in April and significantly negative in May and June. These results are consistent with those reported in section 5.1, table 1, where no adjustment for size was made; (b) after adjusting for systematic risk, the size effect is significant only in April and May and it is negative. This result is consistent with that reported in section 6, table 4, where no adjustment for systematic risk was made.

Note that in May we have both a negative systematic risk premium and a negative size effect. As a result, small firms have, on average, positive returns in May (see table 5). As pointed out by Levis (1985), the city's old saying 'sell in May and go away' seems to be applicable only to larger firms. This conclusion is supported by the results given in the last column of table 5.

8 Concluding remarks

We reported evidence of seasonality in the estimated coefficients of the relationship between average returns and risk on the LSE. We also reported the presence of a size effect which is itself seasonal. We can

Table 6 *Average values of the estimated coefficients of the regression*

$$R_{pt} = \gamma^s_{0t} + \gamma^s_{1t}\beta_{p,t-1} + \gamma^*_{5t}\log(SIZE)_{p,t-1} + \epsilon^s_{pt}$$

based on monthly data from January 1957 to December 1983[a] using the Fama–MacBeth (1973) methodology with an equally weighted market index

Average over	Sample size	$\tilde{\gamma}^s_0$ (intercept)	$\tilde{\gamma}^s_1$ (beta)	$\tilde{\gamma}^*_5$ (size)
All months	324	0.0270 [b] 4.26	−0.0032 −1.44	−0.0008 [b] −1.96
January	27	0.0628 [b] 1.98	0.0169 1.52	−0.0028 −1.32
February	27	0.0388 [b] 1.96	−0.0067 −1.16	−0.0013 −0.89
March	27	0.0093 0.40	−0.0008 −0.10	0.0001 0.04
April	27	0.0258 1.25	0.0157 [b] 2.10	−0.0004 [b] −2.13
May	27	0.0538 [b] 2.95	−0.0150 [b] −2.61	−0.0025 [b] −2.14
June	27	0.0098 0.54	−0.0190 [b] −2.55	0.0001 0.08
July	27	0.0286 1.27	−0.0129 −1.54	−0.0009 −0.68
August	27	−0.0058 −0.32	0.0037 0.68	0.0012 0.97
September	27	0.0269 1.33	−0.0064 −0.96	−0.0014 −1.03
October	27	0.0439 [b] 1.88	−0.0023 −0.33	−0.0021 −1.26
November	27	0.0314 1.31	−0.0123 −1.52	−0.0009 −0.57
December	27	−0.0012 −0.06	0.0012 0.18	0.0010 0.77

Notes: [a]t-statistics are below the average values of the estimated coefficients.
[b]Significant average values at the 0.05 level.

conclude from this evidence that the capital asset pricing model does not provide an adequate description of the historical relationship between average returns and risk on the LSE over the twenty-seven-year period covered by this study (1957–83).

This conclusion can be interpreted either as a failure of the two-parameter capital asset pricing model to provide an accurate representation of how securities are priced on the LSE over the sample period or, according to Roll (1977), as a proof that the capital asset pricing model cannot be tested unambiguously without knowing (and using) the exact composition of the true market portfolio.

Notes

1 See also Keim (1983) and Roll (1983).
2 Results based on the value weighted index are available on request from Gabriel Hawawini.
3 The beta coefficient of individual securities was estimated with the single-index market model (Sharpe, 1963; Fama, 1976) using twelve monthly security returns and the corresponding twelve monthly returns on the equally weighted index.
4 Complete results are available on request from Gabriel Hawawini.

References

Banz, R. (1981) 'The Relationship between Return and Market Value of Common Stocks', *Journal of Financial Economics*, 9, June, 3–18.
Black, F. (1972) 'Capital Market Equilibrium with Restricted Borrowing', *Journal of Business*, 45, July, 445–55.
Corhay, A., Hawawini, G. and Michel, P. (1986) 'Risk-premia Seasonality in U.S. and European Equity Markets', working paper (February), INSEAD, Fontainebleau, France.
Corhay, A., Hawawini, G. and Michel, P. (1987) 'Seasonality in the Risk-Return Relationship: Some International Evidence', *Journal of Finance*, 42, March, 49–68.
Fama, E. (1976) *Foundations of Finance*, New York: Basic Books.
Fama, E. and MacBeth, J. (1973) 'Risk, Return and Equilibrium: Empirical Tests', *Journal of Political Economy*, 71, May/June, 607–36.
Francis, J. and Archer, S. (1979) *Portfolio Analysis*, New Jersey: Prentice-Hall.
Hawawini, G. (1984) *European Equity Markets: Price Behavior and Efficiency*, Salomon Brothers Center for the Study of Financial Institutions, Graduate School of Business Administration, New York University, Monograph 4/5.
Investors Chronicle, (1986) 'Charts, Theories and Systems', 75, 3–9 January, 58.
Keim, E. (1983) 'Size-related Anomalies and Stock Return Seasonality: Further Empirical Evidence', *Journal of Financial Economics*, 12, June, 13–22.
Levis, M. (1985) 'Are Small Firms Big Performers?' *Investment Analyst*, 76, April, 21–7.
Levy, H. (1978) 'Equilibrium in an Imperfect Market: A Constraint on the Number of Securities in the Portfolio', *American Economic Review*, 68, September, 643–58.
Roll, R. (1977) 'A Critique of the Asset Pricing Theory's Test', *Journal of Financial Economics*, 4, March, 129–76.
Roll, R. (1983) 'The Turn-of-the-year Effect and the Return Premia of Small Firms', *Journal of Portfolio Management*, 9, winter, 18–28.
Sharpe, W. (1963) 'A Simplified Model for Portfolio Analysis', *Management Science*, 9, January, 277–93.
Sharpe, W. (1964) 'Capital Asset Prices: A Theory of Market Equilibrium under Conditions of Risk', *Journal of Finance*, 19, September, 425–42.
Smithers, P. (1977) 'London Share Price Data Base', London Business School, February.
Smithers, P. (1980) 'LBS Financial Database Manual', London Business School, March.

Tinic, S. and West, R. (1984) 'Risk and Return: January versus the Rest of the Year', *Journal of Financial Economics*, 13, December, 561–74.

Tinic, S. and West, R. (1986) 'Risk, Return, and Equilibrium: A Revisit', *Journal of Political Economy*, 94, February, 126–47.

IV
THE IMPACT OF STOCK MARKET
REGULARITIES ON EMPIRICAL
RESEARCH

16 The size effect and event studies: a discussion

JOSEF LAKONISHOK

Three of the chapters in part IV, 'The impact of the small firm effect on event studies' by Elroy Dimson and Paul Marsh (chapter 17), 'Performance measurement and performance attribution in less than efficient markets: a case study' by Stan Beckers (chapter 18) and 'A comparison of single and multifactor portfolio performance methodologies' by Nai-Fu Chen, Thomas Copeland and David Mayers (chapter 19) deal with measurement of investment performance. Chapter 20, 'Divergence of earnings expectations: the effect on stock market response to earnings signals' by Dan Givoly and myself examines the impact of divergence of earnings expectations on stock prices and has implications for studies which found that the market does not respond efficiently to earnings announcements.

Chapter 17 by Dimson and Marsh (DM) studies 862 recommendations published in the UK press. DM compute abnormal returns for four periods: year prior to the tip, tip month and one and two years after the tip. The abnormal returns are computed using ten different procedures. All of these procedures are widely used by academics and practitioners and it should be emphasized that they are used almost interchangeably. DM find that if the abnormal returns are computed over short periods (a month) the results are not very sensitive to the different procedures.[1] However, for longer periods (one- and two-year horizons), the abnormal returns are extremely sensitive and for a one-year horizon they obtain a range of abnormal returns of -7.2 percent to $+3.2$ percent. Obviously, it is quite a range. Some of the procedures show that analysts produce valuable recommendations, whereas according to other procedures an investor would probably be better off by merely picking stocks with a pin.

The CAPM procedures to compute benchmark returns (restrict the intercept to its CAPM value), including the version which assumes that all the companies have the same betas, are very much affected by the choice of the market index: equally or value weighted. The reason for this sensitivity is that in the UK, like in the US, small companies outperformed large companies. A tipped stock was four times the size of a typical UK stock. However, the probability of a stock being tipped is less than proportional to its capitalization. Therefore, recommended stocks in the DM study are typical neither of an equally weighted nor a capitalization weighted index. To deal with the size issue DM propose two procedures. These procedures were not previously utilized by researchers and they are appealing when an adjustment for size is called for. After adjusting for size the recommendations seem to be neutral.

DM also compute abnormal returns using the market model to compute benchmark returns. This procedure seems an ideal way to adjust for size because the size effect is captured in the intercept. However, this procedure, as pointed out by DM, is subject to biases. First, to estimate the coefficient of the market model we need time series data and hence we assume that the size effect is constant over time. Previous research indicated that it is not a good assumption. Second, we assume that the size of the company is the same for the estimation and prediction period. This assumption is questionable as well.

The main contribution of chapter 17 is to spotlight how sensitive are abnormal returns (for longer period horizons) to various assumptions about benchmark returns. Reading the chapter one becomes very skeptical about 'significant' abnormal returns reported in many of our empirical studies. I think that after reading chapter 17 we will exercise much more care in computing abnormal returns.

However, based on chapter 17 we should not jump to a conclusion that an adjustment for size should always be made. Whether to perform the adjustment or not depends on the extent to which size was a decision variable for financial analysts. If size was a decision variable and financial analysts had an insight that small companies for the period of this study, 1975–82, will outperform large we should give them credit for it. Most of the period studied was before the first serious academic paper was published on the size effect. Should we now give credit to financial analysts for whom size is a decision variable? Many of us are very doubtful if small companies will outperform large in the future. For example, in the last three years small companies did not perform well. Therefore, we should not automatically adjust for size.

In this particular study if the analyst would recommend stocks whose composition would correspond to a value weighted portfolio they would end up mentioning very few companies or would have to give portfolio weights to the different companies that they recommend. Giving weights is not a common procedure and mentioning few names is also very uncommon. Hence in the setting of chapter 17 it is very questionable whether the analysts should get credit for giving more weight to small companies than in a value weighted index but, at the same time, recommending companies which were on the average four times larger than a typical UK firm.

In chapter 18 Beckers examines recommendations made by a UK firm which publishes monthly a list of 'recovery' and 'downside' stocks. Using the CAPM methodology to compute abnormal returns the performance of the two lists is identical, around half a percent per month, which is not statistically different from zero. (Many fund managers would be very pleased with the abnormal return of 0.5 percent per month over a period of thirty-one months. Howevever, because of the high volatility of stocks such a performance is not statistically significant.) The interesting part of the chapter deals with performance attribution. Using the Rosenberg and Marathe (1976) procedure a multifactor model for the UK equity market was developed. The model applied in this study has forty-eight factors; twelve factors are common to all the stocks (size, beta, earnings/price, book/price, etc.) and the rest are industry factors. The coefficients were estimated monthly by a cross-sectional regression.

This procedure allows us to break down the total return in terms of crucial decision variables. Analysis of such results will help us to understand which factors gave rise to the differential performance which in turn will enable us to evaluate the skills inherent in the management process. In many cases a portfolio manager is restricted to some universe of stocks (high yield companies). Decomposing the performance in the way suggested in this study will enable us to focus on the contribution to performance made by such a manager after adjusting for the constraint.

The results reveal that the two funds benefited from a bias towards high book/price companies. The industry composition of both funds had a positive impact on the returns. The 'downside' fund was adversely affected by the specific returns (residuals after adjusting for the forty-eight factors). It should be emphasized that the specific returns from such a multifactor model cannot be used as a measure of performance, because some of the factors are probably decision variables. For example, a manager can have a neutral performance in selecting stocks within an industry, but can have an insight in selecting industries.

I think that the procedure of finding specific rates of return from a multifactor model can be very useful in event type studies. For example, in a study that examines the returns of companies after a merger, using a multifactor model can potentially reduce the noise and result in a more powerful test.

Chapter 19 by Chen, Copeland and Mayers (CCM) examines the performance of *Value Line Investment Survey* and companies ranked by size using a single factor and multifactor model. The factors and factor loadings for the multifactor model were extracted from the variance covariance matrix of weekly rates of return. Five 'mimicking' portfolios for the factors were formed. Weekly abnormal returns, for all the portfolios, were estimated using the single index model and the multifactor model as benchmarks. In terms of cumulative abnormal returns the two procedures yielded for all practical purposes very similar estimates. From the average cumulative returns and the *t*-values we can calculate the standard error of the estimate. There is no indication that using five factors instead of one improves the precision of our estimates. To compare the two models, CCM also use the mean square error (MSE) criterion. The cumulative abnormal returns for the various periods are squared and averaged for each of the two models. It is not clear why a smaller MSE indicates superiority over a larger value. It is quite possible that the abnormal returns are not constant over time. For example, Value Line recommendations may be more useful in some periods than in others. The results of the MSE comparison are ambiguous. One cannot infer from the results that the multifactor model produces smaller MSE.

In general, this paper does not produce support for the use of multifactor models to compute abnormal returns. The relatively lackluster performance of multifactor models in such a setting is probably caused by the instability of factors and factor loadings over time.

To summarize briefly the results of the above three chapters, DM found that abnormal returns are very sensitive to various procedures used to compute normal returns; Beckers provides a useful way for performance attribution; and CCM find very little support for the use of a multifactor model over a simple one factor model. It is refreshing, especially now, when so many recent studies indicate how inefficient is the market, to find three studies which indicate that professionals do not find that to generate abnormal returns in the stock market is a piece of cake. DM do not discover that recommendations in the UK press are useful. The buy and sell recommendations studied by Beckers generated identical abnormal returns. And the Value Line rankings produced only one portfolio with marginally significant abnormal returns which probably would disappear if some allowance for transaction costs would be made.

Chapter 20 by Givoly and Lakonishok (GL) focuses on earnings uncertainty derived from forecasts of financial analysts. This measure appears to contribute to our understanding of the stock market response to unexpected earnings. The higher the value of the uncertainty measure the weaker becomes the association between price changes and unexpected earnings. There are many studies which found that the stock market does not react efficiently to accounting earning and to revisions in analysts' forecasts of earnings. The various trading rules designed in these studies should consider incorporating earnings uncertainty as well.

The results of the GL study are preliminary. Earnings uncertainty measures are widely disseminated through various investment services and are used by practitioners. There is a need for further studies to understand the importance of this measure.

Note

1 The only exception is when the abnormal returns computed for the various recommendations were weighted according to the size of the recommended company. However, this procedure is statistically inefficient, in spite of its consistency attraction.

17 The impact of the small firm effect on event studies

ELROY DIMSON and PAUL MARSH*

1 Introduction

In this chapter we evaluate event study methodology in the presence of the size effect, using an original study of newspaper recommendations as a cautionary tale. We show that the size effect can distort longer-term performance measures, and hence event study results, unless it is explicitly taken into account in research design; and we propose an alternative methodology which takes account of the size effect. We then use this approach to examine the efficiency of the UK stock market with respect to press recommendations.

The standard event study procedure involves the use of Sharpe's (1963) market model or of various versions of the capital asset pricing model (CAPM). Questions have been raised regarding the integrity of this approach, since it is recognized that event studies entail a joint hypothesis about market efficiency and the validity of the benchmark employed. Nevertheless, in simulated event studies, the gains from using more complex models appear small, and most researchers in this area suggest that simple adjustments for market movements are usually adequate. Indeed, Brown and Warner (1980) conclude that 'Beyond a simple, one-factor market model, there is no evidence that more complicated methodologies convey any benefits'. Most event studies therefore continue to use the CAPM or market model.

However, there has been a growing awareness of the importance of other factors in the return generating process. As explained by Keim (1987), these extra-market factors include company size, potential for tax-loss selling, dividend yield, price-to-earnings ratio, price-to-book ratio and a wide variety of other factors. The most important empirical regularity so far observed is the size effect (the tendency, first noted by Banz (1981), for small capitalization stocks to outperform their larger counterparts) and the turn-of-the-year effect (the tendency for outperformance to occur at the beginning of the tax year). Consequently, an event study which focuses on smaller (larger) firms is likely to witness positive (negative) abnormal returns relative to the market index; and this problem is potentially exacerbated by event date clustering at the turn of the year.

This view seems at odds with the evidence from Brown and Warner's (1980, 1985) simulated event studies. However, Brown and Warner are careful to point out that their research is based on randomly selected samples which are designed not to have unusual exposure to extra-market factors. Methodologies which are reliable for such representative groups of securities may nevertheless perform poorly for samples which differ substantially from the market index, and which, in the absence of an event, exhibit 'abnormal' performance. Where these problems are likely to be severe, Schwert (1983) points out that event studies should give explicit consideration to the size effect. Yet very few studies make any attempt to do so.

Schwert (1983) also argues that when the market model is used 'the size effect is not a problem'. The assumption here is that market model alpha estimates encapsulate any size effect. However, the use of historical alphas introduces considerable noise, and both Brenner (1979) and Brown and Warner (1980) find the market model the least efficient of the standard event study methodologies. More seriously, we know that the small firm effect varies considerably over time, and, for US data, exhibits a turn-of-the-year seasonal (see Keim, 1983; Brown *et al.* 1983). Thus if events are clustered in a particular calendar time period, the mean size effect may differ between the estimation and prediction periods, introducing bias into the market model alphas. A similar problem will arise from seasonality in the event dates, if this coincides with a seasonal in the size effect. For these reasons the market model will not usually eliminate problems introduced by the size effect.

Like its American counterpart, the UK size effect is very marked. The difference between the compound annual rate of return on the shares of small companies and that on large companies was some six per cent over the period 1955 to 1986 (see Dimson–Marsh 1987). The magnitude of the small firm premium varies considerably from year to year: Levis (1987) estimates that it is nearly as volatile as the return on the underlying small stocks, though he finds no evidence of US-type seasonality. While the UK size effect remains an empirical regularity for which only partial explanations have been offered, it is too large to be dismissed, for it may well dominate the results of empirical studies of stock returns.

The size effect does, in fact, appear to be a major influence on the abnormal returns estimated in the present study. When a capitalization weighted index is used as a performance benchmark, we witness significant longer-term outperformance; with an equally weighted index the pattern is reversed and longer-term performance is very poor; and when the market model is used, the results are influenced by the choice of estimation and test periods. When we control for the capitalizations of the event securities, however, performance appears to be neutral. Thus the choice of methodology, index and weighting scheme are all critical in this study, and explicit consideration has to be given to at least one additional factor, namely company size, when longer-term performance is being evaluated.

The plan of the remainder of this chapter is as follows. The sample is described in section 2, and our experimental design is presented in section 3. In sections 4 and 5 we evaluate performance using a variety of alternative methodologies, and demonstrate the importance of controlling for size. In section 6, we identify some of the broader implications of our results, and our conclusions are presented in section 7.

2 Sample description

Our study deals with stock recommendations published in regular features in the British press between 1975 and 1982. The recommendations fall into two groups. New Year tips appear in late December/early January, and consist exclusively of purchase recommendations. Portfolio tips, on the other hand, appear throughout the year in journals which run paper portfolios, and include advice on sales as well as purchases. In total, 862 recommendations are identified from eleven publications which give regular, unambiguous buying or selling recommendations. The sources, and the percentage of total recommendations from each, were the *Economist* (6 per cent) and *Investors Chronicle* (15 per cent), which are financial journals; the *Sunday Telegraph* (6 per cent), *Observer* (6 per cent), *Sunday Times* (4 per cent) and *Sunday Express* (2 per cent), which are all Sunday papers; the *Daily Telegraph* newspaper (12 per cent); the *IC Newsletter* (7 per cent) and the *Fleet Street Letter* (3 per cent), the two leading stock market letters; and finally three investment magazines, namely *Financial Weekly* (2 per cent), *Mr Bearbull* (a pseudonym for regular staff reporters writing in the *Investors Chronicle*) (34 per cent) and *Money Observer* (2 per cent).

The first nine sources provide New Year buying recommendations. These generally have a one-year horizon, though the *Sunday Express'* tips were given as 'shares for the decade'. The portfolio tips, however, come exclusively from the final group of three investment magazines, and make up 38 per cent of our sample. They include fewer

Table 1 *Exposure of recommended securities to size, yield and risk deciles*

Decile of ranking variable	Percentage of recommended securities falling in each decile			
	Market capitalization deciles	Dividend yield deciles[a]	Beta deciles[a]	Residual risk deciles[a]
Largest	32	11	16	6
9	18	13	15	5
8	13	11	14	6
7	10	14	12	10
6	7	10	12	8
5	8	8	9	11
4	6	11	8	14
3	4	9	8	14
2	2	7	5	15
Lowest	1	6	2	11
Load factor[b]	3.81	1.02	1.19	0.95

Notes: [a]Dividend yield is estimated as the gross dividend for the share paid over the year terminating at the end of November immediately prior to the recommendation, divided by the end-November share price. Beta and residual risk are estimated using the trade-to-trade method with sixty months' stock returns terminating one year before the time period of the recommendation (see Marsh, 1979).
[b]The load factor is defined as the equally weighted mean value for the ranking variable for the recommended securities, divided by the equally weighted mean value of the same variable for all UK listed securities.

sale (70) than purchase (253) recommendations, since sales can be selected only from the current portfolio, and also because new paper portfolios are initiated periodically, while termination of the old portfolio is not interpreted as a sale recommendation.

Our sample is distributed fairly evenly over time, with most years containing around a hundred tips. The actual number of tips in each calendar year is 1975, 50; 1976, 88; 1977, 134; 1978, 118; 1979, 121; 1980, 176; 1981, 113; and 1982, 62. The sample also represents each industry sector in rough proportion to the number of equities listed in each sector of the UK market. The percentage of tips (percentage of listed UK equities) in each sector is capital goods 34 (30); consumer goods 32 (30); other industrials 13 (13); oil and natural resources 8 (7); financials 12 (11); and investment trusts 1 (10). When one takes into account the underrepresentation of investment trusts (i.e. closed end funds), the conformity of the sample to the overall market is striking.

Clearly, our sample is well distributed over the sample period, and is representative in terms of industry classification. However, it is differentiated in terms of the factor of prime interest, namely company size. This can be seen if we rank all UK stocks by their capitalization at the previous year-end, and assign them to deciles containing equal numbers of stocks. As can be seen in the second column of table 1, the highest two deciles by market capitalization contain over half of the recommendations, and the next two deciles contain a further quarter. A small proportion are in the middle deciles, while only very few tipped stocks are in the smallest capitalization classes. The last row of table 1 shows the load factor for the ranking variable. This is defined as the equally weighted mean value of the variable for the sample securities, divided by the corresponding mean for UK equities as a whole. As can be seen, the recommended securities are on average some four times the size of a typical UK share.

However, while recommendations are more likely to be for large companies, the probability of a stock being tipped is less than proportional to its capitalization. Although one-third of tipped stocks come from the largest decile, this decile accounts for no less than 83 per cent of the value of the *Financial Times* – Actuaries All Share (the FTA) index. Similarly, although nearly half of the tipped stocks come from the bottom eight deciles, these deciles account for only 8 per cent of the index value. In terms of capitalization, therefore, recommended stocks are typical neither of an equally weighted nor a capitalization weighted index, a feature which assumes considerable importance in our empirical work.

Recommended stocks may, of course, be non-typical in terms of factors other than capitalization. The remaining columns of table 1 therefore analyse the sample in terms of a representative set of factors which the literature suggests may play a role in the return generating process, namely dividend yield, beta and residual risk. The sample has a more balanced exposure across yield deciles and across risk deciles than is the case for capitalization. Nevertheless, there is a tendency for tipped stocks to have a higher yield, higher beta and lower residual risk than the average UK stock. The final row of the table shows that the largest difference is for beta, with tipped stocks having a beta which is nearly one-fifth higher than for an investment in the overall share market.

The above-average beta of the sample securities may reflect a focus by tipsters on shares with relatively high risk. Alternatively, it may be an unintended consequence of the size distribution of the recommended shares, arising from the tendency of large UK companies to have higher betas than small companies. This characteristic has been verified using a variety of methodologies by Dimson (1979: aggregated coefficients estimation), Dimson and Marsh (1983: trade to trade estimation), Pountain and Fitzgerald (1980: OLS with a trading frequency filter), Beckers *et al.* (1983: fundamental beta estimation) and Levis

(1987: quarterly differencing intervals), all of whom adjusted for thin trading. In this study the mean beta for the constituents of each capitalization decile has perfect rank correlation with the mean size of companies in the decile.

To investigate the link between size and beta, we calculate the mean beta for tips which fall in each capitalization decile, from the largest to the smallest. Relative to the mean beta for all constituents of the decile, the tipped stocks have betas which are larger (smaller) by (0.03), 0.05, 0.07, 0.08, 0.03, 0.08, 0.02, 0.13, 0.21 and (0.08) respectively. The weighted average beta of the recommended stocks is only 0.03 above that of UK equities of similar size, where the weights are the proportions of the sample falling in each of the capitalization deciles. Thus the observed differences in beta disclosed in table 1 appear to be a by-product of the size distribution of the tips. Other than through their markedly different capitalizations, the sample stocks are not deviant in terms of beta.

To sum up, our study examines the performance of 862 published stock recommendations drawn fron 12 different sources. The recommendations are evenly distributed over the sample years, and they are representative in terms of industry sector, dividend yield, residual risk and beta. However, they are not representative in terms of the month of the year, or in terms of equity capitalization. It is therefore necessary to take full account of event timing and of company size, while failure to adjust for dividend yield, residual risk or even beta would appear to be of lesser importance.

3. Methodology and data

Our procedure in this study involves estimating pre-and post-recommendation returns on the tipped securities using middle-market quotation prices, from the London Business School's share price database. We utilise eight different methods for evaluating performance. First, we estimate abnormal returns using as a benchmark the usual market indexes, with and without risk adjustment. Second, we develop two size-controlled methods, in which we measure differential performance of the event securities relative to companies of similar size. Finally, we compare these approaches with the widely used single-index market model.

The performance measure used is in each case the difference between the realised return R_{jt} on recommended security j and the expected return $E(R_{jt})$ which is predicted by the benchmark employed. The overall performance measure is thus defined as

$$u_t = \bar{u}_{jt} = \bar{R}_{jt} - \bar{E}(R_{jt}) \tag{1}$$

where the bar signifies the mean over all the event securities. The predicted return $E(R_{jt})$ for each security is generated by using one of four benchmarks: the Financial Times-Actuaries ("FTA") All Share Index without and with risk adjustment (equations 2–3 below); an equally weighted ("EW") index without and with risk adjustment (equations 4–5 below); a control portfolio ("CONTROL$_{jt}$") of stocks with a similar capitalisation to the event security, without and with risk adjustment (equations 6–7 below); or the single index market model ("SIMM"), using either the FTA or EW Index (equations 8–9 below). Our definition of the predicted return is thus one of the following:

Predicted return	Type of benchmark	
$E(R_{jt}) = FTA_t$	FTA Index	(2)
$E(R_{jt}) = (1-\beta_j)R_{ft} + \beta_j(FTA_t)$		(3)
$E(R_{jt}) = EW_t$	EW Index	(4)
$E(R_{jt}) = (1-b_j)R_{ft} + b_j(EW_t)$		(5)
$E(R_{jt}) = CONTROL_{jt}$	Control	(6)
$E(R_{jt}) = CONTROL_{jt} + (\beta_j - \bar{\beta}_j)FTA_t$	portfolio	(7)
$E(R_{jt}) = \alpha_j + \beta_j(FTA_t)$	SIMM	(8)
$E(R_{jt}) = a_j + b_j(EW_t)$		(9)

where FTA_t and EW_t are the respective index returns during period t; α_j, β_j and a_j, b_j are the respective alpha and beta estimates relative to these two indexes; R_{ft} is the return on treasury bills during period t; $CONTROL_{jt}$ is the return on the control portfolio for security j during period t; and a bar denotes the mean across all constituents of the control portfolio. In this study, the control portfolio for security j is defined as the equally-weighted portfolio of stocks in the same capitalisation decile as the security (see Dimson and Marsh, 1986). The α_j, β_j coefficients are estimated using the trade-to-trade method (Marsh, 1979), while the a_j, b_j coefficients, which are subject to greater problems of nonsynchronicity in index returns, are based on the aggregated coefficients method (Dimson, 1979). In all cases we use 60 months' data prior to a 12-month pre-event exclusion period.

When an n-month performance statistic is computed, equation (1) is used wherever possible with the interval length of period t being equated to n months. This avoids rebalancing bias (see Roll, 1983, and Blume and Stambaugh, 1983). With the single index market model (equations 8–9), however, an n-month prediction error is estimated by cumulating a sequence of n observations of the single-month performance measure.

The significance of the measured performance is evaluated from the following test statistic:

$$z_t = v_t / \sqrt{\mathrm{Var}(v_t)} \tag{10}$$

where v_t is in most instances (ie, equations 2–7) equal to the difference between the realised and the predicted continuously-compounded returns over the n-month period represented by t, namely $v_t = \log_e(1+R_{jt}) - \log_e(1 + E(R_{jt}))$. When the SIMM (equations 8–9) is used, v_t is equated to the n-month prediction error described in the previous paragraph (see Dimson and Marsh, 1986). The variance v_t is estimated from the sequence of estimates of this variable estimated for each of the individual event-time months throughout the sample period other than the pre-event month and the event month. A z_t statistic which refers to performance spanning a period of n months is distributed Student-t with n–1 degrees of freedom.

4. Pre-recommendation and tip-month performance

Table 2 summarises the performance of recommended stocks evaluated using all eight methodologies described in the previous section. The monthly post-publication performance is plotted in figure 1 below, while month-by-month returns are listed in Dimson and Marsh (1986).

We begin by discussing the prior year and tip month performance. Our qualitative conclusions here are insensitive to the choice of methodology. For ease of exposition, we therefore focus on panel A: this contains results based on the first two methodologies, namely simple market adjustment [equation (2)] and CAPM [equation (3)] using the capitalisation weighted FTA. We defer our discussion of the differences between methodologies until we evaluate post-publication performance.

The first column of table 2 summarises the performance of our sample over the period from one year before the recommendation month until the precise date of the recommendation. As can be seen from panel A, over this period recommended stocks outperform the market, as proxied by the FTA Index, by 15 percent. The equivalent CAPM abnormal return is very similar, indicating that, as in many previous studies, risk adjustment has only a small effect. A glance at the prior year figures for alternative methodologies (panels B to D) show that, despite substantial variation, all the abnormal returns are positive. Clearly, tipsters appear to favour stocks which have outperformed the market in the recent past.

Post-recommendation returns are calculated assuming purchase on the date the journalist selects the stock. The column of table 2 headed 'Tip

Table 2: *Pre-publication and Tip-month performance of recommended stocks using alternative benchmarks*

Panel	Performance benchmark[a]	Equation no.	Prior year %	(t)	Tip month %	(t)
			Abnormal return up to tip month[b]			
A	FTA Index only	Equation (2)	14.8	(7.0)	4.6	(10.1)
	CAPM using FTA	Equation (3)	15.1	(7.2)	4.7	(10.5)
B	EW Index only	Equation (4)	7.9	(3.5)	3.7	(7.7)
	CAPM using EW	Equation (5)	3.5	(1.6)	3.3	(7.2)
C	Size control only	Equation (6)	12.4	(7.4)	3.9	(10.8)
	Size and beta	Equation (7)	11.1	(6.5)	3.9	(10.6)
D	SIMM using FTA	Equation (8)	4.7	(2.4)	4.4	(7.7)
	SIMM using EW	Equation (9)	5.3	(3.1)	3.3	(6.8)

Notes: [a] The abbreviations used here are as follows: FTA denotes the capitalisation weighted Financial Times-Actuaries All Share Index; EW denotes our Equally Weighted Index of the returns on all UK equities; CAPM denotes the Capital Asset Pricing Model; SIMM denotes the Single Index Market Model. The t-statistics corresponding to each return are shown in parentheses
[b] The prior year return is an average of 862 abnormal returns measured over the period from 12 months before the tip month to the date of the tip. The tip month return is an average of 792 abnormal returns on buy recommendations plus 70 abnormal returns from taking a short position in stocks recommended for sale, measured from the date of the tip to the end of the tip month

month' shows that by the end of the publication month, the tips achieve an abnormal return of some 4 percent. If financial journalists do not 'cheat' (for example, by withdrawing a tip from publication after the selection date) and if deals are executed at the middle market prices used in computing returns, then this could be interpreted as a violation of strong form market efficiency.

The magnitude of the abnormal performance is, however, relatively small, and any potential short-term profits from following tipsters' recommendations would be more than consumed by the transaction costs which prevailed in the UK at the time of this study. Furthermore, investors cannot expect to deal at the price quoted by the journalist. Market makers read the recommendations, and adjust prices before any post-publication trading takes place. It is therefore possible that the subsequent quotation represents a switch from an average of the bid-ask prices to an effective ask-only price. If so, we expect to witness a swift reversal of the initial abnormal returns once the impact of publication is abated. In fact, we observe neutral performance in the month after publication (see Dimson and Marsh, 1986). Thus the 4 percent abnormal

Table 3: *Cumulative performance of Mr Bearbull's recommended stocks on a daily basis*

Event day[a]	Day of week	Cumulative performance around day of tip[b]				Cumulative performance after day of tip[b]			
		Buys %	Sells %	Overall %	(t)	Buys %	Sells %	Overall %	(t)
−14	Tuesday	0	0	0	(0)	–	–	–	–
−7	Tuesday	−0.3	0.2	−0.1	(0.2)	–	–	–	–
−2	Friday	−1.6	0.2	−0.9	(1.2)	–	–	–	–
−1	Monday	−2.1	0.6	−1.0	(1.3)	0	0	0	(0)
0	Tuesday	−0.9	0.4	−0.4	(0.5)	1.2	−0.2	0.6	(2.8)
1	Wednesday	−0.7	0.8	−0.1	(0.2)	1.4	0.2	0.9	(2.9)
2	Thursday	0.4	2.0	1.0	(1.1)	2.7	1.4	2.1	(5.3)
3	Friday	2.2	1.8	2.0	(2.2)	4.4	1.2	3.1	(6.9)
7	Tuesday	3.8	1.0	2.7	(2.6)	6.0	0.5	3.8	(6.0)
14	Tuesday	5.2	1.5	3.7	(3.1)	7.4	0.9	4.8	(5.6)
28	Tuesday	4.0	6.5	5.0	(3.1)	6.2	5.9	6.1	(5.1)
42	Tuesday	4.0	5.6	4.6	(2.8)	6.3	5.0	5.7	(3.9)

Notes: [a] The event days are defined as follows: Day −1 is the day on which the recommendation is made, and the tip is published using the day's closing price; Day 0 is the day when the magazine is sent to the printers; printing continues throughout Day 1; the publishers receive physical delivery of the magazine on Day 2; finally, the morning of Day 3 is the first time at which the magazine is normally available to the public.
[b] Performance is measured as a risk-adjusted return relative to the FTA All Share Index, using the CAPM (equation 3). Note that the cumulative performance of the sell recommendations is the abnormal gain resulting from a short position in these stocks (ie, a positive abnormal return is recorded when the share price of these stocks falls). The overall performance is thus an average of the 52 abnormal returns on buy recommendations plus 34 abnormal returns from taking a short position in stocks recommended for sale. The absolute t-statistics corresponding to the overall returns are displayed in parentheses.

return in the tip month appears to be attributable to the journalists' selection skills.

Several days may elapse between selection by the journalist and publication. During this period, the underlying information content may find its way into market prices. This is illustrated by the UK share recommendations made in the Investors Chronicle by Mr Bearbull during the period January 1980 to December 1981. The Investors Chronicle becomes available to the public on Friday. The publishers take delivery from the printers the previous day, and the recommendation (press) date is three days before this. A study of daily returns over the seven days following recommendation reveals a four percent abnormal return over the week following recommendation (see table 3). Of this, one quarter to one half is realised prior to the publishers taking delivery, and three quarters has been realised by the day the journal is distributed to the public.

Either tipsters tend to recommend stocks which are expected to experience a swift flow of favourable information, or they acquire information which leaks to the market. Additionally, there may be investment opportunities for the tipsters themselves, although the editors of the periodicals represented here indicated that pre-publication dealing would constitute grounds for dismissal. Whatever the explanation, it is clear that this short-term performance is not available to the public. If investors follow tipsters' advice, they must buy at the post-publication price.

5. Post-publication performance

Panel A of table 4 shows that over the one-year period from the end of the recommendation month, the mean abnormal return using either of the FTA based methodologies is around three percent. This rate of outperformance is maintained over the following twelve months, and the two-year abnormal gain is 6.9 percent with simple market adjustments and 8.5 percent using the CAPM. The two-year outperformance is significant at the 5 percent level.

It seems unlikely that British tipsters can predict such substantial abnormal returns, with as much accuracy for months 13–24 as for months 1–12. In addition, the pattern of month-by-month cumulative abnormal returns displays a consistent upward drift, rather than sudden jumps (see figure 1 below). These observations would, if methodologically correct, represent a violation of market efficiency. However, inappropriate conclusions on market efficiency are quite possible in the presence of the size effect, and these results may be misleading because of our choice of weighting scheme and index.

Table 4: *Post-publication performance of recommended stocks using alternative benchmarks*

Panel	Performance benchmark[a]	Equation no.	Abnormal return after tip month[b]			
			One year		Two years	
			%	(t)	%	(t)
A	FTA Index only	Equation (2)	2.5	(1.4)	6.9	(2.2)
	CAPM using FTA	Equation (3)	3.2	(1.8)	8.5	(2.8)
B	EW Index only	Equation (4)	−5.6	(2.9)	−14.1	(4.0)
	CAPM using EW	Equation (5)	−7.2	(3.8)	−18.9	(5.6)
C	Size control only	Equation (6)	−0.5	(0.4)	−1.3	(0.5)
	Size and beta	Equation (7)	−0.4	(0.3)	−1.3	(0.5)
D	SIMM using FTA	Equation (8)	−2.6	(1.4)	−4.8	(1.8)
	SIMM using EW	Equation (9)	−3.2	(2.0)	−6.4	(2.8)

Notes: [a] The abbreviations used here are as follows: FTA denotes the capitalisation weighted Financial Times-Actuaries All Share Index; EW denotes our Equally Weighted Index of the returns on all UK equities; CAPM denotes the Capital Asset Pricing Model; SIMM denotes the Single Index Market Model. The t-statistics corresponding to each return are shown in parentheses
[b] The one-year and two-year returns are an average of 792 abnormal returns on buy recommendations plus 70 abnormal returns from taking a short position in stocks recommended for sale, measured from the end of the tip month until 12 or 24 months later

When small companies outperform their larger counterparts, randomly selected equally weighted portfolios generally outperform a capitalisation weighted index, since capitalisation weighting gives greater weight to the worse performing securities (see Dimson and Marsh, 1987a). Our sample has a lower weighting on large companies than the FTA (see section 2 above), and given the marked UK size effect over this period, this may explain our results.

One solution would be to apply consistent weightings, and compare capitalisation weighted event security returns with the similarly weighted market index. If event securities were drawn randomly from the population of index stocks, the expected abnormal return would then be zero. When each stock is given a weight proportionate to its market value, the apparently superior performance of panel A is indeed transformed into statistically insignificant (though now slightly negative) performance of some −2 percent per year over the two-year post-publication period. Though this procedure is statistically inefficient, it provides further evidence that the findings of tipsters' longer term selection skills may be biased by the size effect.

An obvious alternative to capitalisation weighting, which meets the

Figure 1 Cumulative performance of recommended stocks using alternative benchmarks

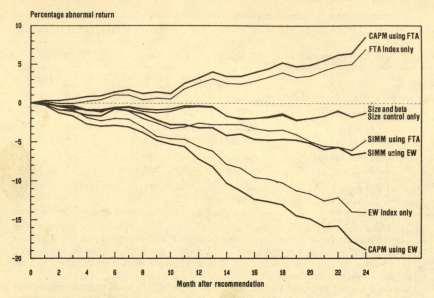

Note: Abbreviations and definitions are as specified in the footnote to table 4 (page 231)

same 'consistent weighting' criterion but provides greater statistical efficiency, is to use equal weighting for each security but to evaluate results against an equally weighted index. Panel B of table 4 therefore presents abnormal returns computed using the EW Index as the benchmark [equations (4) and (5)]. The results reinforce the above conclusions: recommended stocks significantly underperform the EW Index by over 14 percent over the two years after publication, and by 19 percent on a risk adjusted basis. Far from displaying selection ability, the analysts now appear to exhibit perverse forecasting skills.

We have thus evidence of both statistically significant overperformance by recommended stocks relative to the FTA, and statistically significant underperformance relative to the EW Index. As can be seen from figure 1, the abnormal returns are larger in absolute magnitude the longer the post-publication period examined. Ball (1978) points out that when trading strategies offer apparent abnormal returns which increase steadily over time, it suggests a deficiency in the model of expected returns, and from this point of view, the CAPM is clearly an inappropriate benchmark. This is true whether the model uses estimated betas, or assumes betas of unity; and it is true regardless of whether the index is equally or capitalisation weighted.

The major misspecification is the failure of the benchmark to reflect the size composition of the sample. Panel C of table 4 presents abnormal returns computed using the size control portfolio approach. Over all periods, the switch to size adjustment pulls the abnormal returns to an intermediate figure between that obtained using the FTA (panel A) and the EW Index (panel B). These size adjusted results cast an entirely new light on our earlier conclusions: performance is virtually neutral, disclosing evidence of neither longer-term forecasting skills nor perversity. Over the one- and two-year post-publication periods, recommendations underperform similar sized companies by only 0.5 and 1.3 percent, respectively. Neither figure is statistically significant. Given that the betas of tipped stocks are representative of their size decile (see section 2 above), the abnormal returns remain virtually unchanged when we adjust for beta as well as size. Thus, when abnormal returns after the publication month are measured on a size adjusted basis, there is no evidence of market inefficiency.

The last panel of table 4 shows the abnormal performance estimated from the market model using either the FTA or EW Index. In a single month, the alpha contributes relatively little, so that SIMM results resemble the corresponding CAPM results based on the FTA and EW Index (equations 3 and 5 respectively); see table 2 above. Over longer periods, however, the alpha plays a more important role, causing market model results to deviate from their CAPM counterparts (see figure 1). As in Brown and Warner (1980), longer-term SIMM performance is largely insensitive to the choice of index, and the cumulative abnormal return is −3 percent over one year, and −5 to −6 percent over two years.

The general expectation in using the market model is that each sample will act as its own control, with the mean alpha estimate encapsulating factors such as the size effect. The SIMM two-year performance figures, however, are statistically significant at the 10 percent (FTA Index) and 1 percent (EW Index) levels. By contrast, the corresponding CAPM results (equations 3 and 5) are more extreme and more significant, at the 1 percent and 0.1 percent levels. In this study, the market model avoids some of the bias which afflicts the CAPM-type methodologies, but the SIMM results are not as neutral as those obtained with size adjustment.

By definition, the SIMM takes account of the sample's sensitivity to a *single* factor, the market return, while also incorporating an estimate of the mean non-market return per period via the constant term, alpha. If there are other, extra-market factors at work, then the SIMM is misspecified. The magnitude of any resulting bias depends on the stochastic nature of the omitted variables (we focus here simply on the size effect). It also depends on the stability of any omitted coefficient, or in this case, the sample's sensitivity to the size factor, as measured by the average size of the event securities. At one extreme, if the size effect is constant, and the average (relative) size of the event securities remains stable over time, then the estimated SIMM alphas will purge abnormal returns of all size-related bias. On the other hand, if the size effect is volatile and/or non-stationary, then the mean alphas will vary over time. Unless event dates are spread evenly over a very long sample period, this can lead to biased performance measures. Similarly, bias may arise if the average size of the event securities changes between the estimation and prediction periods.

A detailed analysis of pre-event, size-adjusted performance is given in Dimson and Marsh (1986). Our evidence suggests that the SIMM alpha estimates are biased due to an abnormal return over and above the size effect during the estimation period. This pre-event abnormal return may be a consequence of an inevitable form of survivorship bias arising from estimating the SIMM parameters for only those stocks which have (by definition) survived to the event date. Alternatively, it may indicate that tipsters tend to recommend stocks which have performed well over a very long prior period. Unfortunately, we can find no exclusion period, not even one of seven years or more, which leaves us with unbiased alphas according to our size adjusted criterion. We therefore urge caution when using the single index market model, especially when there is event-date clustering and/or the sample period is of limited duration.

6. The impact of the size effect on event studies

The most striking feature of our results, as shown graphically in figure 1, is their very obvious sensitivity to the design of the experiment. Overall performance can appear significantly positive or negative, depending on the choice of index and methodology. Unless tipsters are to be credited (or debited) with a market wide phenomenon, the size effect, performance must be evaluated using a methodology which adjusts for size. On this basis, tipsters exhibit no evidence of stock selection skills.

Unlike the simulations in Brown and Warner (1980, 1985), our research is equivalent to only a single observation from the population of event studies. Yet, to the extent that our results are representative of the impact of the size effect, they have important implications for past and future empirical work. They may go part way towards explaining some of the anomalies in the market efficiency literature and to resolving other disagreements between empirical researchers [see Jensen (1978, 1983)]. They also raise a puzzle about why so many event studies, which ignore the size effect, nevertheless conclude that the market is efficient. To judge the efficacy of previous work, and to ensure that future studies are appropriately designed, it is worth clarifying the circumstances which induce bias. The most serious problems will arise when (1) the measurement interval is long, (2) the event securities differ systematically in size or weighting from the index constituents, (3) the size effect is large and/or volatile, and (4) CAPM-type methodologies are used.

Taking these considerations in turn, it is firstly clear that the magnitude of any bias depends on the length of the measurement interval. Our benchmarks define a normal rate of return; and the importance of this normal rate, and of any misspecification, declines rapidly as the period length tends to zero. For studies using daily data, and focussing only on the immediate post-event period, bias from benchmark misspecification is likely to be small relative to event related returns and noise. However, as the measurement interval is extended, any bias will be steadily magnified and can soon become dominant. Numerous event studies report longer-term performance, and often this seems appropriate. Such studies are potentially susceptible to size related bias.

Second, when there is a size effect, problems can arise if event securities differ in their size or weighting from the index constitutents. In spite of this, most event studies treat the choice of index as inconsequential. Capitalisation weighted indexes, for example, are widely used in the literature – see all previous UK studies, other studies of stock recommendations [e.g. Bjerring, Lakonishok and Vermaelen (1983)], and many other well-known event studies [e.g., Kaplan and Roll (1972), Gonedes, Dopuch and Penman (1976), and seven of the fourteen studies in Jensen's (1983) 'Symposium on the market for corporate control']. Yet if stocks experience an event with a probability less than proportional to their capitalisation, then when there is a positive size effect, a capitalisation weighted index can always be expected to underperform an equally weighted portfolio of event securities. However, we have yet to identify any published study in which the probability of an event is at least proportional to capitalisation.

Similarly, an equally weighted index will produce biased results if event securities are larger or smaller than the typical index constituent. Again, this appears to be the rule, not the exception. For example, stock recommendations and acquisitions are more prevalent for large companies, while initial public offerings and financial distress are typically experienced by smaller firms. In addition, event securities may be non-random with respect to size because of sample selection requirements (e.g., the availability of prior stock price histories or supplementary accounting data), pre-event abnormal returns (as with stock splits or rights issues), and the partitioning criteria employed (e.g., acquirors versus acquirees, or large versus small changes in dividends or earnings) Clearly, size mismatching is a potential problem in many event study settings.

Third, the severity of any bias will depend on the magnitude and volatility of the size effect. Event studies carried out in countries and periods in which the size effect is negligible will avoid these problems. This seems unlikely to be the norm, however, given the considerable evidence that the world's stock markets are characterised by substantial small firm effects, which vary considerably over time (see the references cited in Bowers and Dimson, 1987). Event studies spanning short periods, or in countries with narrowly based stock markets, are likely to suffer most from bias (e.g., Holland and Switzerland, where the three largest companies represent over half of the equity market value). In countries such as the USA, where the size effect has a seasonal, analogous problems may arise, particularly when events cluster around the turn of the year. Similarly, event studies may experience problems from extra-market factors other than size, in markets such as South Africa, Australia and Norway where gold, natural resources and oil companies are heavily represented.

Finally, of the benchmarks investigated here, the most serious problems arise with CAPM-type methodologies. This is because bias in CAPM based abnormal returns is proportional to the magnitude of the small-firm premium, and our sample period coincides with a large size effect. While many previous studies employ the CAPM [e.g., Ball (1972), Kaplan and Roll (1972), Mandelker (1974) and Jaffe (1974)] others use the market model, partly on the grounds that the alpha estimates encapsulate any size effect. Unfortunately, market model results are still distorted if the mean alpha during the estimation period is a biased predictor of the expected value in the post-event period. This can happen because of exclusion period problems, variability and/or seasonality in the size effect, or non-stationarity in event security sizes. Thus while the market model may perform better than the CAPM, in the presence of a volatile size effect it will not necessarily be free of bias.

Problems posed by the size effect extend beyond event studies, and may potentially afflict all studies of longer-term performance, such as mutual fund evaluation and portfolio performance measurement in general. Of all the factors which influence stock returns, size is especially important, partly because of its strong and established relationship with ex post returns, but also because a mismatch of capitalisations is commonplace. However, since the inclusion of sufficient factors in our benchmark would enable us to explain away all abnormal returns in an event study, we have to take a view as to which factors are event related.

In this study, we assume that tipsters forecast stock-specific security returns, and that their outperformance against the FTA is not derived from insights into the size effect. The alternative view begs the question of why they generally recommend larger stocks: if tipsters are to be credited with the outperformance of small stocks, we must ask why they did so much worse than would be expected if they had merely picked small stocks with a pin.

7. Conclusion

This paper evaluates UK press recommendations made over the period 1975–82. While recommended stocks significantly overperform the capitalisation weighted FTA and underperform the equally weighted EW Index, this reflects the size effect and provides no information on tipsters' selection skills. When the size effect is taken into account, recommendations provide an abnormal return of 4 percent (before transaction costs) between the selection date and the end of the publication month. Thereafter, performance is neutral.

We conclude that performance measures can be seriously distorted when (1) the measurement interval is long, (2) event securities differ in size or weighting from the index constituents, and (3) the size effect is large and/or volatile. The biases are likely to be greater with CAPM-type methodologies, although the market model is not an automatic panacea. Clearly, considerable care is required in interpreting conventional, long term performance measures. The danger is that abnormal returns may tell us more about the appropriateness of the benchmark than about true, event related performance.

Under the conditions enumerated above, our evidence suggests that researchers should avoid using all of the techniques described in Brown and Warner (1980). Instead, they should estimate abnormal returns using a methodology which explicitly controls for size.

Our research provides fresh insights into the impact of the size effect on event studies, and demonstrates the importance of taking this pervasive phenomenon into account. Two conclusions emerge, one methodological, the other empirical. The methodological conclusion in that longer-term performance measures which ignore the size effect may be of no value to researchers. The empirical conclusion is that published UK stock recommendations may be of no value to anyone.

Note

This chapter draws on an article by the authors (Dimson and Marsh, 1986) and on an earlier unpublished working paper (Dimson and Marsh, 1984).

References

Ball, R., 1972, Changes in accounting technique and stock prices, Empirical Research in Accounting, Journal of Accounting Research 10 (suppl.), 1–38.

Ball, R., 1978, Anomalies in relationships between securities' yields and yield-surrogates, Journal of Financial Economics 6, 103–126.

Banz, R. W., 1981, The relationship between return and market value of common stock, Journal of Financial Economics 9, 3–18.

Beckers, S., K. Reid and A. Rudd, 1983, BARRA's model of the UK equity market, London: Barr Rosenberg Associates, March.

Bjerring, J. H., J. Lakonishok and T. Vermaelen, 1983, Stock prices and financial analysts' recommendations, Journal of Finance 38, 187–204.

Blume, M. and R. F. Stambaugh, 1983, Biases in computed returns: An application to the size effect, Journal of Financial Economics 12, 387–404.

Bowers, J. and E. Dimson, 1987, Introduction to E. Dimson (Ed.) Stock Market Anomalies, Cambridge University Press.

Brenner, M., 1979, The sensitivity of the efficient market hypothesis to alternative specifications of the market model, Journal of Finance 34, 915–929.

Brown, P., A. W. Kleidon and T. A. Marsh, 1983, New evidence on the nature of size-related anomalies in stock prices. Journal of Financial Economics 12, 33–56.

Brown, S. J. and J. B. Warner, 1980, Measuring security price performance, Journal of Financial Economics 8, 205–258.

Brown, S. J. and J. B. Warner, 1985, Using daily stock returns: The case of event studies. Journal of Financial Economics 14, 3–31.

Dimson, E., 1979, Risk measurement when shares are subject to infrequent trading, Journal of Financial Economics 7, 197–226.

Dimson, E. and P. R. Marsh, 1983, The Stability of UK risk measures and the problem of thin trading, Journal of Finance 38, 753–783.

Dimson, E. and P. R. Marsh, 1984, The impact of the small firm effect on event studies and the performance of published UK stock recommendations, Paper presented at the nineteenth meeting of the Western Finance Association, Vancouver.

Dimson, E. and P. R. Marsh, 1986, Event Study Methodologies and the Size Effect: The Case of UK Press Recommendations, Journal of Financial Economics, 17, 113–142.

Dimson, E. and P. R. Marsh, 1987, The Hoare Govett Smaller Companies Index for the UK, London: Hoare Govett, February.

Dimson, E. and P. R. Marsh, 1987a, The Risks and Returns of Smaller Companies, London: Hoare Govett, April.

Gonedes, N. J., N. Dopuch and S. H. Penman, 1976, Disclosure rules, information-production and capital market equilibrium: The case of forecast disclosure rules, Journal of Accounting Research 14, 89–137.

Jaffe, J., 1974, The effect of regulation changes on insider trading, Bell Journal of Economics 5, 93–121.

Jensen, M. C., 1978, Some anomalous evidence regarding market efficiency, Journal of Financial Economics 6, 95–101.

Jensen, M. C., ed., 1983. Symposium on the market for corporate control: The scientific evidence, Journal of Financial Economics 11.

Kaplan, R. S. and R. Roll, 1972, Investor evaluation of accounting information: Some empirical evidence, Journal of Business 45, 225–257.

Keim, D. B., 1983, Size related anomalies and stock return seasonality: Further empirical evidence, Journal of Financial Economics 12, 3–32.

Keim, D. B., 1987, Stock market regularities: a synthesis of the evidence and explanations (in) E. Dimson (Ed.) Stock Market Anomalies, Cambridge University Press.

Levis, M., 1987, Size related anomalies and trading activity of UK institutional investors (in) E. Dimson (Ed.) Stock Market Anomalies, Cambridge University Press.

Mandelker, G., 1974, Risk and return: The case for merging firms, Journal of Financial Economics 7, 110–120.

Marsh, P. R., 1979, Equity rights issues and the efficiency of the UK stock market, Journal of Finance 34, 839–862.

Pountain, C. C. and A. B. Fitzgerald, 1980, The valuation of risk and return, Edinburgh: Wood Mackenzie, January.

Roll, R., 1983, On computing means returns and the small firm premium, Journal of Financial Economics 12, 371–386.

Schwert, G. W., 1983, Size and stock returns and other empirical regularities, Journal of Financial Economics 12, 3–12.

Sharpe, W. F., 1963, A simplified model for portfolio analysis, Management Science 9, 277–293.

18 Performance measurement and performance attribution in less than efficient markets: a case study

STAN BECKERS

1 Introduction

In a fully efficient market the simple form of the capital asset pricing model holds and active management would be nonsense. There is, however, widespread evidence that most equity markets are not fully efficient in that there appear to be persistent anomalies and empirical regularities. The overwhelming majority of investment managers therefore believe that there is potential for above average performance through selective judgement. Few money managers are market timers (the only form of active management in a fully efficient market); very many concentrate on forecasting the average return to a sector and/or on selectivity among assets in a sector.

Performance measurement and performance attribution can help in evaluating the skill of individual managers reflected in the deviations of their portfolios from the norm. In this chapter we argue that accurate performance attribution is only possible if the norm is well defined ahead of time. In addition, for certain managers who concentrate on 'specialist' market segments (small companies, high yield stocks, etc), the selection of the benchmark will be crucial for the identification of management skill over and above the return arising from the permanent stylistic features of the managers' position. We will illustrate these points using a case study involving a mechanical stock selection rule.

2 Performance measurement in the face of market (ir)regularities

The standard methodology used to evaluate investment performance relies on the market model following the seminal paper by Fama *et al.* (1969) whereby the Sharpe–Lintner capital asset pricing model is used as the benchmark. It is now, however, widely substantiated in the academic literature that other factors in addition to the 'market factor' play a role in investment performance. These extra-market factors include industry effects (King, 1966), company size (Banz, 1981; Reinganum, 1981), dividend yield (Litzenberger and Ramaswamy, 1982) and a multitude of balance sheet and income statement based company descriptors (Rosenberg and Marathe, 1976). These alternative sources of investment performance are, however, rarely explicitly accounted for in performance attribution and analysis. Dimson and Marsh (ch. 17), focusing on the size effect, show convincingly that these omissions can significantly distort the conclusions of performance evaluation. Concentrating on 862 stock recommendations published in UK newspapers and magazines, conventional event study methodology shows the recommended portfolios to outperform significantly a capitalization weighted index and underperform significantly an equally weighted index. When allowance is made for the size effect, however, the authors find post publication performance to be neutral. In other words, the stock recommendations did not appear to contain any value over and above their concentration on smaller companies and the only identifiable 'skill' involved in producing above average performance arose entirely from a play on the size effect. Performance evaluation and attribution methodology therefore becomes much richer when the extra-market factors of investment performance are explicitly taken into account. In the next section we will briefly outline a procedure extending the Dimson–Marsh methodology to take into account multiple sources of extra-market performance within the UK stock market.

3 A multiple factor model of the UK equity market

Following the methodology first outlined in Rosenberg and Marathe (1976), BARRA International Inc. has developed a multiple factor model for the UK equity market. The basic procedure in estimating the model is as follows:

1. For each company which is part of the data base (basically the largest 1250 stocks listed on the London Stock Exchange), fundamental data is retrieved from the EXSTAT data base and a number of 'descriptors' is computed from the available fundamental and market based information. These descriptors are akin to the balance sheet and income statement ratios frequently used by security analysts and are thoughtfully designed to provide valid and relevant measures of asset characteristics. The descriptors are listed in appendix 1 and the descriptor formulas are given in Rosenberg and Marathe (1976). The

descriptors are then normalized so that the capitalization weighted mean is zero and the equally weighted standard deviation is one.

Descriptors are calculated monthly since December 1972 for each company, based upon market related data (security prices, dividends, shares outstanding etc.) and upon fundamental balance sheet and income statement data. Market related data must refer to events on or before the last trading day of the prior month. Fundamental data must have been drawn from an annual report for a fiscal year terminating six months or more before that date. The six month lag allows ample time for the data in the report to be released to the financial community. It is designed to ensure that the data used for the descriptors would have been available as of the beginning of the month.

2. To reduce the dimensionality of the problem, the descriptors are transformed into risk indexes which are continuous variables designed to capture important aspects of the company's operations (and hence permit differentiation among companies). The weights used in the translation of the descriptors into risk indexes are obtained through a principal component analysis of the return series associated with each descriptor. These return series are obtained through (sixty) monthly GLS cross-sectional regressions of a company's excess return as a function of its descriptors and industry affiliation. There are a total of twelve risk indexes – listed in appendix 1 – which contribute significantly to the explanation of return variability in the London market. The risk indexes are normalized in the same way as the descriptors.

3. The residual return for each security is estimated using the conventional CAPM methodology:

$$u_{it} = R_{it} - \beta_i R_{Mt} \qquad (1)$$

whereby R_{it} and R_{Mt} are the excess returns on security i and on the market portfolio proxy in month t after deducting the risk-free rate for which the ninety day yield on T-bills is used. The *Financial Times – Institute of Actuaries* index which is capitalization weighted and captures more than 90 per cent of the total UK stock market – is used as the proxy for the market portfolio.

Individual stock betas are estimated using a five-year history of monthly total returns and are adjusted for fundamental company characteristics as first outlined in Rosenberg and McKibben (1973) and later refined in Rosenberg and Marathe (1975). These 'bionic' betas can be shown to provide better predictions of future systematic risk than those obtained on the basis of the standard regression methodology (Reid and Rudd, 1983; Rosenberg, 1985).

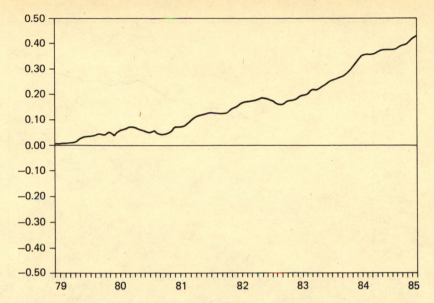

Figure 1   Cumulative factor return: Book to Price
Note: The cumulative return is for a portfolio which is uniquely exposed to this factor (with factor exposure = 1) and neutral with respect to every other characteristic.

4. The residual returns to each of the twelve risk index factors (in addition to the thirty-six industry group factors, defined according to the *Financial Times* – Institute of Actuaries definitions) are estimated monthly using a GLS cross-sectional regression.

$$u_{it} = X_{ijt} f_{jt} + e_{it} \tag{2}$$

where

u_{it} = residual return for company i in month t (from equation (1));
X_{ijt} = exposure of company i to factor j (risk index or industry exposure);
f_{jt} = estimated residual factor return associated with characteristic j;
e_{it} = specific return for company i in month t.

Each company's residual return can therefore be explained as a function of a combination of its exposure to the above-mentioned risk indexes and industry factors on the one hand, and that month's

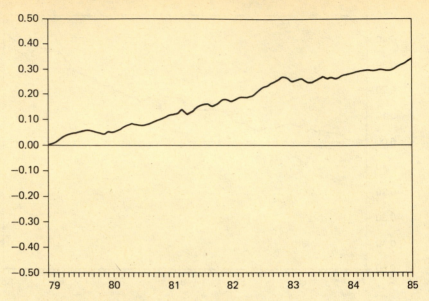

Figure 2   Cumulative factor return: Success
Note: The cumulative return is for a portfolio which is uniquely exposed to this factor (with factor exposure = 1) and neutral with respect to every other characteristic.

estimated residual factor returns on the other, whereby the GLS error term for each stock corresponds to its specific return.

Although the importance of the risk indexes derived from their contribution to explaining total return variability, it turns out that the monthly residual factor returns associated with some of them also have nonzero means. To the extent that these return trends persist over long intervals, they point to significant anomalies in the UK market.

The most prominent of these anomalies are represented in figures 1 through 3. It is important to note that – since these factor returns are the outcome of regression (2) – they capture 'pure' effects (i.e. net of all other factors). This also means that the size effect observed by Dimson and Marsh (1986) in the UK market to some extent appears to be a surrogate for the book to price factor (high net asset value stocks are on average smaller) since the small company factor is much less prominent when all other risk indexes are accounted for (figure 4).

These factor returns are not only intriguing in their own right, they also open interesting perspectives for performance analysis and performance attribution. We will briefly outline their importance in the next section.

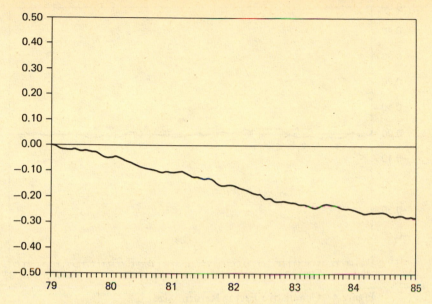

Figure 3   Cumulative factor return: Financial Leverage
Note: The cumulative return is for a portfolio which is uniquely exposed to this factor (with factor exposure = 1) and neutral with respect to every other characteristic.

4 Performance analysis and performance attribution in a multiple factor world

When measuring and evaluating investment performance the traditional point of reference has been a broad-based index which accurately captures overall market movements and can reasonably be claimed to reflect its 'average' performance. Implicit in this comparison is the assumption that the neutral position for the investment manager would be a passive holding in the index. Any deviations from this position usually are transient 'bets' of the manager, the accuracy of which should be evaluated. Detailed performance attribution therefore breaks down total return in terms of a number of crucial decision variables which identify the manager's strategy:

- return due to market timing (beta policy)
- return due to industry selection
- return due to 'type of company bias'
- return due to stock selection

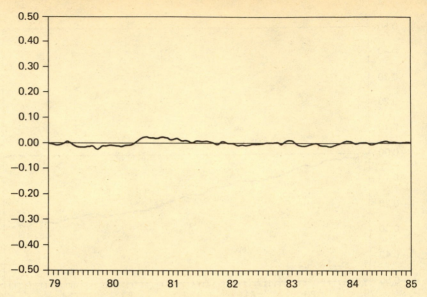

Figure 4   Cumulative Factor Return: Size
Note: The cumulative return is for a portfolio which is uniquely exposed to this factor (with factor exposure = 1) and neutral with respect to every other characteristic.

Through this process it is possible to quantify the return contribution of each component of the investment strategy such that each deviation from the 'neutral' point is evaluated.

Not every investment manager necessarily has the broad-based index as his/her neutral benchmark. Some have a more or less permanent bias in their investment strategy (small company, high yield etc.). In these cases additional insights can be gained by separating performance into the return of the biased (small company, high yield, etc.) universe relative to the market on the one hand, and the return attributable to transient deviations from this (biased) neutral position on the other.

In each case the identification of portfolio strategy in terms of a multitude of factors, which can give rise to differential performance, facilitates the evaluation of the (lack of) skills inherent in the management process. This is illustrated in the following section using an actual case study.

5 A case study

Performance Analysis Ltd, a UK private company, publishes monthly a list of 'recovery' and 'downside' stocks which are expected to respectively outperform and underperform the market. The actual procedure used to

Table 1 *Average factor exposures over the period July 1982 – January 1985*

	Recovery	Downside
Beta	0.98	0.85
Market variability	0.27	0.34
Success	0.15	−1.13
Size	−1.22	−1.72
Research orientation	−0.03	0.41
Growth orientation	−0.14	0.00
Earnings/price	−0.20	−0.99
Book/price	0.47	1.59
Earnings variability	0.75	1.01
Financial leverage	0.44	0.85
Foreign income	−0.09	−0.01
Labour intensity	0.62	0.70

Note: Except for the beta which is an absolute number, all other characteristics are standardized and expressed in number of standard deviations away from the (capitalization weighted) market average

construct these lists derives from a modified Z score procedure which is discussed in detail in Taffler (1982, 1983). No further distinction is made between the stocks within each category, and each stock therefore would get an equal weight in each portfolio.

Our analysis covers the period from July 1982 through January 1985. During this period a total of one hundred different stocks figured in the recovery portfolio whereas there were ninety-five different companies represented in the downside fund. A stock would typically stay in the recovery fund for twelve months (eleven months in the downside portfolio). On average there were thirty-seven stocks in the recovery portfolio and thirty-three in the downside fund, although these numbers varied from a maximum of forty-five (fifty-six) to a minimum of twenty-nine (twenty) in the recovery (downside) portfolio.

Given the above characteristics the portfolio composition changed slowly over time with a few additions and deletions to each portfolio from month to month. The actual construction of these portfolios would therefore incur only limited transactions.

The typical portfolio structure was obviously very unlike the market average. Firstly Performance Analysis excludes the financial companies which make up roughly between 20 and 25 per cent of the total market capitalization. In addition, by the nature of constructing equally weighted portfolios, the industry distribution of the two funds could at times be significantly out of line with that of the market. In particular the recovery portfolio tended to be heavily overweight on the construction and miscellaneous sectors (typical portfolio weight 20 per cent and 15 per

Table 2 *Monthly portfolio returns*

	Recovery			Downside		
Date	Total actual	Total market model	Residual market model	Total actual	Total market model	Residual market model
8207	3.86	4.59	−0.73	−0.32	4.11	−4.43
8208	2.31	4.70	−2.39	−2.00	4.20	−6.20
8209	2.25	4.08	−1.83	−9.27	3.65	−12.90
8210	7.41	5.21	2.20	5.52	4.63	0.89
8211	7.78	1.75	6.03	3.21	1.61	1.60
8212	1.32	0.12	1.20	−3.40	0.21	−3.61
8301	5.46	4.31	1.15	4.67	3.89	0.78
8302	3.22	1.98	1.24	5.95	1.83	4.12
8303	4.11	2.83	1.28	13.66	2.55	11.11
8304	5.63	6.99	−1.36	8.90	6.36	2.54
8305	−1.38	−0.79	−0.59	−1.20	−0.65	−0.55
8306	4.35	0.13	4.22	3.67	0.20	3.47
8307	−0.10	3.27	−3.37	3.36	2.90	0.46
8308	2.38	1.64	0.74	2.31	1.52	0.79
8309	−0.61	−0.82	0.21	−0.31	−0.51	0.20
8310	0.22	−1.14	1.36	−1.24	−0.75	−0.49
8311	5.28	5.15	0.13	2.22	4.31	−2.09
8312	3.25	2.61	0.64	7.26	2.31	4.95
8401	11.68	6.58	5.10	11.78	5.85	5.93
8402	2.84	−0.48	3.32	6.54	−0.34	6.88
8403	5.08	5.83	−0.75	5.11	5.24	−0.13
8404	1.17	2.33	−1.16	3.55	2.14	1.41
8405	−11.00	−7.75	−3.28	−9.65	−6.79	−2.86
8406	−0.24	−0.04	−0.20	−0.24	0.03	−0.27
8407	−0.38	−1.34	0.96	−1.57	−1.09	−0.48
8408	9.45	8.96	0.49	8.40	7.80	0.60
8409	−0.13	2.44	−2.57	1.95	2.22	−0.27
8410	5.36	3.16	2.20	3.94	2.82	1.12
8411	3.53	2.94	0.59	1.63	2.69	−1.06
8412	5.86	5.54	0.32	5.59	5.00	0.59
8501	3.93	4.17	−0.24	7.07	3.83	3.24
Mean	3.03	2.55	0.48	2.81	2.32	0.49
S. dev.	4.02	3.24	2.21	5.08	2.79	4.14

cent respectively) whereas the downside fund favoured the mechanical engineering and motor industries (on average 22 per cent and 18 per cent of the portfolio). These sectors have, over the years, never accounted for more than 5 per cent of the total market capitalization.

Not only was the industry distribution of the portfolios out of line with that of the market, the fundamental balance sheet and income statement-based profile of the typical company in each fund was very much unlike that of the 'average' company in the market. Table 1 summarizes the salient features of both portfolios. It is striking that both portfolios

Table 3 *Average factor exposures and corresponding factor returns over the interval July 1982 – January 1985*

Factor	Recovery		Downside	
	Exposure	Return	Exposure	Return
Variability	0.27	0.02	0.34	0.05
Success	0.15	0.08	−1.13	−0.42
Size	−1.22	−0.03	−1.72	−0.03
Growth	−0.14	0.02	0.00	0.01
Earnings to price	−0.20	0.04	−0.99	0.26
Book to price	0.47	0.37	1.59	1.22
Earnings variation	0.75	−0.05	1.01	−0.09
Financial leverage	0.44	−0.13	0.85	−0.25
Foreign income	−0.09	0.04	−0.01	−0.04
Labour intensity	0.62	0.00	0.70	−0.05
Total		0.34		0.68

Note: The factor exposures are measured in terms of number of standard deviations away from the capitalization weighted mean. The factor returns are expressed in percentage terms.

differentiate themselves from the market on almost all characteristics: both funds concentrate on small, high book to price, highly geared companies. In addition the funds differ from each other in that the downside portfolio concentrates on less successful, smaller (and hence lower beta), more highly levered, higher net asset value (book to price) stocks. A priori, one would expect that portfolios which have such different profile from the market – both in terms of their industry distribution and their fundamental characteristics – could obtain a return which could be significantly different from the market.

Applying the CAPM-based single factor model, both portfolios indeed outperform the market on a risk-adjusted basis as evidenced in table 2 (using the value weighted *Financial Times* – Actuaries Index). The average monthly residual return for the recovery and downside fund is forty-eight and forty-nine basis points respectively. Both funds outperformed the market average which raises the intriguing question as to where this extraordinary performance comes from and why it is so similar for both portfolios when their profiles are significantly different. A performance breakdown using the multiple factor framework can provide us with these additional insights.

For each monthly holding period the residual return can be broken down in function of the contribution of industry, 'type of company' and stock specific biases. Specifically each over- or underweighting can be combined with the residual factor return and stock specific return derived from equation (2). This allows for a further analysis of the residual

Table 4 *Monthly residual return breakdown*

	Recovery				Downside			
	Residual return	Ind.	Factor	Specific	Residual	Ind.	Factor	Specific
8207	−0.73	0.59	−0.19	−1.13	−4.43	0.45	−6.48	1.60
8208	−2.39	−1.37	−1.28	0.26	−6.20	−2.34	−2.67	−1.19
8209	−1.83	0.74	−1.41	−1.16	−12.90	−1.29	−5.59	−6.02
8210	2.20	−1.81	−0.36	4.37	0.89	−2.17	−0.87	3.93
8211	6.03	1.80	2.28	1.95	1.60	−0.14	1.79	−0.05
8212	1.20	2.81	−1.09	−0.52	−3.61	3.11	−2.33	−4.39
8301	1.15	−1.60	0.26	2.49	0.78	−1.39	3.21	−1.04
8302	1.24	1.16	1.43	−1.35	4.12	3.45	2.56	−1.89
8303	1.28	−1.36	1.55	1.09	11.11	1.05	1.45	8.61
8304	−1.36	−2.74	−0.42	1.80	2.54	−1.86	4.63	−0.23
8305	−0.59	1.17	−0.58	−1.18	−0.55	1.63	−1.23	−0.95
8306	4.22	3.83	0.63	−0.24	3.47	4.28	1.28	−2.09
8307	−3.37	−7.62	3.09	1.16	0.46	−5.35	3.68	2.13
8308	0.74	−0.90	0.44	1.20	0.79	−0.76	2.25	−0.70
8309	0.21	0.43	0.87	−1.09	0.20	−0.52	2.19	−1.47
8310	1.36	0.44	−0.76	1.68	−0.49	−0.53	−0.35	0.39
8311	0.13	1.45	−0.83	−0.49	−2.09	2.93	−1.43	−3.59
8312	0.64	1.65	0.02	−1.03	4.95	2.32	2.01	0.62
8401	5.10	1.30	2.20	1.60	5.93	1.42	4.52	−0.01
8402	3.32	−0.19	3.81	−0.30	6.88	−0.66	7.58	−0.04
8403	−0.75	0.82	−0.35	−1.22	−0.13	0.71	−0.17	−0.67
8404	−1.16	1.60	0.19	−2.95	1.41	0.76	−0.94	1.59
8405	−3.28	−3.83	0.55	0.00	−2.86	−4.87	2.66	−0.65
8406	−0.20	+3.09	0.00	−3.29	−0.27	3.09	3.23	−6.59
8407	0.96	−0.61	−0.72	2.29	−0.48	−1.11	−1.93	2.56
8408	0.49	0.95	−0.76	0.30	0.60	1.44	−0.28	−0.56
8409	−2.57	−0.36	0.23	−2.44	−0.27	−0.57	1.20	−0.90
8410	2.20	0.71	0.18	1.31	1.12	−0.03	0.18	0.97
8411	0.59	1.62	−0.63	−0.40	−1.06	1.07	−1.31	−0.82
8412	0.32	−0.51	1.42	−0.59	0.59	0.12	2.52	−2.05
8501	−0.24	−0.89	0.83	−0.18	3.24	0.10	−0.17	3.31
Mean	0.48	0.08	0.34	0.06	0.49	0.14	0.68	−0.33
St. dev.	2.21	2.20	1.26	1.68	4.20	2.20	2.93	2.87

portfolio return in terms of the extra-market decision variables.

Specifically, some of the factor exposures summarized in table 1 for each fund have contributed significantly to the average portfolio residual return, as evidenced in table 3. Both funds benefited greatly from a bias towards high book to price companies and indeed the more significant bias of the downside portfolio on this dimension explains the fact that the residual factor return for this portfolio is double that of the recovery fund. Interestingly both funds suffer from an emphasis on highly geared companies and the downside fund loses out because of an emphasis on 'unsuccessful' stocks. It is also worth noting that the significant bias of both funds towards small companies has a negligible and if anything negative effect on their residual performance. In aggregate the profile of the typical company in the downside portfolio had a more positive contribution to its residual performance than that of the typical company in the recovery fund (sixty-eight basis points versus thirty-four). It can therefore be inferred that the discriminant function distinguishing between both types of companies worked in an exactly opposite way from what one would have expected.

An analogous exercise for the industry biases and stock selection skills leads to the performance breakdown of table 4. The industry biases of both funds on average had a positive impact on the residual return and again the effect was larger for the downside portfolio than for the recovery fund (fourteen basis points versus eight). As far as the stock selection is concerned, the recovery fund on average contained stocks with mildly positive idiosyncratic returns (six basis points). The monthly stock specific return for the typical stock in the downside fund however was a surprising −33 basis points.

The above performance attribution allows for a more correct evaluation of the investment manager or adviser's contribution to the overall fund performance. *Ex post* it is very tempting to claim credit for results which support any supposed selection skills and to gracefully ignore less interesting outcomes. To minimize these risks and to gain maximum benefit from the performance breakdown it is crucial to know the neutral or normal position ahead of time.

If in our example the neutral position would be the All Share Index one should rightfully expect the recovery portfolios to outperform and the downside fund to underperform the index on all scores (industry, factor and stock selection). If on the other hand the selection mechanism is such that by definition both funds will be constructed from a biased universe (such as small, high book to price, highly geared stocks), the point of reference could be this biased universe when evaluating the recovery versus the downside portfolios (whereby the performance of the biased universe versus the index should be evaluated separately).

Specifically, in our example, when both funds' total residual return is evaluated there does not appear to be any skill differentiating both funds from each other. If, however, one considers the industry and factor biases as incidental artefacts of the advisory service, then the service does appear to have some value in its ability to identify 'overpriced' companies with perilous idiosyncratic characteristics (although it would be hard to substantiate the reverse claim). The above performance breakdown is therefore meaningless unless the management style is quantified in terms of neutral and active strategies.

Appendix: *Risk indices and descriptors in the UK model*

Risk index	Descriptors
1 Variability in markets	Historical beta Serial dependence Cumulative range Historical beta times historical sigma
2 Success: Market's perception of the companies' prior success	Historical alpha Growth in EPS Recent earnings change Relative strength Dividend cuts (5 years)
3 Size: Composite measure of the company's size	Logarithm of market capitalization Logarithm of total assets Indicator of earnings history
4 Research: Research orientation	Research and development costs
5 Growth: Growth orientation	Current yield Payout (5 years) Yield (5 years) Indicator of zero yield Growth in total assets Capital structure change Earnings/price normalized Growth in Earnings per Share Recent earnings change Payout Earnings/price ratio Leverage at book
6 Estimated earnings to price	Earnings/price ratio
7 Book to price	Book/price ratio
8 Earnings variation	Variance of earnings Extraordinary items Variance of cash flow Earnings covariability
9 Financial leverage	Leverage at book Debt/assets Uncovered fixed charges
10 Foreign income	Foreign income
11 Labour intensity	Net plant/gross plant Inflation adjusted plant/equity Labour share
12 Investment	Authorized and contracted capital expenditure

6 Conclusions

Active investment managers claim to provide a service to their clients by letting them share in the benefits of their superior skills. These skills arise from their supposed ability to identify mispriced sectors, industries and/or companies. It is a matter of professional honesty and academic interest to evaluate whether and to what extent these skills are indeed present. A detailed performance breakdown and attribution in terms of identifiable portfolio strategies can greatly contribute to this exercise.

In this article we have illustrated one possible approach to this problem using an actual case study. Many variables or biases can potentially lead to differential returns and are used by investment managers as 'specialist' tools in their trade. Historically some strategies appear to have consistently led to superior performance. A detailed performance analysis and attribution concentrating on extra market sources of return can hopefully contribute to the transformation of these few remaining market inefficiencies into academically acceptable regularities.

References

Banz, R.W. (1981) 'The Relationship between Return and Market Value of Common Stock', *Journal of Financial Economics*, 9, 3–18.

Dimson, E. and Marsh, P. (1986) 'Event Study Methodologies and the Size Effect – The Case of the UK Press Recommendations,' *Journal of Financial Economics*, 17, 113–41.

Fama, E.F., Fisher, L., Jensen, M.C. and Roll, R. (1969) 'The Adjustment of Stock Prices to New Information', *International Economic Review*, 10.

King, B.F. (1966) 'Market and Industry Factors in Stock Price Behaviour', *Journal of Business*, 39, 139–90.

Litzenberger, R.H. and Ramaswamy, K. (1982) 'The Effect of Dividends on Common Stock Prices: Tax Effects or Information Effects', *Journal of Finance*, 37, 429–43.

Reid, K. and Rudd, A. (1983) 'Prediction of Systematic Risk in the United Kingdom', Proceedings of the European Finance Association Meetings, Fontainebleau, Sept. 1–3.

Reinganum, M.R. (1981) 'Misspecification of Capital Asset Pricing: Empirical Anomalies based on Earnings Yields and Market Values', *Journal of Financial Economics*, 9, 19–46.

Rosenberg, B. (1985) 'Prediction of Common Stock Betas', *Journal of Portfolio Management*, Winter, 5–14.,

Rosenberg, B. and Marathe, V. (1975) 'The Prediction of Investment Risk: Systematic and Residual Risk', Proceedings of the Seminar on the Analysis of Security Prices, University of Chicago, November, 85–225.

Rosenberg, B. and Marathe, V. (1976) 'Common Factors in Security Returns: Micro-economic Determinants and Macro-economic Correlates', Proceedings of the Seminar on the Analysis of Security Prices, May, 61–116 (University of Chicago, Chicago, Illinois).

Rosenberg, B. and McKibben, W. (1973) 'The Prediction of Systematic Risk in Common Stocks', *Journal of Financial and Quantitative Analysis*, 8, 317–33.

Taffler, R.J. (1982) 'Forecasting Company Failure in the UK using Discriminant Analysis and Financial Ratio Data', *Journal of the Royal Statistical Society*, series A, 145, 3, 342–58.

Taffler, R.J. (1983) 'The Assessment of Company Solvency and Performance using a Statistical Model', *Accounting and Business Research*, 52, 295–307.

Taffler, R.J. (1984) 'Empirical Models for the Monitoring of UK Corporations', *Journal of Banking and Finance*, 8, 2.

19 A comparison of single and multifactor portfolio performance methodologies

NAI-FU CHEN, THOMAS E. COPELAND and DAVID MAYERS*

1 Introduction

Efficient methods to measure the economic significance of new information arrival are of great interest to financial economists. In their seminal paper, Fama *et al.* (1969) used the residuals from the single factor market model to measure the unanticipated returns of assets:

$$R_{it} = a_i + b_i R_{mt} + \varepsilon_{it} \tag{1}$$

where R_{it} and R_{mt} are the returns of asset i and a market index at time t, a_i and b_i are asset-specific time-stationary parameters, and ε_{it} is the market model residual for asset i at time t. Thus, the normal relation between the return of asset i and the return of the market is described by $a_i + b_i R_{mt}$, which is the conditional expected return of asset i given the realization of R_{mt}. The conditional residual, ε_{it}, contains the conditional unanticipated return, including the effect of new information.

The advantage of using the conditional residuals comes from removing the unanticipated 'systematic' term, $b_i(R_{mt} - \mathrm{E}(R_{mt}))$, from the residuals. Copeland and Mayers (1982) found that using the residuals from a future benchmark market model methodology (conditional expected returns) produced more powerful tests than using the residuals from the mean return (unconditional expected return) in their study of the information content of Value Line recommendations. Their findings differ from those of Brown and Warner's (1980) simulation study which indicated about equal power between the two choices. A likely reason for the difference is that more efficient market model parameter estimates were obtained in the Copeland–Mayers study using portfolio rates of return as opposed to individual security rates of return as in Brown–Warner.

In this study, we examine the question of whether efficiency is further improved using a multifactor market model for the conditional expected returns. The rationale behind this approach is derived from the empirical regularity that there is more than one source of common covariation among asset returns (see King, 1966; Roll and Ross, 1980). Our approach is quite apart from the equilibrium consideration of Ross' arbitrage pricing theory, which was the focus of the Roll and Ross study. Here, we are merely trying to determine whether extracting more common covariation from the residuals improves the efficiency of measuring the economic impact of new information.

If the multifactor market model is correct and stationary, and if the associated parameters are known with certainty, then the multifactor model will purge more common covariation from the residuals. However, the multifactor model requires more parameter estimates and there are more possibilities for nonstationarity compared to the single factor model. Therefore, if one uses out-of-sample conditional forecast errors, it is not obvious that the multifactor market model will dominate the traditional single factor market model. To facilitate the comparison, we use two data sets. The first is the Value Line data set as in Copeland and Mayers (1982) and the second is a set of five size-ranked portfolios. As all other aspects of our research methodology are held constant, the only difference in the observed residuals comes solely from the single and multifactor specification of the return generating process.

Section 2 of our study provides brief descriptions of the data and our rate of return calculations. Section 3 outlines our experiment and provides a comparison of the single and multifactor models using the future benchmark procedure. We find that the two models yield measures of abnormal returns that are similar. However, there is evidence of systematic differences between the mean square errors of the single and multifactor models. Section 4 summarizes the results.

2 Data description and rate of return calculations

Our Value Line data base was obtained from *The Value Line Investment Survey* (Weekly Summary of Advices and Index) which lists the Value Line rankings for the set of securities contained in their universe.[1] These rankings are entitled, 'Probable Market Performance, Next 12 months,' and consist of Roman numerals I through V assigned to each firm.[2] The announcements of these rankings may constitute information events.[3] Commencing with the November 26, 1965 *Survey*, Value Line performance rankings were obtained at intervals at least twenty-six weeks apart for a total of twenty-four holding periods for all firms that are also contained on the CRSP daily rate of return file.[4] Thus, our study covers a twelve-year history.[5]

Table 1 *Average cumulative raw returns for twenty-four holding periods from November 26, 1965 to February 3, 1978*

(a) Value Line raw rates of return

Week relative to Value Line ranking date	Portfolio number[a]				
	1	2	3	4	5
1	0.0000	−0.0009	−0.0029	−0.0051	−0.0074
2	−0.0037	−0.0051	−0.0093	−0.0144	−0.0167
3	0.0095	0.0061	−0.0007	−0.0069	−0.0116
4	0.0170	0.0135	0.0068	−0.0001	−0.0068
5	0.0123	0.0090	0.0017	−0.0057	−0.0105
6	0.0200	0.0153	0.0074	−0.0019	−0.0099
7	0.0235	0.0182	0.0073	−0.0028	−0.0099
8	0.0246	0.0179	0.0066	−0.0030	−0.0107
9	0.0302	0.0224	0.0103	0.0008	−0.0111
10	0.0369	0.0292	0.0160	0.0035	−0.0097
11	0.0378	0.0301	0.0130	−0.0010	−0.0161
12	0.0404	0.0333	0.0144	0.0009	−0.0183
13	0.0428	0.0359	0.0168	0.0020	−0.0189
14	0.0481	0.0359	0.0162	−0.0020	−0.0222
15	0.0425	0.0375	0.0172	0.0010	−0.0214
16	0.0477	0.0417	0.0212	0.0063	−0.0188
17	0.0494	0.0432	0.0218	0.0073	−0.0167
18	0.0445	0.0392	0.0180	0.0026	−0.0250
19	0.0420	0.0370	0.0149	−0.0005	−0.0313
20	0.0509	0.0449	0.0220	0.0049	−0.0253
21	0.0621	0.0560	0.0337	0.0203	−0.0041
22	0.0576	0.0609	0.0389	0.0285	0.0060
23	0.0711	0.0640	0.0419	0.0314	0.0085
24	0.0723	0.0645	0.0419	0.0298	0.0082
25	0.0712	0.0623	0.0385	0.0266	0.0037
26	0.0738	0.0651	0.0410	0.0270	0.0037

Note: [a]Portfolio numbers correspond to the Value Line rankings of the securities in the portfolios. On average, portfolios 1 to 5 contain 91, 273, 521, 270 and 91 securities. The rates of return are the average (across the twenty-four holding periods) of the weekly rates of return cumulated to the designated week relative to the ranking date.

We also constructed five size-ranked portfolios for each of the twenty-four holding periods. Portfolio 1 represents the smallest quintile of firms on the CRSP daily tape and portfolio 5 the largest. Market values for all NYSE and AMEX listed companies were computed by multiplying the number of shares outstanding on the Value Line ranking date by the price per share at the end of the previous month. There is no reason to believe that firm size on a given Value Line ranking date constitutes an information event. However, size is a well-known CAPM (or single factor) anomaly and is, therefore, a likely basis for distinguishing

(b) Size-ranked portfolio raw rates of return

Week relative to Value Line ranking date	Portfolio number[b]				
	1	2	3	4	5
1	−0.0002	−0.0036	−0.0034	−0.0029	−0.0031
2	−0.0047	−0.0113	−0.0105	−0.0092	−0.0095
3	0.0035	−0.0013	−0.0002	0.0008	−0.0006
4	0.0095	0.0060	0.0087	0.0082	0.0053
5	0.0078	0.0030	0.0044	0.0030	−0.0006
6	0.0107	0.0080	0.0085	0.0078	0.0054
7	0.0146	0.0116	0.0099	0.0081	0.0044
8	0.0210	0.0150	0.0101	0.0074	0.0012
9	0.0253	0.0176	0.0130	0.0097	0.0060
10	0.0303	0.0222	0.0174	0.0151	0.0116
11	0.0322	0.0225	0.0165	0.0137	0.0081
12	0.0351	0.0248	0.0177	0.0159	0.0111
13	0.0388	0.0273	0.0203	0.0179	0.0121
14	0.0377	0.0263	0.0191	0.0160	0.0102
15	0.0375	0.0260	0.0199	0.0171	0.0130
16	0.0436	0.0323	0.0242	0.0211	0.0172
17	0.0485	0.0357	0.0260	0.0214	0.0168
18	0.0452	0.0313	0.0203	0.0169	0.0134
19	0.0386	0.0260	0.0167	0.0143	0.0120
20	0.0386	0.0260	0.0167	0.0143	0.0120
21	0.0684	0.0495	0.0386	0.0339	0.0259
22	0.0795	0.0601	0.0460	0.0385	0.0279
23	0.0866	0.0642	0.0499	0.0409	0.0293
24	0.0902	0.0661	0.0499	0.0407	0.0286
25	0.0924	0.0660	0.0474	0.0381	0.0243
26	0.0964	0.0672	0.0495	0.0406	0.0265

Note: [b]Portfolio numbers correspond to the size quintile of the securities in the portfolios, with 1 designating the smallest size quintile and 5, the largest. On average, portfolios 1 to 5 each contain 406 securities. The rates of return are the average (across the twenty-four holding periods) of the weekly rates of return cumulated to the designated week relative to the beginning of the holding period.

between single and multifactor market model estimates of residual returns.

The daily CRSP rate of return file was converted to a weekly file using a Friday close to Friday close return interval.[6] The rates of return are adjusted, by CRSP, for dividends, splits, etc. A weekly equally weighted rate of return index, R_{mw}, of all CRSP listed securities was constructed as a single factor market index. Justification for this index is provided in Brown and Warner (1980).

We also constructed five weekly factor return indices for the multifactor model, using Chen's (1983) procedure which is outlined in the appendix. We form well-diversified mimicking portfolios, one for each factor, which have high sensitivity to the kth factor and zero sensitivity to all other factors. Chen's procedure first estimates factor loadings for ten factors using the Jöreskog asymptotic maximum likelihood procedure. Then five mimicking portfolios are formed. The weekly rates of return, $R_{1w}. . .R_{5w}$, on these five mimicking portfolios are our factor return indices. Our choice of five factors (rather than some larger number) is arbitrary, but the procedure guarantees that the factor loadings are not biased due to misspecification (so long as there are no more than ten priced factors). We estimated the mimicking portfolio returns separately for the first twelve holding periods and for the last twelve periods in order to allow for nonstationarity in the factor returns.[7] *Test periods* are defined as the twenty-six weeks following each Value Line recommendation date and *benchmark periods* as the twenty-six weeks following each test period.[8] We evaluate weekly rebalanced, equally weighted portfolios of Value Line securities, and equally weighted portfolios based on firm size. There are five portfolios in each set. Both sets are reconstructed at the beginning of each of the twenty-four test periods. For each portfolio ($p = 1,. . .,5$) the weekly raw rate of return is defined as

$$R_{pt} = \ln(1 + \sum_{j=1}^{N_t} \frac{R_{jt}}{N_t}) \tag{2}$$

Here R_{jt} is the weekly rate of return for security j in the portfolio of interest during week t. N is subscripted by t to denote the possibility of delisting or listing.[9] Table 1 gives the raw rates of return for each Value Line portfolio (a) and for each size-ranked portfolio (b) averaged across all twenty-four test periods and cumulated from week 1 of the test period to week n ($n = 1,. . .,26$).[10] Note that the twenty-six week average cumulative returns are positive for all ten portfolios. Also, the difference between the gross returns on the largest and smallest size-ranked portfolios, 6.99 percent, is roughly the same as the difference in returns between Value Line portfolios 1 and 5, 7.01 percent.[11]

3 Abnormal performance using the market model methodology

Description of methodologies

The specifics of the market model methodology are given in the following formulae. Benchmark rates of return are estimated for each week, w, of a given test period, p. The single factor market model benchmark return is

$$B1_{pw} = \hat{a}_p + \hat{b}_p R_{mw}, \quad w = 1,. . .,26 \tag{3}$$

The coefficients $\hat{a}_p$ and $\hat{b}_p$ are estimated from the simple market model regression

$$R_{pt} = a_p + b_p R_{mt} + \varepsilon_{pt}, \quad t = 27, \ldots, 52 \tag{4}$$

estimated over the future benchmark period, i.e. the twenty-six weeks following the test period.[12]

The five factor market model benchmark return is

$$B5_{pw} = \hat{a}_p + \hat{b}_{1p} R_{1w} + \hat{b}_{2p} R_{2w} + \hat{b}_{3p} R_{3w} + \hat{b}_{4p} R_{4w} + \hat{b}_{5p} R_{5w} \tag{5}$$

where the intercept and slope terms are estimated from the multiple regression

$$R_{pt} = a_p + b_{1p} R_{1t} + b_{2p} R_{2t} + b_{3p} R_{3t} + b_{4p} R_{4t} + b_{5p} R_{5t} + \eta_{pt} \tag{6}$$

again estimated over the future benchmark period.

For each Value Line portfolio and size-ranked portfolio, we then estimate the cumulative excess rates of return for period p and the average cumulative excess rates of return

$$CR_p = \sum_{w=1}^{26} (R_{pw} - B_{pw}) \tag{7}$$

$$ACR = \frac{1}{24} \sum_{p=1}^{24} CR_p \tag{8}$$

using both benchmark models, and test for whether the cumulative excess rate of return performance is different from zero. The standard deviation for this test is the usual unbiased estimator calculated with the period-by-period cumulative test period excess returns.[13]

Abnormal performance results

Table 2 and figure 1 contain the abnormal performance results. The table presents the average cumulative excess rates of return (ACRs) and t-statistics for the five Value Line portfolios (a) and the five size-ranked portfolios (b) for both the single-factor and the five-factor market models over the entire twenty-four period history. The figure contains plots of cumulative abnormal performance for weeks relative to the Value Line ranking date using both models.

The results for the single and multifactor market models are practically indistinguishable. For the Value Line portfolios (a) the 3.05 percent ACR reported for the single-factor model for portfolio 5 is marginally significant at the 0.05 level. The 2.89 percent ACR reported for the five-factor model for portfolio 5 is marginally insignificant.[14] Moreover, the differences between the portfolio 1 and 5 ACRs are almost identical for the two market models; 3.38 percent for the single-factor model and 3.42 percent for the five-factor model.[15]

Table 2 *Excess rate of return performance for twenty-four ranking dates from November 26, 1965 to February 3, 1978; single-factor and five-factor market model benchmarks, estimated over a twenty-six week benchmark period*

(a) Value Line excess returns[a]

		Portfolio number				
Market model		1	2	3	4	5
Single factor:	ACR	0.0033	0.0035	−0.0057	−0.0112	−0.0305
	AR	0.0001	0.0001	−0.0002	−0.0004	−0.0012
	t-stat	0.2545	0.3801	−0.5935	−1.1007	−2.1258[b]
Five factor:	ACR	0.0053	0.0058	−0.0005	−0.0071	−0.0289
	AR	0.0002	0.0002	−0.0000	−0.0003	−0.0012
	t-stat	0.3603	0.6704	−0.0699	−0.8054	−1.9640

Note: [a]Portfolio numbers correspond to the Value Line rankings of the securities in the portfolio. ACR is the average cumulative twenty-six-week test period excess rate of return, AR the average weekly excess rate of return and t-stat the t-statistic under the null hypothesis that ACR = 0. Degrees of freedom for t-stats are 23.
[b]Any t-stat greater than 2.069 is significant at the 0.05 level.

(b) Size-ranked portfolio excess returns[c]

		Portfolio number				
Market model		1	2	3	4	5
Single factor:	ACR	0.0031	0.0027	−0.0020	−0.0113	−0.0098
	AR	0.0001	0.0001	−0.0001	−0.0004	−0.0004
	t-stat	0.2272	0.4997	−0.3665	−1.2051	−0.6850
Five factor:	ACR	0.0088	0.0062	0.0004	−0.0065	−0.0045
	AR	0.0003	0.0002	−0.0000	−0.0003	−0.0002
	t-stat	0.5320	0.5916	0.0396	−0.8659	−0.4879

Note: [c]Portfolio numbers correspond to the size rankings of the securities in the portfolio. ACR is the average cumulative twenty-six-week test period excess rate of return, AR the average weekly excess rate of return and t-stat the t-statistic under the null hypothesis that ACR = 0. Degrees of freedom for t-stats are 23. Thus, any t-stat greater than 2.069 is significant at the 0.05 level.

As expected, the results for the size-ranked portfolios (b) show no statistically significant performance at all. The largest t-statistic is only −1.2051, and the difference in ACRs between the smallest and largest size portfolios is only 1.33 percent using the multifactor model or 1.29 percent using the single factor model.

Note, however, that the ACR plots of the size-ranked portfolios for the single factor model reveal negative cross-sectional correlation.

(a) Value Line Portfolio ACRs, Single Factor Market Model

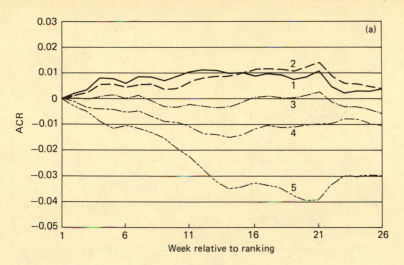

(b) Value Line Portfolio ACRs, Five-Factor Market Model

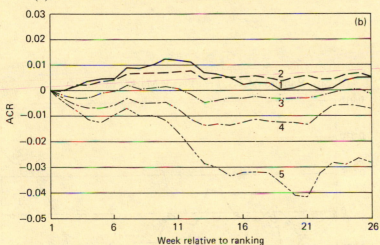

Figure 1   Excess rate of return performance plots for five Value Line rankings portfolios and for five size-ranked portfolios for 24 ranking dates from November 26, 1965, to February 3, 1978. The ACR are the average (across 24 periods) of the weekly excess rates of return cumulated to the designated week relative to the ranking date in the test period (week zero). The numbers 1 to 5 correspond to the Value Line rankings of the securities in the portfolios, in panels a and b, and to firm sizes (with 1 being the smallest quintile) in panels c and d.

(c) Size-Ranked Portfolio ACRs, Single Factor Market Model

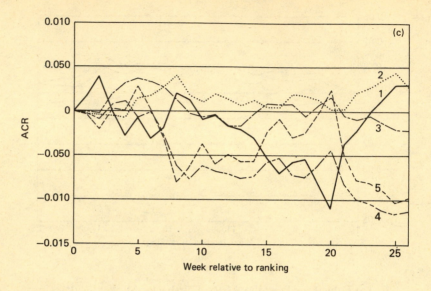

(d) Size-Ranked ACRs, Five Factor Market Model

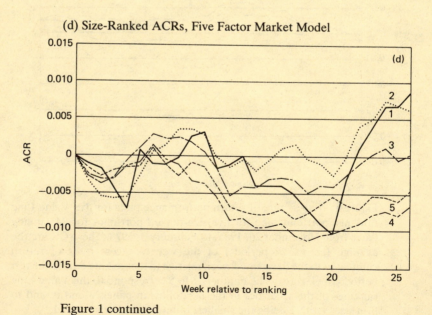

Figure 1 continued

Table 3 *Cross-sectional correlations for excess returns of size-ranked portfolios*

(a) Single-factor correlations

	1	2	3	4	5
1	1.000				
2	0.329	1.000			
3	−0.331	−0.292	1.000		
4	−0.105	−0.662	0.784	1.000	
5	−0.610	−0.762	0.659	0.804	1.000

(b) Multifactor correlations

	1	2	3	4	5
1	1.000				
2	0.859	1.000			
3	0.367	0.359	1.000		
4	0.287	−0.007	0.689	1.000	
5	0.281	0.022	0.670	0.948	1.000

Portfolios 1 and 5, and portfolios 2 and 4, seem to be reflections of each other. This is confirmed in table 3, which presents a correlation matrix of residuals.

The most interesting thing about the correlations is that the large negative correlations between portfolios 1 and 5, and 2 and 4, are reduced from an average of −0.636 to 0.137 when the single-factor model is replaced with the five-factor model. This suggests that there is a left-out variable in the single factor model and that this variable is uncorrelated with the single-factor market index.

Mean square error comparisons

Although the ACRs of the single and multifactor models are similar, the two models may differ in power, especially when portfolios are based on a CAPM anomaly such as firm size. In order to compare the two models, we examine the mean square error criterion, which is defined as

$$\text{MSE} = \frac{1}{24} \sum_{p=1}^{24} (\text{CR}_p)^2 \qquad (9)$$

The results of these calculations are reported in table 4. The multifactor model appears to do better. It has smaller MSE for Value Line portfolios

Table 4 *Mean square error terms for the single-factor model (column 2), the five-factor model (column 3), and their ratio (column 4)*

(a) Value Line portfolios

(1) Portfolio number	(2) Single factor MSE	(3) Five factor MSE	(4) Ratio = (2)÷(3)
1	0.00387	0.00508	0.762
2	0.00196	0.00176	1.114
3	0.00217	0.00109	1.991
4	0.00298	0.00182	1.673
5	0.00567	0.00581	0.967

(b) Size-ranked portfolios

(1) Portfolio number	(2) Single factor MSE	(3) Five factor MSE	(4) Ratio = (2)÷(3)
1	0.10387	0.10315	1.007
2	0.01687	0.04518	0.373
3	0.01724	0.03075	0.561
4	0.05118	0.02594	1.973
5	0.11598	0.02604	4.454

2, 3 and 4, and for size-ranked portfolios 1, 4 and 5. However, we need a significance test.

If the test-period cumulative forecast errors of the two models were independent, the ratio of mean square errors could be interpreted as a doubly non-central F-test. However, as the cumulative forecast errors of the two models are highly correlated, a different significance test must be employed. A procedure introduced by Ashley *et al.* (1980) is used to test the null hypothesis that the difference in the mean square error terms for the two models is zero. To explain their procedure, let ε_{1p} and ε_{5p} be the test period CRs for the single and multifactor models respectively. The difference between the mean square errors is

$$\text{MSE}(\varepsilon_1) - \text{MSE}(\varepsilon_5) = [s^2(\varepsilon_1) - s^2(\varepsilon_5)] + [m(\varepsilon_1)^2 - m(\varepsilon_5)^2] \qquad (10)$$

where MSE is the sample mean square error, s^2 is the sample variance, and m is the sample mean. Now defining Δ_p as the difference in error terms and θ_p as their sum,

$$\Delta_p = \varepsilon_{1p} - \varepsilon_{5p} \quad \text{and} \quad \theta_p = \varepsilon_{1p} + \varepsilon_{5p} \qquad (11)$$

Table 5 *Results of the OLS regression* $\Delta_p = A_1 + A_2[\theta_p - m(\theta_p)] + \mu_p$ *for each of the five portfolios*

(a) Value Line portfolios

Value Line portfolio	Parameter estimate	t-test	r^2/DW	F-test
1	$A_1 -0.0020$	-0.2386	0.0541	1.26
	$A_2 -0.0747$	-1.1214	1.9809	
2	$A_1 -0.0023$	-0.2994	0.0068	0.15
	A_2 0.3780	0.3874	2.2257	
3	$A_1 -0.0052$	-0.7804	0.1766	4.72^a
	A_2 0.1989	2.1721^a	2.1433	
4	$A_1 -0.0041$	-0.5535	0.1082	2.67
	A_2 0.1365	1.6636	2.3342	
5	$A_1 -0.0016$	-0.1573	0.0014	0.03
	$A_2 -0.0140$	-0.1752	2.1340	

(b) Size-ranked portfolios

Size-ranked portfolio	Parameter estimate	t-test	r^2/DW	F-test
1	$A_1 -0.0057$	-0.7250	0.1263	3.18
	$A_2 -0.1002$	-1.7831	2.7603	
2	$A_1 -0.0034$	-0.5673	0.4490	17.93^a
	$A_2 -0.3658$	-4.2338^a	2.3643	
3	$A_1 -0.0024$	-0.4106	0.3289	10.78^a
	$A_2 -0.3003$	-3.2832^a	2.3138	
4	$A_1 -0.0047$	-0.6668	0.0791	1.89
	A_2 0.1322	1.3750	2.3993	
5	$A_1 -0.0054$	-0.7407	0.3750	13.20^a
	A_2 0.2444	3.6334^a	2.6903	

Note: ^{a} The variable is statistically significant at the 5 percent confidence level or better.
DW is the Durbin–Watson statistic.
F-test degrees of freedom are (2,22) with $F>3.44$ being significant at the 50 percent confidence level.

equation (10) can be written as

$$MSE(\varepsilon_1) - MSE(\varepsilon_5) = [COV(\Delta,\theta)] + [m(\varepsilon_1)^2 - m(\varepsilon_5)^2] \qquad (12)$$

where COV is the sample covariance. From equation (12), a significant difference between the MSEs for the two models is indicated if we can reject the joint null hypothesis that COV $(\Delta,\theta) = 0$ and $m(\Delta) = 0$ in favor of the alternative that both quantities are non-negative and at least one is positive. This joint hypothesis can be tested by running the OLS regression

$$\Delta_p = A_1 + A_2[\theta_p - m(\theta_p)] + \mu_p \qquad (13)$$

where μ_p is a mean zero error term and is independent of θ_p. Equation (13) also assumes no significant autocorrelation. The null hypothesis of no difference in the MSE is equivalent to the joint hypothesis that $A_1 = A_2 = 0$. The two simple null hypotheses of no difference in prediction bias and of equivalent prediction variances are the same as $A_1 = 0$ and $A_2 = 0$ respectively.

Table 5 shows the results of regression (13) for the five Value Line portfolios and for the size-ranked portfolios. The intercept term, which is an estimate of the difference in excess returns between the single and multifactor models, is insignificant in all regressions. The slope term is significantly positive for Value Line portfolio 3 and size-ranked portfolio 5, indicating superiority of the multifactor model. However, the slope is significantly negative for size-ranked portfolios 2 and 3, indicating superiority for the single-factor model. These results are consistent with the ratios of mean-squared errors which were reported in table 4. From the pattern of the results, we conclude that the advantage of extra factors in the multifactor model makes it superior for well-diversified portfolios, but that this advantage is lost (and even reversed) when portfolios have greater idiosyncratic risk. The multifactor model is superior for Value Line portfolio 3 which has over 500 securities but not for portfolios 1 and 5 which have less than 100. Similarly, it does well for a portfolio of large firms (size-ranked portfolio 5) but worse for portfolios of smaller firms (portfolios 2 and 3). Presumably the more diversified portfolios provide more efficient parameter estimates for the benchmark returns allowing the potential gains of the multifactor model to be realized.

4 Summary and conclusions

We have compared single and multifactor portfolio performance evaluation techniques in a specific application to determine if a multifactor model improves on the more familiar single factor model. The ACR measurements were unbiased and similar whether using a single factor or a multifactor model. Upon reflection it should not be too surprising that the abnormal performance estimates were not different. The future benchmark methodology is essentially a market model technique, whether one uses a single or a multifactor index. Consequently, the intercept term accounts for potential misspecification of the factors. Our results show no significant differences in the average cumulative returns. However, when portfolios were based on a CAPM anomaly, namely firm size, the patterns of ACRs were considerably different. The single factor ACRs exhibited significant negative cross-sectional correlation while the multifactor residuals did not.

Even though the single and multiple factor methodologies give the same point estimates of abnormal returns it is still possible that their mean square errors are different. A priori, one might expect the multifactor model to be more powerful. However, we find that the additional factors result in greater power only for portfolios with relatively low idiosyncratic risk. The multifactor model actually has less power for explaining the excess returns for poorly diversified portfolios.

Appendix A: How to form the mimicking portfolios

Assume that returns for assets ($i = 1,. . .,I$) are generated by a k-factor ($k = 1,. . .,K$) linear model such as

$$\tilde{r}_i = E_i + b_{i1}\tilde{\delta}_1 + . . . + b_{iK}\tilde{\delta}_K + \tilde{\epsilon}_i \tag{A.1}$$

where E_i is the expected return during the next time interval; $\tilde{\delta}_k$ are the mean zero factors common to all assets; b_{ik} is the sensitivity of return on asset i to the fluctuations in factor k; and $\tilde{\epsilon}_i$ is the idiosyncratic risk for the ith asset with $E(\tilde{\epsilon}_i, \tilde{\delta}_j) = 0$ for all k.

Chen (1983) has shown that there exists a unique linear transformation that can generate the factor sensitivities, i.e. the b_{ik} for all assets corresponding to a fixed set of common factors. Chen's theorem enables us to form well-diversified 'mimicking' portfolios, one for each factor, which have high sensitivity to the kth factor and zero sensitivity to all other factors. The subperiod (e.g. weekly) returns on these mimicking portfolios may be used as estimates of the factor returns (analogous to a K-factor market index), and then employed in a multi-index market model to estimate subperiod abnormal portfolio performance.

The procedure we used for estimating the weekly rates of return on the mimicking portfolios is:

1. Compute the variance–covariance matrix for the weekly rates of return of the first 180 securities on the CRSP tape which had weekly returns every week.[16] The data were separated into two halves. The first half began with Friday November 19, 1965 and ended with Friday May 4, 1973, thereby spanning the first twelve holding periods. The second half began on Friday August 4, 1972 and ended with Friday October 26, 1979. It spanned the second twelve holding periods.[17]
2. Compute ten factor loadings for the 180 stocks by using the Jöreskog asymptotic maximum likelihood method.[18]
3. Based on the factor loadings, form five mimicking portfolios.

Note that although ten factor sensitivities for each of the original 180 securities were produced by the Jöreskog routine, we created only five mimicking port-

Table A1 *Summary statistics for five mimicking portfolios chosen from 180 securities. Factors estimated using the first half of the returns data (April 1965–January 1972)*[a]

(a) Factor sensitivities, $\Sigma W_{ip} b_{ik}$. For example, row 1 – column 1 is the sensitivity of the first mimicking portfolio of the first factor.

Mimicking portfolio number	Factor number				
	1	2	3	4	5
1	−0.4154E+00	0.3169E−06	0.4556E−06	0.4999E−07	−0.4398E−08
2	0.6694E−06	0.2000E+00	0.1146E−06	0.2002E−06	−0.4398E−08
3	−0.1544E−06	0.15464E−06	−0.2000E+00	0.5945E−07	−0.7503E−09
4	0.2792E−06	0.1824E−06	0.9242E−07	0.1500E+00	−0.5650E−07
5	−0.4028E−07	0.1214E−07	−0.4060E−08	−0.4736E−07	0.1682E+00

(b) Correlations among the five mimicking portfolios

Mimicking portfolio number	Factor number				
	1	2	3	4	5
1	1.00000	−0.00164	−0.00023	−0.00398	−0.00766
2		1.00000	−0.03076	−0.06202	0.00450
3			1.00000	−0.02809	0.01286
4				1.00000	−0.00993
5					1.00000

Note: [a]The second half factor sensitivities and correlations among the mimicking portfolios were very similar.

folios. There are two reasons. First, no one knows the exact number of true underlying factors, but Roll and Ross (1980) suggest there are at least three and probably four 'priced' factors. Hence, our choice of five factors is arbitrary, but is probably reasonable. The second reason has to do with a possible misspecification problem. So long as the eleventh and higher-order factors are immaterial (and there is good reason to believe that they are) we can be sure that the first five factor loadings are not contaminated by misspecification by setting the loadings for the sixth through tenth factors to zero.

A linear programming model (using 180 securities) was used to determine sets of weights for five mimicking portfolios.[19] The objective was to minimize departures from a well diversified, equally weighted portfolio, subject to constraints that (a) the mimicking portfolios should be uncorrelated with each other and (b) that the weights in the first portfolio should sum to one while the weights in the remaining four portfolios sum to zero. This procedure was repeated twice to produce first half and second half matrices of mimicking portfolio returns (where there were 390 weeks in the first half and 378 weeks in the second). Table A1 shows summary statistics for the mimicking portfolios: the matrix of sensitivities, and a correlation matrix for the first half data.[20] Table A1(a) shows that the pth portfolio has high sensitivity to the kth factor when $p = k$ but virtually zero sensitivity to all other factors where $p \neq k$. Table A1(b), the correlation matrix, provides a way of checking the quality of the mimicking portfolios. The non-diagonal elements should ideally be zero. The largest two correlations are 6.202 percent and -3.070 percent.

Notes

* We benefited from comments and suggestions of Eugene Fama, Michael Hanssens, Richard Roll, Myron Scholes and George Tiao. Our thanks to Glenn Graves, Professor of Mathematical Methods, Graduate School of Management, UCLA, for lending us the use of his mathematical programming system.

1 Since April of 1965, Value Line has published performance predictions using their present ranking system. They rank stocks from 1 to 5 with 1 being the most favorable. Currently, they are the world's largest (based on number of subscriptions) published advisory service, employing over 200 people. Security rankings result from a complex filter rule which utilizes four criteria: (1) the earnings and price rank of each security relative to all others, (2) a price momentum factor, (3) year-to-year relative changes in quarterly earnings, and (4) an earnings 'surprise' factor. Roughly 53 percent of the stocks are ranked third, 18 percent are ranked second and fourth, and 6 percent are ranked first or fifth.

2 Value Line indicates in a pamphlet entitled *Investing in Common Stocks* that for rank I stocks, 'Expect the best price performance relative to the other stocks covered in the survey.' Similarly, for rank V one should expect the poorest.

3 See Copeland and Mayers (1982) or Stickel (1985) for evidence concerning the information content of Value Line rankings.

4 The CRSP (University of Chicago Center for Research in Security Prices) file contains daily returns for all New York and American Stock Exchange listed securities, since July of 1962.

5 Exact ranking dates are in Copeland and Mayers (1982). The intervals are occasionally irregularly spaced because the early data were originally collected for a slightly different experiment. The intervals always contain at least twenty-six weeks. There are three occasions when the intervals are greater than twenty-six weeks.

6 Of some concern is the timing of Value Line activities and when the clients actually have the Value Line recommendation. The construction of our weekly rate of return file assumes investors buy or sell at the closing price on the date of the recommendation, which is always a Friday. Value Line staggers mailings so they will arrive on the recommendation date. The recommendations are actually printed over the weekend preceding the ranking date. Thus, Value Line analysis is completed the week prior to the week that the recommendation arrives and recommendations are one week old when received.

7 Mimicking portfolio weights were also estimated from the entire twelve-year variance–covariance matrix. The results, which are reported in note 14, lead us to conjecture that nonstationarity may be a problem.

8 Copeland and Mayers (1982) refer to this as the *future benchmark technique*. Picking a future benchmark period avoids selection bias problems associated with using historic benchmarks to evaluate managed portfolios. However, it has problems of its own. For example, future benchmarks may be biased if the manager's predictive ability extends into the benchmark period. These problems (as well as others, e.g. the effects of statistical dependencies on significance tests) are discussed in detail in Copeland and Mayers (1982).

9 The amount of listing and delisting was minor. For a discussion of their possible impact on measurement of Value Line performance, see Copeland and Mayers (1982, pp.

27–8). In addition, the possibility of delisting explains why we formed portfolios before measuring abnormal returns rather than measuring individual security abnormal returns and then averaging them. It is impossible to obtain a future benchmark return for a delisted security. Hence, selection bias would be introduced if we were to purge delisted securities when using a procedure based on individual security benchmarks.

10 Copeland and Mayers repeated all of their performance experiments in non-log form also. The results were practically identical to the log form. Thus, we do not replicate our experiment in the log form.

11 Copeland and Mayers (1982) found the Value Line portfolio 1 and 5 firms not significantly different in size.

12 Coefficients were also estimated over a fifty-two week benchmark period, following the test period. Results for the Value Line portfolios are reported in note 15.

13 The formula is

$$SD(CR) = \left(\frac{\Sigma(CR - \overline{CR})^2}{24-1}\right)^{1/2}$$

14 Recall that the mimicking portfolio returns for the five-factor model in table 2 were estimated separately for the first twelve and the second twelve holding periods in order to allow for possible nonstationarity. The results given below are estimated using an identical procedure except that the mimicking portfolio returns were estimated over the entire twelve-year period, not allowing for nonstationarity.

| | Value Line portfolio residuals | | | | |
	1	2	3	4	5
ACR	0.0193	0.0218	0.0117	0.0084	−0.0105
AR	0.0007	0.0008	0.0004	0.0003	−0.0004
t-stat	1.4580	1.8696	1.1853	0.8438	−0.8528

| | Size-ranked portfolio residuals | | | | |
	1	2	3	4	5
ACR	0.0243	0.0186	0.0141	0.0103	0.0112
AR	0.0009	0.0007	0.0005	0.0004	0.0004
t-stat	1.2261	1.5939	1.0946	1.0413	1.2414

The difference between portfolios 1 and 5 remains about the same but the ACRs for all portfolios have shifted upward.

15 We also repeated the experiment using fifty-two-week rather than twenty-six-week benchmarks. In this case, the difference between portfolios 1 and 5 for the Value Line data set was 4.49 percent for the single factor model and 3.25 percent for the five-factor model. This was the greatest difference which we found and it was not large.

16 Of the 4063 companies on the CRSP tape, 999 had weekly returns for each of the 861 weeks between the beginning of July 1962 and the end of December 1978. Of these, we used only the first 180 stocks (chosen alphabetically) because we were constrained by the processing capacity of the IBM 3033 in use.

17 The mean weekly rate of return for the *i*th security in the *t*th year was used to compute the mean deviations that year. This was done yearly in order to emphasize the covariability among securities.

18 The software package EFAP II, written by Jöreskog was utilized.

19 This is the GUB routine within the elastic programming in the XS mathematical programming system developed by Glenn Graves, Professor of Mathematical Methods, Graduate School of Management, UCLA.

20 In order to save space we have not printed either the entire period or the second half tables. They are essentially the same except that the maximum correlations which

resulted from fitting over the entire period were as high as 16.8 percent and 11.6 percent. This is further evidence that nonstationarity was a problem.

References

Ashley, R., Granger, C.W.J. and Schmalensee, R. (1980) 'Advertising and Aggregate Consumption: An Analysis of Causality', *Econometrica*, July, 1152–9.

Brown, S. and Warner, J. (1980) 'Measuring Security Performance', *Journal of Financial Economics*, September, 205–58.

Brown, S. and Weinstein, M. (1983) 'The Use of Derived Factors in Event Studies' working paper, University of Southern California, November.

Chen, N. (1983) 'Some Empirical Tests of the Theory of Arbitrage Pricing', *Journal of Finance*, December, 1393–1414.

Copeland, T.E. and Mayers, D. (1982) 'The Value Line Enigma (1965–1978): A Case Study of Performance Evaluation Issues', *The Journal of Financial Economics*, November, 298–321.

Fama, E., Fisher, L., Jensen, M. and Roll, R. (1969) 'The Adjustment of Stock Prices to New Information', *International Economic Review*, 10, February, 1–21.

Huberman, G. (1982) 'Arbitrage Pricing Theory: A Simple Approach', *Journal of Economic Theory*, October, 183–91.

King, B. (1966) 'Market and Industry Factors in Stock Price Behavior', *Journal of Business*, January, 134–90.

Reinganum, M. (1981a) 'The Arbitrage Pricing Theory: Some Empirical Results', *Journal of Finance*, 9, May, 313–21.

Reinganum, M. (1981b) 'Misspecification of Capital Asset Pricing: Empirical Anomalies Based on Earnings Yield and Market Value', *Journal of Financial Economics*, March, 19–46.

Roll, R. and Ross, S. (1980) 'An Empirical Investigation of the Arbitrage Pricing Theory', *Journal of Finance*, December, 1073–103.

Roll, R. and Ross, S. (1983) 'Regulation, the Capital Asset Pricing Model, and the Arbitrage Pricing Theory', *Public Utilities Fortnightly*, May 26, 22–8.

Ross, S.A. (1976) 'The Arbitrage Theory of Capital Asset Pricing', *The Journal of Economic Theory*, December, 343–62.

Stickel, S.E. (1985) 'The Effect of Value Line Investment Survey Rank Changes on Common Stock Prizes', *Journal of Financial Economics*, March, 121–43.

20 Divergence of earnings expectations: the effect on stock market response to earnings signals

DAN GIVOLY and JOSEF LAKONISHOK*

1 Introduction

The research on the information content of earnings, stimulated by the work of Ball and Brown (1968), relied heavily on the prediction error or the 'unexpected' earnings. Empirically, unexpected earnings were defined as the difference between realized earnings and some point prediction produced by an assumed expectations model.

More recently, several works have attempted to explain price response to earnings disclosure by additional factors. Among the factors examined are the precision of the earnings signal relative to the precision of prior expectations of investors (Verrecchia, 1982; Holthausen and Verrecchia, 1983).

This chapter represents another attempt to depart from sole reliance on unexpected earnings for the explanation of the information content of earnings releases, by suggesting and testing another explanatory factor—earnings uncertainty. Similar to previous research, the information content is measured here as the abnormal return that could be obtained from a foreknowledge of the content of the earnings report, and is therefore measured over the period preceding and immediately following the earnings announcement. Uncertainty is represented by two alternative measures: dispersion of earnings expectations and earnings unpredictability. Both measures are derived from earnings forecasts of financial analysts. (For a discussion on the quality of analysts' forecasts see Givoly and Lakonishok, 1984.)

With the enhanced availability of data on economic forecasts, the use of the dispersion of forecasts has increasingly attracted the attention of researchers. In particular, dispersion of analysts' forecasts is used by Friend *et al.* (1978), Malkiel and Cragg (1980) and Friend and Westerfield (1981) as an additional measure of risk with quite promising results, while Figlewski (1981) analyses the implications of dispersion of forecasts for equilibrium prices.

Information on earnings uncertainty is perceived by investors as valuable, apparently as a proxy for security risk. Earnings uncertainty measures are widely disseminated through various investment services. For example, Value Line publishes regularly the uncertainty ratings of companies' earnings; and Lynch Jones & Ryan supplies investors with such measures as the range and standard deviation across analysts of one and two year ahead earnings forecasts.

Many studies explored the price reaction to accounting earnings. In general, these studies do not support market efficiency. For example, Rendelman *et al*. (1982) examined the price reaction to quarterly unexpected earnings. They found a gradual price response and a substantial difference in returns between the stocks with the highest and lowest unexpected earnings. Givoly and Lakonishok (1979, 1980) explored the price reaction to revisions in earnings forecasts made by financial analysts. Their results are inconsistent with the efficient market hypothesis; some of their trading rules based on publicly available information produced abnormal returns in excess of 10 per cent (annual basis) after adjusting for transaction costs. The studies mentioned above, as well as all the others in this area, concentrate only on the earnings forecast and ignore the uncertainty surrounding the forecasts. The various trading rules motivated by the gradual adjustment of stock prices to unexpected earnings could possibly be improved by considering earnings uncertainty as well.

The organization of the chapter is as follows. In the next section we describe the methodology. Section 3 describes the data and section 4 describes and analyses the results. Concluding remarks are provided in the final section.

2 Methodology

Two alternative measures of earnings uncertainty are examined: divergence of forecasts from the mean forecast and the cross-sectional error of earnings forecasts. The first measure, dispersion of forecasts, is defined here as (time and firm subscripts will be omitted for simplicity)

$$D_1^2 = \frac{1}{n-1} \sum_{i=1}^{n} [\ln(F_i) - \overline{\ln(F)}]^2 \tag{1}$$

where F_i is the forecast made by forecaster i and $\overline{\ln(F)}$ is the sample mean of $\ln(F)$ over n forecasters.

The second measure, unpredictability, is

$$D_2^2 = \frac{1}{n-1} \sum_{i=1}^{n} [\ln(F_i) - \ln(A)]^2 \tag{2}$$

where A is the realization, and the expression in parentheses corresponds to the percentage forecast error of forecaster i.[1] As suggested by Cukierman and Givoly, D_2^2 is, under fairly general conditions, the correct empirical counterpart of the uncertainty surrounding earnings. The two measures will be referred to collectively as uncertainty measures.

The measures D_1^2 and D_2^2 closely correspond to the widely used coefficient of variation and the deflated prediction error respectively. Nonetheless, the logarithmic transformation has certain advantages (such as avoiding asymmetry problems). For a discussion of the advantages of this transformation see Theil (1966).

The research question to be addressed is whether the information content of earnings is associated with the degree of uncertainty of earnings expectation, and, if so, what is the direction of this association. To test this question, we partitioned the sample of stocks each year into portfolios, ranked first by the sign and magnitude of the earnings signal and then by the measure of uncertainty. The prediction error was defined as

$$E = \ln \frac{A}{\bar{F}}$$

where

$$\bar{F} = \frac{1}{n} \sum_{i=1}^{n} F_i$$

The normal relationship between return of a given stock and market returns was estimated using the following time-series regression:

$$R_{it} - R_{ft} = \alpha_i + \beta_i(R_{mt} - R_{ft}) + \mu_{it} \tag{3}$$

where R_{it} is the return of stock i in month t, R_{ft} is the risk-free rate in month t measured by the yield on thirty-day treasury bills and R_{mt} is the market return measured by the value weighted index of the NYSE.[2]

The estimation period for the α_i and β_i coefficients for any given year was the forty-eight months preceding April of that year.

The estimated monthly abnormal returns were derived as

$$\varepsilon_{it} = (R_{it} - R_{ft}) - [\alpha_i + \beta_i(R_{mt} - R_{ft})] \tag{4}$$

where α_i and β_i are the estimated coefficients. The abnormal return was accumulated over the twelve months from April to the following March (only December 31 firms are included in the sample – see section 3), and calculated as

$$\text{CAR} = \sum_{t=0}^{11} \varepsilon_{it}$$

In line with most of the research on the information content of earnings, the association between the earnings variables and stock prices is measured over a period of one year.[3]

The stocks were ranked each year according to their prediction errors (E) to form four groups. The stocks in each group were then ranked according to the uncertainty measure (D) (for each of the two values of D separately) to form four subgroups. The procedure yielded sixteen subgroups (or portfolios) each year.[4] To check the robustness of the results to the grouping procedure, the grouping was repeated with stocks ordered first by D (for each of the two values of D separately) and then by E. By aggregating securities into portfolios, we reduce the measurement error inherent in the estimation of the beta and the uncertainty measures.

Two cross-section regressions of the following form were estimated each year:

$$\text{CAR}_p = \alpha_j + \beta_{1j}E_p + \beta_{2j}D_{jp} + e_p \quad \text{for } j = 1, 2 \text{ and } p = 1, \ldots 16 \quad (5)$$

where E_p is the mean prediction error of portfolio p, and D_{jp} is the average value of the uncertainty measure D_j in portfolio p.

Since the directional effect of uncertainty on abnormal returns may depend on the sign of the prediction error, the regression in equation (5) was estimated twice: once for sixteen portfolios constructed by grouping cases with positive prediction errors, and once for sixteen portfolios formed by grouping cases with negative prediction errors (the number of companies with negative and positive prediction errors was very similar).[5]

Each yearly cross-section regression results in estimates for α, β_1 and β_2. The final statistical test of the coefficients is based on their average and respective standard derivation over the years, a standard procedure in finance (see for example, Fama and MacBeth, 1973).[6]

Given the previous evidence on the association between the sign (and magnitude) of earnings prediction errors and price movement (see, for example, Ball and Brown, 1968; Beaver *et al.*, 1979), we expect the coefficient β_1 to be positive. In addition, if uncertainty is important in explaining the association between stock price movements and the earnings signal, β_2 would be different from zero.

3 Data

Financial analysts' forecasts of earnings of a sample of companies were evaluated in each of the eleven years 1969 to 1979. The source of the forecasts was the S&P's *Earnings Forecaster*.[7]

Strictly speaking, financial analysts' forecasts of earnings (hereafter FAF) reflect only the expectation of the respective analysts. Yet, their wide dissemination and the reliance of the public on the advice of financial analysts suggests that analysts' expectations may be shared by a wide group of investors.[8]

Considered each year were the FAF of that year's earnings as of the beginning of April.[9] The time of the forecast is between the release of the annual report for the previous year (which is made, on average, in early February – see Givoly and Palmon (1982)) and the release of the first quarterly report (typically late April).

Included in the sample each year were companies which satisfied these criteria:

1   existence of at least four forecasts (by different forecasters) of the current year's earnings;
2   availability of monthly return data for the forecast year and the preceding four years;
3   fiscal year ending December 31;
4   NYSE listing.

The first criterion was introduced to allow the derivation of reliable measures for the average or 'consensus' forecast and for the uncertainty measures. The second criterion was needed to allow the estimation of the market model's parameters. The third criterion ensures convenient intratemporal, cross-sectional comparisons. The fourth criterion was imposed to ensure availability of monthly return data.

The first criterion apparently was responsible for eliminating most of the companies and introduced a sample selection bias in favor of large and established companies which are more actively followed by investors. The effect of this selection bias will be discussed in the next section.

The final sample consists of 1,247 cases (company-years) with a total of 6,020 forecasts. The number of cases in each year differs and ranges from 95 (1972) to 173 (1969). This sample represents 424 distinct companies.

4 Results

Table 1 and figure 1 describe, for the eleven-year period, the distribution of the two uncertainty measures, D_1 and D_2 (square roots of the measures in equations 1 and 2) and the error measure E. The average D_1 is 5 per cent which is actually the standard deviation of the percentage deviation of forecasters from the mean forecast. The magnitude of the earnings unpredictability measure, D_2, is much larger (average of 19 per cent) than that of D_1, suggesting a strong commonality between the sign and the size of the errors of individual forecasters.

Table 1 *Mean and standard deviation of the uncertainty and error measures, by year*

Year	D_1		D_2		$|E|$	
	Mean	SD	Mean	SD	Mean	SD
All years	0.050	0.045	0.190	0.202	0.163	0.215
1969	0.037	0.025	0.134	0.157	0.115	0.170
1970	0.046	0.030	0.240	0.240	0.212	0.248
1971	0.044	0.037	0.189	0.211	0.162	0.211
1972	0.046	0.037	0.128	0.140	0.098	0.126
1973	0.037	0.037	0.199	0.194	0.174	0.194
1974	0.061	0.049	0.257	0.221	0.216	0.200
1975	0.080	0.065	0.249	0.251	0.216	0.289
1976	0.064	0.056	0.165	0.151	0.130	0.172
1977	0.044	0.040	0.183	0.196	0.157	0.204
1978	0.047	0.048	0.183	0.218	0.167	0.258
1979	0.051	0.051	0.202	0.209	0.180	0.247

The magnitude of the measures appears to be time-dependent. The yearly mean absolute error measure $|E|$ ranges between 0.115 (in 1969) and 0.216 (in 1974 and 1975). Undoubtedly, some years are more difficult to predict than others. Furthermore, the relationship between the variables might assume different forms in different years. These considerations led us to estimate the regression in equation 5 for each of the eleven years separately.

Table 2 reports the rank correlation between the value of each uncertainty measure in one year and its value in subsequent years. For this purpose we ranked each year's firms according to the variable under examination and formed five equal sized portfolios. (The investigation was conducted at the portfolio level to reduce the biases that arise from measurement errors in the explanatory variables.) We then followed these same groups (portfolios) of firms in subsequent years and ranked them again according to the new average variable's value of their firm members. The first row of table 2(a) displays the rank correlations between the mean values of D_1 of portfolios formed in 1969 and the mean values of D_1 of the same groups of firms in subsequent years. Similarly, the second row in table 2(a) displays correlations between values of portfolios formed in 1970 and the values in subsequent years.

The mean correlation of each column is reported at the bottom of each part of the table. The results suggest that there is a long-term persistency in the portfolio's values of D_1 and D_2. The mean rank correlation between two adjacent years is 0.70 for D_1 and 0.79 for D_2. The rank correlation declines as the compared years are further apart; however, it

(a) Relative frequency distribution of the dispersion measure (D_1)

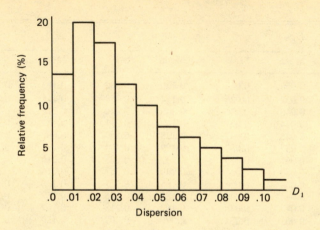

(b) Relative frequency distribution of the unpredictability measure (D_2)

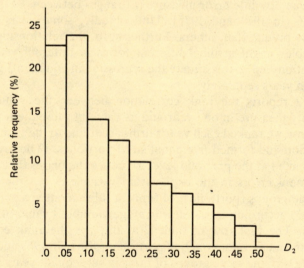

Figure 1   Relative frequency distribution of the dispersion and unpredictability measures

remains fairly high for as long as seven years after the initial formation of the portfolios.[10]

We now turn to the examination of the relationship between the uncertainty measures and other stock properties, particularly risk char-

Table 2 *Rank correlation of portfolios formed by D_j with D_j in subsequent years*[a]

(a) Results for the Dispersion Measure (D_1)

Portfolio formation year	Years following the portfolio formation year									
	1	2	3	4	5	6	7	8	9	10
1969	1.0	0.3	1.0	0.7	0.9	0.8	1.0	0.1	0.3	0.7
1970	0.8	1.0	0.5	0.1	0.9	1.0	−0.5	0.2	−0.1	
1971	0.7	0.7	−0.1	0.5	0.5	0.0	0.2	0.9		
1972	0.7	−0.3	0.3	0.5	0.1	0.0	0.8			
1973	0.4	0.8	0.7	0.5	0.1	0.8				
1974	0.9	0.8	0.8	0.8	0.7					
1975	1.0	0.7	0.4	0.2						
1976	0.6	0.9	0.7							
1977	1.0	0.7								
1978	−0.1									
Mean over years	0.70	0.68	0.54	0.47	0.53	0.52	0.38	0.40	0.10	0.70

(b) Results for the unpredictability measure (D_2)

Portfolio formation year	Years following the portfolio formation year									
	1	2	3	4	5	6	7	8	9	10
1969	1.0	0.2	1.0	0.3	0.6	0.7	0.9	−0.9	0.5	0.6
1970	0.8	0.7	0.8	0.6	0.9	1.0	0.3	0.1	−0.2	
1971	1.0	0.0	0.1	0.1	0.2	0.1	−0.4	0.6		
1972	0.1	0.4	0.5	0.6	0.0	−0.2	0.1			
1973	0.8	0.6	0.0	0.7	−0.3	0.7				
1974	0.9	0.7	0.3	0.9	0.9					
1975	0.9	−0.6	−0.3	−0.4						
1976	0.9	0.9	0.9							
1977	0.6	0.8								
1978	0.9									
Mean over years	0.79	0.41	0.41	0.40	0.38	0.46	0.23	−0.06	0.15	0.60

Note: [a] The Spearman rank correlation is used (see Conover, 1971, pp. 245–9). All values of 0.80 and over are significant at the 5 per cent level.

acteristics. Table 3 presents the mean correlation (over the eleven yearly coefficients) between D_1 and D_2 and five other firm variables: beta, standard deviation of the residuals (both computed over the forty-eight months preceding the year for which the correlation is compared), marketability (shares traded during the year as a percentage of shares outstanding), size (natural logarithm of the market value of the firm's

Table 3 *Mean correlation coefficients between the dispersion of forecasts* (D_1), *unpredictability of earnings* (D_2) *and selected firm characteristics[a]* *(t-values in parentheses[b])*

	D_1	D_2
β^c	0.19	0.15
	(4.50)	(4.97)
σ^c	0.20	0.18
	(5.10)	(6.63)
Marketability[d]	0.21	0.23
	(4.09)	(8.47)
Size[e]	−0.06	−0.05
	(−1.80)	(−0.83)
Earnings growth variability[f]	0.35	0.27
	(10.35)	(8.95)
D_2	0.48	—
	(11.37)	

Notes:
[a]The results in the table are based on individual cases.
[b]The *t*-value is computed by dividing the table's value (the eleven-year mean) by its standard deviation.
[c]σ and β are estimated from the forty-eight months preceding the year for which the other variables are computed.
[d]Marketability is defined as the number of shares traded divided by the (average) number of shares outstanding.
[e]Size is defined as the natural log of the market value of the equity at the beginning of the year.
[f]Earnings growth volatility is the standard deviation of the earnings growth rates over the sample years.

equity at the end of the year) and earnings growth variability (measured as the standard deviation of the rate of growth in EPS over the years 1961–80).

The table reveals a positive and significant association between D and the traditional market-based risk measures (β and σ) and the accounting-based risk measure (earnings growth variability). There is a negative, although insignificant, correlation between the uncertainty measures (D_1, D_2) and size. The table also shows that the two uncertainty measures are correlated (correlation coefficient of 0.48). This is also expected from their functional relationship (see equation in note 1, p. 287).

The association between the abnormal return, the prediction error, and the uncertainty measures are presented in table 4. The table shows the coefficients, the *t*-values of the independent variables (prediction error and the uncertainty measures) and the R^2 of regression (5) for each

Table 4 *Summary results of the regression of cumulative abnormal
return on the earnings prediction error and dispersion of earnings
forecasts (t-values in parentheses)*

(a) Results for dispersion[b]

Year	Cases of positive errors[a]			Cases of negative errors[a]		
	β_1	β_2	$R^2(\%)$	β_1	β_2	$R^2(\%)$
1969	0.53	−1.26	11.0	0.83	0.52	59.0
	(0.88)	(−0.97)		(3.65)	(0.34)	
1970	−0.17	1.15	4.2	0.30	2.09	44.0
	(−0.29)	(−0.73)		(2.66)	(2.75)	
1971	0.35	−0.17	4.0	0.50	0.96	55.0
	(0.71)	(−0.11)		(3.90)	(1.18)	
1972	0.09	−1.35	12.5	−0.07	−0.43	0.5
	(0.22)	(−1.34)		(−0.19)	(−0.24)	
1973	0.78	2.38	73.9	0.55	1.48	24.6
	(4.49)	(2.19)		(1.44)	(0.77)	
1974	0.12	−1.07	8.6	0.69	1.82	27.4
	(0.59)	(−1.07)		(2.10)	(1.53)	
1975	0.28	1.51	23.8	0.10	2.13	43.4
	(0.42)	(1.50)		(0.67)	(2.82)	
1976	0.91	−0.48	63.5	0.37	0.84	11.8
	(4.35)	(−0.67)		(1.21)	(1.17)	
1977	0.81	−2.28	25.3	0.29	1.47	12.9
	(1.95)	(−1.62)		(1.33)	(1.20)	
1978	0.58	0.24	48.8	−0.02	−0.34	3.7
	(3.08)	(0.25)		(−0.14)	(−0.48)	
1979	0.55	−0.53	39.6	−0.24	−0.62	11.9
	(2.92)	(−0.69)		(−1.18)	(−0.61)	
Mean over years	0.44	−2.17	28.7	0.30	0.90	26.3
Overall t-value[c]	(5.80)	(−0.53)		(4.64)	(3.12)	

Notes: [a]The regression is specified in equation (5) and is estimated each year from a sample
assigned to sixteen portfolios.
[b]In some years, there were too few observations for sixteen portfolios. As a result,
regressions based on individual cases were used.
[c]Derived by dividing the mean t-value over the years by its population standard deviation
over the n-years, $\sqrt{n}$.

Table 4 (*continued*)

(b) Results for unpredictability[b]

Year	Cases of positive errors[a]			Cases of negative errors[a]		
	β_1	β_2	$R^2(\%)$	β_1	β_2	$R^2(\%)$
1969	—	—	—	—	—	—
1970	—[d]	—[d]	—[d]	0.29 (2.15)	0.80 (1.95)	9.9
1971	0.51 (0.92)	0.00 (−0.01)	4.8	0.36 (2.87)	0.17 (0.64)	23.4
1972	0.47 (1.18)	−0.79 (−2.43)	17.8	0.25 (0.74)	−0.11 (−0.33)	5.1
1973	0.61 (2.23)	0.21 (0.47)	13.5	0.36 (1.02)	0.45 (0.65)	12.0
1974	0.17 (0.87)	−0.28 (−1.58)	8.1	0.63 (2.40)	−0.51 (−1.10)	31.0
1975	1.22 (2.16)	0.69 (3.69)	47.7	−0.00 (−0.00)	0.23 (1.18)	4.0
1976	1.46 (3.34)	0.01 (0.04)	31.0	0.20 (1.07)	0.22 (1.75)	11.5
1977	0.70 (1.74)	0.04 (0.10)	15.9	0.07 (0.47)	−0.43 (−1.73)	8.5
1978	1.30 (4.91)	−0.24 (−1.42)	43.0	0.01 (0.13)	0.03 (0.16)	0.1
1979	0.79 (3.13)	−0.24 (−1.15)	20.5	−0.05 (−0.38)	0.26 (1.46)	11.5
Mean over years	0.72	−0.07	22.5	0.21	0.11	11.7
Overall *t*-value[c]	(6.84)	(−0.75)		(3.32)	(1.46)	

Notes: [a]The regression is specified in equation (5) and is estimated each year from a sample assigned to sixteen portfolios.
[b]The bias term of D_2 (see footnote 1) used in year t is that observed in year $t-1$. As a result, the regression could not be estimated for the first year, 1969. In some other years, there were too few observations for sixteen portfolios. As a result, regressions based on individual cases were used.
[c]Derived by dividing the mean *t*-value over the years by its population standard deviation over the n years, $\sqrt{n}$.
[d]Insufficient number of observations (fewer than ten).

year. The mean coefficients across the eleven years and the corresponding *t*-statistic are shown at the bottom of each part of the table.

As expected, and in conformity with previous research, the *t*-value of the coefficient of the prediction error is positive in almost all years. That is, the abnormal return is positively related to the sign and size of the prediction error. The mean coefficient across the years of the prediction error is positive and significant at the 1 per cent level in both panels, for positive and negative error cases.[11]

To analyse the coefficients of the uncertainty measures we will turn first to the cases with negative prediction errors of earnings. A positive β_2 coefficient is consistent with the conventional wisdom which suggests that earnings uncertainty reduces the impact of the earnings report. Based on the results in table 4(a) (uncertainty defined in terms of dispersion), the mean of β_2 over the years is 0.90 and the t-statistic is 3.12 indicating that β_2 is significant. In addition to the statistical significance, β_2 has a substantial effect on abnormal returns. For example, a company whose dispersion measure is one standard deviation (0.045, see table 1) from the mean will have a return higher by 3.85 per cent (0.045×0.9) than a company with an average dispersion measure (keeping the magnitude of unexpected earnings constant). Looking at individual years, the β_2 coefficient has the predicted sign in eight (out of eleven) years, and is statistically significant at the 1 per cent level in two of these.

The results for the second uncertainty measure, earnings unpredictability, are contained in table 4(b). The overall mean of the β_2 coefficient is 0.11 and the t-statistic is 1.46, which is associated with a significance level of 7.2 per cent. Turning to individual years we find that β_2 has the predicted sign in seven out of ten years and is statistically significant at the 5 per cent level in two years. The results for the unpredictability measure are not as strong as the results for the dispersion measure. Two explanations can be put forward: first, fewer observations were available to estimate the coefficient of the dispersion measure. (Only companies with two consecutive sets of earnings forecasts could be included.) Second, because there were fewer observations, the coefficients were estimated using individual companies rather than portfolios. Therefore, the results for the unpredictability measure are subject to greater measurement errors leading to a more pronounced downward bias in the coefficient estimates and thus less significant results.

Overall, the results from negative earnings prediction errors are consistent with the notion that earnings uncertainty mitigates stock price movements that could be expected from the prediction error.

Turning to the positive prediction errors, we find that the mean coefficient of β_2 is negative in table 4(a) and (b); however, the results are not statistically significant. On a year-by-year basis, seven out of the eleven β_2 coefficients are negative in table 4(a) and five out of nine in table 4(b).

To explain the difference in the observed effect of dispersion on stock price behaviour between cases of favourable and unfavourable earnings signals, one needs a model relating both earnings dispersion and earnings signals to stock price movements. In the absence of such a model one can only speculate about the reason for this difference. One plausible (yet by no means exclusive) explanation is that earnings uncertainty stems both from 'genuine' uncertainty concerning future cash flows and from noisiness of the accounting reporting system.

Resolution of real uncertainty (relating to future cash flows) will have, ceteris paribus, a positive effect on stock prices (assuming risk averse investors), due to the reduction of the risk premium.[12] The greater is the uncertainty of this kind, the stronger is the favourable impact on the price. The information content of earnings, measured over the period before and after the earnings release, will thus be affected by the resolution of real uncertainty in the following way: a more favourable market response is expected for positive unexpected earnings and a less unfavourable response is expected for negative unexpected earnings.

When most or all uncertainty concerning future earnings is due to the noise of the reporting system rather than to unpredictability of cash flows, unexpected earnings will be only loosely related to real economic developments and therefore weakly associated with stock price movements. We therefore expect that the less noisy is the earnings number the greater is the information content of a given magnitude of unexpected earnings. In other words, when earnings uncertainty is due to 'noise', high earnings uncertainty will tend to mitigate the impact of unexpected earnings. The notion that noise is inversely related to the informativeness of signals is developed in a recent paper by Verrecchia (1982).[13]

Although this distinction between different types of uncertainty is not formally modelled the results for the two subsamples of favourable and unfavourable news are consistent with the notion that earnings uncertainty may stem both from 'genuine' uncertainty concerning future cash flows and from noisiness of the accounting reporting system.

The results presented so far about the uncertainty measures probably underestimate the importance of the uncertainty measures. There are at least two elements unique to the setting of our experiment that may result in underestimating the importance of the uncertainty measures: measurement errors in estimating the uncertainty variables and the sample composition.

The measurement error could stem from at least two sources. First, the uncertainty measures are estimated based on a relatively small number of forecasts (typically four to seven). Second, the observed forecasts are, strictly speaking, not perfectly contemporaneous. There is a continuous process of forecast revision. It takes S&P (our source of forecast data) a week or two to collect and publish new forecasts, hence, any given issue of the *Earnings Forecaster* inevitably contains forecasts that are outdated

Table 5 *Distribution of observations by the market value of the corresponding firms*

	(Million dollars) Our sample[a]	All NYSE[b]
First quartile	425	41
Median	864	144
Third quartile	2147	358

Notes: [a] Market values are averaged over the eleven years of the study (1969–79).
[b] Estimated from Stoll and Whaley (1983), table 1. Market values are averaged over the twenty years 1960–79.

to a varying degree. Both uncertainty measures could be contaminated by this publication lag.

In addition to the potential measurement error, the sample, by construction, might be poor in terms of the cross-sectional variability of the uncertainty measures. It is evident from table 5 that the sample companies are very large. The median firm has a market equity value of $864 million, compared to $144 million in the population of the New York Stock Exchange which itself consists of relatively large firms. The sample composition was dictated by the selection criterion whereby firms with less than four contemporaneous forecasts were excluded (due to the poor quality of the estimates of the uncertainty measures when based on very few forecasts). The number of forecasts available at any given time probably mirrors the extent of interest of investors in the stock. We expect large companies to be watched closer by investors and therefore to be followed by more analysts. Table 6 provides a strong support for this notion. The table presents the average number of earnings forecasts that are reported by the *Institutional Brokers Estimate System* (IBES) for firms of different sizes. IBES is a publication of Lynch, Jones & Ryan, a Wall Street firm.[14] The table shows that the number of available forecasts increases with the size of the firm. In part, this is a reflection of the percentage of institutional holdings which is also shown by the table to be positively associated with size.

The deletion from the sample of small companies might eliminate companies with a high forecast dispersion or high earnings unpredictability. The resulting reduction in the cross-section variability of these measures in the sample might have led to less efficient estimates of their coefficients. In addition, it has been shown empirically that the stock market response to the release of earnings of small companies is more

Table 6 *Number of earnings forecasts available by IBES and percentage of institutional holdings by firm's size*

Capitalization (million dollars)	Average number of earnings forecasts	Average of percentage institutional holding[a]
Below 100	6.7	26.4
100–200	8.4	35.5
200–400	9.8	38.1
401–1000	13.1	41.0
1001–5000	16.9	47.4
Over 5000	21.8	44.1

[a]*Source:* Computer Directions Advisors, Inc. (1981).

pronounced than the response to earnings releases by large companies (see Grant, 1980). This phenomenon might also bias the results against significance of the uncertainty measures.

5 Concluding remarks

The paper introduces another element to the examination of the information content of earnings – the uncertainty of earnings expectations. The results suggest that there is an association between the uncertainty measures and stock price movement. In particular, for unfavourable earnings the evidence supports the notion that earnings uncertainty mollifies stock price response to earnings signals. The results are statistically significant and the impact of the uncertainty measures on returns is substantial. A company with a dispersion measure of one standard deviation above the mean would experience a return of 3.85 per cent above the return of a company with an average dispersion measure. For favourable earnings, there is some indication that earnings uncertainty tends to mollify stock price response to earnings. The results, however, are not statistically significant. The asymmetric response to favourable and unfavourable earnings is an interesting finding that should be further explored.

The results suggest that studies based on trading rules triggered by the gradual response of the stock market to earnings announcements and to revisions in analysts' forecasts, may benefit by incorporating earnings uncertainty.

Notes

* The financial support of the Israel Institute of Business Research is gratefully acknowledged.

We would like to thank Yakov Amihud, Elroy Dimson, Richard McEnally and Eli

Talmor for their helpful comments. The paper was presented at the Financial Management Association Meetings and Western Finance Association Meetings.

1 The very few cases with negative or zero earnings were discarded. The measure D_2^2 can be written as

$$D_2^2 = \frac{1}{n-1} \sum_{i=1}^{n} [\ln(F_i) - \overline{\ln(F)}]^2 + \frac{n}{n-1} [\overline{\ln(F)} - \ln(A)]^2$$

Note that while the first term on the right-hand side is known to investors who have access to analysts' forecasts, the second (the bias) term is, obviously, unavailable at that time. In this sense this measure is, strictly speaking, not an *ex-ante* measure. The second term has to be estimated, and we estimate it from the most recent experience.

2 The natural logarithm was used to measure the rate of return.

3 The use of a shorter period (e.g. the last quarter preceding the earnings announcement) would have resulted in a much smaller forecast dispersion (see Brown *et al.*, 1984) that could be overshadowed by a measurement error (to be discussed later).

4 The selection of the number of portfolios was made by balancing the need to have large enough portfolios so as to produce meaningful portfolios' averages against the wish to have as many portfolios (observations) as possible. The particular selection of sixteen portfolios is, of course, arbitrary.

5 An alternative approach would be to run a single regression by creating dummy variables for the sign of unexpected earnings. However, such a procedure assumes that the distribution of the error term in equation (5) does not depend on the sign of the unexpected earnings. If this assumption does not hold, the significance tests based on the single regression would be biased.

6 Long time-series data reduce the multicollinearity problem that may arise in cross-sectional regressions, since the standard deviation of the average coefficient is $\sqrt{T}$, where T is the number of periods. Multicollinearity does not bias the coefficients, of course, but reduces their estimation precision.

7 A weekly publication that first appeared in 1967, the *Earnings Forecaster* lists in every second issue the outstanding EPS forecasts for about 1500 companies. The forecasts are those made by S&P itself and by about seventy other security analysts and brokerage firms.

8 For example, the report of the Securities and Exchange Commission (1977) Advisory Committee on Corporate Disclosure suggests that financial analysts' expectations may be shared by a wide group of investors. The notion that FAF might proxy for market expectations gains support from recent studies that show that FAF have a substantial influence on stock prices (see Elton *et al.* 1981; Fried and Givoly, 1982; Givoly and Lakonishok, 1979, 1980).

9 All the contemporaneous company forecasts were for primary EPS before extraordinary items. When a forecast was for another definition and no conversion to primary EPS number could be made, the observation was discarded. The number of such cases was negligible.

10 The mean correlations for years 8, 9 and 10 after the portfolio formation year are not very meaningful as they rely only on three, two and one observations respectively.

11 The results in table 4(a) are for portfolios formed by ranking firms first according to their earnings predictions error (E) and then within each group according to their dispersion measure (D_1). The results for the reverse procedure were essentially similar.

12 Note that, under CAPM, resolution of firm specific earnings uncertainty would not be expected to cause any price reaction. Nonetheless, some of the earnings uncertainty may well be connected with general market or industry-related factors and its resolution may thus affect stock prices. In addition, there is considerable evidence and theoretical support to the notion that unsystematic risk may be priced in the market. For relevant evidence see Basu and Cheung (1982), Friend and Westerfield (1981), Levy (1978) and Lakonishok and Shapiro (1986). The theoretical explanations – existence of transaction cost, heterogeneous expectations and information asymmetry – are provided by Levy (1978) and Mayshar (1981, 1983).
In fact, a number of studies have examined the process and effects of information

generation in detail. The general assessment is that temporal resolution of uncertainty has a positive effect on stock prices (see, for example, Epstein and Turnbull, 1980; Robicheck and Myers, 1966).

13 The relationship between stock price response to unexpected earnings, earnings uncertainty and the noise concerning the earnings signal can be formulated as follows: Assume that investors' a priori expectations about E, the uncertain future earnings, is normally distributed with mean m_a and variance σ_a^2 (those parameters are estimated in this paper by the mean and the dispersion of analysts' forecasts). Investors receive signal m_s drawn from a normal distribution with a variance σ_s^2 (the latter representing the 'noise' of the reporting system). The posteriori distribution of expected future earnings, assuming Bayesian revision, has a mean of m_p

$$m_p = \alpha m_s + (1-\alpha)m_a \tag{6}$$

where

$$\alpha = \frac{\sigma_a^2}{\sigma_a^2 + \sigma_s^2} \tag{7}$$

and a variance

$$\sigma_p^2 = \frac{\sigma_a^2 \sigma_s^2}{\sigma_a^2 + \sigma_s^2}$$

Market response to the new signal is positively correlated with the magnitude of $m_p - m_a$ (see Beaver *et al.*, 1979). Now from (6) we get

$$m_p - m_a = \alpha(m_s - m_a) \tag{8}$$

which suggests that market response is an increasing function of α (and of the difference $m_s - m_a$ which is independent of α). From (7) it is apparent that α is an increasing function of the dispersion of the a priori distribution of expected earnings, σ_a^2, and a decreasing function of the 'noise' in the reporting system, σ_s^2.

14 IBES covers more companies and more forecasts per company than our sample; however, these data are available only for the last six years. Furthermore, individual forecasts are not provided.

References

Ball, R. and Brown, P. (1968), 'An Empirical Evaluation of Accounting Income Numbers', *Journal of Accounting Research*, Autumn, 159–78.

Basu, J. and Cheung, S. (1982) 'Residual Risk, Firm Size and Returns from NYSE Common Stocks: Some Empirical Evidence', working paper, McMaster University, January.

Beaver, W., Clarke, R. and Wright, W.F. (1979) 'The Association Between Unsystematic Security Returns and the Magnitude of Earnings Forecasts', *Journal of Accounting Research*, Autumn, 316–40.

Brown, F, Foster, G. and Noreen, E. (1984) *Security Analyst Multi-Year Earnings Forecasts and the Capital Market*, Accounting Research Study Series No. 21, American Accounting Association.

Computer Directions Advisors Incorporated (1981) *Spectrum 1* and *Spectrum 2* Publications, June, Maryland.

Conover, W.J. (1971) *Practical Nonparametric Statistics*, 2nd edition, New York: John Wiley.

Elton, E.J., Gruber, M.J. and Gultekin, M. (1981) 'Expectations and Share Prices',*Management Science*, September, 975–87.

Epstein, L.G. and Turnbull, S.M. (1980) 'Capital Asset Prices and the Temporal Resolution of Uncertainty', *Journal of Finance*, June, 627–43.

Fama, E.F. and MacBeth, J.D. (1973) 'Risk, Return and Equilibrium: Empirical Tests', *Journal of Political Economy*, May, 607–36.

Figlewski, S. (1981) 'Capital Asset Pricing Under Heterogeneous Expectations and the Importance of Restrictions on Short Sales', *Journal of Financial and Quantitative Analysis*, November, 463–76.

Fried, D. and Givoly, D. (1982) 'Financial Analysts' Forecasts of Earnings: A Better Surrogate for Earnings Expectations', *Journal of Accounting and Economics*, October, 85–107.

Friend, I. and Westerfield, R. (1981) 'Risk and Asset Prices', *Journal of Banking and Finance*, September, 291–315.

Friend, I., Westerfield, R. and Granito, M. (1978) 'New Evidence on the Capital Asset Pricing Model', *Journal of Finance*, June, 913–20.

Givoly, D. and Lakonishok, J. (1979) 'The Information Content of Financial Analysts' Forecasts of Earnings: Some Evidence on Semi-strong Inefficiency', *Journal of Accounting and Economics*, Winter, 165–85.

Givoly, D. and Lakonishok, J. (1980) 'Financial Analysts' Forecasts of Earnings: Their Value to Investors', *Journal of Banking and Finance*, September, 221–33.

Givoly, D. and Lakonishok, J. (1984) 'The Quality of Analysts' Forecasts of Earnings', *Financial Analysts' Journal*, September–October, 40–7.

Givoly, D. and Palmon, D. (1982) 'Timeliness of Annual Reports – Some Empirical Evidence', *The Accounting Review*, July, 486–508.

Grant, E.B. (1980) 'Market Implications of Differential Amounts of Interim Information', *Journal of Accounting Research*, Spring, 255–68.

Holthausen, R.W. and Verrecchia, R.E. (1983) 'The Change in Price Resulting from a Sequence of Information Releases', working paper No. 54, University of Chicago.

Lakonishok, J. and Shapiro, A. (1986) 'Systematic Risk, Total Risk and Size as Determinants of Stock Market Returns', *Journal of Banking and Finance*, March.

Levy, H. (1978) 'Equilibrium in Imperfect Market: A Constraint on the Number of Securities in the Portfolio,' *American Economic Review*, September, 643–58.

Malkiel, B. and Cragg, J.G. (1980) 'Expectations and the Valuation of Shares', Working Paper 471, National Bureau of Economic Research, April.

Mayshar, J. (1981) 'Transaction Costs and the Pricing of Assets', *Journal of Finance*, June, 583–97.

Mayshar, J. (1983) 'On Divergence of Opinion and Imperfections in Capital Markets', *American Economic Review*, March, 114–28.

Rendelman, R., Jones, C. and Latane, H. (1982) 'Empirical Anomalies based on Unexpected Earnings and the Importance of Risk Adjustments', *Journal of Financial Economics*, 10, 269–87.

Robicheck, A.A. and Myers, S.C. (1966) 'Valuation of the Firm: Effects of Uncertainty in a Market Context', *Journal of Finance*, December, 727–30.

Securities and Exchange Commission (1977) *Report of the Advisory Committee on Corporate Disclosure*, Washington.

Stoll, H.R. and Whaley, R.E. (1983) 'Transaction Costs and the Small Firm Effect', *Journal of Financial Economics*, March, 57–79.

Theil, H. (1966) *Applied Economic Forecasting*, Amsterdam, North-Holland Publishing Company.

Verrecchia, R.E. (1982) 'Information Acquisition in a Noisy Rational Expectation Economy', *Econometrica*, November, 1415–30.

Index